PENGUIN BOOKS
PERFECT WIVES IN IDEAL HOMES

Virginia Nicholson was born in Newcastle-upon-Tyne and grew up in Yorkshire and Sussex. She studied at Cambridge University and lived abroad in France and Italy, then worked as a documentary researcher for BBC Television.

Her books include the acclaimed social histories *Among the Bohemians: Experiments in Living 1900–1939*, *Singled Out: How Two Million Women Survived Without Men after the First World War*, and *Millions Like Us: Women's Lives During the Second World War*, all published by Penguin.

She is married to a writer, has three children and lives in Sussex.

Perfect Wives in Ideal Homes

The Story of Women in the 1950s

VIRGINIA NICHOLSON

PENGUIN BOOKS

PENGUIN BOOKS

UK | USA | Canada | Ireland | Australia
India | New Zealand | South Africa

Penguin Books is part of the Penguin Random House group of companies
whose addresses can be found at global.penguinrandomhouse.com.

First published by Viking 2015
Published in Penguin Books 2016
001

Copyright © Virginia Nicholson, 2015

The moral right of the author has been asserted

Typeset in Bembo by Palimpsest Book Production Ltd, Falkirk, Stirlingshire
Printed in Great Britain by Clays Ltd, St Ives plc

A CIP catalogue record for this book is available from the British Library

ISBN: 978-0-241-95804-9

www.greenpenguin.co.uk

Penguin Random House is committed to a
sustainable future for our business, our readers
and our planet. This book is made from Forest
Stewardship Council® certified paper.

For my daughter, Julia

Contents

11. A Living Doll

List of Illustrations

Integrated illustrations

Inset illustrations

Foreword

A few years ago I wrote a book about women's lives in the 1940s.* I tracked the experiences of dozens of women whose lives were turned upside down by the Second World War, and who entered the post-war world forever changed by the international upheaval through which they had lived. This book follows the fortunes of their 1950s successors, and it adopts the same approach.

There have been many books explaining, analysing and illustrating our post-war world – and I am in debt to their authors, David Kynaston, Peter Hennessy, Paul Addison, Steven Humphries, Dominic Sandbrook, John Montgomery, Geoffrey Gorer, Christopher Booker, Stephanie Spencer, Ina Zweiniger-Bargielowska, Jane Lewis and others, who have trodden this path before me. They are mostly men. I hesitate to make the claim that it is because I am a woman that this book may come at its subject from a different angle to theirs. Still, this is a book about women, which theirs are not. It is also a book which – like its predecessors – prioritises personal experiences over generalisation, human narrative over attempts to be comprehensive. While my reader may be denied a panoramic sweep, I hope that she (or he?) will feel compensated by the insights to be gained from hearing so many authentic voices and memories from the past. And yet this is not what is commonly described as 'oral history'. Although much of the raw material of this book comes from interviews, the challenge has been to weave a readable narrative from multiple threads; to unravel and reveal the particular

* *Millions Like Us – Women's Lives in War and Peace 1939–1949.*

story from the impersonal context of dates, facts and events
which make up the blanket of history.

*

In 1950, my mother was thirty-four, working as an exhibitions
organiser for the Arts Council. At the time of writing, she is
ninety-seven, living out a comfortable old age, well looked after
in a house with central heating, a washing machine, a steam
iron, a dishwasher, a food-mixer, a toaster, an electric kettle, a
fridge-freezer, a vacuum cleaner and a television. When she
married early in 1952, she had none of those things. With a
degree in Art History, she resigned from her job, and turned
instead to the task of caring for husband, home and three children born in 1952, 1955 and 1959.

For the next fifteen years, until she resumed work, my mother
exclusively shopped, cooked, cleaned, mended, scrubbed, laun-
dered and baby-minded with very little help. My earliest
memories are of my mother aproned, in front of the kitchen
window, her strong working hands plunged in the sink as she
scrapes carrots, scours her frying pan, or rubs and rinses her way
through a mighty pile of dirty washing. Or she is carrying her
heavy basket home from the shops, peeling cooking apples for a
pie, shovelling coal into the coal-scuttle, pegging out nappies to
blow in the breeze, sitting by the fire at the end of the day darn-
ing a frayed sleeve. My father, who undoubtedly felt himself
fortunate to have married a good cook and housekeeper, is
either at work, or in his study. In all these things, my mother
was absolutely typical of her generation.

In the context of all that drudgery, the title of this book is a
nod towards an omnipresent and inescapable 1950s fantasy world;
for a generation of women – and men – marriage and home were
the twin pinnacles of aspiration. Traumatic destruction and loss

in the war worked a suggestive change on blitzed and battle-scarred Britons. The possession of one's own precious hearth, with a pair of cosy slippers lovingly placed beside it to warm by an angelically attentive wife, became imbued with an ineffable mystique. This image was a resilient one, for both sexes. A culture of sex discrimination, inhibition, conservatism, hierarchy and economic prosperity all favoured it. It withstood the waning of class privilege, systematic racism, sexual delinquency, murder, nuclear threat, rock'n'roll and a fledgling feminist movement. Even today, it will not lie down; we carry it with us, we listen to politicians and pundits extolling the virtues of the stay-at-home wife. It is worth exploring the nature and power of that image, and what it meant to women at that time.

The following chapters will open windows on to their lives, revealing some of the conflicting pressures and strains under which they lived in the 1950s. We will meet women of talent renouncing their careers and a 'don't-talk-about-it' culture breeding distress and loneliness. We will meet sexism, prejudice, poverty and ignorance, alongside secret lives, class deference and powerlessness. We will meet a perfect Queen and a not-so-perfect Princess. But, as I also hope to show in this book, the post-war world was – gradually but inevitably – becoming more accommodating to young women who wanted to pursue their dreams.

Since 1970s second-wave feminism gave my own generation a new language of rights and equality, the unquestioning assumption that hearth and home were a woman's destiny has shifted massively. A journey into the 1950s – though it is within my own lifetime and my mother's, and that of countless women alive today – can seem like alighting on another planet. In so many ways their era was extraordinarily different from that of my two twenty-plus daughters, born in the early 1990s, and now launched into university and beyond.

I wanted, in writing this book, to uncover what it actually felt like, sixty-odd years ago, to be a young woman entering adult life. What did our mothers or grandmothers think? What did they want? What was it like to be them? To make their voices heard I ransacked memoirs, archives and the internet, and nosed in diaries and newspapers, but above all I asked numerous women to talk to me about their memories. From housewives to unmarried mothers, air hostesses to academics, immigrants to debutantes, I have set out to uncover and reconstruct many of their stories, telling them against a roughly chronological back-drop of their times. (Some of the women who agreed to be interviewed were impressively frank, and have asked to have their identities disguised.) Theirs will be at times a narrative of fears, frustrations and deep unhappiness, but it will also be one of ambitions, dreams and fulfilment. And because I was born into that decade it will also be something of a self-indulgence to resurrect the manners, styles and material aspirations on to which my own young eyes were first opened: Spangles, Shippam's fish paste, Pond's Cold Cream, Orlon cardigans, Morris Travellers, Player's Navy Cut, holiday camps, hostess trolleys – and, of course, Coronation Chicken. I grew up in a world of farthings, twelve-sided threepenny bits and russet ten-shilling notes. One pound felt like untold wealth.

Researching the 1950s has often felt like time travel.

1. Elizabethans

The Post-war Blues

We love the 1950s. Today, we look back on it as a decade of black-and-white movies, retro decor and secure values. The images of 1950s women show them always smiling, posing in flattering frocks and high heels in front of a batch of freshly baked fairy cakes. For many, an enchantment still lingers over those years, which seem washed with gaiety, innocence and grainy colours.

But if you are in your eighties, as Valerie Gisborn now is, you may remember them differently. In 1999 a community history unit published a memoir she had written, under the title *Post War Blues*. She was born in 1934 and grew up in the Midlands manufacturing city of Leicester. Her parents had married young. Mr Gisborn worked as a boilerman at Wilson's Dye Works and Mrs Gisborn, a fastidious housewife, took house-keeping seriously, spending her days in a never-ending battle against cockroaches, and against the soot and dust that dropped from the adjacent factory. The family was poor. Valerie's clothes were always second-hand, and as a covetous thirteen-year-old she knew that if she wanted anything new she would have to earn her own money. On raw spring days, along with batches of her classmates, she was bussed out to work in the fields picking potatoes. During the six-week harvest period the children laboured at this back-breaking muddy task for five hours a day, and only attended school three days a week. 'The money – three shillings a day – was a great temptation to keep going. Dirt and soil were ingrained into our fingers and nails for weeks afterwards.' Valerie also took on a newspaper round. Six days out of seven, starting at 6.45 in the morning, she shouldered her load on a daily two-mile circuit, for seven and sixpence a week. Years later the figures of those early wages are branded on to Valerie's memory, as only the earnings of the truly necessitous can be. But already, inchoate dreams of promise and adventure hovered within her reach. A treasured copy of *Wuthering Heights*, bought over four months at sixpence a week, still occupies her bookshelf, 'a constant reminder of those days'.

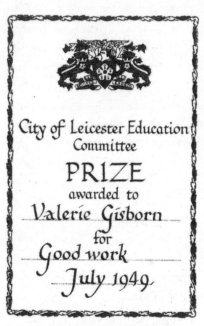

City of Leicester Education Committee
PRIZE
awarded to
Valerie Gisborn
for
Good work
July 1949.

Valerie's school results held out the prospect of a rosy future.

For Valerie was a bright girl, responsive to art, music and literature, and a hard worker at school. Her teachers were full of praise for her drawing and craft projects; she excelled in needlework too. An undefined dream started to form in her head. Might there be a life beyond Leicester, a life beyond her mum's poverty and domesticity? At the age of fifteen, having come top of her class and overall second in the examinations, she was summoned by her headmistress to discuss her future.

She was of the opinion that my schooling should continue until the age of 18 years.

It was a waste of time because I knew Mother was committed to me earning my living as soon as possible. When I gave the

Headmistress's message to my parents they listened and, after a
moment's thought, poured forth the excuses . . .

The good part of my life came to an end when school finished
for the summer in July 1949.

There was nobody to whom Valerie could turn for guidance;
once the decision was made that she would leave and seek work,
her teachers lost interest in her. There was disappointment, and
shame too, for her classmates had all regarded her as something
of a prodigy who would go on to higher things. Now, with no
diplomas or certificates to prove her value, Valerie was worth
only what she could offer to the local factory: her skill at the
sewing machine. But she was young and buoyant. A new possi-
bility came to her.

At least, I thought, it was a start. I had ideas of specialising
and starting my own business but until then I had to learn the
trade . . .

Somehow, I meant to better myself in the future.

Early on a Monday morning in August 1949, Valerie started
work. She was employed, initially, to do a ten-hour day, five
days a week, for £1 5s.* From then on, she posted her card daily
into the clocking-on machine which recorded the workers'
times of arrival and departure. More than three minutes late and
you lost a quarter of an hour's pay. Soon, she was well versed in
the intricacies of fitting zips, stitching collars and overlocking
seams.

Valerie's long working days at Trafford Knitwear were spent
in an environment of deafening clatter; women sat in lines at
their benches, heads bent over the machines, their drab everyday
clothes covered up with capacious aprons. Clouds of steam rose

---

* A sum worth £37.42 in 2014. The hourly rate (take away an hour for lunch,
leaving a nine-hour day) would thus be the equivalent of a miserly £0.83p an
hour. Today the national minimum wage is £6.50 an hour.

from the pressing area; beyond, men laboured tugging the huge rolls of fabric and bales of finished garments to load up for delivery to the shops and fashion houses. Week-in, week-out, there was little to interrupt the monotony. For Valerie, work only varied when she graduated to the overlocking machine, or when a new fashion came in for pin-tucking. There were also occasional work dramas, as when a sewing machine needle impaled her finger; one of the other women had to extricate it with pliers. She soon got used to performing the same operation for her fellow workers – 'We were all caught eventually.' But prospects of escape from her repetitive job were slim, and it looked like she might be tied to the factory floor for the rest of her working life.

By now, Valerie's half-formed ambitions had shifted. Gone was the dream of starting her own business. Self-effacing as she was, the pinnacle of her ambition was to become a sample hand, a machinist whose job it was to interpret one-off new designs which would then go into mass production. But two young, healthy women were already working for the firm as sample hands, and promotion seemed impossibly distant.

> I was bored out of my mind. There was nothing glowing ahead to look forward to. It seemed I was destined to be a machinist all my life and it went very much against my feelings. I withdrew into myself, becoming more depressed and quiet as the weeks went by . . .

Unspecific though they were, Valerie's dreams refused to lie down, and occasionally she still allowed herself to imagine a different life. But how could an uneducated girl like her defy the unwritten rules of her sex and class, and step into a world outside the factory gates?

> I felt I could become someone better in a more satisfying job.
> Inwardly I knew I was capable of better things if given a chance. But at what . . . ?

Valerie Gisborn was entirely typical of many thousands of young women in the 1950s who, leaving school at fifteen, went straight into low-status employment without training or higher education. At this age 62 per cent of girls were in full-time work; even by 1959, only 1.3 per cent of girls would leave school to pursue higher education. For most girls like Valerie, the bright light on the horizon was marriage: 'the ultimate goal of every rational female who seeks happiness . . .' as one woman's magazine writer put it. Every film, advertisement and shilling romance aimed at women sent out the same message – that to be a wife was to be complete. But Valerie could not, would not aspire to be like her mum, a sharp-tempered, anti-social woman, controlling and often inflexible, whose life was bounded by the four walls of her damp and uncomfortable rented home next to the dye works. Mrs Gisborn's confined life was reflected in an absence of leniency when it came to her daughter. Valerie could go to the cinema – 'but my parents accepted no excuses if I was late home. My mother worried about the people I would be associating with and felt she had to keep a strict control on my activities.' Mrs Gisborn's neurotic restrictiveness was soon to be put to the test. Soon after starting the job at Trafford Knitwear, Valerie took the unforgivable step of falling in love.

Under duress, Valerie was allowed to go dancing weekly, provided her behaviour with men was irreproachable, and she was home on the dot of 10.30. The dances were a regular part of her life and, inevitably, led to dates. Her favoured dancing partner, Brian, was 'tall, slim, smart, good looking and charming'. Their evenings together, waltzing beneath the ceiling mirror ball, whose flickering lights reflected the coloured jets of the ballroom's central fountain, were the highlight of her week. Swept into Brian's embrace, freed from the leaden hours in the factory, Valerie's feet – in silver sandals – were as light as her heart. 'I was thrilled. I had really fallen for this one.'

In working-class Britain in the 1950s the social codes were explicit: walking a girl home was an unmistakable declaration of seriousness, and so it was a few weeks before Valerie permitted Brian the liberty of escorting her back to her house. In due course, convinced that he was 'quite the gentleman', and with the rhythms of the band lending buoyancy to her steps, they set out on the short, lamplit walk back to Nottingham Road. Valerie was glowing. Reaching the gate in the wall, Brian took her in his arms and kissed her there, lingeringly.

And then, the gate opened; there, to her appalled gaze, stood her mother. What time did he call this? She smacked her daughter in the face, and ordered Brian to get off home promptly. The brown eyes that had gazed upon Valerie so meltingly were transfixed with amazement. Disappearing into the darkness, he called out to her, 'Bye, see you Wednesday . . .' 'But I knew by his look of horror that I should be lucky if I saw him again.' Howling in shock, despair and humiliation, Valerie was dragged back into the house.

By now it seemed to Valerie Gisborn that for a girl like her, life held little in the way of fulfilment. Such pleasures as she experienced were either prohibited by lack of money, curtailed by her mother, or else such brief windows on to a monotonous life that they served only to accentuate the everyday tedium and hardship. She was not alone. At the beginning of the 1950s the chill post-war fog of austerity had barely lifted. Rationing was still in force. Few people travelled, the cities were scarred by bomb damage and there was a chronic housing shortage, while stirrings in the Far East indicated that conflict was again a likelihood. In this context, our rulers decided that the people of this country needed something to cheer them up.

In 1951, Trafford Knitwear decided that their annual thank-you gesture to their employees, of hiring coaches to take them on an outing to Skegness, would surpass those of previous years.

That summer, the girls were booked to go to the Festival of Britain.

For Valerie, it was the most wonderful excursion of her life: a day of laughter, fun and companionship, a wonderworld of irresponsibility detached from the wearisome imperatives of everyday clocking on, clocking off and wage-earning. The women arrived, bright-eyed and shiny-haired, gay in their floral frocks and comfortable shoes, ready for an early morning start from Leicester. The first British motorway had yet to be built, and at six o'clock that June morning the coaches rolled off down the A6, on through Bedford to Luton, where they joined the A1 to London – a journey of over five hours. On arrival Valerie and her gang of four made straight for the Battersea pleasure park. There, the lovely weather had brought out the crowds; they milled in the Gardens, admiring the novelty Guinness clock with its spinning menagerie, Lockheed's naked bronze mermaid fountain balanced on a water-spouting turtle, and the Grotto sponsored by Schweppes.* It seemed a fairyland. The Pleasure Park Parade also incorporated a bewitching 'Ladies' Powder Room' (sponsored by the cosmetics company Leichner) fully supplied with eye-shadows, powders and lotions – a feast for the make-up-deprived women of austerity Britain. How many of them had spent the war years dabbing their lids with Vaseline or eking out a lipstick's final days by melting it down with cooking oil? The sense of a treasure trove was enhanced in the shopping parade, where elegant boutiques laid out the kind of wares unseen since pre-war days, in carefully gendered displays:

> . . . bright adornments for my lady – earrings and necklaces of pearl and brilliants, costume jewellery of every description.

* There was political and press controversy over the overt commercialism and advertising permitted in the Battersea Pleasure Park, in contrast to the high-minded and educational tone of the exhibits on the South Bank site, where sponsorship had been barred.

> And while madam yearns over gems and fine perfumes, elegant
> slippers and diaphanous underwear, the mere male can comfort
> himself with the contemplation (and purchase) of pipes, snuff,
> fountain pens, cameras, watches or electric razors . . .

The day was hot. By late afternoon, meandering among the
attractions and exhibits, the girls from Leicester had walked for
miles and were parched with thirst. While her friends made for
the lovely Powder Room, Valerie unthinkingly joined a queue
in one of the beer gardens sponsored by the Worshipful Company of Brewers and, under pressure to decide, impulsively
bought a clutch of green bottles without reading the labels. It
was not until she swallowed a thirsty draught, and spluttered at
its fizzy bitterness, that she discovered what she'd bought: four
pints of extra-strong Double Diamond, marketed as 'The Beer
That Men Drink'. Never mind. It was a day for fantasy – and
folly. A few bottles later, the girls all discovered that they liked
it anyway, and the evening firework display over the Thames
seemed like a dazzling hallucination. At 11.30, in a state of helpless giggles, Valerie and her chums, now hysterical with drink,
hailed a (barely affordable) taxi; one of the girls simply sprawled
out on its floor, incapable of hauling herself on to a seat. With
minutes to spare they made it back to the rendezvous, just as
their coach was pulling out. 'We were going without you!' cried
the others . . .

> We did not care. We stood in the aisle trying to explain what
> had happened in the taxi but it was so funny we collapsed with
> laughter again. No one could get any sense out of us . . .

At 4.30 in the morning the coach pulled up outside the Trafford
works; by now the mist was clearing and the midsummer sun
was rising. Intoxicated with her day of delights, and beer,
Valerie walked home through the empty streets, let herself in
and went straight to bed. In memory, nothing would ever, ever

compare to the fun of that Festival of Britain day trip. And on Monday morning it was back to the factory.

Cheated hope, a sense of futility and depression are common themes for all too many women of the post-war era. For thousands of others like Valerie Gisborn, fulfilment was elusive. Bright and capable as she was, her life was circumscribed by the undeviating routine at Trafford Knitwear. 'I knew I was capable of better things . . . But what . . . ?' Intermittently, there were glimpses of pleasures on offer, promises of greater satisfactions, richer experiences. But it was to be another six years before Valerie's formless, ever-receding dream of 'better things' would finally – as we shall see – become excitingly tangible.

Coronation Fever

How can we capture the aspirations and attitudes, the fears, ideals and desires of Valerie's generation? To start with, I propose to step back from chronology, and take a snapshot of the female psyche as it encounters an emblematic national moment. Arguably, the Coronation was, for women, the defining event of the decade. Tracking its stately progress through the spring of 1953, we will become acquainted more closely with some of them, focusing by turns on the working woman, the schoolgirl, the teenager, the student, the secretary at her typewriter, the young wife in her kitchen, each in her own way illuminated by history's bright lamp.

*

During the spring of 1953, a momentous decision hung over Miss Prudence Moss.

I am toying with the idea of having a Television Set.

Miss Moss was a teacher at a girls' secondary school in the Wirral. That year, for the first time, women in such posts were awarded equal pay with their male counterparts; nevertheless, the most she could have earned that year would have been £676.* A television could cost up to £80,† depending on the model, but then there would be the installation, and the licence to pay for: £2. After school, on the evening of Friday 24 April, Miss Moss took the bus to the town centre with her friend and colleague Daphne Goddard, to find out from the local showroom what her money could buy. They were demonstrating models.

> We both liked the Ferranti – of those that were within my reach financially. Now I'm pondering about it. It seems a lot of money to pay out – but when I think that I have only had one holiday abroad since the war ended, maybe it wouldn't be such an extravagance after all. It's seeing the Coronation on Television that is the special attraction . . .

This was not a decision to be made in a hurry; the Coronation, scheduled for 2 June, was still more than five weeks away. Miss Moss went home and pondered over what to do. Life had been hard; in the war she had been bombed out. She had never married, worked hard at her job, and lived in an upstairs flat. The temptation was growing on her to do something indulgent, something for herself. In those pre-credit-card days it would take a bit of scrimping and saving, but the desired object could be hers. On Saturday morning she 'shopped most frugally' for food, and bethought herself of

---

* Worth about £16,974 in 2014. The average salary for a school teacher in the UK in 1953 was £676. The average salaries for a female secondary school teacher were £536 (in a secondary modern school), £622 (in a secondary modern school with a graduate degree), and £645 (in a grammar school).
† Worth about £2,009 in 2014.

her store cupboard, where a supply of tinned food lay in wait for emergencies, left over from wartime perhaps? If she were to live off Crosse & Blackwell's Cock-a-Leekie soup, toast and processed peas for a few weeks, maybe that would release the £2 needed for the licence?

On Tuesday, again with her companion Miss Goddard, Miss Moss's footsteps strayed in the direction of another showroom. This time the Pye table-top model – cheaper than the Ferranti – caught her fancy, and the prospect of saving a few shillings on aerial installation was a further inducement. By now Coronation fever was upon her. The shops, she noticed, were putting her purchases into specially designed Coronation bags, and beginning to dress their windows with souvenirs: you could buy a Coronation jigsaw puzzle, a Coronation tin of biscuits, Coronation stationery, toffees, handkerchiefs and crockery adorned with our monarch's image – on horseback, in ermine, with or without Prince Philip. Red, white and blue Union Jacks, golden crowns were everywhere, on cars and on dustcarts. On Friday 1 May, Miss Moss succumbed:

> Dashed off this afternoon to see the Pye Television Set – and have decided to have it!

No sooner said than done. The deal was concluded, and arrangements made for an aerial to be fixed to her chimney the following Tuesday. The set itself would be installed on Wednesday.

A new dilemma now presented itself. Miss Moss became agonisingly aware that, as the possessor of a television set, she would become an object of envy to everyone she knew – the majority – who did not. And with The Day fast approaching, barely a month to go now, how was she to decide on whom to confer the privilege of an invitation to watch the solemnities in her small sitting room? 'An agreeable few' was the most she could manage. On Tuesday 5 May she casually mentioned in the staff room that she was getting a TV. 'A gleam of interest shot from everyone's eyes.' Twenty-five teachers intimated unmistakably that, *were* she disposed to ask them round on The Day . . .

But I can't have 25 people can I?

Miss Moss felt besieged. She was going to have to narrow it down somehow. The problem was solved the following day when she unexpectedly ran into two ladies who back in the dark days of war had kindly given her shelter when her accommodation had been bombed. Along with Daphne Goddard, these good Samaritans were the best possible choice of guests, and her invitation to them to view on 2 June was met with alacrity. She got home to find that the electricians had put the set in place. 'Yes – it is here.' That was incredible enough. But the brandnew machine with the recessed, myopic-looking ovoid screen now occupying a place in her sitting room filled Prudence Moss with awe. She was much too nervous to touch any of the jutting control buttons at the base of its boxy wooden framework. That would have to wait until Friday, the earliest that an electrician could be available to instruct her. On Friday he duly came:

> There are two gadgets on the front – the On/Off switch which controls volume and the other 'switch' which controls brightness. At the back of the set, there is a lever which is labelled Focus and four small knobs labelled 'Horizontal Hold', 'Vertical Hold', 'Contrast' and 'White Spot Suppressor'. I don't think I've grasped the function of the last-named.

So had it all been worth it?

> The TV programmes, which of course I have now been studying, aren't very good, so I shan't be tempted to 'view' very much.

★

Prudence Moss's Pye table-top model was one of 526,000 TV sets sold in the run-up to the Queen's big day – increasing by over a quarter the number of televisions in British homes, which at the beginning of 1953 had numbered fewer than 2 million.

Six years of bombs, fuel economies, tinned beans and make-do-and-mend had intensified the longings of Prudence Moss and thousands like her for the graces and femininity of a bygone era. Under Britain's grey austerity skies, lovely queens and golden coaches were a beckoning mirage, like a phoenix rising from the ashes. In spring 1953, expectations ran high, festivity was in the air. For many, buying their new televisions, eagerly awaiting the spectacle, life seemed to wear an unaccustomed gloriousness and glow. The inauguration of a new reign brought with it a celebration of womanhood. Queen Elizabeth II – a pretty, clear-skinned, averagely bright upper-class twenty-seven-year-old with a handsome husband, two children (a boy and a girl) and a passion for horses and dogs – embodied the aspirations of her nation.

Cynics were rare. Even Joan Bakewell – then Joan Rowlands, a hip party-going undergraduate at Newnham College Cambridge, in her Juliette Greco-influenced black polo-necks and tight black trousers – found it hard to resist the young Queen's glamour:

Now she would be queen . . .

she remembered wistfully –

– a woman on the throne, and one not much older than ourselves. There was a sense of lightheartedness about that: it felt, well, sort of contemporary, the turn of our generation.

Janet Bourne, her contemporary at Girton, felt the same. Janet was reading Music and as a talented singer was a star of the prestigious Cambridge Madrigal Society. Yet despite having just purchased her first pair of super-fashionable and liberated side-zipping jeans, she was thrilled to be invited to take her Norman Hartnell debutante frock out of mothballs, ready to don for a pre-Coronation concert of specially composed English songs at the Festival Hall. In this full-length white gown, with frills around the bust, Janet would feel touched by royal stardust.

Where glamour and Elizabethan mystique were concerned, a generation of women wanted their slice of the action. In 1953 more debutantes were presented at court than ever before. A privileged minority of these were on the guest list for Miss Elizabeth Ward's coming-out ball that spring, to which the Queen herself had been invited, accompanied by the Queen Mother. A canopied dance floor was laid out in the garden, on which both royal ladies were to be seen waltzing, their partners in white tie and tails, heavily encrusted with orders and decorations.

Observing these details was 'Jennifer', aka Mrs Betty Kenward. As a social diarist and national institution Jennifer's secret was her unflagging energy (that season she was out every single night, often attending three or four engagements) and her blanket veneration for class. If you were out of the top drawer, there was little risk in inviting Jennifer to your party. Infallibly grateful and respectful towards her hostess, she would also take good care to record the finer points of your attire and jewellery. But the American journalist and divorcée Emily Kimbrough had less to lose, and fewer scruples. Emily was making her second big trip from the USA to Europe. She arrived in London in early May, timing her arrival in London to coincide with the run-up to the British Queen's Coronation. She admired the ladies' jewels at the parties to which she was invited, but lamented the sad state of their gowns. Clothes rationing had ended in 1949, but in 1953 many women were still feeling the austerity pinch:

> The clothes of many of them had seen long wear. They had a look of having been too often cleaned and pressed. But how superbly

every Englishwoman carries herself. It gave me a twinge in my heart; they stood so straight, the dresses of some of them so out of style, and the jewels of nearly every one of them so magnificent.

The Ward ball was one of the last private functions graced by the Queen before the Coronation.

White-flowering Days

So the lead-up proceeded. On 14 May sixty-one-year-old Betty Hodge went to a cookery demonstration at the Electrical Circle in her home town of Morecambe in Lancashire. 'It was all fancy things for Coronation Day parties,' she reported in her diary for Mass Observation.* The demonstrator explained how to make easy-to-serve, previously prepared cold dishes, a boon to the hostess who wanted to share feeding her guests with watching TV. These included a remarkable dessert

> – a Union Jack jelly, a foundation of red jelly – the blue parts filled in with blue-tinted desiccated coconut & white icing piped on for the white crosses . . .

With reckless abandon, rations were consigned to the past.

That same day, gulls' eggs and salmon mayonnaise were on the menu when Frances Partridge, a highly educated pacifist and intellectual aged fifty-three, took the train to London to lunch at the Ivy with her old friends the art critic Clive Bell and the literary critic Raymond Mortimer. Over the meal they talked of the apparent contradiction that could arise between an artist's life and his or her work. But the imminent royal rites

---

* Started in 1937, the Mass Observation project was an initiative by three young men to create 'an anthropology of ourselves', by calling upon ordinary members of the public to submit diaries of their everyday lives, as well as responding to surveys. The work continued until the early 1960s.

Piccadilly Circus, May 1953. This artist's impression of the Coronation
decorations is loaded with period detail.

were impossible to ignore – 'roaring towards us like a lorry heard approaching up a steep incline'. Lunch over, Frances walked up Regent Street and took a dim view of the Coronation decorations – the swags of fake-looking pink roses made a 'fussy and sad' impression. Through them, the grey buildings seemed to her to peer anxiously.

Emily Kimbrough didn't agree at all. The floral settings – banks of blooms spilling over fountains, street corners and lamp-posts – earned her most fulsome praise, along with their creator, Constance Spry:

> They were masses of beauty that none of us who were in London during those days will ever forget.

At the age of sixty-six Constance Spry was invited to join the Coronation planning committee as honorary consultant on floral decoration. Her company, Flower Decorations, had been hugely successful among the wealthy and fashionable for over thirty years. Together with her friend Rosemary Hume she founded both the Cordon Bleu Cookery School and Winkfield Place, a domestic science college 'for the hostesses of tomorrow'. But at heart Connie was an influential democratiser and pioneer who believed that everyone, not just those who could afford tuberoses and gardenias, had the right to beautify their living space. A woman of boundless energy, combative and determined, she dedicated her working life to bringing the decorative possibilities of wild and garden flowers, vegetables and foliage to a wide public. In private too she was unconventional; though officially married, her long-term partner was the cross-dressing flower artist Hannah Gluck.

Despite early hesitations by the male Ministry mandarins, who huffed and puffed at the prospect of anything other than a rigid geometry of scarlet geraniums to decorate the royal route, confidence in Connie's abilities soon became unshakeable. Thus she was entrusted not only with adorning the processional route, but also with organising a grandiose post-Coronation luncheon for visiting dignitaries. With Rosemary Hume she drew on all her reserves of ingenuity and taste in devising a tightly budgeted menu and decor for this occasion. Then there was the logistical challenge posed by entertaining hundreds of international potentates in the sombre, bomb-damaged shell of Westminster School Hall. How, in this environment, could she create splendour and festivity? How would she serve them, and what on earth could she feed them all on?

By now, Constance Spry's name was on everyone's lips: 'the greatest artist of all in flower arrangements'.

*

Another name, that of Jean Metcalfe, would have been familiar at that time to a generation of devoted listeners to BBC Radio's General Forces Programme, for whom she had compèred the much-loved request show *Two-Way Family Favourites* between 1943 and 1950. In 1950, aged twenty-seven, Jean married her *Family Favourites* co-presenter, Cliff Michelmore, and afterwards joined *Woman's Hour* on the Home Service.

In Coronation year the top brass (male) at BBC Radio were intent on achieving the best possible coverage of the royal celebrations. A team of twenty commentators (nineteen men, just one woman) would provide listeners worldwide with dawn-to-dusk reports. But it was thought appropriate that four 'back-up girls' should be found to cover the lighter, human-interest side of the occasion. To her astonishment, Jean discovered that on the day she would be broadcasting from <u>inside</u> Buckingham Palace, posted close to the Queen's own private apartments, and would be expected to report on every detail of the royal send-off from the Palace:

The ensuing weeks of April and May were a nightmare of stage-fright . . .

Shortly before the day, a confidential memo landed on Jean's desk, marked 'Not for use until June 2nd. For Miss Metcalfe only.' The envelope contained the top secret description of the Queen's Coronation dress:

> 'Historic gown of white satin . . . the bodice, sleeves and extreme hem are bordered with an embroidered band of golden crystals, graduated diamonds and pearls.'
> I felt a tingle of excitement like a child at a pantomime.

★

Everyone was hoping for a sunny day – with some justification. May 1953 had been blessed with such prolonged warm weather that it was surely reasonable to expect it to continue into early June? But on 26 May there was a drastic change. The thermometer dropped and an unexpected front brought in violent and persistent showers. By Saturday the 30th, the best the forecasters could come up with was a cautious: 'It will be cool on The Day.'

On Sunday 31 May the British prayed for their Queen in cathedrals and dank country churches across the nation.

On Monday 1 June there were queues outside bakers' shops in every high street, as housewives adopted the siege mentality that commonly precedes all major public events held in this country. Bread ran out. The capital became – temporarily – multi-cultural, as visitors from the various Commonwealth countries appeared in saris, striped robes and elaborate headdresses on the tops of London buses. That evening a delighted audience at the Royal Festival Hall applauded the Cambridge Madrigal Society as they sang

White-flowering Days by Gerald Finzi, and *What is it Like to be Young and Fair?* by Arnold Bax.

*

Over the weeks leading up to the Coronation Mary Whitehouse, a deeply religious Warwickshire housewife, found herself wondering how best to respond to the plea that the young Queen had made in her Christmas broadcast of 1952, asking for her people to pray for her. What could she, Mary, do to help, personally? These musings found their way on to paper, and then into an envelope, which she optimistically posted off to the BBC. Unknown to Mrs Whitehouse, the programme planners had been searching high and low for just such material to broadcast to the nation pre-Coronation. On 19 May a telegram was delivered to the Whitehouse home: 'Script accepted. Please contact immediately.'

I collapsed on the bottom stair, shaking like a leaf . . .

Picking herself up, she telephoned the producers. And so 1 June 1953 saw the forty-two-year-old mother of three in front of the microphone in the *Woman's Hour* studio, where she delivered 'A Housewife's Thoughts on the Eve of the Coronation'. As the producers had recognised, her short essay captured many of the fundamentals of 1950s wifehood. Born in 1910, Mary had been an art teacher for eight years until 1940, when she met Ernest Whitehouse who, like herself, was a follower of the Moral Re-Armament movement. Following their marriage Mary put her career on hold and settled down to keep house and raise her family. But what she did not desert was her faith. The *Woman's Hour* piece was a genuine attempt to reconcile 'pots and pans, ration books and children fast growing out of their clothes' with making a constructive and spiritual contribution to 'the great world outside our homes'. As she saw it, men in their important worldly activities were the conduit through which women could influence events, whether positively or negatively. An argumentative, exacting wife will drain and deplete her man. He will feel tired out by her insatiability, by her grumpy moans and groans about the domestic load. By the same token, a good wife will send her husband out happily in the morning, and welcome him home gladly when he returns from his office or factory. Women must take the new Queen as their model:

> The Queen will live to make our nation great, and in my own way I want to do the same. While hers may often be in more spectacular ways my dedication may just be in the caring I put into the details of my everyday life, even into the washing up and in the thought and preparation that goes into cooking:
>
> > *Each meal a sacrament, a feast,*
> > *And many who may never know our care,*
> > *Will feel it and be glad. . .*

At this point in her life Mrs Whitehouse, like millions of others, took for granted that her home was the only environment over which she exercised control. Her home, and herself. Her sense of powerlessness in combating the manifold afflictions of humanity caused her to look inwards:

> At least there I can fight it, and in my heart and home I need to build a citadel against these things.

*

'There were about eight or ten of us, men and women . . . We had walked into the Festival Hall in evening dress. We came out in jeans: the first time I'd ever worn them . . .' remembers Girton student Janet Bourne. Like Cinderellas, the Cambridge Madrigal Society singers packed away their ball gowns and black ties after the concert, handing them to others who were returning from London, before resuming their casual student identities. It was a chilly, darkening midsummer night with rain in the air. Clutching knapsacks of sandwiches, they made their way past the South Bank Festival site and over Westminster Bridge into Parliament Square. There they made camp outside the Treasury Office door.

> My friend John and I lay down with his knapsack for a pillow – we squashed the sandwiches! And then about three o'clock in the morning, we heard the noise growing in volume round the square . . . the news vendors were calling it out: 'Everest has been climbed . . . Everest has been climbed!' It was absolutely marvellous.

That night Angela Austin from Golders Green came into town with her parents. Despite being bright, vivacious and academic, twenty-year-old Angela had opted not to go to university. 'What would I do with an English degree? Be a teacher? No thanks! I had no careers advice. Anyway, one was expected to get married . . .' Instead she left school at sixteen, signed up for a two-year shorthand and typing course, and graduated top of her class in just twelve months. 'To begin with I just wanted to GO TO WORK. I wanted to be one of those people who went off dressed in business clothes and got on buses, wearing a hat <u>of course</u>!' But beyond Angela's more immediate horizon of secretarial glory hovered half-formed dreams of travel and romance. 'Like everybody else I thought one day I'd get married, but before that I wanted to see the world. And there's an awful lot of world to see.'

For now, in 1953, Angela had a 'lovely' job as a secretary with

Yardley Cosmetics at their company headquarters in Bond Street. Yardley held the royal warrant, and Angela was proud to be employed by such a blue-blooded firm. And the eve of the 2 June public holiday saw her, as a good patriot, down by the Mall:

> I'd gone because it was a momentous event in British history. And I did feel such an affection for the Queen . . . She was young, and beautiful. Also it was the feeling that it had been thrust upon her – she could have expected another twenty years before she had to rule.
>
> It was drizzly wet. We stayed out in the Mall all night; we'd taken blankets – didn't want to lie on bare earth! And they'd set up public lavatories all along the Mall. Actually I don't recall having any need of them – or of needing to eat or drink.

VIPs had reserved seats in the stands but, like Angela and her parents, everyone else had to take their chance. The meteorologists continued gloomy. Their recommendation was –

Take raincoats and umbrellas with you . . .

– advice which was taken to heart. The crowds brought tarpaulin groundsheets, spirit lamps, thermoses, packs of sandwiches and Union Jacks, and pitched wherever they could find a space. By the evening of Monday 1 June half a million people had taken up their places along the processional route. One of these was seventy-three-year-old widow Zoe Neame from Speen in Buckinghamshire. Mrs Neame had sat it out for every royal occasion – jubilees, weddings and funerals alike – since 1921. Bearing just a package of egg sandwiches and a bag of fruit, she had arrived in Trafalgar Square at 8 a.m. on Sunday 31 May, with the intention of staying there till Tuesday night. 'My two sisters think I'm barmy, but I'm loving every minute of it,' she cheerfully told the *Daily Sketch*, who pictured her on their front page edition of 1 June. 'I do it for the thrill of it. I never get tired. I never catch cold. If it rains? Oh, it will dry!'

All This I Promise to Do

Coronation Day dawned chilly, gusty, overcast and decidedly damp.

On that raw, wet morning of 2 June at her home in St Albans, Hertfordshire, Miss Rosamund Essex had risen at five-thirty. Rosamund was fifty-three; portly and plump of feature, she was a saintly woman devoid of personal vanity. But this was not the occasion to appear modestly retiring. She washed, put on an evening dress with an ample, fluttering, hooped skirt and pinned a floaty nylon veil decked with artificial mimosa flowers to her headdress, then climbed with difficulty into the waiting car. Rosamund described herself as 'a woman in a man's world'. Now three years into her significant post as Editor of the *Church Times*, she was the first woman to be appointed to run a London journal not aimed exclusively at a female readership. In this capacity she was bidden to attend the ceremony itself, wearing suitable finery.

A downpour was now setting in. At six-thirty the junior clerical staff of Sun Insurance arrived at their offices on the south side of Trafalgar Square, bearing special passes, and were allowed to climb to the topmost floor of the building, from where they had a pigeon's eye view. Their managers provided breakfast, and as the rain came down the secretaries and girls from the typing pool felt a pang for the 'poor sailors' lining the route. 'The blanco ran off their white caps and streamed down their uniforms.'

Towards seven in the morning Rosamund Essex's car approached Westminster Abbey; along with hundreds of other equipages laden with guests the vehicles crawled around the

perimeter of Hyde Park in a holding pattern until their occupants could be disgorged at the Abbey entrance. Peers and
goose-pimpled Peeresses were to be seen hoisting their robes out
of the puddles, coronets tucked under their arms to protect
them from the showers: 'Very silly they looked.' Gradually, the
multitudes filed into the Abbey under a canopied aisle, to be
ticked off on lists by resplendent Guardsmen as they entered.

By 8 a.m. Rosamund was in her seat among the other journalists (also in evening dress), on the upper tier of a constructed
gallery in the north transept.

> I regret to say that the first and absorbing topic of conversation
> among us was what lavatory accommodation was provided for
> us. It was only human. We had a huge wait before us . . .

The guests wandered off in dribs and drabs to locate the toilets
down twisting narrow corridors of scaffolding; this entailed
clambering over the cramped knees and treading on the toes of
the back row of invitees with many an apology. 'That's quite all
right: no trouble at all,' they responded. But the courtesies wore
thin as the hours passed. Many had brought discreet snacks,
malted milk tablets and barley sugar, hip flasks and thermoses of
coffee, and over time these contributed to their bodily needs.
People were heading for the lavatories 'not singly, but in droves'.
The torments of the back row now became incessant; they
started to sweat, swear and protest. It was bedlam. Nobody paid
any attention, any more than they respected the hierarchical
edicts ordaining WCs to be used by 'Peeresses', 'Ladies' and
'Bishops'. Rosamund 'became an unrepentant peeress for the
occasion . . .' The bishops' toilet was invaded by proletarians; in
turn the bishops themselves grew unruly. The flustered ushers
were powerless. It was each for their own.

★

Inside Buckingham Palace, broadcaster Jean Metcalfe was feeling unnerved. Overnight on Monday Jean had occupied an uncomfortable billet on BBC premises; on Tuesday she rose at five and applied a reviving facepack in the Ladies. She was aware of the duffle-coated crowds pressing their faces to the railings as she crossed the puddled Buckingham Palace forecourt, her new shoes hurting; aware of their interest as she waited for the powdered flunkey to admit her. Breakfast was being provided in the Steward's Dining Room, where she found her engineer and his microphone. But now?

> Below the window the State Coach was waiting with its patient horses. The Inner Courtyard was as quiet as a country Sunday. That was the unnerving part. Everything was ready for the party but would anyone turn up?

'Mama, Mama, Mama!' The children, released from their nursery, came tumbling down the corridor. They were being allowed to see their mother in all her glory before she set off for the Abbey. Charles, nearly five now, would see some of the ceremony, but Anne wasn't yet three. She was too little. 'The Queen was actually there, behind that door . . .' Outside it, the seamstresses whose needles had stitched the golden crystals, diamonds and pearls to the hem of her dress were waiting to see their creation. Then she emerged. A wafting scent of lilies-of-the-valley, a gracious 'Good morning', and she was on her way down to take her seat in the golden coach.

Half-past ten was approaching. 'And now we join Jean Metcalfe within Buckingham Palace . . .' White terror. With three words – 'The Coach moves . . .' – Jean's voice was the cue for the entire procession, all two miles of it, to set off.

★

High above Admiralty Arch, the Sun Insurance girls caught their breath and craned their necks as, at last, they glimpsed the splendour they had waited all morning to see, emerging from the arch below.

Among the hurrahing crowds lining the processional route that morning was an excited teenager from Bethnal Green. Florence Fell's parents were strict Congregationalist church-goers; her father a cobbler, and her mother – like the majority of Cockney mums – a housewife. The family, with six children, lived in a three-bedroom flat in a block behind the fire station in Roman Road. Florence grew up with low expectations. 'I never thought past where I am now. I had no ambition, no future thinking. I did as I was told. I went to church twice on Sunday.' Her protective, implacable mother kept her on a short rein, with no pocket money, and boy-friends off limits.

But on that day in 1953, Florence was given permission to see the royal pageant. Philip was the one she had come to see: 'You don't get ugly princes do you? I always thought he was handsome. I always loved him.' Westminster was a long way from Bethnal Green, and generally speaking few East Enders made the journey, but Florence felt happy among the hundreds of well-wishers good-naturedly shouldering each other on the chilly Victoria Embankment. As the grandiose baroque coach rumbled ever closer, the uproar swelled – 1,000 onlookers waving and clamouring, among them Florence Fell. There they were: the Queen herself, and beside her Philip the Duke of Edinburgh in his full-dress uniform of Admiral of the Fleet, glittering with medals and plaited gold braid. And then, to her astonishment, Philip noticed her in the crowd:

He waved to me. He spotted me, and he waved to me. To <u>me</u>.

In a life that was to bring more than its share of pain and heart-ache, Florence would never feel so special again.

★

'The Queen had the longest train of all, and she had six train-bearers. The Queen Mother had four little boys. But I had to carry Princess Margaret's train all on my own.'

As the Princess's lady-in-waiting, Iris Peake's worst ordeal on that momentous day was ensuring that she did not fall flat on her face while carrying this 'exceptionally long' train, in purple velvet trimmed with ermine. They had been rehearsing for this moment for weeks.

> There were five steps when we got to Westminster Abbey – and Princess Margaret was going to get to the top of these steps before I reached the bottom. And, you know, you had this train in front of you, and you couldn't exactly look down to see where you were stepping, or put the train aside to have a look, so it was pretty nerve-racking.

That wasn't the end of Iris's preoccupation with this unwieldy garment, which had to be folded up like a concertina while Princess Margaret took her seat in the Royal Gallery. It turned out that the only person who knew the arcane pleating technique for doing this was Princess Alice, no longer young, but an aristocrat of blood royal:

> She told us how to arrange it over her arm with the right side showing. Well we practised like anything, and thankfully all went well on the day.

With her view of the aisle screened by the organ loft, Mrs Felicity Fisher, daughter-in-law of the Archbishop of Canterbury, had no chance of seeing any of the unfolding drama below.

Instead, she consoled herself with glimpses from above of the array of extraordinary finery in which the invited grandees were smothered. It was eleven o'clock when, at long last, craning her neck, Felicity was able to catch sight of the royal entry into the Abbey. There was her father-in-law, Doctor Fisher, the Archbishop of Canterbury, supporting the Queen to one side; to the other, the Bishop of Bath and Wells ('the least good-looking man I had ever seen'). Then they were lost to view. After that Felicity had to content herself with the sonorities of Doctor Fisher's 'lovely speaking voice', the piping, almost strangled tones of the young woman's responses: 'All this I promise to do . . .'; and the reverberating crescendos of *Zadok the Priest*. Halfway through the ceremony her neighbour, the Mayoress of Bradford, offered her a fortifying nip of brandy. The glum-faced lady on the other side of her was mutely unsociable.

Outside the Abbey, it was like November; that day, the temperature barely topped 12°C. Numb and frozen, deeply grateful for her heavy winter suit, raincoat and galoshes, Emily Kimbrough sat, exposed to the elements, in the journalists' stand opposite the entrance. She had caught a glimpse of the Queen as she entered, but from the point at which the service began she was able to follow it only via loudspeakers and an announcer's commentary. Shivering, she began to feel she might as well have been listening to the proceedings on the radio. Would it be regarded as lèse-majesté to take a surreptitious gulp of hot coffee from one's thermos while the solemnities were taking place?

But then came the moment which, as Emily said, would be 'recorded in my memory for all the rest of my life . . .':

Our announcer said, 'The Archbishop of Canterbury is holding the Crown above her head. He is lowering the crown. He places it. Elizabeth is a Queen.'

And simultaneously, without a word, but with a sound like a breeze through a field of corn, every person in every stand as far as my eye could stretch around Parliament Square, rose to his feet . . . I have never before seen a spontaneous rising of thousands of people as I saw that day. Nor do I know why I rose. But I think I would have done so had I been alone. And that is what happened to all of us.

For millions of her subjects, Elizabeth II was a receptacle for hope. She was just twenty-seven, small and slight, and for many of them there seemed a special poignancy in seeing 'one who is little more than a girl . . .' receive on her head the weighty crown, symbol of the unending duty now awaiting her. The Defender of the Faith seemed, herself, defenceless and innocent, alone among the multitude filling the Abbey, in sore need of her people's prayers and comfort. Among those present, many wept; touched, tremulous and awed by the solemn moment they had just witnessed.

The service was three hours long. At its end, the newly crowned and anointed Queen and her close retinue retired to a special annexe, before rejoining the buzzing throng of crowned heads and commoners, nobility and newspapermen from around the world, gathered to greet the royal family in Westminster Hall. Amongst them was the Comptroller of the Queen Mother's Household, Group Captain Peter Townsend, a man of charm and intelligence with a touch of the film star about his sculpted features and blue-grey eyes. Townsend had married in 1941; there were two young sons, but by the end of the war his marriage was starting to crack. It finished in divorce in 1952. Since 1945 Townsend had worked as closely trusted equerry to the Queen's father, George VI, and it was in this capacity that he met – and fell in love with – the radiantly pretty Princess Margaret, sixteen years his junior. She returned his love, but until that day both believed their relationship to be secret from the world at large.

Princess Margaret came up to me; she looked superb, sparkling, ravishing. As we chatted she brushed a bit of fluff off my uniform.

It must have been a bit of fur coat I picked up from some dowager in the Abbey. I never thought a thing about it, and neither did Margaret. We just laughed over it. But that little flick of her hand did it all right. After that, the storm broke.

Black and White

But first, it was time for lunch.

I doubt whether many of the 300-odd guests at the Coronation luncheon detected [the presence of curry powder] in a chicken dish which was distinguished mainly by a delicate and nutlike flavour in the sauce . . .

recalled Constance Spry. Of faintly bilious appearance, the recipe for this impeccably 1950s dish had been devised by Connie's working partner Rosemary Hume, who had risen to the challenge of providing food that was both appetising and distinctive, but could also be prepared ahead of time and served cold. The mayonnaise and cream sauce was daringly enlivened not only with curry powder but also with lemon juice, apricot purée and red wine. On the menu, in keeping with the Frenchifying tendencies of haute cuisine of the day, it was described as *Poulet Reine Élizabeth*, and served alongside a salad of rice, diced cucumber and peas. The dish was the centrepiece of a spectacularly successful lunch.

From that day on, as Fiona MacCarthy tells us in her memoir of her debutante days, 'Coronation Chicken was inevitably on the menu . . . The recipe remained a staple of upper-class entertaining for many years to come.'

★

It was estimated that in Britain 27 million people watched the Coronation live on television for at least half the day. In the heart of the Derbyshire mining country, at Langwith Junction near Mansfield, where she has lived all her life, Audrey Alssebrook's experience was typical:

> We had a nine-inch television, and we paid weekly for it. And we were t'first in our street to have a television. And then, not many days after, Mrs Leach had one, and then Mrs Brittles, she had one.
>
> And we had t'neighbours in to watch t'Coronation – in black and white, you know? But it were brilliant. You had to dress up – ooh, definitely! Clean pinners on! We thought we were everybody didn't we? And they were even sat on t'floor. They were all miners – and t'little kids were sat at t'front. There were our Frieda, and Malcolm, and Cheryl from Glossop. And you could see t'Queen walking down there, on that little tiny set! And ooh, it were brilliant. We thought we were t'cat's whiskers, we thought we were everybody, didn't we? Ooh, we thought we were <u>everybody</u>, duck.

In Leicester Valerie Gisborn was grateful to be given a day off from the factory. 'A great number of people had television sets, but we were not one of them.' So the family crossed town to watch television at Auntie Pat's. By 9.30 a.m. they were seated with a crowd of neighbours in front of the fourteen-inch set:

> [Auntie Pat's] front lounge was packed . . . We followed the proceedings in silence, broken occasionally with an 'Oh' or an 'Ah' . . . Auntie Pat supplied us with drinks and sandwiches periodically . . .

In Liverpool the public holiday meant that sixteen-year-old Sheila McKenzie had a day off from her job in the accounts office of a big department store. Her family rented a TV for the occasion. Sheila remembers being entranced by the Queen's dress. But she also remembers feeling distressed at the thought of her monarch's new and burdensome responsibilities:

> She'd become Queen at such a young age hadn't she? I can remember thinking when she had that crown on her head, how heavy it must have been. There was a kind of sorrow . . . I couldn't help putting myself in her situation, and thinking about all that she had to cope with at that time.

In Sussex Elizabeth Monnington felt the same. On the day, she and her husband David, a farmer, joined forces with the in-laws:

> We watched the whole thing on television, enthralled. And yet, as well as being wonderful, it was really quite a sobering occasion.
>
> Because you know I felt so sorry for the Queen, that her happiness and her private life had ended so quickly. But at the same time I was full of admiration; I had complete confidence that she would make a wonderful job of it, which she has!

Liz had known David since childhood, and both had been regulars at the local Young Conservatives and Young Farmers' Club. She had married him the previous year at the age of nineteen. Did something in Queen Elizabeth's bitter-sweet predicament resonate with her namesake – a vivacious twenty-year-old who at such a young age had forsaken her journalistic ambitions and a carefree, sporty social life when she accepted David Monnington's terms for their relationship? 'He didn't really approve of women playing tennis or frivolling away going out to coffee or horse-riding, so I gave all that up.' Perhaps even then Liz sensed that she would need to draw on a similar sense of confidence in order to make a wonderful job of being wife to this uncompromising man.

Drawn together across the nation, viewers gaped at the

spectacle of a young, pale, small woman in 'unexpectedly bridal' attire, bowed beneath the weight of the 'huge, hideous, sacred St. Edward's Crown', and dwarfed by the barbarously ornate golden juggernaut which bore her back to the palace under a downpour. The Sun Insurance girls had also watched the ceremony on TV, but they were back up on their rooftop eyrie to wave and cheer the royals as, far below them, the coach turned out of Whitehall and back down the Mall.

At a quarter past five in the afternoon the new Queen made her appearance on the palace balcony. Iris Peake was there too, accompanying Princess Margaret. Still clutching that wayward train, Iris stood respectfully behind her mistress listening to the thundering cheers of the crowd, gasping along with them as 168 RAF jets in formation performed a perfect fly-past.

*

In the down-at-heel Birmingham suburb of Sheldon, grumpy thirteen-year-old Brenda Nash was less than enraptured by the day's festivities. She was indignant at being forced by her mum into an outsized patriotic frock patterned geometrically in red, white and blue. 'The day lost some of its magic for me as I contemplated this monstrosity . . .' Brenda felt resentful, put-upon: a familiar enough response to life in the Nash household, where as a daughter she had grown accustomed to accepting unfairness in a spirit of resignation. Brenda was a clever girl – the only child on her estate to attend grammar school – and already she felt like a freak, 'something of a fairground attraction'. And though Brenda's dad was a skilled worker, 'Mom' was a bad manager; the family's daily life was haunted by the spectre of debt. At times, indeed, the 'monotony, poverty and lack of hope that seemed to make up [the] daily round' left Brenda feeling that life was unbearable:

> To be born a girl was to be born a second-class citizen. [Boys] were something in [our] world; girls were nothing.

Birmingham was even colder and more miserable than London that day. The rain came down in sheets, and Westcott Road's planned celebratory Coronation street party was relocated to a school hall. Earlier, Brenda had traded the Union Jack get-up for a fancy-dress costume. 'I was Miss Correspondence 1953.' The dress was a jokey collage of postcards, telegrams and letters. The downpour left this creation soggy and dripping, but the competition – Hawaiian dancers half-frozen in their grass skirts, pirates with streaked make-up and a medieval knight whose cardboard armour had been reduced to mush – were in a worse state, and Brenda was triumphant. 'I won first prize – a brush, comb and mirror set, with a regal picture of our new Queen on the back.'

That wet afternoon in 1953, it was impossible for Brenda Nash to imagine any more glittering prize than this.

*

Over 4,000 miles away in Kingston, Jamaica, 2 June was blazing hot. In the shade of their houses, everyone who had a radio was listening in. One of them, Gloria Walker, remembered her feelings that day:

> The broadcast made us feel connected . . .
>
> We felt we were like part of England, in spite of we were so many miles away. We thought England was the Mother Country. I grew up to love the National Anthem, in those days it was <u>our</u> National Anthem. And we believed England would look after us, because it always did . . .

Vilma Owen, whose story we will follow later in this book, also lived in Jamaica. She was only eleven years old at the time of the

Coronation. Her mother, a dressmaker – separated from her father, who drank – cared devotedly for Vilma and her two younger brothers. As a strict Seventh-day Adventist, she brought her children up on puritanical principles. From sunset on Friday to sunset on Saturday the family observed the Sabbath. Saturdays were given over to church and all meals had to be prepared in advance. But though life could be a struggle, Vilma and her brothers grew up carefree and secure. Their island life was blessed with sunshine and fruit; but paradise, to Vilma, would always be the holidays spent with her extended family at her grandmother's house. Spacious and welcoming, with a fruitful orchard, it was an adventure playground for small children. Chickens scratched in the yard. You could chase lizards or a mongoose. There were birds to shoot, naseberries to gather and crabs to catch.

Socially, however, Vilma lacked confidence. She was a shy and sensitive child, who still remembers being confused and overwhelmed by the scale of the Coronation celebrations:

> I found it very frightening. We all had to go to a huge children's jamboree in a park. It meant leaving home, getting on a bus and going to this vast place where there were thousands and thousands of children doing some kind of activities. I felt – well, it was just too much!

But the source of the festivities was clear to her. Distant as it was, Vilma knew that her country was inseparably tied to England and its Queen.

> I knew my country was linked to England. And yes, we knew that she was head of the Commonwealth, Queen of England – Queen of Jamaica, you know? I admired her. I remember feeling sad that she'd lost her dad, and that's how she came to the throne.
>
> I often imagined England. I can remember thinking, I wonder what the people are like? I wondered, for instance, what

snow is like? I'd heard of snow but I hadn't seen snow. And I wondered about the Queen, and what would it be like to be her? What she ate, how did *she* feel? These were the thoughts that went through my head, you know?

The Empty Vessel

Not everyone was swept up in the fervour. Back in England, ex-debutante Anthea York had grown up in an entrenched Establishment family, in which reverence for the Monarchy was taken for granted. By extension, where emotional matters were concerned, 'not talking about things was a way of life'. In 1950 Anthea spent a year being 'finished' in Paris before making her debut and then accepting an offer to read History at Cambridge University. Through family connections she and her sister Helena found themselves on Coronation Day freezing to death in privileged seats overlooking the processional route along the Mall. But Anthea was underwhelmed by the occasion:

> I associate the event with cold, damp and boredom; hours of waiting for the procession to begin. I remember being puzzled. Was it really such an influential event, could it really contribute something to Britain?
>
> The Queen had such a funny voice didn't she? But I suppose one accepted her as being just there. It is convenient to have a nominal head of state who is not party political . . .

What caused her to question the ceremony? At twenty-one, Anthea felt that there were many pieces in the jigsaw of her own life that didn't quite fit, and that couldn't be talked about. Her grandfather had been a high-up officer in the armed services; her father was also a service officer; her mother was a pillar of the local Conservative party, and she herself had been presented at court. And yet – 'I felt like a fish out of water . . . and I kept thinking I would get back into the pond. But I was lonely, and an outsider. In fact I now recognise that I was in denial and confusion.' For all her top-drawer upbringing, Anthea York found that the pattern of womanhood offered up by the new Queen, with her good-looking husband and bonny children, bore no congruence with her own life. The missing piece in the puzzle was her own sexuality. 'The rest of society was just so heterosexual. It was simply assumed that you couldn't do anything unless you had a man to do it with. But I didn't know I was lesbian till I was thirty . . .'

Another Cambridge student, Joan Rowlands, was in no doubt at all about where her priorities lay that day. The Amateur Dramatic Club in Cambridge had cast her in a new play, due to open on 3 June. For Joan, Coronation Day was Dress Rehearsal Day. Yes, she thought, on balance, the new young Queen was a good thing; but twenty-year-old Joan went with the crowd in being blithely disdainful of such Establishment junketings, dismissed by an Oxford contemporary of hers as 'this maypole nonsense'. Along with her fellow actors she cold-shouldered the celebrations, to spend the day 'rehearsing heartily'. The only side benefit of the royal occasion was that the pubs had been granted extended opening hours, so after the rehearsal Joan and her gang spent considerably longer than usual in the Eagle, just off King's Parade.

> We took it no more seriously than that.

In 1953 Flora Calder was working as a graphic artist in a Glasgow advertising agency. This twenty-five-year-old Scot felt that her race was too independent-minded to be taken in by Hanoverian high jinks:

> Sure, we watched it on television on a tiny wee screen – jeering slightly . . .

Like many Scots I was never a royalist. You'd get some royal coming up to Clydeside to launch a ship or whatever, and there'd be none of the wild cheering – just a whole crowd of people standing there quietly listening, as if to say, '*You* shouldn't be on the throne anyway, you're House of Hanover, *we're* House of Stuart!' Actually, the whole thing left me cold, and I was not alone.

But Flora's nonconformity went beyond a Scottish reluctance to respond to English royalty. In 1952 this exceptionally pretty, artistic, liberated young woman had escaped from her inhibited, social-climbing parental home, and set out to see the world. She travelled to France, and to Holland:

I sat in a canal-side café in Amsterdam, and I felt free for the first time.

And I thought, 'Ooh! This is the way lots of people in the world live! I don't have to stay in a gloomy northern city where their idea of a night out is standing in a tenement with a bag of chips, and that's it!

Within a year or two, that realisation would transport her to an even more unimaginable way of life, in the heart of London's bohemian art world.

*

Coronation Day was a day consecrated to family values, and it couldn't have come at a better time for Britain, reaffirming collective morality, national unity and post-war optimism.

But more than that, the 1953 Coronation attested to female values, speaking eloquently of our nation's attitude to women. At its heart was their personification, Queen Elizabeth, our nation's revered paradigm of beauty and blamelessness. In that moment when Elizabeth Alexandra Mary Windsor silently submitted to the yoke of sovereignty, she also relinquished any claim to idiosyncrasy, human fallibility or selfhood. This young woman would, in future, speak little, and never (in public) of her personal or private opinions. She would go to church on Sundays. To all appearances her marriage would be entirely happy, faithful and fulfilling. Through her husband, the epitome of masculinity, she would bring into the world three boys and a girl, who would also be expected to grow up in her image. She would wave and smile, and at all times appear perfectly groomed; her 'work' would be above all an expression of her femininity. She would be an empty vessel, waiting to be charged with our ideals of womanhood.

From 1953, Princess Margaret's love life was the antithesis of her sister's virtue and irreproachability. It is tempting to view the Townsend affair – in which two people who loved each other were driven by innumerable social pressures to renounce that love – as a dark reminder that the 1950s were not as comforting and cosy as they often appear to be. Divorce, guilt, hypocrisy, subversion and unhappiness were the flip side of the flag-waving, forelock-tugging patriotism, conservatism and adulation that coloured the Coronation celebrations. But the case of Princess Margaret also challenges the traditional model of womanhood. In Westminster Abbey on that day, with the flick of a hand, events were set in motion that would line up the forces of modernity, tolerance and liberalism against those of reaction, convention and the Establishment.

*

In 1953, in Establishment circles, divorcés of both sexes were still given the pariah treatment; they were not invited to royal garden parties, nor were they invited to any occasion where royalty might be present.

Just eleven days after her sister's Coronation, the *People* ran an 'exclusive', indignantly informing its readership of the story that, it appeared, readers round the world already knew: the young Princess, twenty-two years old and third in line to the throne, was contemplating a scandalous act that would 'fly in the face of Royal and Christian tradition . . .', namely, marriage with a man of thirty-nine who had been dragged through the sordid quagmire of the divorce courts.

The Prime Minister, Winston Churchill, the Cabinet and the Commonwealth Premiers were united in pronouncing that the Princess should not enter into a marriage which the Church could not recognise. This sledge-hammer judgement was all the more hypocritical in coming from a number of cabinet ministers who themselves had been involved in divorce cases.* The view was taken that a cooling-off period was required; the couple would have to wait until Margaret was twenty-five, when she might petition the Privy Council.

It was decided to remove Group Captain Peter Townsend from the Royal Household and banish him to Brussels without delay. On the morning of 29 June, Townsend went to Clarence House to say goodbye:

> The Princess was very calm, for we felt certain of each other . . .
> Her mother – I blessed her for her exquisite tact – left us alone
> for a few precious moments. Then the Princess was gone.

They would not meet again for over a year.

---

* Sir Anthony Eden, Sir Walter Monckton and Mr Peter Thorneycroft.

2. Her True Calling

The Twin Pillars

The hit TV variety show *The Good Old Days* was first screened in 1953, and tapped into a powerful nostalgia for an imagined time before juvenile delinquency, rationing and soulless modernity. Its Leeds audience, decked out in Edwardian boaters and feathered toques, had endured the Second World War. At the City Varieties Music Hall they relived their lost past.

That sense of a vanished prelapsarian world is a common one, but for those for whom the Second World War acted as a dividing line between childhood and adulthood it was, perhaps, unusually poignant.

Writing about her Essex childhood, Kath Langstone from Kelvedon recalled a time of Temperance clubs, horse-drawn carts and hopscotch:

> The pace of life was so much slower and people had so much more time for each other . . . How times have changed!

Bathed in the glow of memory, home, and Mother, were the centre of Kath's world:

> I do not think we appreciated how selfless and hardworking our mothers were, they just devoted their lives to their husband and family and always put themselves last.

In her autobiography *Slipstream*, Elizabeth Jane Howard conjures up timeless 1930s country-house childhood summers spent reading in apple trees, playing tennis and swimming. For Margaret,

Duchess of Argyll, the courtly glamour of her own past seemed irrecoverable:

> The splendour of the 1930s had vanished for ever. Gone were the beautiful evening dresses and the dress uniforms of the men . . .

– while for diarist Nella Last it was the moral certainties of her youth that had gone with the wind:

> . . . there was right and wrong, kindness or cruelty, clear-cut ways of thought . . .

The clammy hand of nostalgia gripped the past, wrapping it in a fugitive radiance.

Millions of British women who had lived through the Second World War knew that this country could never be the same again, but that didn't stop them wanting it to be. Many of them had striven with every sinew to help win the war – not only so that afterwards they might have a better future, but also so that they might resume the old, happy life, the life they had left behind.

At the mid-way point of the war, in 1942, a report written by the liberal social reformer Sir William Beveridge offered a blueprint to improve the post-war lot of every man, woman and child. Beveridge's utopian vision was the Welfare State and, with its emphasis on maternity provisions, rosehip syrup, childcare, and care for the elderly, it read like a manifesto for women.

Nevertheless, embedded within its 300 pages was an assumption about women which – though today we might find it unjust and discriminatory – was absolutely attuned to the mood of the times:

> The great majority of married women [wrote Beveridge] must be regarded as occupied on work which is vital though unpaid,

without which their husbands could not do their paid work and
without which the nation could not continue . . .

and he went on to say:

> The attitude of the housewife to gainful employment outside
> the home is not and should not be the same as that of the single
> woman. She has other duties . . . In the next thirty years house-
> wives as Mothers have vital work to do in ensuring the adequate
> continuance of the British Race and of British ideals in the
> world.

Between 1945 and 1949 the Labour Party implemented Beveridge's proposals, creating the Welfare State, but at the same
time enshrining such assumptions in law. A wife was not
expected to take up paid employment, and any benefits she
might receive would be paid via her husband's insurance. Thus
innovation and reform went hand-in-hand with tradition and
orthodoxy. Institutionally, the post-war world was not unlike
the pre-war world, in seeing Housework and Motherhood as
the twin pillars supporting Britishness.

We cannot dismiss Beveridge and his political confederates
as hopelessly sexist, without recognising the mind-set of
women themselves as they entered the post-war period. They
too were conditioned by their times. They had endured six
years of gruelling anxiety and hard work; they had struggled
to feed their families on rations; many had seen their belongings smashed to smithereens, their homes burned and
destroyed. The austerity Britain of the later 1940s and early
1950s was a nation of rationing, continued belt-tightening,
fuel economy, cold winters, a housing crisis, rocketing divorce
figures, and a baby boom. The future was frightening. It
should not surprise us that women in 1950 were in some ways
backward-looking. The lost world of their youth, irreplaceable

in the national psyche, had a welcoming hearth, four safe walls and smelt of fresh-baked cake. And if bringing it back meant acceptance of injustices, prejudice and inflexibility on the part of men, then that was because many women themselves were conditioned into believing this to be the natural order of things, an order which they too yearned to restore.

Even highly intelligent and self-aware women raised no objection to being sidelined and – by contemporary standards – misused by their male colleagues or associates. Diana Athill, co-director and shareholder of the publishers André Deutsch, noted in a resigned way that she was a better editor, but was paid less than her fellow (male) co-directors doing the same job:

> All publishing was run by many badly-paid women and a few much better-paid men: an imbalance that women were, of course, aware of, but which they seemed to take for granted.

Athill claims that she and many of her contemporaries felt a kind of guiltless inertia when it came to women's rights. 'We could see injustice, but we didn't feel the pinch of it . . .' She felt more a kind of relief at being permitted to do what she liked doing – editing books – and being let off dealing with money and accounts.

The same applies, broadly speaking, to the wider point Diana Athill makes about her generation of women, shaped by their backgrounds to please men, and happy to stick to what they supposed themselves to be good at: motherhood and home-making. In her critical history of women *Lady Into Woman* (1953), Vera Brittain asserts that '. . . the largest scope for change still lies in men's attitude to women, *and in women's attitude to themselves . . .*' (my italics). Feminists like Brittain aside, this is an unavoidable essential to understanding the period, and one that we will encounter repeatedly. As ever, the high-circulation women's magazines had their finger on the nation's pulse. In

Woman's Own, Monica Dickens implored her readers, 'Don't try to be the boss . . .':

> Marriage is the goal of every female who seeks happiness . . . It was not intended by Nature that a woman should have to fend for herself.
>
> The instinctive desire of woman is to attach herself to a man who will be her provider.
>
> The average woman is only too happy to do so, to have the tedious business of coping with the duller mechanics of existence taken off her hands while she gets on with the more satisfying business of looking after a home and children.

It was abnormal and against Nature for women to 'take over the things that should be a husband's job'. Everybody knew that men liked making decisions, paying bills, ordering taxis, tackling plumbers, meeting landlords and signing things, while women preferred childcare and keeping house and were only too pleased to have the administrative burdens of life removed from their slight and pretty shoulders. Even Diana Athill, who was single, entirely uninterested in food and barely able to boil an egg, was given the André Deutsch cookery list to edit:

> I was a woman, and where was the woman's place but in the kitchen? So the cookery list became 'mine'.

In the early 1950s, feminists still had a mountain to climb.

A Better World?

At that time, the imagined 'golden age' of the early twentieth century seemed more irrecoverable than ever, as the world fell under a new threat of war.

On 25 June 1950, Communist North Korean forces invaded

the American-held southern end of the Korean peninsula. The United Nations Security Council immediately authorised military intervention, placing America and her allies head-to-head with a Soviet-aided enemy, thousands of miles from home. Aghast, Nella Last listened to the announcement that Britain was sending troops to Korea. Her gloom intensified at the thought that such a war could so easily escalate into a nuclear exchange:

> America has the A-bomb . . . We would have little or no say whether one had to be dropped in Korea, and if such a dreadful thing *did* happen – and Russia *has* them – all hell could easily be let loose. A terrifying outlook.

'Letter from London', Mollie Panter-Downes's weekly bulletin to the readers of the *New Yorker*, described the lowered morale and nagging uncertainty of that summer of 1950. Thunderstorms and squalls were flattening the crops and destroying the fruit harvest. Holiday-makers were packing their waterproofs for a fortnight by the sea, a brief getaway from grey cities scarred by bomb sites. But reports were that the Brits were displaying their customary phlegm. Overheard: a sprightly shop assistant saying to her customer: 'Well, we don't want another war, do we, just when they've taken petrol off the ration?' Peace seemed very fragile, but weary Londoners broadly supported the military intervention and the increased defence expenditure it entailed, while recognising that it would not make their lives any easier. Another visitor from America, the political theorist Hannah Arendt, noted the 'dull blanket of fear [which] lies over the country . . . softened, though, by the fact that they've been eating too little for such a long time that they barely notice the difference anymore . . . Everything [is] scarce. Everything [is] of bad quality.'

In 1950, rationing of soap and petrol ended; other foods

released from rationing that spring were chocolate biscuits, dried fruit, syrup and treacle, jelly and mincemeat. Cake-makers were among the happy few – if you could get the sugar that is – but tea remained controlled until 1952, sweets and sugar till 1953, and a number of other foods until 1954. Among Joan Rowlands's memories of Newnham College in 1951, austerity, cold and cheeseparing loom large. The wind blew in from Siberia and she and her friends froze walking to lectures. Their rooms were unheated, and with just two buckets of coal a week one only lit a fire in extremity. Any student who did so might expect to be invaded by a cluster of girls who would huddle around it to share warmth and cocoa. Joan was allocated a small portion of butter, a modicum of sugar and an ounce of cheese a week.

The wartime make-do-and-mend ethos persisted. Growing up in west London post-war, Virginia Ironside recalled a culture of thrift:

Fulham Road . . . was full of repair shops – shoe repairers, electrical repairers, furniture repairers, pen hospitals, doll hospitals. There was always someone available to enable you to eke a few more months out of any gadget or article you possessed.

We had no car, no television and only one big radio. The doors were always closed in winter to keep the heat in, the lights always turned off whenever we left a room. If the toast was burned, as it frequently was, it was scraped over the sink and eaten. Mould that developed on cheese was simply cut off, and if the pork smelled a bit, it was just washed thoroughly and cooked for a rather longer time than usual. Nearly every meal consisted of 'remains' cooked up in some ingenious way with Bisto to make them edible . . .

It is hard to describe the bleakness of the London landscape. Nearly everyone was thin and white. Their teeth were often bad, their hair was, like mine at the time, only washed once a week, and everyone smelled, it being long before the days of deodorant . . .

Everyone in the street, in their worn, dingy clothes, looked horribly unattractive and not at *all* beautiful.

★

Would rationing never end? Two years after the austerity budget of 1948, a mood of disillusionment with the Labour government was creeping over the nation, and the Conservative Party was preparing to battle it out in the 1950 election.

Liz Jones was seventeen that year, growing up as a bubbly, spirited teenager in the Conservative-held county town of Lewes in Sussex. Though the word 'feminist' was not in her vocabulary, Liz was clever, talented, and enjoyed teamwork and participation. Her father, an accountant, was the family bread-winner; her mother diverted her excess energies to supporting the local Conservative party, and young Liz followed enthusiastically in her footsteps. Though only twelve at the time of the 1945 Labour landslide, she remembered great family concern at the thought of Mr Attlee coming to power, and when another election was called for February 1950, Liz was of an age to do her bit. The Conservative Party at this time held a 4 per cent lead among women; Lewes too was a safe Tory seat, represented since 1945 by the patrician Sir Tufton Beamish,★ and Liz was thrilled to be allowed to help with his campaign. Though still not eligible to vote, she joined him on canvassing trips, sporting a blue rosette, knocking on the doors not only of the more gracious neighbourhoods, but also of dilapidated terrace houses in the more slummy areas of town:

★ A dynasty of Tufton Beamishes served the people of Lewes. Sir Tufton's father, Tufton Percy Hamilton Beamish, represented the town as MP from 1924 until 1931 and again from 1936 until 1945.

It was a 100 per cent canvass. We'd do every household, and if somebody was out when we called we'd go back again. Some of the electorate were really hostile – they would throw stones at you. Actually I found that all rather exciting.

Sir Tufton was wonderful. He was really quite fearless – and in fact a lot of the working classes greatly respected and liked him. He would have a pint in the pub with anybody . . . It was a very good experience going round with him – I was so lucky!

Then it was back to HQ at the Constitutional Club to tick off the registers. On Election Day, 23 February 1950, Attlee's government were the victors, but with a massively reduced majority. In Lewes, the turnout topped 80 per cent, and Sir Tufton nearly doubled his majority, to over 15,000.

The following year, when the crippled Attlee government called another General Election for 25 October, Liz and her mother were back on the stump. This time, they were full of hope for a Tory victory. Like many women, they accepted the opposition's argument against Labour's economic controls and austerity measures. That autumn – a full six years after the end of the war – and with the meat ration at its lowest ever, both the major political parties were pitching hard for the housewife vote. Churchill's candidates were still finding it hard to win seats in the industrial north, but across south-east England, women voters were putting crosses by Tory candidates' names, helping Sir Tufton Beamish in Lewes to win his biggest majority yet: 17,263. In October 1951, seventeen women candidates gained seats in parliament – six of them Conservatives, eleven of them Labour. Sixty other women were unsuccessful, including twenty-six-year-old Miss Margaret Roberts, who had fought the safe Labour seat of Dartford. The *Daily Graphic* ran a picture of Britain's youngest woman candidate on polling day, wearing a trim buttoned-up suit and a plumed hat, smiling arm-in-arm with Mr Denis Thatcher, under the headline 'And they voted for romance . . .' They had just announced their engagement.

★

The future Mrs Thatcher was beaten in the polls by Labour's Norman Dodds. It was the first time twenty-two-year-old Maureen Johnson had voted and in Dartford, Kent, she was one of Mr Dodds's most enthusiastic supporters. Maureen dates her passion for the Labour cause to the day when she stood in the crowd in July 1945 and cheered the visiting Clement Attlee to the echo. Surely socialism would sweep away the ills of the past?

Maureen needed to believe in a better post-war world. Tragedy had visited the Johnson family twice within the space of one year when her two elder brothers were both killed – one shot down over Malta in 1943, the other on the bridge at Arnhem in 1944. When the second telegram came Maureen, then aged just fifteen, was alone in the house. She read it, and fled terrified to her room:

> [I] shut myself in. I didn't come out for about two days just because I was frightened of my mother breaking down. And we never really talked about it until very much later, and even then not very much. In a way it was too painful.

Maureen's parents were shopkeepers who kept a general store in Dartford. Her father was laddish and lackadaisical, fond of the pub, and an avid reader of the *Daily Mail*. Her gossipy, uneducated mother was always loving, yet disappointed that her bookish daughter wasn't more feminine and interested in clothes. The war had interrupted Maureen's education, and left to her own devices she developed an inner life and a rebellious streak. Back at school, this evolved into a talent for debating, and before long into a passionate interest in politics. But neither of her parents encouraged this, perhaps because she brought her disputatious tendency home to the family fireside, furiously challenging her father's *Daily Mail*-influenced ideas. They had terrible rows:

> It was explosive . . . How I stuck it – and why he didn't kick me out – I don't know. From a very early age I read everything I could.

At the earliest opportunity Maureen joined both the Labour Party and the Labour League of Youth.

> I was an idealist in those days. We really thought that we could build a better world. That it didn't have to be the way it was, that people didn't have to be brought up in poverty, that everyone should have the opportunity for the education that they needed, and healthcare. And in fact some of what we wanted came true . . .
>
> It was inspiring. We had endless debates in our group . . . But it never entered my thoughts to continue my education past school – because I literally didn't know anyone who'd been to university . . .

Brian Nicol was the first person she ever met with college ambitions. One day in 1950 the members of the Bexleyheath branch of the Labour League of Youth came over to meet their counterparts in Dartford for a combined debate . . .

> – and that was it. He said it was because I wore a plunging neckline.

Their mutual attraction, love, respect and shared commitment to the cause would be the basis for a life together.

But right from the start, Maureen found that her new boyfriend was not always going to be there for her. As soon as he had finished his National Service he took up a place at Fircroft

College in Birmingham. Brian was nurturing embryonic political ambitions, and in 1951 he upped his educational game by enrolling at Ruskin College, Oxford. Meanwhile, Maureen was living at home back in Dartford and working in a secretarial post in London, neither of them had any money, and they were only able to see each other during the vacations. Something had to give, and by now marriage seemed the only answer. As to whether Maureen's independence and intellectual hunger would find an outlet once she took on her wifely duties, only time would tell.

★

When the Conservatives won the 1951 election Brian Nicol and Maureen Johnson were far from overjoyed. But with Winston Churchill back at Number 10 Downing Street, there was huge relief both in the Jones household and at 9 Ilkley Road, Barrow-in-Furness:

> Gradually a feeling of security stole over me . . .

wrote Nella Last in her diary on the Friday after the election. In 1950 Churchill's defeat had reduced her to tears. But now:

> . . . difficult to explain except a feeling that competent people would soon be in command. Mr Churchill has a place in our hearts . . .
> I was amazed at the light-hearted feeling that came over me.

Labour was destined to remain in the political wilderness for another thirteen years, as Britain's electorate voted against socialism and everything it stood for.

Less reflective, full of the joie de vivre and optimism of her eighteen years, Liz Jones was, if she was honest, more motivated by parties than by party politics. Nationally, Young Conservative membership peaked at around 170,000 in the 1950s, and Liz was a card-carrying member:

> I think probably I did join for the social side ... There were speakers who came to talk to us about politics, but mainly it was just young people being sociable and chatty.
>
> Most of us went to private schools. We used to meet in the town, and go to the Southdown Tennis Club. The Young Farmers' Club was very popular too ...

Liz loved nothing better than gathering with her girlfriends at the various approved Young Conservative hangouts round Lewes: Plumpton Racecourse, hunt meets, the Southdown Tennis Club, the Tatler Tea Rooms in town. Pubs weren't considered suitable for young ladies, but coffee mornings were seen as cheery and elegant, so the Tatler was the preferred venue for everyone's birthday celebrations. Having left school at sixteen, Liz was spending a year at Mr Box's Academy in Brighton – ('practically *all* the girls of my generation went there ...') – gaining basic secretarial and accountancy skills ...

> ... but most of the girls weren't expected to have a career and earn their living. They were expected to marry and settle down.

Despite this, a dream lingered in Liz's mind of going to university, perhaps – who knows? – training to be a journalist. But those expectations that she would 'settle down', her parents' as well as her own, were to prove hard to resist.

At that time the high spots of Liz's week were the YC or Young Farmers' Club dances. Saturday evenings would see her hooked into a full-length taffeta ball gown – 'rather meringue-ey' – clutching her wrap and handbag. Make-up was forbidden by her mother but, once safely round the corner of the street, out would come her secret supply of lipstick, and in keeping with her friends Liz would appear suitably enhanced with a coat or two of Yardley's Rose Pink. Everybody in her group had been to dance class, and up at the Town Hall the atmosphere was dizzy as the Gordon Ryder band from Rottingdean played waltzes, quicksteps and old-time favourites like the Gay Gordons. Liz, with her pretty looks, enthusiasm, and lively sense of enjoyment, rarely suffered the fate of the 'wilting wallflower'; in any case, she had started going out with David Monnington when she was sixteen, and he now claimed her for most dances.

David was the son of a local farmer and landowner:

> I'd known him when I was at nursery school, and thought what a horrid little boy he was. He and another boy used to chase us home from school. They were nasty little bullies.
>
> But he improved!

Brought together through the Young Farmers and YCs, it was now the easiest thing in the world for Liz to be swept away by his potent, unwavering presence. Here was a man who knew what he wanted – and he wanted her. Soon she was 'besotted, infatuated . . .' Without a backward look she jettisoned her secret longing to try for university. Going away to college, being anywhere far from David, suddenly seemed impossible. She was living for their dates, for the Saturday dances when she would whirl in his arms till past midnight. Afterwards, pushing his bicycle, he'd walk her home. The skimpy finery barely kept her warm, but once at the garden gate he'd take her in his arms . . .

> I was terribly physically attracted to him. But I didn't know anything; I thought if you kissed a boy you'd have a baby. I can't tell you how ignorant I was. Somehow, much as I might have wanted to, I was scared of going beyond the bounds. I felt one should wait till one was married.

Fuel rationing ended that year, and on other days David borrowed his father's battered Land Rover and took Liz out to explore the Sussex countryside. They joined the YC crowd at point-to-points, or sometimes went alone and picnicked on the Downs. It was on one of these occasions that David proposed, and it was here that he laid down his conditions for their marriage:

> We met, and we drove up on to the race course at Lewes. And he said, 'I would like to marry you. But I don't think I could marry anyone who leads the sort of social life you lead – hunting, playing tennis, going out to coffee. You know, wasting time.'
>
> He implied that if I continued to do all that sort of thing he wouldn't marry me. Like his father, he was very serious and Victorian. He believed in hard work. Well I certainly did that for about forty years!
>
> I was so besotted with him I just gave up doing all the things I liked. And I think I should have known then what I know now – you can't change a person . . .

★

For thousands of young women like Maureen Johnson and Liz Jones in the early 1950s, the dreams of education, career, achievement and fulfilment were within reach. The war had exploded the inequality myth. The doors were opening. But for too many, their own ignorance, fears, confining desires and expectations were bred-in-the-bone. If Maureen had had any notion that a working-class girl like her could make it to university, she would surely have tried to go. 'A waste, really . . . But I didn't go to a private school, and I had missed two years of education in the war. My mother never bothered to question why I'd slipped through the net. She lived with the working-class assumption that one submitted to authority, that "they" know better than we do . . .' And if Liz could have had a no-strings boyfriend, if she had not said 'Yes' to David Monnington at the age of nineteen, if she had not been able to negotiate her own conditions for their marriage, if she had not given birth to six babies over eleven years, above all if she had had more confidence in herself, her life might also have been very different. As it was, there were too many 'ifs':

> I was much too subservient. Perhaps I should have stood up for myself. But sometimes it didn't seem worth it. I just thought – anything for peace and quiet.

Houseproud

In 1951 22 per cent of married women had jobs – a figure set to increase by almost 10 per cent over the decade – but stay-at-home mothers like Liz Monnington were still the norm. That year Mass Observation reported that a sample of housewives surveyed in the London suburban area spent fifteen hours a day on domestic activities. In 1948, just 4 per cent of British households owned a washing machine, and 16 per cent owned some form of electric water heater. Forty per cent of households had invested in a vacuum cleaner by 1948 – but in the early 1950s a quarter of homes were still cooking on coal ranges. The historian Caroline Davidson uses such figures to demonstrate that 'in 1950 most women in Britain were still cleaning their houses with the same basic equipment and materials that their ancestors had used 300 years earlier'.*

The steady reduction in numbers of domestic workers also put new pressures on middle-class housewives who had no

---

* Caroline Davidson, *A Woman's Work is Never Done: A history of housework in the British Isles 1650–1950* (1982).

servants. How were you to go on living the life you knew without the cook, housemaid, and parlourmaid of your pre-war childhood? Victorian standards persisted; homes had to be spring-cleaned, rooms 'turned out', carpets beaten, paintwork washed. Indeed, the work never seemed to get done. In the hope that their burden might be eased, they might have turned to manuals and magazines for guidance. *The Housewives' Pocket Book* was one which set out the average wife's day with the exactness of a railway timetable. She will rise at 7.15. Breakfast is a rolling meal. She and her husband will eat theirs first, before he leaves for work at 8.15, at which time the children come on stream. Once fed they are packed off to school at quarter to nine. Then the real work begins: turning down beds and opening windows, washing up, dusting and tidying, followed by 'weekly work'. This is elaborated on the following page:

Monday:	Laundry.
Tuesday:	Clean out bedroom and landing. Ironing in evening.
Wednesday:	Clean out children's bedroom and do stairs. Mending in evening.
Thursday:	Clean out hall, bathroom, w.c., cooking stove.
Friday:	Clean out living rooms ready for weekend; baking for weekend, cleaning silver.
Saturday:	Weekend shopping; change all linen, towels etc.

However, at eleven the housewife <u>must</u> have a short rest, *with her feet up*. Then she must go shopping, after which she must have her own lunch and another rest, followed by 'personal recreation' – but only for forty-five minutes, because tea must be on the table at 4.15. After tea she must 'tidy herself', and serve the evening meal at 6.30. Children in bed by 7.30. Then, unless occupied with the ironing or mending (see above), her time was her own until bedtime.

The evidence is that many women took such prescriptive routines extremely seriously. It was a matter of pride for the self-respecting housewife to have her whites blowing on the line where everyone could see them by Monday lunchtime – an image important to the marketers of the new washing detergents. My own mother always washed on Mondays, ironed on Tuesdays.* For her, there still remains something almost depraved about washing on any other day. As a young wife in the Derbyshire mining village of Langwith Junction, Audrey Alssebrook was another who took such domestic diktats to heart:

> I used to worry if things weren't perfect. Monday was always washday. And your kitchen floor tiles all had to be washed on washday as well. And you had a fire underneath your copper to heat the water, and that fire had to be cleaned out. Well then I'd got to do my ironing on the right day an' all.

And Nella Last recorded her chagrin after helping her daughter-in-law to do a big wash on a Saturday evening, and hanging it all out to dry overnight. What would the neighbours think? She was half amused, half horrified at this transgression, and early on Sunday morning crept guiltily down to the garden in dressing gown and slippers to unpeg the offending articles from the line before anyone noticed them.

Morally and physically, washing, drying and ironing dominated women's lives. The young East End midwife Jennifer Worth often had to fight her way through 'a forest of flapping linen' stretched across the backyards of her Bethnal Green patch.

---

* The weekly wash routine is enshrined in a nursery rhyme, familiar to the 50s generation, which begins: 'They that wash on Monday, have all the week to dry . . .', and ends 'And they that wash on Saturday, Oh! they are sluts indeed.'

'Once in the house or flat, there would be more washing to duck and weave through, in the hall, the stairways, the kitchen, the living room and the bedroom.' Blankets, sheets, curtains and clothes were all hand-washed, using water boiled up in a vast copper, rinsed and put through an unwieldy wrought-iron mangle before being hung out to dry. Why, asks Caroline Davidson, did more women not send their linen out to commercial laundries, which were competitively priced and widely available? 'The explanation is a moral one,' she argues. Women's sense of righteousness was bound up in washing, in an almost

Illustration from a 1950s manual on housework, which devoted a whole chapter to the Dos and Don'ts of Laundrywork.

religious way. Cleanliness was next to godliness. Virtue could not be bought; like charity, it must begin at home.

Audrey Alssebrook's self-respect depended on the domestic face she presented to her community:

> And we had our steps down to the street, and they'd got to be all scrubbed.

Even more than your washing-line, a clean front doorstep conferred street credibility – quite literally. Scoured and white, the external, public area of a woman's home blazoned messages of industry, moral worth and good repute to the passing world. But such status symbols cost much in the way of hard work. Weekday mornings would see rows of women in wrap-around pinnies, bottoms bobbing, genuflecting in front of their doorsteps. Donkey-stoning, the arcane ritual on which they were engaged, has long disappeared, but until the mid-1950s was an essential part of working-class life. One boy who grew up in a Pennine valley community recalled how it was a matter of pride for every housewife to keep her steps white:

> ... you could tell whether you were going into a house-proud woman's abode by glancing down at the doorstep. If it was donkey-stoned you were very likely in for a good tea with plenty of home-made sweet stuff. If not you might have to make do with a cream cracker or a rich tea biscuit.

By the same token, if the woman's step wasn't donkey-stoned, the neighbours would brand her as sloppy – or go in to see if she was ill.

The donkey-stone itself was a tablet of ground stone-dust, cement, water and bleach, mixed and compressed, then stamped with the image of a donkey. The stone doorstep, and sometimes the surrounding flagstones, would be scrubbed clean, then – while still wet – treated by rubbing with the donkey-stone, which brought them out in an attractive pale cream. The effect was pleasing, but fleeting. If anyone stood on it, or if it rained, the impermanent colour came off. You might wonder why they bothered, since it would all have to be done again so soon. But donkey-stoning not only ensured your reputation, proving to the world that you were conscientious in 'bottoming' your house, it was also an opportunity for women to spend time together, outside the confines of their homes. Indoors, they were isolated. On their front steps, they became an important conduit for information; they could gossip, caution, advise and set the world to rights. This was a community. When donkey-stoning died out, an outlet for female communication was lost.

Another young middle-class health worker – nurse Jennifer Craig – did some of her training in the slums of Leeds in the early 1950s. There, working-class families were crowded into 'one-up one-downs', with no bathrooms, shared outside toilets, and one cold-water tap per household. But Jennifer was able to judge by appearances. 'Despite the lack of running hot water the steps of most of the houses are well scrubbed and the lace cur-tains at the windows gleam white against the grimy brick walls.'

These clean curtains, visible from the street, were further evidence to the passer-by that the female occupant was respectable and took her work seriously. It was not unusual for the houseproud wife to own two sets of curtains for each window. One set would get taken down and washed, and replaced with a second pair. Nets had many advantages, being fashionable, dis-creet and conspicuously white – but they too were high-maintenance.

It might appear from the above that the excessive toil needed to present whitened doorsteps and fresh curtains to the world was, in its way, fulfilling. For some maybe, but not for Mrs Phillips, who wrote to writer and broadcaster Amabel Williams-Ellis after hearing her on *Woman's Hour*:

Few brides foresaw the incessant grind that awaited them once the orange blossom had faded.

Day by day I become more warped, bitter and almost hysterical with frustration. Why? Life's door is shut – there's time for nothing but chores, chores, chores.

And writing her Mass Observation diary one day in 1950, a forty-eight-year-old Sheffield housewife gave voice to millions like her who simply felt wearily resigned to their Sisyphean task:

26th June
Never was I so barren of anything for this diary as today. I have washed. And being a good drying day, also ironed; been to the library, bought rations, typed a letter, had 2 cups tea, and here I am. Shall presently see what the Dale family* have been up to and as I listen change into housecoat, sans corset, and relax properly.

Stewed fruit for tea, so no cooking to do, only b[read] & b[utter] to prepare, and a potta tea. Then to my book, and thankfulness that my life is as it is. 'Twas not always so.

Housework is endless. Thank goodness a woman can do it in her own time and leave it if she wishes. That is the only thing about it which makes life bearable to a woman such as I, who hate housework and have to be for ever driving myself to do the bit I do. Ugh.

Past Praying For

But in 1950 Eileen Hawe from Kilkenny felt free as a bird. She was twenty that year. Her nursing training in London was coming to an end, and her plan was to qualify, get a job, and see something of the world. Settling down would come, but not yet.

* The radio soap opera *Mrs Dale's Diary* – centred on the wife of Dr Jim Dale – began in 1948. By 1950 59 per cent of British women were listening in daily; it would run for over 5,000 episodes, until 1969. Mrs Dale and her world were safe, comfortable and middle-class; her repeated line 'I'm rather worried about Jim . . .' would become a national catch-phrase.

Sparkling and pretty, with auburn hair, green-grey eyes and a trim, shapely figure, Eileen exuded radiance and energy. She had arrived in London in 1946; her idyllic Irish childhood had not only endowed her with a peachy-bright complexion, but had also given her an eager love of the outdoors. 'I was a very good golfer – that was in my blood – and I grew up wanting to be a gym mistress.' But the Hawes were Catholics, and with eight children to support, her father, a town clerk, couldn't afford to send her to college.

It was not the only time that primitive Irish Catholicism was to prove an insurmountable obstacle in Eileen's life. In the mid-twentieth century, Ireland was a country still dominated by its priesthood and their doctrine of guilt. Mrs Hawe was devoutly Catholic in the old-fashioned way: daily prayers, novenas, church on Sunday, confession. She sent her daughter to be educated by a 'useless' order of French nuns, who extinguished any academic thirst she might have had. Languages were a love – had it not been for the French teacher Mother Gerard. Then there was the dancing. Eileen was a talented dancer in the Irish country tradition, who did performances to raise money for the Kilkenny Athletics Association. When one of these was reported in the local paper, Mother Gerard hauled her from her desk, stood her on the teachers' dais, and railed at her in front of the whole class: 'Will you all look at her? Will you look at her! Now we know why she can't speak French, because all her brains are in her feet!' Only Mother Rosaria inspired in her a love of poetry – Keats, Byron and Yeats – that has stayed with her for life.

Not surprisingly, the pupils at this school were given no information whatsoever about the facts of life. Instead, they were brainwashed:

There was this special talk by a Dominican or a Jesuit for the school leavers. He started shouting from up there on the altar, and he said: 'I've *seen* them at the railway stations, with their <u>dripping talons</u> – (meaning their nail varnish) – and their <u>congealed blood</u> – (meaning their lipstick)!' And then he said, 'On the day of judgement, I shall be saying *Dear God, Dear God, it's not my fault, I warned them, but they wouldn't listen to me.*'

And when I heard him saying that from the altar, something turned inside me, and I thought, 'My God, you think you're so sure you're going to be up there?' And it just sickened me.

Eileen felt she had to get away. Her PE teaching dream had evaporated, and instead she opted to do nursing. At seventeen she set off for London and enrolled as a trainee nurse at St Mary Abbot's Hospital in Marloes Road, Kensington. The change from green Kilkenny couldn't have been more abrupt:

Everything they gave me to eat made me sick. It was dried egg, and horse meat and bread and dripping – a horrible diet! And back home we had had our own fresh vegetables and everything . . . I got a crop of boils, and I got German measles and everything you could possibly get. And everybody looked to me starved, they all looked so hungry and grey. I couldn't believe what London was like! When I went down to Shoreditch and those places, that had all been bombed, it was like another planet.

It was here in London that Eileen finally lost her faith. The last straw for her was watching the officious Irish Catholic hospital chaplain conducting his visits to her patients. He would scurry up the stairs, buttonhole Eileen and loudly demand, 'Hello there *Mary-Ellen*, which beds are the *Catholics* in?' He had no time for anyone else, though the wards – post-war – were full of displaced persons from all over Europe. Sickened by his rudeness and lack of compassion, Eileen gave up going to church.

Nursing training was tough. She was on her feet for twelve hours on the trot; matrons and ward sisters were famous for their ferocity, and Eileen got her share of being shouted at. Even when the ward wasn't busy, the lower orders like Eileen were obliged to scrub out the sluice with Lysol and carbolic, to the ruination of her hands. As in a nunnery, hospital life had its own monastic rules. You had to get a pass to go out, and curfew was 10.30 p.m. Once, she joined a gang of other nurses to go dancing at the Hammersmith Palais, where there was a big band playing. In 1950s Kilkenny, that wasn't the way good Catholic girls behaved; you had a young man call by and collect you, and see you home safe, so when her mother heard, she was scandalised. 'I may as well have told her I was a prostitute, she thought it was *appalling*.'

Nonetheless, Eileen loved her time in London – the buzz of the big city around her was exhilarating, and she made close friendships in the nurses' home. After she qualified, her scanty wage was £3 12s 6d a month, but even without much money, she adored having mornings off to walk in Kensington Gardens, or to trip down Exhibition Road and visit the museums for nothing. Extravagances were out of the question, though Eileen's love of finery occasionally got the better of her. The shops in High Street Kensington were almost sinfully tempting, and Eileen skimped on necessities to purchase her first 'New Look' Norman Hartnell coat from a boutique there: it meant paying it off over weeks, 7s 6d at a time, but eventually the coat was hers. Later, when she left St Mary Abbot's, she went straight to Oxford Street and tried not to feel guilty at blowing the entire lump sum they gave her on an irresistible black tight-waisted suit. 'I admired clothes *so much*, and I thought – For Once, *for once*, <u>for once</u>, I'm going to have a *really* nice outfit – it had a pencil-slim skirt and the most lovely little jacket. Och, I really *loved* that suit!'

London was awash with all kinds of vicious temptations for a pretty girl – a factor that had her mother begging her to return to Ireland ('she was terrified I'd meet someone who wasn't a Catholic ...') – but in every other way, Eileen exercised restraint. 'I was in London for five years and I didn't put a foot wrong ...' But much as she loved her life there, her mother's pleas finally got through. 'She wouldn't shut up about me coming home, so I gave in ...' Eventually, charity towards her family prevailed.

In 1951 she returned to Kilkenny, a qualified nurse. Here she survived a few months at the local hospital, but it was run by nuns, and by now anything of an overly Catholic nature was intolerable to her, so at the earliest opportunity she accepted a post at a newly opened tuberculosis sanatorium in Phoenix Park, Dublin. It wasn't London – but life in the Irish capital had much to offer. She joined a hockey team, and picked up with old Kilkenny acquaintances, among whom she soon found herself a boyfriend, Brian Shankey. Brian had been at Trinity College Dublin, and was headed for a business career in South Africa: 'It's true he was very sweet on me ...' Nevertheless it was a light-hearted, non-committal relationship. At the end of a long day on the wards Eileen would smarten up and meet Brian at the Metropole Bar in O'Connell Street. But Brian often brought a friend along: George Mooney.

> He was a Protestant, you see, George was. So inevitably there were going to be difficulties ...

In time, Brian departed to look after his interests in South Africa ...

> – and when he left, George came round and he said, 'I've been asked by Brian to look after you.'

George, like her, was twenty-three, and had a decent job as a travelling salesman with Rowntrees' confectionery. To start with, it was a casual arrangement. They were both avid about sport, and Eileen enjoyed going on dates with him to rugby matches. When they talked she found that, like her, he was highly intelligent with a love of theatre and literature. But George Mooney shared something else in common with Eileen Hawe: 'He had charm, and he was good-looking. They were like flies around a jam-pot wherever he went.' Eileen was captivated; she soon fell head over heels in love with him, and he with her.

But neither had any intention of making a future together. For his part, George Mooney was struggling to come to terms with an unsettled background. He was the illegitimate son of an unmarried governess who in her predicament had given him away as a baby; he never knew his parents, and had been fostered by an unsympathetic and austerely Protestant family in Tipperary. The charm and sexy good looks masked a troubled personality; he was intermittently depressive, and out of his depth when it came to family responsibilities. Despite their love, from the outset his relationship with Eileen was founded on shaky ground.

It was one evening in September 1953 that George and Eileen met up to go to a rugby club dance together. George had been on his travels in the west of Ireland, and had returned to Dublin in possession of a bottle of the illegal, highly alcoholic Irish moonshine liquor known as poteen. And to this day Eileen remembers nothing of what happened after she drank it:

> It was the first time ever. And I was a nurse! I knew the facts of life!

Because of this, she felt unable to blame George for the outcome:

> Didn't I get myself pregnant? I'd come back to holy Ireland to *get myself pregnant* . . .

Provincial Ireland in the early 1950s was a country caught in a time-warp, gripped by tribalism, superstition and prohibitions. Personal vanity was the route to hellfire; non-Catholics were seen as untouchables; pregnancy out of wedlock was a sin.

And Eileen Hawe had broken every rule in the book.

Forbidden Facts

What was she to do? At twenty-three, facing the formidable consequences of her one slip-up, Eileen owned that she knew the facts of life. But she was in a minority. A survey conducted in the mid-1950s* reported that among women born between 1924 and 1934 – Eileen's generation in other words – a full 23 per cent had been given sex education by 'no one in particular'. Only 18 per cent had been given any information by their own parents. Anecdotally, the evidence is that most of our mothers and grandmothers were woefully ignorant about how their bodies worked. Richard Hoggart's assertion, in his account of proletarian Britain in the 50s, that 'few working-class parents seem to tell their children anything about sex . . .' is borne out by the vivid memories of women like Derbyshire miner's wife Audrey Alssebrook:

> Honest to God, I didn't know nothing.
>
> I were fourteen, and I were watching this wedding at the church in Scarcliffe village, and the bride were in white velvet. And I started my periods on the way. And I went rushing home to tell me mum. And she says, 'Well, now you'll have this every month,' and she says, 'Well now you keep away from t'lads.'

* Dr Eustace Chesser, *The Sexual, Marital and Family Relationships of the English Woman* (1956).

> I wish I'd have known a little bit more. She were a good mother, but all she ever said were, 'Just you behave yourself, me lady!'

Equally typical was Janet Lee from Leicester, whose mother was a market stall worker:

> I shall never forget when I started my periods. Me mum had never discussed it with me . . . so I thought oh dear, what am I going to say to me mum? I was SO embarrassed, I really was, 'cos you didn't discuss them sort of things in those days. Anyway, I finally plucked up courage and I told her — and she gave me an old vest and two big safety pins — and they were the sort of things that you wore. And then they'd wash them! And hung them on the line . . .

Such information as Janet received took the form of prohibitions:

> You *didn't* play with boys, you didn't wash your hair, you didn't walk about with no shoes on — and you NEVER sat on a cold doorstep! This is what they used to say when you had your periods.

Mothers would tell their daughters, 'Now you're a woman, take care of your three "F's": your feet, face and fanny.'

However, in rural Wales the onset of puberty in a girl might be a golden opportunity for the entire community to indulge in its favourite activity, gossip — as fifteen-year-old Joan Hilditch found out to her cost. She started her periods without noticing, and then inadvertently left her soiled knickers on the back of the kitchen chair. Mam found them and, bursting into Joan's bedroom (which she shared with her sisters), set up a full-volume rant, the gist of which was that she could now 'catch babies' and that she had probably caused permanent damage to her insides by washing her hair and rinsing it in cold water. 'Her words terrified me . . .' The following day Mam calmed down and issued instructions. She supplied Joan with sanitary pads, which she was told she had to wash out herself. She was also told not to bath during her period, nor ever to put her hands in cold water, and she was told on no account to permit any man to touch her 'down there'. Then Mam went off to tell the whole village.

'I hear you're a woman now,' said Auntie Betty, the grocer lady . . .

'Growing up now, aren't you?' said Dai the Fish.

It seemed I could go nowhere my womanhood hadn't already been discussed. Even callers to the door, nudge, nudge, said, 'Woman now she is,' and Mam would wink.

Soon after, to her horror, hair began to bush out from unexpected areas of Joan's body. Worse was to come: she began to grow small breasts, which itched and burned:

I heard the whispers: 'Ahh! Growing up she is . . . shy' and 'She will be proud of them soon enough.'

I wanted to die . . . I would never be happy as a woman.

In Birmingham, teenager Brenda Nash's mother was barely more helpful, since it appeared that her own knowledge of sex and puberty was hazy. Menstruation, she explained to Brenda, was caused by 'bad blood, that has to come away'. Apparently if it didn't, terrible unwished-for consequences would ensue. From this, Brenda took away an awareness that sex was a subject fraught with peril and unhappiness: 'marital disharmony and unwanted pregnancy'. Though her mum told her how babies got out, Brenda was left completely vague as to how they got in.

Jennifer Craig was well into her nursing training before she found out how 'It' happened, and then only because a friend managed to lay hands on an off-the-syllabus anatomy book.

Until then she had a vague idea that the man inserted his penis into the woman – but remained unsure how he got the floppy thing in. 'It must have been like pushing toothpaste back into the tube.'

Dr Chesser's survey cited a figure of 21 per cent as having received their sex education from teachers or doctors, but well into the 1950s many grammar-school-educated girls like Mary Evans were left equally perplexed. Her mother was educated, emancipated and open about most things with her clever daughter, but where sex itself was concerned there was silence. 'We learnt our minimal lessons about reproduction in mammals from a somewhat garbled account of the activities of the rabbit . . .' she recalled. Biology lessons were almost wilfully imprecise when it came to detail:

> The male rabbit did, at some point, 'deposit' his sperm in the female rabbit but why the female should have been used as a kind of sexual lost property office remained an unanswered, and unasked, question. We simply had no idea how these processes occurred in human beings.

For a girl like Florence Fell, puberty when it came was worse than embarrassing, it was terrifying. Florence had never felt close to her mother – a forbidding, sullen and religious woman who had resented becoming pregnant with a fifth child late in life. Mrs Fell had mistaken the symptoms for early menopause, and in 1937 there was little rejoicing at Florence's arrival in the Bethnal Green tenement where the family lived, seven of them and a grandmother now crowded into two floors in Corfield Street. A couple of years later a brother arrived, further confirming Mrs Fell's inadequate knowledge of her own fertility, and bringing the number of children to six.

Florence grew up unconfident, unsupported, and – in her own description – 'a slow learner'; English and arithmetic seemed especially daunting. Socially she was always on the edge of the crowd; she was, however, a caring, tender-hearted child who loved to bandage her dollies' hurt arms and legs. One day, she thought, she might be a nurse. Somehow, Florence made it through the eleven-plus exam to grammar school, which brought its own challenges, among them the fearful ordeal of catching a Number 8 bus to Bishopsgate – 'I'd never been out of Bethnal Green.' But nobody in her family made her aware of the opportunities her new school presented, and her education never took root.

Florence yearned for intimacy, but barely knew the meaning of the word. Church dominated the family's social life; authority was embodied by the stern and unbending figure of the minister. The Congregationalists' values were hard work, decency, respectability and propriety, and the Fell children were sent to Sunday school and an evening service weekly. Sometimes Florence would join a small group of teenage church-goers who would gather afterwards in a Victoria Park café. But a bicycle, which would have offered freedom, was denied her:

> I don't think my parents wanted me to stray very far. They were far too protective – but they never told me why.
>
> I never had any sex education. I did biology at school, and I knew about animals and birds. But babies never crossed my mind.
>
> One day I came home from an evening walk with the group, and I started getting ready for bed, and suddenly there was blood everywhere. I was terrified. I rushed into the lounge screaming, 'Mum, mum, I'm bleeding, I'm bleeding.' But all Mum did was, she just padded me out with lots of towels to go to bed with, and in the morning she wrote me a note which I had to go and hand to the chemist. It was for S.T.'s – she wouldn't even write the word 'sanitary'! – and I had to go round there myself, all padded up with the towels. The point is she

didn't bother to explain to me. She had the opportunity then to tell me, 'This is going to happen to you every month, and these are the things you need to pad yourself with and be prepared.' But I had none of that.

As deeply religious people, the Fells certainly meant well by their daughter and, as we have seen, in the early 1950s it was common enough for sexual matters to fall into an exclusion zone. But far from protecting her, her ignorance exposed her. Only a few years later her vulnerability would lead Florence into a terrible predicament which causes her sorrow to this day. And she remains angry with her mother for keeping her in the dark:

> I don't think I liked my mum very much really. She didn't care for me enough to tell me about things.
>
> And when eventually I had boyfriends, we weren't allowed to kiss outside the front door – in case we did anything else I suppose. But she never told me what the 'anything else' *was*. She <u>should</u> have told me what it means when boys start feeling round you and all that. But she didn't.
>
> And I left school still ignorant.

★

In post-war Britain, there were many thousands of girls like Florence Fell, Liz Jones, Audrey Alssebrook, Brenda Nash, Mary Evans and Joan Hilditch who had no understanding of sex. They had no understanding of its satisfactions, its power, its danger or its consequences. But what many – most – of them *did* understand was the fundamental importance to every girl of attracting a man. While the unspeakable secrets of male lust, the terrifying, uncontrollable realities of physical desire were things that the majority tried hard not to contemplate, ignorance, fear and social expectation simultaneously caused many a young woman to do her utmost to incite those same passions. Monica Dickens was not out on a limb in expressing the ineradicable assumption that marriage and motherhood were woman's destiny: 'The instinctive desire of woman is to attach herself to a man who will be her provider.' In this world view, a woman who didn't try her hardest to secure a man was running the risk not just of unhappiness, but also of destitution, even death. Thus beauty, sex appeal, allure – the entire panoply of feminine qualities – were to be deployed in the cause not just of meeting and mating, but in the greater cause of survival itself. This was a decade in which, for all the contradictions that came in its wake, femininity carried the imperative of an absolute life force.

3. Lovely in Every Way

How to Get Your Man

The man in the pin-stripe suit cowers. He is looking wary, almost frightened. With an alarmed glance behind him he is concentrated on escape; his body language – arms raised and tensed, legs positioned for flight – tells us he is about to make a run for it. He has every reason to fear. Above his head, a lasso is poised to descend, tightening around his cringing frame.

The woman who wields the end of the rope, by contrast, has the appearance of a film star Valkyrie. Her posture is erect, and despite her vertiginously high heels she is both steady and dynamic. Her pointed bosom, like her whirling lasso, defies gravity, and she beams with all the confidence of imminent victory. She will certainly catch him. She knows exactly what to do, because she has read the pamphlet whose title is blazoned across the image I have just described: HOW TO GET YOUR MAN! For Women Only!

In 1951, just one shilling could make any aspiring female the possessor of eleven pages of this indispensable knowledge. In compressed form, the pamphlet takes its reader through the various stages of man-hunting: what to do when you meet your ideal man, how to arouse his curiosity and make him want to meet you again, how to get him interested in you, take you seriously and respect you, how to court him and kiss him, how to secure him and how – having once snared him – to ensure that he does not escape.

But if, having paid up, the female reader hoped to find

This pamphlet stressed female submission and guile: 'Fan the flames of his ardour gently, but always leave him a little unsatisfied. Thus you will lead him to the altar.'

instructions that would transform her into the superwoman predator depicted on the cover, she might have asked for her money back. The strategy outlined in *How to Get Your Man* had little to do with conquering him, and everything to do with wily, pseudo-submissive manipulation. For example:

- It is often necessary to lose in order to win. Men do not take kindly to being beaten by women at games . . .
- NEVER TALK ABOUT YOURSELF.
- Never at any time . . . suggest that you have any claim on his time . . .
- Be childlike and feminine at all times.
- Don't talk 'cleverly' to him . . . Men are terrified of brainy women.

– Love him, feed him, sympathise with him, soothe him, admire him.

In the 1950s, advice of this kind was readily available in pamphlets, books and magazines. All of these were agreed that there was no substitute for femininity.

Perhaps the most compelling advocate for its old-fashioned, passive virtues was, and remains, the writer Barbara Cartland. Today she is largely remembered as the flamboyant neon-pink-clad author of over 700 effusive romances with titles like *A Rhapsody of Love* and *Passions in the Sand*, peopled by brooding strangers and raven-haired beauties. But Cartland was more complicated than her literary output suggests. There was a down-to-earthness and frankness about her, and her character was marked by qualities of charity and compassion. Her penchant for schmaltz was tempered in private by a taste for the bawdy, and also by an entirely thought-out position on sexual and above all marital relationships. In the 1950s Barbara Cartland published over twenty-five romances and other titles. One of these was *Marriage for Moderns*, a book which argues with eloquence and conviction for a rigidly traditional view of the sex divide. Man owns, Woman belongs; Man desires, Woman needs. In an arsenal of certainties, Cartland's biggest gun was her unshakeable belief in the natural order of things, in which our male ancestors roamed the plains and mountains, hunting and fighting, leaving their females minding the cooking pots on the floor of the cave. The Neanderthal, she claimed, knows no better. He is unsubtle, he has no homing or paternal instincts. The only thing that draws him back is 'the magnetism of a woman's love'. For her part, the artful woman should not attempt to upset that natural order, but should marshal her own array of weaponry to ensure he always returns to her: beauty, passivity, dependency, inferiority, subordination. However clever or talented she may be, the woman must learn to yield to the man in order to gain her end, the happy marriage.

*Every girl ought
To love sport,
But if she wants to be wise
and adorable
and completely feminine
She will let meniwin
ALWAYS*

According to the advice book *The Years of Grace*, tennis, golf, show-jumping and diving were all competitive sports suitable for girls – provided they didn't actually *compete*.

She must <u>not</u> be cleverer than him, and she must never, ever beat him at tennis. For equality was a chimera:

> However much women believe in emancipation, however much they talk of careers and professions, they all of them know that unless they can capture a husband and have a child they have failed – as a woman.

The vacant room, the empty vessel, the hollow shell – defined by the void. We will meet, again and again, this assumption that women have no independent identity, that only men could confer meaning on their nonexistence.

So much was at stake, and such warnings fed insecurities. Today, we agonise about negative body-image and the fears – often exploited by the media – that we are insufficiently thin, curvaceous or youthful. But the 1950s female had her own panoply of body-image vulnerabilities, fuelled by journalists, marketing men and all-round busybodies. Writing about her teenage years, the author Fiona MacCarthy admits to her own 'avid if anxious' reading of an instruction manual entitled *The Years of Grace*. This volume covered every eventuality for the adolescent girl, stating at the outset:

> Every girl cannot be beautiful, but every girl can – and must – be attractive.

There were so many things to remember: 'I want you to be lovely in every way. When you wake in the morning, always jump out of bed, never crawl. Go straight to your window and get some fresh air into your lungs. Smile . . .' And then – for this was a time when cinemas and public transport reeked of unwashed bodies and it was thought necessary to remind women to take a bath and to shampoo their hair weekly – there was hygiene. 'Halitosis and Body Odour are "lethal to glamour".' The makers of the new 'anti-perspirants' played on such warnings. 'Hasn't she ever heard

of ODO-RO-NO?' ran the strap-line of a memorable advertisement. Meanwhile, observe armpit drill: 'plenty of soap is essential'.
Wash 'between your legs'. Clean your neck and your navel. Cher-
ish your teeth. One good bowel action daily please, preferably
after breakfast. Clean underwear was imperative, even in times of
soap shortage – 'Suppose you were in an accident?' So many hints
and pressures: Watch your posture! *Tuck your tail in. Stand tall.*
'Poise will make you look somebody instead of nobody . . .'

Glorify Yourself by Leonore King was another book-form
training course in self-improvement, whose mission was to get
women to make the most of themselves. The stakes were high:

> [Collectively], these little matters of personal attractiveness . . .
> mean the difference between riches and poverty, marriage or
> spinster-hood, and wedded bliss or broken homes. And these
> differences are not trifles.

Its pages contained diagrams that showed how to prevent your
bust wobbling as you went upstairs, and demystified a range of
essential techniques such as: how to carry your gloves and handbag, how to wear coats and (fascinatingly) how to turn
decorously in a doorway, this last speciality being described as
'. . . one of the most beautiful movements which any woman
[can] execute . . .' Loveliness didn't just happen, it involved
exertion. Rotate your ankles for ten minutes daily to keep them
slim. Slap yourself under the jaw every day with a flannel to
prevent a double chin. And no slouching at bus stops.

> Walk with purposeful strides; send out vibrations which indi-
> cate that you are a live, unique and interesting personality.

Being glorious was exhausting.

Take heed, too, of products that assist in snaring the elusive
male. Ryvita for example – 'makes you fit – keeps you slim'. The
Ryvita-eating woman's 'fairy-tale figure' is part of her romantic

secret – 'she has everything it takes to make a man a happy captive'. Perfume was even better. For as little as two-and-sixpence Bourjois' 'Evening in Paris' will irresistibly lure tweedy pipe-smoking football-playing he-men towards its wearer: 'You'll soon see what we mean!' urged the advertisers. In the *Glorify Yourself* world view, men are helplessly in thrall to slender ankles, exquisite grooming and an upright posture; every woman a Grace Kelly of perfection.

Did Muriel Spark have some such training course in mind, when she introduced us to Selina Redwood in her novel *The Girls of Slender Means*? Selina, the beauty among her peers at a post-war Kensington hostel, has subscribed to the Poise Course – twelve correspondence lessons for five guineas – which recommended a twice-daily repetition of the following mantra:

> 'Poise is perfect balance, an equanimity of body and mind, complete composure whatever the social scene. Elegant dress, immaculate grooming, and perfect deportment all contribute to the attainment of self-confidence.'

Morning and evening, the top floor of the hostel falls silent while Selina recites the mystic words . . .

Muriel Spark had first-hand experience of Poise. For a brief period in 1950, the as yet unknown novelist worked in the offices of *Model* – a photographic model directory – with its director, Leslie Kark, and his assistant Evelyn Gordine, both of whom were to become business leaders in the field of Charm, Beauty and Deportment. Post-war, photographic models suddenly found there was as much magazine work as they wanted. The year 1949 saw the end of clothes rationing, and the ready-to-wear industry started to boom; the end of paper rationing in 1950 meant more features, and more gloss.

The success of *Model* led soon after to Kark's acquisition of the Lucie Clayton Model and Charm School and Agency; under that name, Evelyn would be its principal, based at the School's premises at 449 Oxford Street. Here, the aristocracy of elegance – fashion models Barbara Goalen, and Cecil Beaton's favourite, Fiona Campbell Walter, as well as a bevy of aspirant lookalikes – came to walk with books on their heads and learn the essentials of grooming.

Jennifer Hocking,* another of Clayton's stable of models, looked back from the 1960s on what it meant to be a 1950s fashion model:

> Most of us were [married], and I think it made a difference.
>
> We didn't go around with our hair all over our face wearing cheap, kooky clothes – partly, I think, because we were so much taller! When you're very tall you have to be dignified. Somehow you can't be tall *and* cute . . .
>
> We couldn't have looked sexy. It wouldn't have been allowed. We were Belgravia ladies.

Later, in the 1960s, that glossy image would become tarnished. But not all the Lucie Clayton students could become mannequins (if you were under five feet six you were not considered) and the college did much of its business as a finishing school for top-drawer Henriettas and Belindas. Even so, Evelyn Gordine – who, having married the boss, was now Mrs Evelyn Kark – was strictly selective. The Clayton students were lined up in shorts and brief white midriff-exposing shirts to do energetic, balletic exercises of the 'must-increase-my-bust' variety. Their hairstyles and beauty routines were evaluated and criticised. Then they were weighed, their 'vital statistics' carefully measured, and their social skills and that crucial deportment assessed. Once qualified, the girls would emerge with such essential skills as flower arrangement, how to climb in and out of a car, and curtseying. Call it Poise.

---

*Jennifer Hocking (1929–2011) graduated to become fashion editor on *Harper's Bazaar*, where she hired Anna Wintour as an office junior.

Razzamatazz

The Lucie Clayton school was hugely successful, at a time when there were few criticisms of those who cashed in on women's vulnerabilities. In the early 1950s, there seemed nothing unusual in schooling young women for the marriage market, nothing patronising in implying that a model in a swimsuit would cheerfully trade in her career if a husband happened along. Take this commentary over a 1951 Pathé Cinemagazine* feature, for example. The pictures show curvaceous fashion models in two-pieces on a sandy Bournemouth shore: 'When they've developed all their charms they'll be *far* too good to work as mannequins! They'll be parading in their own wedding gowns, if the men-folk get half a chance . . .' The male tone is all too typical of its genre, as it follows this with: 'Who *wouldn't* be a beachcomber on a beach like *this*?'

Thus in 1951 – the year of the Festival of Britain – it seemed obvious to suggest that the nation should celebrate femininity, alongside architecture and town planning, industry, agriculture, science, technology, design and the arts. And so it was that in the run-up to the festivities, a demobbed Captain of the Royal Fusiliers – having a flair for enterprise and a taste for pretty women, and being now employed by the dance hall and catering group Mecca Limited as publicity sales manager – found himself with a new project. His name was Eric Morley.

Mecca's centre of activity in London was the Lyceum ballroom, barely half a mile from the Festival of Britain's South Bank site. The managing director of Mecca catering, Group

---

* Pathé's Cinemagazines, lighter and more entertaining than their newsreels, targeted the female audience with shopping items, home improvements, scantily clad beauty contests and fashion shows, which (for today's viewer) makes their lascivious tone and jokey all-male commentary sound all the more dated.

Captain Pickard, was approached by another ex-army man, Squadron Leader Phipps, who was then organising the Festival's publicity, to see how Mecca could add some 'razzamatazz' to the Festival scene. 'My man Morley will come up with something,' responded Pickard. So Phipps and Morley met for lunch at the Savoy, where with military efficiency they hatched a plan. Beauty contests on a local scale had already proved hugely popular at Mecca ballrooms across the country. Morley himself had originally struck on the winning formula of placing fashion shows in his dance halls, tapping into the post-war hunger for glamour, femininity and pretty clothes. Bathing beauty contests in dance halls were simply another step along the same road – and had quickly become a huge, money-spinning attraction. Morley knew that it could work, and over lunch he now proposed a spectacular contest on a national and international scale, with a £1,000 prize for the winner, which would both promote Britain and draw in contestants from many countries. In a daringly up-to-date move, he suggested that the entrants should all wear the popular and newly fashionable two-piece swimsuits; the competition to be entitled The Festival Bikini-Girl. Morley's proposal met with enthusiasm. The contest would be held at the Lyceum, and Morley immediately set about organising and publicising it. Attracting international entrants at short notice proved problematic, however, and only five foreign girls took part in what the press were, nevertheless, soon dubbing the 'Miss World' contest; their numbers had to be made up to thirty by inviting British beauty queens to compete. But getting publicity was easy – as Morley later recalled: 'the newspapers and magazines with large circulations were delighted to publish shots of the girls in these whispy [*sic*] outfits'.

However, when the contestants filed in on the night, Morley got a shock. For all his pugnacious enthusiasm in organising the event, the actual sight of thirty semi-naked women parading past him on white high heels was scarily sexual in its impact. And yet by today's standards, the women's 1951-style bikinis disguised and covered more than adequately. There was not a nipple in sight, the briefs were relatively modest in their cut, and the top halfs – in conformity with the fashionable brassière-style of the day – distorted the women's breasts into geometrically rigid cones. But Eric Morley was dumbstruck:

> When I first saw the bikinis which some of the girls were going to wear I had to take not only a big gulp but a big grip on myself . . .
>
> It was not until I saw all the contestants together in their tiny two-piece costumes that I realised [my] decision might have been a big mistake. All the girls were attractive, some of them were highly voluptuous and when they were seen en-masse they provided an almost overwhelming picture.

Morley claims to have been alone in his misgivings: 'The only person who seemed to be worried about it was me!' But his doubts lingered over the sheer eroticism of the spectacle he had invented. For its creator, the 1951 Miss World contest was the realisation of male fantasy on an almost alarming scale. In the event, despite the vast majority of contestants being British, it was a Swedish beauty queen, Kiki Haakonson ('[she] filled a bikini more perfectly than anyone I have seen, before or since . . .') who was proclaimed winner that night and took home her £1,000 prize.* The occasion was generally agreed to be such a success that it should become annual. But in future caution prevailed. Bikinis were too hot to handle, and from then on one-piece swimsuits were the rule.

*

* Worth nearly £27,000 in 2014. In subsequent years the prize was set at £500.

The Miss World pageant, created for the Festival of Britain, long outlived its origins. Eric Morley had created a winning formula.

The infrastructure already existed. By the early 1950s there was barely a seaside resort in the country that did not hold its own Bathing Beauty contest around the local swimming pool or lido, whether under the auspices of Mecca, local newspapers, charities or the Town Council. From Ilfracombe to Morecambe, from Penzance to Scarborough, the contests attracted lucrative sponsorship from banks, cinema chains and womenswear companies keen to get in on the act. The judges were celebrities – often local, sometimes national. For the women themselves, there were enticing cash prizes. But according to Eric Morley, the standard was shocking:

> A few of the contestants were absolute 'scrubbers' while the odd one or two were not even clean!

If Miss World was going to flourish as a British-run competition, national pride demanded a British winner. But as title-holder Kiki Haakonson was followed in 1952 by May Louise Flodin, also from Sweden, it seemed to Eric Morley that it was not going to be so easy to find a British girl sufficiently professional to hold her own against the lovely Scandinavians. He was determined to prove that Britain could not only compete, but win, and with this determination came an unshakeable personal beauty credo:

> The ideal British entry would have to be at least five feet five inches tall (ideally 5 feet 7½ inches), weigh between eight stone ten pounds and nine stone six, have a neat waist of 22 to 24 inches, be 35 to 36 inches in the hips and have a 36 or 37 inch bust – no more, no less. Her legs had to be perfectly shaped whether they were seen from the back or the front, all the way up (in other words, she must not have fleshy thighs), and naturally, she

would have to have a lovely face and good teeth. I didn't care if her hair was badly set, provided she had plenty of hair, if she walked like a camel, provided she was not perpetually round-shouldered, or if her make-up was badly applied, provided she had a genuinely good complexion. The hair could be properly styled to suit her in the hands of a decent hairdresser, her walk could be ironed out at a modelling or deportment school and her make-up could be taken care of by a cosmetics expert. In a nutshell, as long as we had the correct *basic* material we could turn the girl into the *perfect* material for the international contests, including the Miss World competition.

These are indeed the words of a farmer presenting his prize-bred heifers at a cattle show. Here, in Morley's memoirs, was every pretext the feminists of nearly twenty years later might have needed for their actions, when they hurled flour-bombs in the Albert Hall at the occasion of the 1970 Miss World contest. Eric Morley saw the women's bodies that fell under his gaze primarily as commodities, saleable merchandise that had to conform to exacting standards or be rejected. But in 1951 nobody saw anything strange or offensive in this.

★

Certainly, Leila Williams didn't. For this painfully shy ugly duckling, the world of beauty queens was a ladder out of the neglect and lovelessness of her childhood, offering money, admiration and blessed independence.

Leila was born in Erdington, near Birmingham, in 1937. While she was a child her father went missing during the war, never to return. Her mother embraced merry widowhood with enthusiasm, and at the earliest opportunity packed her inconvenient child off as an evacuee. Until she was fourteen, the girl lived with a farming family, treated by them as a second-class Cinderella. She had to do chores and wait on them, while her grudging guardians told her that she was too ugly to be seen in public. However, it was during this time that Leila caught her first glimpses of the brightly lit, entrancing world of the celebrity beauty. The family were early adopters of a television set:

> On Sunday evenings *What's My Line?* was on – and I used to look
> at Barbara Kelly and Lady Isobel Barnett. They were so glamor-
> ous, and they wore all these lovely clothes, and I thought, 'I'd like
> to do that . . .' But I had no idea how I was going to get there.

Barbara Kelly was a gamine blonde while Lady Isobel's crystal-line elegance and pseudo-aristocracy* lent an air of sophistication to the simple panel-game format, in which witty celebrities – the women in jewels and low-cut evening dress, the men in black tie and tux – competed to guess the occupations of members of the public. The *What's My Line?* panellists were to become household names, and the programme entered the life of the nation, as preachers shortened their evening sermons, local pubs emptied, and children's bedtimes were rearranged around the transmission. For the mute, painfully timid and neglected teenager watching them, the panellists' star-quality seemed both infinitely desirable, and infinitely unreachable.

Meanwhile, Leila's mother remarried; she and her new husband took on the running of a Walsall pub, the Wheatsheaf. Here, they needed help at the bar. So, in 1951, Leila was sent for. 'She decided to take me back.'

At this time I was so shy I couldn't speak. I used to go red in the

---

* Isobel Barnett, née Marshall, was in no sense an aristocrat. She took her title from her husband, who had been knighted. She was, however, a qualified doctor.

face, and I could not get a word out. And my mother used to get so angry with me – 'How can you be like this? How can you embarrass me in such a way?' She couldn't understand. I was just tongue-tied.

In the immediate term, Leila's lack of confidence might have been an obstacle to her mother's ambitions, for – as the girl became a woman – it was now becoming increasingly apparent that she was also metamorphosing into a beauty. Though still petite, her posture was erect. Her figure was filling out, her skin was radiant, her red-auburn hair was thick and lustrous. Her features – in a perfectly heart-shaped face – were charmingly girlish, but with the hint of something more sexy. One day in 1952 she arrived home from school, to be told: 'You're not going to school tomorrow. You're doing a fashion show.' Entreaties were in vain; her mother was inflexible. Leila had half an hour's training in how to walk and turn gracefully, 'up and down the kitchen floor with a book on my head', before finding herself, knees knocking with sheer fright, pushed on to the end of a catwalk to model clothes for a teenage fashion show in a works canteen. Somehow, in a daze of terror, she got through – even though the last outfit was a swimsuit.

It led to more. Leila still recoiled at the thought, still hated it, but strutting up a catwalk seemed better than withering away in misery and servitude. And so it was that, soon after her six-teenth birthday, she first dipped her toe into the world of beauty queens.

Bella, the other barmaid, was reading the *Sunday Mercury* one evening while waiting to open up. Leila, as usual, brought in her tea. As she placed the cup before her, Bella looked up from her paper and said, 'Look – you should go in for that. The paper is looking for a girl to be the *Sunday Mercury* Girl. You could win it!' Leila's heart sank. 'Count me out,' she said firmly. 'The modelling is quite enough for me to deal with, thank you.'

But Bella was dead set. She showed the article to Leila's mother, who seized on it. Entry for such shows was by photograph, and without more ado she sent her daughter off to have her picture taken. 'Well, the photographers found out I was photogenic!' After that Bella could barely contain herself, and night after night she pounced on the paper to see if Leila's picture was in. 'Every night, to my relief, it was not.' But then a letter came, informing her that she had been selected for a heat, to take place at a cinema in Walsall; the winner would compete in the final. Leila felt she had been cast to the wolves.

A cocktail dress was bought, her hair was styled. 'I was a nervous wreck.' Fortified with sherry, she stumbled into the makeshift backstage dressing room, milling with girls titivating and powdering. 'It was complete chaos.'

> After what seemed like forever, we were ushered down the stairs to the side of the stage. My heart was pounding. It felt as if I would have a heart attack. Then it was my turn to go on the stage.
>
> The moment I walked out, all the fear drained away. The warmth that came from the audience was amazing. I loved every second of it. We all had to line up on stage for the winner to be announced. What a shock and a thrill when I realised it was me.

It was a watershed moment. Reporters flocked round her; as a schoolgirl beauty queen, they wanted to hear what she had to say, and her confidence soared.

> Well, I didn't win the whole contest. But the publicity it attracted – well, my mother absolutely *loved* it! Because it brought people into the pub didn't it?
>
> But it also changed things for me. I realised it could be a way to escape. For now I could see that it was a way of earning money, getting publicity, and a way of getting out of Birmingham . . .

Gradually, her career accelerated. With her photograph in the *Sunday Mercury*, Leila was offered a lucrative short-term modelling contract by the top fashion retail chain, C & A Modes. Propelled by her earning power, by a new sense of purpose, and abetted by her mother, Leila started to enter more beauty contests around the region. At seventeen she left school, and got a secretarial job in an estate agents' office. Her mother sent her for elocution lessons to eradicate her Birmingham accent, but in between she was still washing glasses and pulling pints. Success as a beauty queen was slow in coming, and Leila waged a constant battle against fear and self-consciousness:

> If you're not a natural exhibitionist, you have to get used to being stared at. The first time I ever walked round a swimming pool was in Morecambe – and it was huge. And I suddenly felt this trepidation: 'Why is everyone staring? What's wrong with me?' I started almost to run. They had marshals at each corner of the pool, and when I got to the end the man stopped me and said, 'For goodness' sake, slow down! You'll overtake the girl in front of you!'
>
> And while I was standing there, I could hear some of the spectators saying 'What a *shame* . . .' By now I was beginning to think I was deformed. But what they were actually saying was, 'What a shame she's so *thin*!' So I went back home and fattened myself up.
>
> And I was determined, because now I could see that this was my ticket out of the environment that I was in. I just wanted to get out of it.

Money, and escape, were Leila's twin goals. Never during her career as a beauty queen did she regard herself as a sex symbol. Her new task was to master the complexities of her chosen profession with all possible thoroughness. And she was driven by an almost desperate desire for independence – an independence that only the crowning success of her career could offer. By 1954, Leila had her sights set on a new target:

> I gave myself a deadline. I was going to win Miss Great Britain by the third attempt. And if I failed – well, that would be the end of the line.

Who is This Beautiful Princess Going to Marry?

Being crowned winner of a beauty contest would be the accomplishment of a dream. But it was more than that; that showy piece of diamanté was an ersatz pledge of worth in a world where women were constrained to believe that their chief or only value lay in pleasing men. Its mesmerising glitter enticed countless women like Leila Williams into joining the beauty parades, into mincing and smiling their way round swimming pools with fear in their hearts, and the warnings ringing in their ears: '. . . personal attractiveness means the difference between riches and poverty, marriage or spinster-hood . . .' A simple premise lay at the heart of the beauty myth, that loveliness in men's eyes made you Somebody – and that without it you were Nobody. It was a myth as worthless as the diadem itself.

And yet it was barely questioned. Leila Williams was pressured into it – though in the end, with few options open to her, she bought into it willingly enough. But so too did those privileged beings whose tiaras boasted genuine diamonds and pearls. Our royal princesses, for all their golden crowns, were just as much heifers in that cattle market – in which all women were judged on how correctly and desirably they measured up.

Everyone agreed that for her part Princess Elizabeth had done everything right. In 1950, she was a demure newlywed, living in domestic contentment at Clarence House with her handsome husband and small son – a household to be perfected that year by the addition of a baby daughter, Princess Anne. 'So lucky, Philip and I . . .' was the *Daily Mirror*'s headline the day after the birth, going on to reflect on how the royal couple tried 'to follow the pattern of ordinary British life in every way . . .'

Princess Margaret couldn't, or wouldn't, be that kind of Princess. But what kind could she be? From the age of sixteen Princess Margaret's beauty, her wardrobe, her quasi-bohemianism, her appetite for fun and her intoxicating femininity had singled her out. She had arty leanings, remarkable blue eyes, and a flirtatious manner. She was sexy. All this and more made her a social magnet:

> During the post-war years there were a lot of parties, and Princess Margaret was the star in the middle; a planet round which everyone revolved. She simply sparkled . . .

recalled her cousin, Margaret Rhodes. Soirées at the American Ambassador's house in Regent's Park often went on till four in the morning, with the Princess, fox-trotting unstoppably, at their centre. She drank, she smoked, she was an outrageous mimic, she sang risqué popular songs. The press pack soon dubbed her group the 'Margaret Set'. The Princess's biographer claimed that media interest in her – and above all in her love life – 'far exceeded anything Diana, Princess of Wales, was to experience thirty years later . . .' And like the ill-fated Diana, she too would find herself besieged, a fashion icon for her times, a daring charmer, everybody's darling, everybody's martyr.

Her lady-in-waiting Iris Peake had to go ex-directory:

> If I hadn't it would have been a nightmare; the press would have been ringing me up every time they spotted the Princess at a night club with somebody.
>
> The thing is, she was just so beautiful. She had a tiny waist, a lovely figure. She looked so glamorous in those New Look dresses.
>
> And so of course the question everyone wanted the answer to

was, 'Who is this beautiful Princess going to marry?' That was *all* the press ever wanted to talk about.

Who she was, was defined by who would be her husband. By the time she was twenty-one, no fewer than thirty-one young men, many of them earls or sons of earls, had been mentioned in the newspapers as eligible contenders for her hand.

And then her father died. From childhood Margaret had adored this gentle, anxious, inhibited man. They rejoiced in a closeness of two opposites – her outgoing, physical gaiety complementing the King's reserve.

In the early hours of Wednesday 6 February 1952, at the age of fifty-six, cancer claimed him. Grief consumed his younger daughter. She sobbed uncontrollably, refused food, and could only sleep when prescribed sedatives. For years afterwards she would ask, 'Why did he have to die so young?'

George VI was almost as well loved by his people as by his family. The day his death was announced (interrupting the broadcast of *Mrs Dale's Diary*), shops, cinemas, theatres, sports fixtures and the money markets all closed as a sign of respect. Church bells tolled, and an ever-growing crowd gathered outside Buckingham Palace.

Nella Last, when she heard of the King's death, experienced a 'rush of sympathy' for Princess Elizabeth, 'whose youth dies at 26'. On Saturday 9 February in Barrow-in-Furness Nella did a quick tidy round and dusted her house, then she and her son Cliff picked up their neighbours – Jessie and her little daughter Kath – and set off to the Town Hall. Today, they would have stayed at home and watched the ceremonial of the Queen's accession on live television. But that morning in 1952, communities across the nation put on their coats and hats, and gathered in front of castles, town halls and Mansion Houses to witness the solemn proclamation read aloud by mayors, sheriffs, or Lord Lieutenants in full regalia from steps and balconies, accompanied by trumpet fanfares. In Barrow the dark red brick of the Victorian neo-Gothic clock tower dominated the square on Duke Street; its flag, lowered to half-mast since the King's death, was temporarily raised again to full-mast, where it fluttered in a sharp wind. 'It's years since I've seen such a crowd in Barrow,' reported Nella in her diary that evening. Cliff took little Kath up on his shoulders to get a better view. There were prayers and cheers, and the Shipyard Band played the national anthem. Before about 1,000 citizens Queen Elizabeth II was proclaimed Queen. Kath said: 'I'll 'member it all to tell my Daddy when he comes home.'

Two days later the royal coffin was transported from Sandringham to Westminster Hall to lie in state. The dim medieval cavern was silent, scented with white flowers. In 1952 vocal outpourings of grief were unheard of; in hushed decorum, more than 300,000 men and women filed past it to pay their respects. Among them was twenty-year-old secretary Angela Austin from Golders Green, with her parents:

> We queued up for hours. We just queued and *queued* and <u>queued</u>. We were somewhere on the south side of the river, beyond Westminster Bridge. And at last we walked through Westminster Hall and saw the coffin. I was very impressed. But being British of course we didn't show our emotions. I was always told, 'Never show your feelings in public, ever. It's only foreigners who do that.'

In time, Angela would indeed discover that British reticence had its limits, but in 1952 she had barely travelled. Her experience of irrepressible foreigners was still non-existent. London was her life, and its royal ceremonials and pageants represented a brief, if unemotional, respite from her typewriter.

Four days later, on 15 February,* George VI's coffin, loaded

---

* This was to have been the date set for my parents' wedding. The registrar

on to a gun-carriage drawn by 100 naval ratings, and followed by the Grenadier Guards with their arms reversed in sign of mourning, processed through the streets of London. The late King's heavily veiled widow and two daughters travelled behind in the Irish State coach to Paddington Station, where his mortal remains were loaded on to the Royal Train to be conveyed to Windsor.

That crisp winter's morning, thirteen-year-old Rose Hendon was attending her school as usual in Wornington Road in North Kensington. The west coast main line ran directly behind the school buildings, and she was never to forget how classes were suspended, with the pupils all made to stand as they witnessed the funeral train rolling solemnly past carrying the dead monarch to his last resting place in Windsor's Royal Chapel. The Hendon family were old-fashioned royalists. Rose, vivacious and pretty, was one of eight children; the family lived in Southam Street, just the other side of the tracks from her school. Her dad was a lorry driver; her mum balanced looking after her large brood with a job cleaning trains at Willesden Junction. Money was tight. Rose shared one bed with three other sisters, and the slummy terrace houses in Southam Street were infested with rats. But despite hardship Rose's mum dressed well. She would wear a glamorous shoulder-cape with a fox's face inlaid into its lustrous fur; she owned a coat with yellow buttons, a pair of high-heeled shoes and a jauntily plumed hat. Rose would grow up with a strong but unsatisfied interest in appearances – and in her case, that meant clothes. But respectability also demanded the family's compliance with regal occasions, and Rose's dad always insisted on complete quiet for the duration of the Christmas Day royal broadcast. And so on 15 February 1952 Rose stood, obediently silent

---

decided it should be cancelled as a mark of respect, and it took place instead the following day, 16 February 1952, in Liverpool Road Registry Office in north London.

behind her desk, as the majesty of a reign came to an end, and
royal death exerted its ineffable mystique.

*

Iris Peake, who had only recently been taken on as Princess
Margaret's chief lady-in-waiting, was inevitably concerned with
the sartorial implications of the King's death. Both of necessity,
and by inclination, this was another young woman who had a
serious relationship with clothes. The court went into complete
mourning. Iris recalls three months of wearing total black,
'morning, afternoon and evening', after which they graduated to
semi-mourning. But by June, the prospect of dressing for four
days of racing at Royal Ascot was still worrying her:

> I went to stay at Windsor and our entire wardrobe had to be grey,
> white, black or mauve. I did get an extra clothes allowance when
> the King died, but nevertheless it really was quite hard work . . .

Becoming a royal lady-in-waiting was a process shrouded in
mystery. Iris still has no idea how she was selected for the job:

> I've never really known how I was appointed. I did know Prin-
> cess Elizabeth and Princess Margaret a little bit. We shared a
> social background I suppose. I just got a letter one day saying
> my name was down, amongst others, and would I come and be
> interviewed by one of the Queen's ladies-in-waiting? I went to
> stay at Sandringham – in fact it was just before the King died. I
> sat next to him at dinner one night – so I did just know him.

She appears to have passed.

Iris's working day started after she left her Belgravia 'bach-
elor girl' flat and drove the short distance around Green Park
to Clarence House, where the Princess now lived. In a tiny
office, partitioned off from the ground floor drawing room,

she performed the functions of a rather grand secretary/PA, attending to the minutiae of royal visits to hospitals, Girl Guide packs or private dress fittings, working out a minute-by-minute programme for each appointment. Train schedules were plotted; timings had to be estimated for ribbon-cutting, speech-making and hand-shaking sessions. Then the royal post-bag underwent a kind of triage. The Princess removed her own private letters, while lunatics' letters went in the waste-paper basket. All others were dealt with by Iris.

Most days, the Princess and Iris were both on duty, opening motor shows, launching tankers, planting trees, accepting bouquets. For Iris, the icing on the cake was foreign trips, away from the hothouse of London. This was at a time when most people's idea of travel was the annual migration to Bournemouth or Scarborough by train or charabanc. Few people flew.* Iris was already from the class that had been further afield; but during her time with the Princess, she made two journeys to the West Indies, one to Mauritius and Zanzibar, a coast-to-coast trip across Canada, and several shorter excursions to European countries. 'Sometimes we just flew for the day – on the Royal Flight of course. It was so exciting just to fly to Germany and then come back again in the afternoon!'

The thrill of flight in the 1950s also lent glamour to air crew and aviators. Peter Townsend was one of these. He had become a Wing Commander in 1941, and during the war had displayed super-hero qualities of courage. In 1941, after flying 300 missions, Townsend was grounded. It was during that period of enforced rest that he met Rosemary Pawle: 'I . . . stepped out of my cockpit, succumbed to the charms of the first pretty girl I met and, within a few weeks, married her.' Post-war he was

---

* British European Airways (BEA) was formed in 1946; in the first month of its operation it carried 9,300 passengers. Ten years later it would exceed this number in a single day.

employed as equerry to the King. The two men quickly became close; it was an easy, forthright, human friendship based on natural compatibility. But his absence on royal duties put a strain on his marriage to Rosemary, who found consolation in the arms of export merchant John de Laszlo.

At the time of George VI's death, Townsend was posted to Clarence House; he was thirty-eight and his marriage was collapsing. The Townsend divorce took effect in December 1952. By then Princess Margaret and Townsend were growing in intimacy. They were thrown together by constant proximity, and the twenty-two-year-old sought solace for the loss of her father in his closest confidant. One afternoon in April 1953 they found themselves alone together in the red drawing room at Windsor Castle:

> It was then that we made the mutual discovery of how much we meant to one another. She listened, without uttering a word, as I told her, very quietly, of my feelings. Then she simply said: 'That is exactly how I feel, too.' It was, to us both, an immensely gladdening disclosure, but one which sorely troubled us.

It is a huge measure of social change that as recently as 1952, two people ardently in love should so immediately feel the icy blast of Establishment censure stifling their flame. A Princess could not do what a commoner could do. This Princess in particular. The expectation was that among Margaret's string of aristocratic escorts an eminently suitable consort would come to the fore, one who would bring the skittish Princess to heel, dampen her excesses, recast her as wife and mother – and make her like her sister. Townsend did not fit this model. He was middle-class, far too old and, worst of all, divorced.

Both must have known that the Church would see their relationship as transgressive. Both, too, would be all too aware of the events of only sixteen years earlier, when the King's relationship with double-divorcée Wallis Simpson had precipitated a constitutional crisis. Decidedly, in 1953, royals were not free to love whomsoever they chose.

When Townsend broached the subject of their relationship with the Queen's private secretary, Tommy Lascelles, his reaction was, 'You must be either mad or bad.' A couple of months later, in June 1953, Lascelles appears to have been instrumental in Townsend's banishment. It was now made clear to the couple that the Princess could not marry without the Queen's consent until she was twenty-five, nor – since her sister was proposing to marry a divorcé – could that consent be given without the endorsement of the Prime Minister. And – 'that, then, was that'.

The Wages of Sin

Eileen Hawe was no princess, but she was just as powerless when it came to taking control of her own destiny. She was not besieged by newspaper reporters when, being the unmarried daughter of a devout Catholic mother, she fell pregnant to a Protestant man. But the strictures of her Church – pitilessly reactionary in cases of female disobedience – were as harsh if not harsher than those imposed on Princess Margaret, and certainly caused her as much mental distress.

The moral consensus of the 1950s was guided by a powerful squeamishness about sex. If the word 'divorcé' invoked panic-stricken associations with Jezebel and Messalina, how much more did the word 'abortion' call forth outrage and venom against the perceived sinner? In this country, the procedure was illegal except in cases where it could be proved that a woman's mental or physical health was in danger. In the Republic of Ireland *all* abortions were illegal (most still are). An attempt in 1953 by parliamentarians to amend the British law was met with righteous scorn by the Catholic clergy: 'This Bill seeks to legalize practices in direct contravention to the natural law,' declared Cardinal Griffin, Archbishop of Westminster. 'The Christian principle is: Thou shalt not kill . . . We Christians must defend the right of the individual and the laws of God.' Meanwhile, 85,000 desperate women sought abortions behind the scenes each year.* Listen to some of them, writing in the early fifties to the campaigning Abortion Law Reform Association:

> I am one of those unfortunate women who do not want a child. My mental state is that I am going to a back street doctor or take a bottle of aspirin, but I would far rather have it done legally. I have cried and cried but my tears have got me nowhere . . .

> I am one of the unfortunate girls to be in trouble, and I can assure you it was against my wish and it was the first time. I am 21 years old and it is a case where I cannot get married . . . I am so worried I just don't know what to do.

> As the result of a criminal assault my daughter became pregnant and in her despair has made two attempts on her life. She is 16 years old . . .

> I met a man whose child I am having now . . . I thought he was so different. I had never known such happiness for such a long time. [Then] I received the terrible truth, he was married. Why are men so cruel, so heartless?

---

* It is notoriously hard to determine a figure for illegal abortions. In 1947 the Abortion Law Reform Association (founded 1936) published a booklet entitled *Back-Street Surgery – A Study of the Illegal Operation, which is performed probably about 100,000 times a year in England and Wales*. In 1966 the ALRA arrived at the following figures: 31,000 illegal and 9,000 legal abortions over the twenty years 1946-65, with about 85,000 abortions attempted each year (cited in C. B. Goodhart, 'Estimation of Illegal Abortions', in *Journal of Biosocial Science*, Vol. 1, Issue 3 (July 1969), pp. 235–45).

Every day it gets worse to bear, I cannot stand it much longer, the thought of people finding out, the shame . . .

When I was two months pregnant I went to my Doctor, as I had to talk to someone, I felt so ill with worry. I thought he might have helped me. He just said, 'You cannot do a thing like that.' Is it because he is an Irish Doctor?

I am 24, and single, and 10 weeks pregnant. The man responsible is already married, which I didn't know until it was too late, and he refuses to help me. If I told my mother, I think she'd have a heart-attack. She feels so strongly about sex in general . . .

I don't want to go to a 'back-street abortionist', but I'm so terribly desperate that I'll have to although I know how dangerous it is. If I have this child my whole life will be ruined . . .

This twenty-four-year-old was right to dread seeking help from a back-street abortionist. In *Call the Midwife*, through the eyes of Mary, a prostitute, Jennifer Worth relates the gruesome case of her co-worker Nelly, who found herself pregnant and fell into the hands of an illegal practitioner:

[They held] her legs open while this woman stuck what looked like steel knitting needles inside her . . .

It was dreadful. The woman went on poking and scraping. Then suddenly there was blood everywhere. All over the bed and the floor, and the woman. She said, 'That's all she needs. Just keep her in bed for a few days. She'll be all right.' They cleaned up, and threw the mess into the bomb site . . . [Nelly] was dead white, and still in dreadful pain . . .

Sometimes she knew who I was, sometimes she didn't. She got terribly hot. Her skin was burning up . . . All the time she was bleeding, till the mattress was soaked with blood. I sat with her all day and all night, and the pain never left her. In the early morning, she died in my arms.

Some women took matters into their own hands. You could buy steel and pennyroyal from the chemists, or tincture of ferric chloride. Taken orally, such home remedies could bring about a painful and often bloody abortion. When Jessie Butler, Brenda Nash's neighbour in the suburbs of Birmingham, found herself pregnant with a sixth child, she stuck a knitting needle up her own cervix and soon after started to bleed to death on the kitchen floor. There Brenda's mum found her, and saved her life by calling an ambulance.

In Dublin, Eileen Hawe was anguished by her predicament, but she was not going to be like Nelly or Jessie. She certainly considered the option of termination, and having qualified as a nurse in London, she knew where she could get a safe abortion if she went back there. What stopped her was not her love for George Mooney, nor wanting to be married, but that same hesitation regarding the taking of life. Despite all her efforts to shake it off, the Catholic mindset was encoded in her genes: 'I just thought, if I had an abortion, I'd feel guilty every time I looked at a kid – or else I'd never have a kid, 'cause I'd be feeling so guilty every time I looked at it. And I love children. I wanted to have children . . .'

There was also the reality that her mother, pious Catholic as she was, was distraught at her daughter's lapse. Mrs Hawe clung to the prospect of redemption through holy matrimony. 'I knew she wouldn't die happy if her daughter wasn't married in a Catholic church.' The clock was ticking. Eileen didn't wait for a romantic proposal from George. Though they were in love, marriage hadn't been part of the plan. But with a baby on the way, both of them now accepted that they had to become man and wife. Next she had to brave it out with the priest, but even so she was unprepared for the dressing-down she got. 'He lambasted me. He told me to go back to England – he told me that I wasn't fit to be in Ireland.' Her need gave her courage. She stood her ground:

I said, 'I'm staying in Ireland, and I'm going to get married, and I want to get married in a Catholic church.' Well he told me he wouldn't have me getting married in his parish, I'd have to go over to the other end of Dublin where the dog track is, and I'd have to get a dispensation from the Bishop of Dublin which would cost me thirty shillings.

Eileen and George were married from her Dublin flat in December 1953. It was a hole-and-corner, makeshift kind of wedding. The night before, George slept on a sofa in her lounge. The early morning ceremony was booked at the Church of the Holy Rosary in Harold's Cross. People were coming out of eight o'clock Mass as they arrived, but their little solemnity had been allocated to the sacristy round the back – so small it could accommodate no more than eight people. As Eileen's family numbered ten, the couple cut their losses and decided to get married without guests. And as it turned out, the priest officiating had no intention of taking this trifling occasion seriously. As they waited for the ceremony to start, he turned to George and said: 'Listen now! Would you like to see some dirty postcards that someone's sent me from France?' Eileen blenched. Was *the priest* really intending to show them pornographic pictures? George's face was like thunder. 'I thought George would kill him. I thought, "God, what kind of an idiot is this?" We were getting married for God's sake.' With a look of knowing amusement the priest thrust his hand between the folds of his black soutane, and pulled out a sheaf of plain white postcards – with mud smeared on them. Eileen was speechless with shock and mortification. Was this his idea of a joke? Had he no respect for them on their wedding day? To her, it seemed he had not.

It turned out that they needed witnesses. In the churchyard an old lady wearing a shawl and an elderly boy named Paddy Prendergast agreed to play their parts. Then they were wed.

The Hawes coped with their daughter's new situation with a good grace. Clinging to straws, they took the view that she had always been a tearaway – and at least now she was safely married. With his charm and good looks George Mooney proved popular, not least for his surname, which to Mrs Hawe provided irrefutable evidence that his shadowy antecedents *must* have been Catholic 'somewhere along the way'.

As for Eileen:

> It wasn't the way I wanted it at all. But you can't turn the clock back. I'd have liked to have travelled before I settled down but it wasn't to be . . .

With very little money, the newlyweds moved in with her sister Peg in a small flat in Cardiff. George got what travelling jobs he could pick up; Eileen was taken on for some night shifts at the local hospital. In May 1954, their daughter Marie Therese was born.

Every Child a Wanted Child

As Eileen Mooney discovered, there was no 'right' time to have a baby. Lorna Arnold's remarkable career was also to bring that reality into focus, both professionally and personally.

A small auburn-haired woman of delicate beauty and acute intellect, Lorna was born Lorna Rainbow in 1915, and grew up on a farm in the Surrey countryside. At Guildford County School for Girls she was a scholarship pupil, always at the top of her class. Sensitive and shy, she was from an early age a conscience-stricken vegetarian, and also gave much puzzled thought to her own future:

> Was my success in school a good thing, or was being clever something that should be hidden? Was I sufficiently modest and well-behaved? It was not clear what ideas of girlhood (and later

womanhood) I should adhere to, and those doubts lingered for me many years . . .

Hidden or not, her cleverness got her into Bedford College London in 1934 to read English Literature. The Second World War, and her precarious health, saved her from the fate – common to so many educated, unmarried women of her generation – of becoming a teacher or secretary. From 1940 to 1944 she had a desk job at the War Office, where her talent and intellect saw her taking on increasing responsibility. 'I was in a big, complex, powerful, and almost entirely masculine organisation, dealing with huge issues . . .' After D-Day she was promoted again. With victory in sight she was needed by the Foreign Office to work on the planning of the Allied occupation of Germany, and in June 1945 she was sent to Berlin to work with the Control Commission that administered the defeated nation. In the lawless early days following the occupation, with Russian troops on the rampage across the wasted city, Lorna slept with a revolver under her pillow.

In Berlin her scanty social life took place in the British officers' clubs. And it was at one of these, one day in August, that she received the reports of an event whose implications were to resonate through a large part of her later career. In the bar, the wireless was on. Together with a group of military officers Lorna listened, appalled, to the historic announcement of the bombing of Hiroshima:

> They were a tough lot, those army officers, they'd fought their way across Europe, and here they were sitting in ruined Berlin. And one of them said, '*That* is a dishonourable way to make war. *That* is wrong!' They were all shocked. They all thought it was disgraceful.
>
> And I was horrified too. I still think the bomb was not only wrong in itself, but it was wrong because it opened the way to a

new and terrible world. You know, people forget that those weapons are all still there. They're still as great an existential threat today as ever they were. They're very difficult to get rid of, and they've proliferated. But memories are pretty poor and for people who didn't live through the bomb, they don't really feature very large. As T. S. Eliot said, 'Humankind cannot bear very much reality.'

That always seems to me one of the things that is so terrible about history: that things that would be unspeakable, unimaginable, absolutely beyond all possible acceptance, can become seen as just normal.

Lorna stuck it out in Berlin for over a year, before finding herself suddenly required in Washington, where a financial deal for German reconstruction was being hammered out between the British and the Americans. She was employed by the Foreign Office, but as such she was an anomaly: 'The whole assumption which pervaded – almost unspoken – was: "You're a bit of a freak, doing a man's job, but thanks a lot . . ."' She was indeed one of our very first woman diplomats, and the only one in her unit. At one glitzy gathering called to celebrate a milestone passed in the negotiations, the host, who was the US Secretary of State, opened his speech of welcome with the words, 'LADY and Gentlemen . . .'

For the next three years Lorna divided her time between the British Embassy and the Pentagon, putting all her efforts into meeting Germany's urgent needs. At the Embassy one of her colleagues was the young Donald Maclean: 'a golden boy', as she described him, clever, highly regarded and popular, with an elegant American wife. But why was he so jumpy, nervous and quick-tempered all the time? His later treachery and defection to the Soviet Union would come as no surprise to her.

Settled in a pleasant house in Georgetown with two girlfriends from the Embassy staff, Lorna now found time to pursue her love of music. She joined a choir based in downtown Washington,

and soon found that her nationality made her an object of fascination to the choir's organist and director, Bob Arnold. Bob was
handsome and intelligent; he was also in love with all things
English, the music, the architecture, the traditions and, before
long, with Lorna.

> He seemed like a kindred spirit. And well, he so seldom met
> anybody who was interested in early English church music – so
> for him I represented all the wonderful old traditions of Europe.
> We got on so well . . .

For Lorna, however, there was no romantic quality to their relationship at this time; but Bob's sensitivity, vulnerability and
loneliness made her feel needed. Bob's life dream was to go to
London to study Tudor church music and composition; he was
eligible for a grant to study at the Royal College of Music, and
she willingly offered him introductions to her friends and
family. Bob left for London; she remained in Washington for
another year. The final momentous event of Lorna's time in
America was the historic ceremony to mark the signing of the
North Atlantic Treaty in April 1949.

Today, a diplomat of Lorna's experience – male or female –
would probably have a glittering career ahead of them. So why,
in 1949, did she hand in her resignation? The reasons speak eloquently of women's self-estimation in those post-war days, and
of a moment when the pull of the female stereotype was as
strong as at any time in history. Lorna felt, now that German
restoration was virtually accomplished, that the job she had
been temporarily employed to do was at an end. There was an
awareness that life was returning 'to what we used to regard as
normal'. For women, normality did not encompass high-flying
jobs in international diplomacy. Young ex-officers had returned
to their colleges and were ready with their Oxbridge Firsts to
fast-track into the Foreign Office. With her 2:1 in Eng. Lit. from

Bedford College, and despite three years of first-hand experience in a most precise and exacting job, Lorna did not feel able to compete:

> My contract was clearly worded. My job was a temporary one – 'for the emergency'. It never occurred to me that I had established any right to a special position in this man's world. I never felt it was a career path.
>
> In the Embassy there were no other women I could talk to and say, 'Look, when this aftermath-of-war period is over, and all the men come back, what do you think *we* ought to do?' I was out on a limb, partly because I was the only diplomatic woman, and partly because I wasn't really part of the Mafia in the Embassy. They were *all* men, nearly all toffs, all very nice – but from another world. When I left I had a letter from the Embassy saying 'Goodbye, good luck, thank you so much.' But they never said, 'Why don't you stay on?'
>
> And I did think, 'Really this does seem a waste when I've got some quite useful experience . . .'

It was a thought that, lacking confidence, she felt unable to put into words.

Spring 1949 found Lorna in London. She was not unemployed for long. Scanning *The Times*, she spotted an advertisement to work as general secretary for an organisation new to her: the Family Planning Association. 'I wasn't exactly dedicated to family planning or anything, but I thought, this looks interesting and worthwhile. I applied thinking it would be something quite new and challenging, and I might meet some interesting people.'

Now that she was home, her friendship with Bob Arnold re-awakened, and intensified. But he was anxious and highly strung, and increasingly emotionally dependent on her. At the same time . . . she was reluctant to identify what it was, but

Lorna had begun to realise that there was also something un-declared, unadmitted, about her good-looking admirer.

> It's not that he concealed his homosexuality, I just didn't realise
> what the implications were. When I was young you read books
> about young men having terrible pashes on other young men,
> and you thought, 'Oh that's a phase that a lot of them go
> through, especially at public school – but they grow out of it.
> They meet a nice girl and get married and all is well.' That's the
> way most people thought of the gay world. And Bob was long-
> ing for a family and a nice home life . . .

Soon after she got the job at the FPA, Bob proposed. Lorna accepted, from a real fear that if she didn't he might have some kind of nervous collapse. And that summer they were married.

★

The year that Lorna spent with the FPA before she had her first child and stepped off the ladder is worth attention not so much in respect of Lorna's career, but as a window on to sexual atti-tudes at the beginning of the decade, and on to the pitiable conditions endured by innumerable women with respect to their sexual health. We have already seen something of how the dreadful prospect of an unwanted pregnancy could induce heartache, shame and despair. In this new job Lorna now encountered poverty, ignorance, squalor and ill health among women, on a shocking scale.

The FPA had been founded in 1930 as a much-needed resource to help poor couples limit the size of their families. When Lorna joined in 1949, the National Health Service and Welfare State were still in their infancy. Soon after she started work with the Association, they moved their offices from Victoria and, ironi-cally, took over the premises of an up-market illegal abortionist's clinic in a swish Sloane Street town house. Upstairs, Lorna helped to answer the mass of correspondence from bewildered and distressed women, organised committees and arranged meetings, while in the basement a group of volunteers cheerfully parcelled up and despatched mail-order condoms. Meanwhile the various volunteers, medics and committee members came and went: 'We had a lot of very "do-gooding" great ladies – Lady-this, Lady-that and Lady-the-other . . .'

But there was nothing up-market about the FPA's clientele. A survey taken in 1951 showed that 47 per cent of families in this country survived on less than £8 a week; of the sample, 10 per cent managed on under £5 a week.* Lorna accompanied some of the FPA doctors to visit the poverty-stricken families crowded into insanitary King's Cross tenements, who lived in utter dread of the arrival of another mouth to feed. 'Really, you wouldn't believe what those slums were like then . . .' The tenants often lived one family to a room, having to get their water from a tap on the landing one floor down. It was the same story in the East End, as related by midwife Jennifer Worth:

> I often wondered how [the] women managed, with a family of up to thirteen or fourteen children in a small house. Some families of that size lived in the tenements, which often consisted of only two rooms and a tiny kitchen.
>
> Contraception, if practised at all, was unreliable. It was left to the women, who had endless discussions about safe periods, slippery elm, gin and ginger, hot water douches and so on, but few attended any birth control clinic and, from what I heard, most men absolutely refused to wear a sheath.

Not all men were wilfully obtuse about birth control. 'My wife is on staff, earning £11. She has no time for having a baby,' said one, pragmatically. But traditionally, the working-class husband

---

* About £216 and £135 today, respectively.

regarded contraceptive practice as falling into the wifely domain, while ignoring the consequences of his short-term gratification. Having sex with a condom 'was like having a bath with your socks on'. 'They take away the pleasure . . .' Withdrawal was by far the commonest form of family planning – if you can call it that:

> He couldn't always time it proper so I got caught more times than I wanted . . .

recalled one Lincolnshire wife . . .

> In the end, we didn't do it so much. I couldn't stand it any longer, it was too much of a worry you see. I had nine. I didn't want no more . . .

However, a Lancashire couple successfully practised coitus interruptus for eight years before starting a family – even though it didn't sound like much fun:

> It was like getting off at the roundabout instead of going on to Morecambe.

A working-class woman would usually have her babies at home. Lorna Arnold described seeing a young mother going through her labour on a mattress on the floor while her small children looked on, frightened and hungry, with nobody to get their meals. Such mothers would later suffer from severe gynaeco-logical complications caused by repeated pregnancies: 'prolapses down to their knees . . .'

But many doctors neglected such cases – seeing the area of women's health and family planning as 'social work' rather than 'proper medicine', so the FPA plugged a vital gap in information and assistance. 'This was the sort of thing that we were trying to deal with: these poor women, in this awful state – and *still* the husband would insist on his rights, and that was that.'

The mantra at the FPA was 'Every child a wanted child'. A clear enough objective, but not only did the Association have to contend with reluctant doctors, it had to fend off public controversy in order to pursue its activities:

> There was a great deal of persuading to be done, and the persuaders had to break through a huge barrier of resistance, made up of principled opposition as well as prejudice, Puritanism, and misogyny.

It was common for the Association's representatives to be on the receiving end of enraged abuse, as Lorna discovered when she spoke at the opening of one volunteer-run FPA clinic. As she concluded, a man broke into a torrent of insulting language, yelling out that the activity of the clinic was 'against the will of God'. This attitude – all too typical – meant that the FPA could not be seen to condone sexual activity outside marriage. The onward march of universally available contraception was being achieved at a crawling pace.

> Many clinics stuck to a 'Married Women Only' rule. If you turned up and you weren't married it was standard practice to say 'Where's your engagement ring? What date are you getting married, and can I see your licence please?'

But the goal of preventing unwanted children ran up against a folklore founded on the myth of women's own powerlessness. A study of unmarried mothers carried out towards the end of the decade explored the reluctance of young unmarried women to take any steps to safeguard against pregnancy. It revealed a view among many of them that the use of contraceptives implied a degree of calculation and premeditation regarding sex that was seen by women themselves as heartless – or at best as unfeminine. In the 1950s, setting out on a date with a condom in your handbag was definitely not what you did if you wanted to be thought ladylike. The preferred option was irresponsibility, and the result was a slow but steady increase in the number of illegitimate births.*

As we have already seen, prejudice, ignorance and bewilderment about sex and its consequences were still a default position in the 1950s. The tidal wave created in 1948 by Alfred Kinsey's report *Sexual Behavior in the Human Male* – and its companion volume on the Human Female (1953) – would take another decade to break on the shore. For now, the message of 'How to Get Your Man' remained unchanged: that for women, the only clever thing was stupidity.

*

Lorna Arnold worked at the FPA until three weeks before the birth of her legitimate, well-planned son in October 1950. She had had an uncomplicated pregnancy and everything seemed to favour a straightforward, middle-class birth. One sunny morning, she strolled among the bright autumn leaves in Kensington Gardens; later the same day her contractions started and she was taken to St George's Hospital at Hyde Park Corner. From then on, everything started to go horribly wrong, in a way revealing of the prevailing male climate in obstetric wards at that time. A medical student who was being examined on obstetrics tried to raise concerns that the baby appeared to be in the breech position, necessitating a Caesarean operation. But he was smartly ticked off by the doctor:

> ... this poor nervous young man told the old consultant all kinds of things about how dire my situation was, and this old medic was saying 'Yers, yers, yers ...' And then he said, 'My boy, you're not paid for how many complications you can find.

---

* Between 1955 and 1958 the figures in England and Wales rose from 31,145 to 36,174 – a 16.1 per cent increase, and 10,000 more than the pre-war 1938 figures.

I shan't fail you if you just say, "Here's a healthy young mother with a healthy baby."' So the poor boy was absolutely shattered. But *everything* he said actually came true.

Hours, days of excruciating pain followed; eventually forceps were used, causing a huge tear. Lorna nearly died. The baby, scraped and dented, with a semi-paralysed arm, and only fortunate in having escaped brain damage, was taken away. Bonding hadn't been invented. Wretched, ill and desperate, Lorna believed him dead. Nobody would enlighten her until one night a compassionate nurse smuggled a tiny bundle in to see her. 'Don't tell anyone,' she whispered, 'or I'll be in terrible trouble.' It was a fortnight before mother and baby were allowed home. Little Geoffrey soon recovered, but Lorna was battered, exhausted and disillusioned:

> What the future held for me as a new wife and mother I could not see, but clearly my life's work was not to be social betterment through family planning.

4. Paved with Gold

The Game

At the start of the 1950s Angela Austin, aged eighteen, was happily embarked on her secretarial post at the London office of Yardley's Cosmetics. A more acceptable job for a middle-class girl could hardly be dreamt of. As an only child, growing up in respectable Golders Green, Angela had made her parents proud by passing top in her year at Pitman's Secretarial College, qualifying her to apply for the Yardley's job, but in no way rocking the boat by seeming overly careerist. 'No one in my family encouraged me to pursue my interest in English literature at university. No one said, "With that degree you could work for a publishing house, or a magazine . . ." Nobody said it. Because married women didn't have careers, and I would be getting married, wouldn't I?' Until that day came, Angela set out each morning in hat and gloves and took the 13 bus to Piccadilly, where for nearly seven years she sat in an upper floor office on Old Bond Street typing standard replies to teenage customer correspondents who wrote in to the Customer Club: 'Dear Worried of Basingstoke, Pimples are normal for a girl your age. Have you tried Yardley's . . . ?'

But Mayfair was a neighbourhood of contrasts. Angela's parents might have been surprised to learn how their irreproachable daughter and her three young colleagues in the cosmetics company spent their tea breaks. Pure and perfumed, the Yardley offices overlooked an opposing establishment a few doors down Stafford Street. Its ground floor was occupied by a butcher's shop. From their vantage point the Yardley girls could see the occupants of the busy brothel above these premises slowly surfacing as the day wore on, waking up to the many business opportunities passing on the street below. The sign hanging above the butcher's entrance read 'Fresh Meat Daily'.

It was quite an eye-opener . . .

remembered Angela.

The Messina brothers, who were Maltese, ran many of the brothels in London. And this was one of theirs. And I and the other nineteen- and twenty-year-olds would look out of our window, and one girl would always be the one to look up and say, 'Hello – first one's out – five past four, right on time!' And then we'd hang about near the windows, waiting until we spotted a deal taking place: 'Look! She's got a customer!'

These girls were top professionals. The Bond Street furriers would persuade them to wear their best coats as an advertisement, because some of them were really very beautiful. One of them was less so – she was short and dumpy and wore glasses, which I found bewildering. But someone who was a bit more wise in the ways of the world than I was explained: 'Probably she's attractive to a man who wants a mother figure!'

And then we used to time them, to see how quickly they'd be in and out. We never actually worked out how much money they were making, but they did go in and out pretty fast.

As it happened, the Messina girls in Stafford Street did indeed operate under the strictest of time regimes. One of them, Marthe Watts, the 'slave' of Eugenio ('Gino') Messina, later recalled:

I could not spend more than ten minutes with a client at a session, even if the latter spent a great deal of money. This was a rigid time limit. It brought me many slaps and blows, for, if I stayed with a client even eleven or twelve minutes, it led to scenes . . .

Unsurprisingly, first-hand accounts by 1950s prostitutes are rare. As women on the margins of society, held in contempt by the mainstream, their personal stories did not rank high. In any case, the Obscene Publications Act of 1857 (reformed in 1959), under which immorality was grounds for book-banning, would have ensured their stories could only be partial ones.

Marthe Watts's story is one of just a couple, and unmasks the frightening and distasteful reality of life with the Messinas, who, post-war, ran their illegal racket unchecked. In 1950, aged thirty-seven, this attractive Frenchwoman was one of the prostitutes based at the Messina premises at 7 Stafford Street, who Angela Austin might have seen selling herself to everyone from guardsmen to airline pilots, drug addicts to dukes, between the hours of 4 p.m. and 4 a.m.* The ten-minute rule she described had of course been instituted by Messina to maximise profits. Though expensive at £3 a time, it was a no-frills service. The clients were given cursory attention in a small room containing a wooden bench. But where the über-pimp Gino was concerned, Marthe was slave to his master – and early in their relationship he had her branded. For fifteen years she bore tattooed on her left breast the legend L'HOMME DE MA VIE – GINO LE MALTAIS. Gino's business rules were law, and isolation was the key. No smoking. No looking at other men. No being friendly to customers. No over-revealing clothes.

* In *The Men in My Life* (1960), Marthe tells how on VE night, May 1945, she serviced 'more clients than I ever had on any other day during my life in London'. By the early hours of the morning she had clocked up forty-nine clients, but despite staying on the streets till 6 a.m. she failed to top the number up to a round fifty.

Moreover, we were never allowed to look at cinema or film magazines in which there were pictures of male film stars in an undressed state . . . The reason was, I imagine, that Gino was afflicted with an inferiority complex and was evidently afraid of our comparing these wonderful people with him. It was probably for a similar reason that he would not let us stay too long with a client, for fear that we might find someone with more prowess than his own in bed.

The penalties were severe. The girls at Stafford Street took it in turns to service Gino himself; he, depending on his mood, rewarded them either by beating them with an electric light flex or buying them fur coats, for money was no object. Gino ran a customised yellow Rolls-Royce, and in those days of strict food rationing, the racketeering Messinas were able to feed their girls well on as much butter, meat and alcohol as they could wish for. The girls stuffed the pound notes they were paid into a saucepan in the kitchen, each girl being expected to keep careful records of her earnings, while Gino for his part maintained meticulous accounts.

In 1951 the law started to catch up with the Messina brothers. Alfredo Messina was fined £500 and jailed for two years, having been found guilty of living on the immoral earnings of a certain Mrs Hermione Hindin, and of attempting to bribe a police officer with offers of a turkey and champagne lunch and £200 in cash. His brother Gino fled abroad.

Over fifteen years with Gino Messina, Marthe Watts calculated that she made £150,000 for him (over £4m today). A mixture of fear and loyalty kept her and her co-workers in his thrall. In the mid-1950s Marthe's health broke down; she left Gino, who was brought before a Belgian court and sentenced to six years' imprisonment. Finally in her mid-forties Marthe put street life behind her, lived quietly and respectably, and wrote her memoirs. They were published soon after the recommendations of the Wolfenden Report were adopted as the Street

Offences Act (1959), which outlawed visible prostitution, driving it underground.

Another woman who recorded her experiences on the streets preferred to remain anonymous, simply calling herself 'Jay'. Like Marthe, Jay is an outsider, driven into prostitution by need and neglect. Both are women persevering in a perfidious world to eat and keep a roof over their heads. But Jay's story, *Streetwalker* (1959), is very different in tone to Marthe Watts's book. It is atmospheric in its descriptions, acute in its characterisation, telling of internal anguish and a personal journey. Embroidered with a rich vocabulary, *Streetwalker* reads almost like a novel, but appears to be authentic. By way of endorsement its publishers quoted Sir John Wolfenden, saying:

> One of the difficulties we had while the Departmental Committee was sitting was to get a first-hand account of the life and attitude of the prostitute herself. I only wish this book had been available then.

Listen to Jay's account of a typical night's work. She has done a deal with a man in a Jaguar cruising along Piccadilly, and brought him back to her 'gaff':

> 'Oh, Colin darling, would you mind very much if I had the money first? It's sort of a rule, you know . . .'
>
> Now to business . . .
>
> I strip, from the waist down only, and lie on the bed, stretching cat-like in the warmth from the fire. The red light throws the room into deep rose shadow and the gas hisses cosily . . .
>
> Colin joins me on the bed, kissing me with shy, boy's kisses. I hate the intimacy of a kiss, as most of us do, and shift my head slightly, at the same time lying close to him and pulling myself against him, to hide my rejection of his lips. The reflex is immediate. No need for further caresses, whisperings, promises, undressings.

I remember the time, when I first went on the streets, that an old hand at the game gave me advice. She told me that there is no quicker nor surer way of speeding up the love-making process than to pretend an enthusiasm as great, if not greater, than your partner's. It saves time, trouble, embarrassment, and produces excellent results in the way of return visits or – extremely profitable – extended ones. This tip has proved invaluable . . .

I murmur in Colin's ear, using every trick of voice and action that I have learned instinctively and from experience. In a matter of another thirty seconds it is over.

If this is not an authentic reminiscence, it is surely drawn from somebody who had lived such a life? And even if ghosted or lightly fictionalised, Jay's story – detailing the techniques, the payments, and the awful dangers of her profession – carries conviction. She tells of the hours spent on her beat, of finding 'the most comfortable section of wall to lean against when the minutes drag . . .'; of 'Willie, the contraceptive man . . .' who plies his trade in Hyde Park; of streetlights and neon, criminals and derelicts, of physical and emotional insensibility, of running for her life from a rough customer. For a brief spell she finds salvation with Pete, who reawakens dormant emotions. But he turns out to be an ex-jailbird and gambler, rapacious and violent: 'Those doses of affection and passion, rare though they are, have become as necessary to me as heroin to a junkie . . . Fear, the need to belong to someone however bad that person may be, and apathy – these three have enslaved me.' Pete's final frenzied attack on her, in which he scars her face with a nail file, lands him back in prison, and causes Jay, at twenty-three, to abandon her old way of life forever:

I cannot, no, I cannot – not in the most minor degree – go back on the game.

*

While the sight of prostitutes haggling on the Mayfair pavements may have been titillating to the demure girls in the
Yardley offices, their ever-increasing presence on the streets of
London caused deep offence among the morally inclined.*
Convictions for street offences had risen steadily over a decade
– perhaps more indicative of the moral climate of the time than
of an actual increase in the numbers of prostitutes working the
streets. Dr Wand, the Bishop of London, alarmed at the prospect of thousands of foreign visitors flocking into the city for
the Festival of Britain who might be dismayed at the turpitude
of our capital, led a deputation to the Home Secretary in 1951,
extracting from him a promise to do everything in his power to
stamp out visible vice in the West End. His proposals had been
drafted by residents of Paddington, under the banner of the
Paddington Moral Reform Council, that borough being particularly plagued by the incidence of streetwalkers and
kerb-crawlers after dusk.

By 1955 as many as 12,000 of them had been arrested on the
capital's streets: a 600 per cent rise since the early days of the
war. The women themselves were not deterred, regarding the
inevitable thirty-shilling fines as a regular business expense.
One local commented that lots of the girls might as well have
taken out season tickets to Marlborough Street court. They'd
shrug their way to the magistrates' and say, 'Oh well, Thursday's my day to be collected.' But – assuming that the actual
numbers of prostitutes had not risen dramatically since the war

* In 1951 the philanthropists Seebohm Rowntree and G. R. Lavers, with the
assistance of the Metropolitan Police and a journalist, came up with a figure
of 10,000 prostitutes in London (2,000 of whom worked in the West End) and
a maximum of 60–70,000 in the whole of Britain. But investigations by the
research worker Rosalind Wilkinson showed that this was little more than
guesswork, and the figures might well be a great deal higher. See Helen J.
Self, *Prostitution, Women and the Misuse of the Law*, Hove, Psychology Press
(2003).

(when, anecdotally, women were for sale on the streets as never before) – these later, faint-hearted attempts to clamp down on the trade reflect a characteristically gutless hypocrisy around the topic of sex. For every dozen virtuous marriageable maidens looking down from their offices on high, for all those embodiments of decency – paragon wives like Mrs Whitehouse perfecting themselves in the kitchen over their pots and pans – the swirling underworld of the 1950s harboured hundreds upon hundreds of hookers and hustlers. They were the living manifestation of the all-too-familiar double standard by which men continue to separate their lusts from their loves. At a time when decent women were expected to be domestic, demure and dependent, their menfolk reacted with bogus outrage as the plumed and painted objects of their deeper desires paraded in the parks and streets. And rather than find ways to control or condemn her clientele, it was the gaudy, visible, threatening streetwalker herself who was not only penalised and outlawed, but beaten up and whipped.

They were everywhere. A teenager up for an evening out from the suburbs recollected the overwhelming impact of seeing the Soho streets crowded with women for sale:

> It was twilight time. Winter late afternoons. Not nights. The girls being on the street was a revelation to me, really, because there were so many of them. Whatever direction you went, they were there . . .
>
> The girls seemed extraordinarily attractive and well made up, and had very attractive, sexy clothes. They handled themselves almost like a dance routine. They'd come up, sashay up to someone, move over to the side, go round them . . . It wasn't just a case of standing there waiting for guys to come up to them . . . It was almost as if they were sweeping.
>
> They seemed to be very practised in everything they did, obviously . . . And what was intriguing, and sexual, and mysterious to

us was that it seemed matter-of-fact to them, a job, and that was one of the most remarkable things about it. You have a job selling your body.

If Angela Austin had a lunch date in a nearby Shepherd Market pub, she would notice that the tarts were already swarming around by midday. Here in Mayfair women like Jay and Marthe were 'the aristocrats of street prostitution',* 'charming and sympathetic women, who dress well and reasonably tastefully'. Many of them were accompanied by fluffed-up and manicured French poodles. Like courtesans, they were often kindly and concerned listeners who, if they were not operating under the strict time constraints imposed by the Messina gang, took a sympathetic interest in their client and his problems. These, the ones watched by Angela striking deals in Stafford Street, were likely to be professionals from the upper echelons of society. The £3 which these well-heeled men paid for a short session created another rung of the prostitution economy, the maids, who were often superannuated prostitutes themselves. It was the maid's job to book appointments, to time the men's visits and knock on the door to tell them to hurry up and get their

---

* Cited (as are a number of the following examples) from a study published in 1955 entitled *Women of the Streets: A Sociological Study of the Common Prostitute*, edited by the largely humane and sympathetic author, journalist and police officer C. H. Rolph. His allusion to 'aristocrats' is the cue for a seditious contemporary ditty doing the rounds:

> *It fairly broke the family's heart,*
> *When Lady Jane became a tart,*
> *But blood is blood and race is race,*
> *And so to save the family face,*
> *They bought her an expensive flat,*
> *With 'Welcome' written on the mat . . .*

– and so on, for another four increasingly smutty verses.

trousers on if they overran. She would also intervene with awkward or troublesome customers, and provide any necessary equipment – like canes, if the customer requested flagellation, or black lace underwear and high-heeled boots for the men who liked to dress up in women's clothing. Then she tidied up afterwards.

In Soho the prices were lower – £1 10s or £2 – and the atmosphere was raucous. On Friday nights noisy fights broke out in its whore-infested alleyways between Big Jean and Stout Sally, their 'protectors'. Nor could you expect much in the way of youthful freshness down near Victoria Station; the women there were drunk and embittered but the prices were still high, up to thirty shillings, while in Waterloo a client might get himself a quick one with a disaffected or unstable adolescent for less than ten. In Euston you got the criminals, in Hyde Park the younger type ('ten bob and find your own railings'); they were often ex-Borstal, though admittedly they were often pleasant and chatty. In Paddington you got more of the same, turning tricks in the backs of cars in the Bayswater Road. The streetwalkers here held their clients in contempt: 'They are like rats in holes . . . if a wife knew what her husband was really like she'd never live with him no more.'

Stepney and the East End was a destination known to be frequented by young runaways, whose customers would be sailors, dockers or men who had strayed in from the Essex suburbs. A girl might arrive there from Wales or the north of England and get picked up by procurers – often Maltese like the Messinas, foreign seamen or immigrants. In the early fifties Caribbeans were mainly men responding to the call for a labour force. Following the 1948 *Windrush* pioneers, they made the voyage to Britain in increasing numbers, leaving their womenfolk behind them. Here, lacking family or a mate, they often found consolation – and sometimes a lucrative business – with the deprived, uneducated, drifting young women washed up on those estuary shores where the ships docked. You could get good money for a virgin. As midwife Jennifer Worth described it, the vice industry descended on the East End like a plague in the 1950s. Whole tenements became brothels, prostitutes were living four or five to a room, corner shops were turned into cafés and drinking dens. For any families remaining in such buildings, this was a living hell of 'noise and loud music, parties, swearing, fights . . . The trade of prostitution goes on all night and all day, with men tramping up and down the stairs, and hanging around the stairways or landings, waiting their turn.' If there was nowhere else, alleys, doorways and the numerous bomb sites were put to use. Nationally too, dockland prostitution was seen as an all too visible menace. Liverpool shop assistant Joyce Kearney was waiting for a rendezvous with her boyfriend at the Mersey Pier Head when she found herself accidentally occupying a streetwalker's beat: 'This woman came up to me and she said, "Move off this spot, it's mine." I'd been standing on one of their places. You had to be a bit careful.'

The survey *Women of the Streets* gave detailed case histories of some of its subjects, a typical one being that of 'Bridget', a Hyde Park prostitute born in 1930. Bridget's background, set against the Depression and the War, was characteristically bleak: abused by her unemployed father, she lived in poverty with feuding parents. In her teens she had a variety of low-status jobs as a kitchen-maid or waitress, and at fourteen was sent to 'approved school' for two years. On her return home she became pregnant, but abandoned the baby to her mum and fled to London at the age of eighteen. Within six months she had become a professional prostitute. As with Jay, the author of *Streetwalker*, her ponce was her boyfriend, who represented the only point of security in her troubled life. He was a feckless, good-looking twenty-four-year-old who bullied her to earn more.

Bridget existed within a cycle of dependency, where sex and money were interchangeable, where men were simultaneously abusers, lovers, providers and exploiters, and where women were submissive, inferior and subordinate. From childhood, sex had been the only measure she had by which to calculate her own worth. Perhaps, despite her degraded and deprived circumstances, Bridget was not, in this, vastly different from the models, beauty contestants and man-hunters described in the last chapter, whose self-esteem found endorsement through male projections of 'femininity' (like those of Eric Morley). Their selling points were the perfect hairdo, the 37-inch bust, the beautifully-turned thigh; hers were unmentionably carnal. But in the male-dominated marketplace of the early 1950s they existed on the same spectrum.

Good-time Girl

And yet, Bridget adored her trashy boyfriend. '[She] said she would murder anyone who tried to part them.' Her threat may not have been an empty one. The famous case of prostitute, night-club hostess and convicted murderer Ruth Ellis remains a subject of controversy but, as details gradually accumulate about Ruth's life, cataloguing abuse, beatings, ill-health, abortions, miscarriages and depression, the balance is tipping towards an assessment that she could and should have been saved from the gallows in 1955. Had a defence of diminished responsibility been available to her then, she probably would have been.

Ruth (née Neilson) was twenty-four in 1950; as a young child her father probably terrorised and abused his young daughter.*

---

* An excellent recent book, Carol Ann Lee's *A Fine Day for a Hanging* (2012), explores and contextualises Ruth Ellis's story with the introduction of much new material.

She was under-educated and left school at fourteen. Still in her teens during the war, she had the misfortune to succumb to the blandishments of a married Canadian serviceman. She fell deeply in love with him, and got pregnant by him. The baby was born in 1944, but Ruth had finished with the duplicitous father. 'I no longer felt any emotion about men,' she recalled later. 'I was cold and spent.'

To support her son Ruth found work as a photographic model (occasionally nude); it paid £1 an hour. Again, luck was not on her side when one of the cameramen took her out for a drink at the Court Club in Mayfair, a brothel in all but name, owned by another infamous crook and vice king, Morris Conley ('ugly as a toad'). It was not difficult for Conley to persuade her that £5 was good pay for sitting chatting with the late-night drinkers at 58 Duke Street; and, for his part, he may have recognised Ruth's restless ambition and emotional disengagement. Sleeping with Conley as part of the deal was not to her taste, but she liked the glamour, the female company, and the income.

For Ruth, glamour and its trappings were a means to an end. As the author Carol Ann Lee points out, she was unusual for her time, in being a woman who not only needed but wanted to pursue aims outside the home. To this end she was prepared to leave her young son to be cared for by her parents, while she followed other ambitions. 'Sex was a commodity, financial security the goal, and along the way she intended to enjoy life.' Her tragedy was that her stock-in-trade attractions were calculated to tempt a range of selfish, worthless and brutal men.

In 1950 Ruth became pregnant by one of the club's clients, and had an illegal abortion. Towards the end of that year George Ellis, a divorced dentist who also frequented the club, persuaded her into marriage. She saw him as offering stability – but he was a chronic alcoholic who terrorised her with violence. She gave birth to their daughter in October 1951 but the marriage was disintegrating. Desperate, in poor health and unable to make ends meet, she was soon back at the Court Club.

Towards the end of 1952 Ruth Ellis suffered an ectopic pregnancy and spent a fortnight in hospital. At the time of the Coronation, she was emerging from a year of fear and ill-health.

Summer 1953. 'You know how it is – you look in the mirror one morning and decide that you must do something to change that drab old hairstyle.' Reborn in the likeness of Marilyn Monroe, ash-blonde waves now framed Ruth's pretty face. In this new guise, her life started to look up. Conley paid her £15 a week, plus a £10 entertainment allowance, to run the Little Club in Knightsbridge; she lived above the premises in a glamorous flat decorated in white. It was there that she became involved with the ill-fated racing driver David Blakely. Upper middle-class, passably handsome, work-shy, fickle and utterly unreliable, David was an habitué of the racing set who formed Ruth's clientele. A fortnight after he first showed up at the Little Club, David moved in with her; but within weeks he was chasing other women. Ruth became pregnant a fifth time early in 1954, and in March she had the foetus aborted – it would have been David's child. Their relationship was a roller-coaster of flare-ups and reconciliations. One day she would be the exhilarated passenger in David's souped-up HRG, lapping 100 m.p.h. on the track, the next he'd be bullying her in the bar at the Little Club as she plied admirers like the reserved and morose Desmond Cussen – another of the motor-racing boys – with her attentions. Desmond often gave her money; he was rewarded when she slept with him to punish the worthless David, who had typically failed to return from Le Mans for a birthday party she'd organised.

But her real affection for David Blakely was shifting into another gear, to the extent of subsidising his extravagant lifestyle and cars. 'I thought the world of him. I put him on the highest of pedestals . . . If he had cut his finger, I would have gone to the ends of the earth to bandage it.' By contrast, David had started to become aggressive and violent towards her; the jealous scenes escalated, David's uncontrollable temper fuelled by heavy drinking, and by snobbery at his mistress's tawdry employment. David never allowed her to meet his 'respectable' Home Counties family; while she persisted in believing that they might one day marry, he seems to have regarded the social gulf between them as unbridgeable. And yet '[he] was always urging me to give up my job'. Ruth, who was also drinking heavily by now, was often black and blue from bruises. He would hurl her down flights of stairs, and on several occasions came close to strangling her. 'I took it all because I loved him so much.' At one level, Ruth knew that she had to end the relationship, but she lacked the strength. By the end of 1954, Ruth was becoming less able to run the club. Takings were down, and Conley fired her. Staring poverty in the face, homeless and unemployed, she found refuge with Desmond Cussen. But neither she nor David seemed able to give the other up. 'Although we quarrelled and he beat me, I just could not part from him.' The early months of 1955 were dogged with tempestuous scenes between the couple. In February Ruth paid upfront for a room in Kensington which became the stage set for the next series of rows and recriminations. In March, though she was pregnant again, he was still punching her, smacking her and trying to throttle her. She lost the baby, it is not known whether by miscarriage or abortion, though probably the latter; whichever it was, she was very unwell and suffering blood loss at the end of the month. When David's racing car ('The Emperor') broke down before the British Empire Trophy, he turned on Ruth accusing her of jinxing him. The row ignited another explosion of violence.

The last evening that they spent together ended with them

both being thrown out of a club after David hit Ruth full in the face. He spent the next two days avoiding her, staying with his motor-racing associate Anthony Findlater and his wife Carole, whom Ruth hated, while with Desmond Cussen's help Ruth jealously and obsessively tracked his movements. It seemed to her, in her fog of rage, passion and embitterment, that the Findlaters were trying to drive a wedge between them. On Saturday 9 April Ruth Ellis spent a sleepless night. As she was later to tell a Sunday newspaper, she spent the early hours of Easter morning sitting in her Kensington room reliving her life of the last two years:

> When I first fell in love with David, I was a successful manageress of a prosperous club. I had admirers, money in the bank and a lovely flat. Now all I had was a bedsitting room, no money, no job and a man who swore he loved me one day and couldn't be bothered to collect me on time the next. A man who beat me in private and abused me in public. A man who was relieved when I lost the child he had fathered. A man who, I was convinced, was being unfaithful to me.
>
> I thought and thought. All kinds of things went through my head – all the things he had said to me and all he had done to me . . . I was raging inside.
>
> I had an overwhelming desire to kill David.

There are still uncertainties regarding Ruth's movements on the day of the shooting, Easter Sunday 1955. What is clear is that David Blakely left the Magdala pub in South Hill Park, Hampstead soon after 9.15 p.m. And then (by Ruth's account) as he was about to get into his car he turned, saw her, and turned away again.

Ruth was holding a .38 Smith and Wesson. She fired a total of six shots. Four of them found their target, and one disappeared. As David lay dying in the road, blood spewing from his mouth, a witness saw Ruth hold the gun's barrel to her temple. But she couldn't do it. Her hand fell to her side. The final bullet fired into the pavement and ricocheted off, wounding a passer-by.

Ruth Ellis passed the remainder of her short life in Holloway Gaol. She never made any denial, nor any plea that the charges against her should be altered. She seemed to understand that her actions would merit the death penalty, but was vehement that she did not want her life to be spared. Two and a half months after the shooting, Ruth stood in the dock of Court No. 1 at the Old Bailey, smartly dressed and with her hair freshly peroxided. When a spectator in the public gallery called out 'Blonde tart', she remained composed. Her plea, on the advice of her solicitor, was not guilty.*

The trial was cursory. Desmond Cussen, who may have known more than anyone else about the source of the gun, about Ruth's familiarity with it, about her movements on the day of the shooting, and about her relationship with Blakely, was briefly cross-examined but was not probed on those topics. Anthony Findlater's evidence was despatched in haste; Carole was not called. A witness to Ruth's injuries at David's hands was ignored and forgotten.

Another story could have been told, a story about years of systematic violence, abuse and humiliation, about her state of mind when she killed David, and about the provenance of the gun, but that was not the one which emerged in court. Ruth's defence team succeeded in alienating the jury's sympathies towards her, nor did she do much to help herself on this front, coming across as dispassionate and oddly calm. She did not

---

*Despite insisting that she had killed Blakely, Ruth Ellis cooperated with her solicitor's recommendation to plead not guilty, believing that it would offer her the opportunity of exposing the Findlaters' collusion in Blakely's fate before a jury. In the event, this aspect of the story never came out in court.

behave in the way a wronged woman was expected to behave. How was the idea of a dyed-blonde nightclub hostess, a common harlot, compatible with that of an abused female? To some of the lawyers and spectators present, Ruth was damned by her appearance, by her class, and by her own past career.

At only one point in the proceedings did she break down – when a photograph of David was produced – and the counsel for the prosecution asked her just one question:

> Mrs Ellis, when you fired that revolver at close range into the body of David Blakely, what did you intend to do?

to which Ruth replied:

> It is obvious that when I shot him I intended to kill him.

The following day Ruth Ellis was convicted of murder.

Over the next two months her solicitor worked frantically to try to gain a reprieve. Public appeals on her behalf gained momentum: MPs, literary figures, religious leaders and death penalty abolitionists called for her to be spared, and a petition of 50,000 signatures was sent to the Home Secretary. But their clamour was equalled by that of the group who believed Ruth had broken the rules and must hang. Some of these were fearful men, urging the strictest suppression of viragos like Ruth, liable to boil over or lose control, but many were from women who felt their own sex to be the guardians of public morality. By their book, a 'trollop' who was so unapologetic about her own sexuality, and so seemingly lacking in remorse, deserved the noose. One woman wrote to the Home Secretary to say:

> The fate of this openly immoral and shameless woman will, I feel, prove a deterrent to many who might otherwise have been tempted to let lust rule their lives. Such women are a menace to our national standards, and there is now one such less to corrupt others by her example.

THE WOMAN WHO HANGS THIS MORNING

A 'good-time girl' could not be allowed to get away with freedoms disallowed to the rest of us. Ruth had had sex with many men, she had worked for her living instead of looking after her children, she had decked out her body and adorned her pretty face with scant regard to the proprieties, and she had tried to carve out an existence for herself in the only way she knew how. 'Proper' women were expected not to do these things. They were judged, and they judged themselves, on their conformity with the norms of womanhood: fidelity, modesty, motherhood,

The morning this newspaper headline appeared, Ruth Ellis applied a final dab of lipstick and walked calmly to the scaffold. Her executioner described her as 'the bravest woman I ever hanged'.

care of the home, passivity and submission to men. Thus in their despair, the puritans redoubled their righteous cries for Ruth Ellis to pay the price.

On 13 July 1955, with exemplary dignity, she paid it.

Fourteen years later, capital punishment was abolished for ever in Britain.

Bright Lights

David Blakely didn't deserve his horrifying death. Before he became a murder victim, he was already the victim of his own background. There was violence and infidelity between his own parents, who divorced when he was eleven. He was spoilt, his schooling was unsuccessful, and the only real interest he ever cultivated was motor racing. But David was also a type: the entertaining, cocktail-drinking playboy, complete with fast cars, suave suits and a casual attitude to women. A type it's easy enough to recognise.

Step forward Agent 007, complete with 4½ litre Bentley and a .25 Beretta automatic. James Bond made his first entrance in *Casino Royale*, the first of Fleming's twelve novels based on Secret Agent 007, in 1953. Stunt cars, martinis, high living and misogyny alike, a fine line divides James Bond from David Blakely. And Bond's women conformed to type: they were often victims of abuse and maltreatment, had magnificent figures, were glamorous and sexually available, though as historian David Kynaston points out,* Fleming's take on them was also dismissive: 'These blithering women should stay at home and mind their pots and pans and stick to their frocks and gossip and leave men's work to the men.' For all their glamour and varnish, Vesper Lynd and Solitaire are, after all, playthings, victims, and members of an inferior sex.

Ian Fleming's London merges with the London of Morris Conley, the Court Club, the Stafford Street bordellos. Mayfair, Belgravia and Knightsbridge were his territory. And by 1951,

---

* See *Family Britain* (2009); Kynaston cites *Casino Royale*, p. 157.

despite austerity, the heart of the capital was starting to lose its moth-eaten, crumbling air. The blackout was becoming a memory as neon and sodium lighting burned up the darkness, reclaiming the night-time city for sinners and pleasure-seekers alike. The West End was awake. Outer-city dwellers from Earls Court or Islington headed 'up to Town' to do the sights and the lights – 'it was magic'. Raymond Chandler – an acknowledged influence on Ian Fleming – visited London that year and was struck by its appearance of buzzing prosperity:

> I thought England was broke but the whole damn city is crawling with Rolls-Royces, Bentleys, Daimlers and expensive blondes . . .

He could have been describing the seedy glamorous London of David Blakely and Ruth Ellis: tawdry, titillating, dazzling, opulent, modern.

London was reinventing itself. The ice was cracking. As car ownership increased over the decade, London's streets were bursting at the seams with blaring traffic.

Nobody knew what to do about the congestion. A ban on stopping? Build flyovers? Or tunnels? In December 1952 traffic fumes combined with coal emissions to shroud the whole capital in a hideous phlegmy fog – or 'pea-souper' – the worst incidence of air pollution in history. That year, Dodie Smith returned from America to her homeland for rehearsals of her latest play, and stayed for several months in the Ritz. In the evenings she strolled along Piccadilly and was smitten all over again by the lit-up vulgarity – somehow so touching – of the West End:

> Even Leicester Square, my least-loved London square, looked to me romantic . . .
>
> I went into the little streets between Leicester Square and the Haymarket . . . these were not business streets, people *lived* here, lights were on above the shops, there was laughter and occasional singing. The pubs were busy . . .

It was strange to come out of this little world . . . into the blaze of colour and noise that was Piccadilly Circus. It was crammed with people . . . The many neon signs intensified the blue of the sky and the whole scene was a brilliant raucous jumble, both appealing and repulsive.

The fifties were a boom time for showbiz. Bands were big, chorus lines were bigger. You could choose between the Balladinis and Tommy Cooper who were packing them in for the *Folies Bergère Revue* at the Hippodrome, or George Formby and his ukulele plus Billy Cotton and his Band in *Fun and the Fair* at the Palladium. Writers, actors and American film stars visited London; agents and producers wined and dined them in the burgeoning Soho restaurants and theatreland clubs.

The streets smelt of Polish sausage and French cigarettes. Spaghetti was chic, and after years of wartime confinement it was fashionable to be continental. At bars women sipped Pernod and Cinzano Rosso. The most glamorous of celebrities was Gina Lollobrigida, who gave her curvaceous blessing to the opening of Britain's first Italian coffee bar, the Moka, 29 Frith Street, destination for the hip, cool and bohemian. The coffee bar scene started to explode: Gaggia machines were installed at the Torino (Dean Street), the Bar Italia (Frith Street) and Au Chat Noir (Old Compton Street). The place to see and be seen was seated on one of their chromium pedestal stools, nursing a cappuccino at the Formica and steel counter. In 1954 the first Wimpy bar opened near Leicester Square, serving fast food to suburbanites on a night out 'up West'. But true metropolitans in the swim preferred an espresso doppio and cannelloni alla Parmigiana at Gennaro's.

Under the influence of Dior's New Look, Paris was still king where fashion was concerned. Extravagance and ostentation carried the day: skirts swaggered, petticoats flounced, handbags and heels were black, shiny and patent leather. 'Stake everything on the big, bold effect,' *Woman's Own* told its readers. Then as

'Coffee bars – a craze that's spreading everywhere'. In 1955 *Woman's Own* ran a fashion spread for the cappuccino crowd.

now, the West End of London catered for the grandes dames of society. Bond Street and the Piccadilly Arcades glittered with diamonds, while in Mayfair luxury dressmakers and milliners discreetly opened their glossy doors to the haute couture customer.

★

This is Sally. Have you met her – or her like – come to London from Dundee, Belfast or Penzance, perhaps? At 22 she is fighting for independence, security, contentment . . .

Sally is a child of the twentieth century who came to London, not because she thought the great city was paved with gold. 'It isn't,' says Sally. 'But it has something.' It has something that her own home town – in Scotland, Ireland or the provinces – hasn't got.

The more London resumed its lustre and glory, the more it beckoned to women eager for some of the stardust to rub off on them. Girls 'of slender means' could still afford to live in Kensington. They didn't have to sell their bodies to follow an independent occupation in the capital. Even on a secretary's salary of £4 10s a week, 'Sally' – depicted in the pages of a 1951 issue of *Good Housekeeping* – could dress, keep healthy, share a room with a friend and go to a show. Mary White came from rural Kent. 'It was a golden time to be in London,' she remembered of the years 1949–53, which she spent as a trainee nurse in Whitechapel; 'people were so cheerful and optimistic'. She lapped up all the musical shows. The future looked bright.

Flora Calder never lived in her native Glasgow again. Today the capital city is familiar to her, an easy journey from her trim Kentish commuter village of oak-beamed houses. But in 1954, when she first arrived in London, the style and polish of the women she saw prancing about the West End caused her to marvel, and the view from Westminster Bridge made her catch her breath in wonder:

I loved London. I loved seeing very nicely dressed people walking down Regent Street. And London at night was so scintillating. The Festival Hall, and the lighting-up of public buildings was beautiful. And looking at it all I just felt, Yes, I'm where it's at!

The contrast with Glasgow where she was raised could not have been greater.

Flora had grown up in an upwardly mobile household. Her mother was from the Gorbals, the worst slum in Europe at that time, and had married 'above her' into a seafaring family. But her husband found a career on dry land, and rose to become a bank manager. Thus the family acquired copper-bottomed respectability. Though still hampered by social insecurity (she refused to attend banking 'socials' for fear of being outclassed), Mrs Calder took up playing bridge, became an expert at the game and was appointed President of two bridge clubs. Meanwhile she groomed her two daughters for social success, and for marriage. Flora was sent to Bible class, dancing class, skating lessons and tennis coaching. 'My sister and I felt we were being programmed to marry some Clydeside shipping magnate. I'm afraid we didn't oblige.'

Instead, Flora felt creative tendencies stirring within her. By temperament she was what the Scots call 'douce', biddable, dreamy and 'in a dwam'. It was through the influence of an eccentric family friend that she discovered music, painting and poetry. 'He would wander about the house with a huge gold-tooled book of Milton, reciting "Hence, loathéd Melancholy, Of Cerberus and blackest Midnight born . . .", and would burst into Verdi arias on trams . . .' He encouraged Flora to draw, for by now she had a pencil in her hand all the time. She made up her mind to go to art school.

But Mrs Calder nursed a fantasy of status and material comfort for her daughter. Behind this ambition was a pathological fear of destitution. The bridge teas and the cushioned life of a bank manager's wife masked memories of grinding poverty. A generation earlier her own indigent father had spent every last halfpenny on alcohol. Flora *must* catch a decent upstanding man of the right class who would provide for her.

Paul Weston seemed just the ticket. Paul's aunt played bridge with Mrs Calder. And he seemed to appreciate the finer things of life. 'She finagled a meeting between us . . . and to tell the truth he seemed a very nice young man.' Flora started to go out with him.

> I liked him a lot. He was fond of art and we liked the same sort of things. We had very nice conversations. And it went on like this for a while, and he was very good company.
>
> But something wasn't quite right. He still hadn't so much as put a hand on my knee! Instead, he would talk with great enthusiasm about how we would do up our matrimonial home, and about the design of our bedhead and so on. And I thought, he's still not flung himself on me or attempted anything like that at all.
>
> I remember seeing him in an amateur production of the operetta *Rose Marie*, and he came out afterwards still wearing the make-up – very camp – all sort of lit-up and exhilarated by it. And I thought, hm, this is not really getting anywhere.

Eventually she plucked up courage to end it. Paul drove her home one night, and under the street light by the front gate she told him gently that the relationship appeared to be heading down a cul-de-sac.

> I think he was a bit cut up, but actually he wasn't devastated . . .
>
> And I went back in and I said to my mother, 'I've just had a long talk with Paul . . .' She was so excited. She said '*Yes* . . . ?' And I said, 'I think he's such a nice boy but I really don't think he's the one for me.'
>
> And she cried like a little girl. She said, 'But I've bought wall lights!' And I said, 'What *do* you mean?' Well – it turned out that she had already raced ahead in her mind to the engagement announcement, and wedding presents, and she'd visualised it all. Because in Scotland in those days it was a very big thing, and very competitive as well. You didn't get given furniture, you got given a lot of homewares and stuff. And

wall lights with peach-coloured glass panels were just _the Thing_
at that time, and she'd got them for the illuminated display of
presents that we would have, all to be laid out on black velvet.
And there'd be crystal and dinner sets and so on, and cheques
pinned on.

And she was just so cast down . . .

Flora was undeterred. A feeling that there was more to life than
wall lights drove her back to her paints and her sketchbook,
while half-formed ideas of freedom and a healthy libido sent her
ricocheting from boyfriend to boyfriend. In the late 1940s she
was at art school, and for all its provincial limitations Glasgow
could be fun for a very pretty and lively student. Flora's blooming beauty made her a magnet for the boys at the nearby Medical
School, and at Saturday night dances at the student Union she
was rarely without a partner. Between foxtrots they would
cajole her back into the recesses of a room known as the 'sit-
ooterie' (literally, where you 'sit out' a dance); here, someone
had removed the light bulb, and all that could be seen was the
glowing ends of cigarettes, while all manner of petting and inti-
macies took place under cover of darkness. Flora did have her
limits:

> My upbringing was very typical. There was no question of sex
> before marriage. My mother was a very small woman who had
> had very big babies, and she was preternaturally terrified of
> becoming pregnant. So she decided to frighten me and my sister
> into not becoming pregnant. She told us horror stories about
> the pain. And it was a middle-class thing, because what moti-
> vated her was the thought of the shame, if one of her girls got
> pregnant.
>
> Anyway, I didn't always want to 'sit oot'. I'd say, 'Listen,
> they're playing *The A Train*, oh I'd love to dance to that!' and
> drag them back on to the floor.

But there was an awful lot of what was later called 'petting into climax'. It was very safe. No risk of pregnancy or disease or anything. All you needed was a man with a big handkerchief. And you'd do that nearly every night of the week, and not always with the same bloke. I learnt quite a lot that way.

Flora left art school in 1949 and for the next three years worked as a commercial designer for a Glasgow advertising agency, while taking every possible opportunity to travel. Correspondence with a good-looking Dutch penfriend finally led to the loss of her virginity when she visited him in the Netherlands. One overcast afternoon, overlooking the grey expanse of the North Sea, Flora was seduced on Katwijk beach near The Hague. It was not a satisfying experience. The sand and scrub left painful abrasions on her bottom, and a subsequent nasty attack of cystitis convinced her she was pregnant. 'Frequent urination! I got back to Scotland and drank quite a lot of gin and took a hot bath. Luckily I wasn't . . .'

She was twenty-four when she threw in her job, having sent her portfolio to a company near Nantes in France who took her on. Living abroad changed everything. Gloomy tenements, the legacy of poverty, social expectations, wall lights: she was beginning to realise that one didn't have to live like that. It could all be jettisoned:

When I returned I tried to fit back into Glasgow life, but I couldn't. I had completely changed.

  And that was when I decided to go to London with Myrtle, my friend from art school . . .

The girls picked up their portfolios, headed south and, with the days of respectability and scrubbed doorsteps behind them, threw themselves into London life. In 1954 unemployment was around the 3 per cent mark. Flora went to see a lascivious agent who licked his lips at the sight of her and told her she would have no difficulty finding work in magazine graphics. In a very short time she had secured her dream job, designing for *Woman* magazine, at that time the biggest-selling woman's weekly in Britain. Year-round, the highly-coloured and beatifically smiling girl on *Woman*'s bright cover guaranteed its faithful readers a treasure trove of household hints, health tips, dress patterns, romantic fiction and problems solved. Here, for the next seven years, under the formidable editorship of Mary Grieve, Flora designed illustrations, typography and page layouts. (Myrtle meanwhile got a job in a Chelsea art materials shop.)

Woman offered up a cosy picture of domesticity and femininity. Here were recipes for Crabmeat Puffs and Chocolate Chiffon, suggestions for 'how to make a gay candlewick cushion', beauty advice featuring unblemished virgins, reassuring horoscopes and knitting patterns for cardigan-clad grannies. But Flora's own life in London told a very different story to that depicted in its pages.

Flora and Myrtle had started out sharing a room in World's End. Myrtle was an operator, however, when it came to flat-finding. She soon found them a three-bedroom flat in central London, and the Glasgow network provided them with a flat-mate named Jimmy. Jimmy worked as a technician – or 'roadie' – for the celebrated band leader and matinee idol Jack Parnell, whose career in the mid-fifties was at its height. Taking Parnell's sixteen-piece orchestra on tour, loading and unloading them from gigs, was the everyday job of this easy-going Glaswegian, a guitarist himself. Pre-rock'n'roll, Parnell's strident, percussive ensemble was the headiest, most intoxicating sound Flora had ever heard. She joined Jimmy on some of Parnell's gigs, and soon became familiar with the shifting, smoky, sexy, night-time world of jazz musicians. It was bohemian and glamorous, and Flora, fascinated, became part of it, sitting in on rehearsals, partying with them in basements. Often she would ply the band members with soup while they copied out their manuscript scores longhand, working against the clock before a performance.

At this time, jazz musicians had easy access to drugs. An 'exchange' operated, whereby American performers came to Britain, and in return British musicians would travel to the United States; they would come back bringing with them cannabis and cocaine. (Parnell's star saxophonist was never without his stash, but evaded capture by keeping the weed in a bag which he hung from a string outside the window whenever a raid seemed imminent.)

> I remember very often being at parties where people would go into the bathroom and lock the door: five or six people, very giggly, all laughing away about nothing at all, and the smell of sweet hay coming out . . . But I didn't really hanker after it at all. They're not as funny as they think they are!

But Jimmy took hard drugs. Over time his capacity for work evaporated. All day long he would lie on his bed in the flat, half-dazed with heroin, eyes rolling in his head. Then he lost his job. Flora noticed that money was starting to disappear. One day Myrtle walked in on him and found him with a tourniquet round his arm, injecting himself with a syringe. When Flora found out she took fright and left the flat:

> I couldn't stand the idea of this man with his eyes all over the place, taking money. I left enough for my share of the rent and moved on . . .

But in the mid-fifties, Flora was living life to the full. Soon after her arrival at *Woman* she got chatting to a broad-minded journalist friend about contraception and told him she was using spermicidal tablets. He firmly recommended that she try something safer, and gave her the address of a doctor who fitted her up with a Dutch cap and asked no questions. Thus equipped, and with a steady job that she loved, Flora Calder was ready to taste the pleasures of financial independence, freedom and youth. She went straight out and bought a waisted vermilion velvet trouser suit at a time when trousers were still a crime against femininity, and wore it with matching vermilion shoes. Then she bought an asymmetrical white sheath evening dress embellished with a cascade of fluttering wired organza petals. 'I liked making an entrance. I've had my times of glory . . .' And then there was the ruched number in shocking pink chiffon with matching shoes in which she danced wildly with a handsome and extremely drunk Scottish portrait painter at a Royal Academy ball . . . And the time her false eyelash dropped in the soup at a posh luncheon. And the time *Woman* sent her to Paris to art-edit a photo shoot with top US model Suzy Parker . . .

Giddy with success and love affairs and dancing, glorying in the moment, Flora and the newest in a procession of men make their way to the Embankment. London sparkles. The bewitching night-time city can be seen from the river: a myriad jewelled lights reflected in the eddying Thames – '*so* beautiful'. On the bridge they kiss, a charmed moment absurdly cut short as his spectacles – temporarily deposited on the parapet to allow for a more passionate clinch – are knocked spiralling into the waters below . . .

The Shires

At *Woman* Flora Calder was earning 'more money than I knew what to do with'. London had laid its glorious freedoms before her. The dream of independence had come true. She was playing hard and working even harder, describing herself as 'just a girl who can't say "No" – not as far as sex was concerned, but as far as work was concerned'. Marriage, and babies, were ideas she tried to put from her mind. Her mother, stern and unloving, had instilled in her a morbid terror of childbirth, and a terror of the bourgeois trappings associated with a wedding. Despite her many loves, she replaced emotional commitment with unremitting hours at her desk, at a cost to her health – and, ultimately, to her own stability. Flora was caught in a trap rarely acknowledged in the 1950s – but all too familiar to many women today – in which the path of professional achievement is pursued at the expense of marriage and motherhood. Her twenties were passing . . .

★

The impulse towards freedom and independence felt by 'Sally', and nurse Mary White, and by Flora Calder couldn't always find expression by packing your suitcase and catching the train to London. If, like Dorothy (Dot) Maskell, you were painfully poor and trapped in the provinces, merely surviving from Friday to Friday was enough.

Things might have been different for Dot, who was naturally curious and independent-minded, had she not fallen in love with a farm worker. Today we might call her move from Brighton to a rural village 'down-sizing'. In 1947 it felt more like culture shock.

During the war Dot had worked on a farm as a landgirl, and it was there that she met Ron Medhurst. They married in 1947 and proceeded to have five children over the next twelve years, living on Ron's £8-a-week wage as a herdsman. In truth, Dot was used to poverty. Her father was an engineer, who had received a leg wound in the First World War. After the financial crash in 1929 he was unemployed, and the family was close to desperate. Her mother's powers of endurance, intelligence and pride were a lifelong inspiration to Dot; and it was owing to her that she grew up to love reading, to become thoughtful and self-reliant. But once married, there was no time for mental pursuits. Every day was dominated by laundry:

> An average day? Getting all the children up, seeing that they had their breakfast, getting them off to school. And I suppose I'd start doing some washing then. 'Cos Ron would get his overalls filthy on the farm.
>
> There was *always* washing to do. I had a mangle to squash all the water out and put it out on the line in the garden, but if it was raining you'd have to try and dry it in the house.
>
> And Ron used to come home at lunchtime, 12 o'clock, so I had to get a hot meal on during the morning. Then in the afternoons it would be washing up, and ironing, and gardening. We grew all our own veg . . .
>
> I'd catch the bus into town once a week to do the shopping, because the village shop was too expensive. Bread came round in a van. We had milk from the farm, and we kept our own chickens for eggs.
>
> And I used to knit all the children's clothes, and make their dresses. You just spent the whole day cleaning and washing and cooking. There weren't enough hours in the day.

They finally got a washing machine when she was expecting her fourth child.

City-bred, Dot felt herself to be an outsider in her husband's village. The entire community was involved in the labour-intensive work of farming, and few villagers felt any need to travel beyond the confines of their little tribe. Doors were shut at 10 p.m., and anyone coming home late was viewed with suspicion verging on hostility. Whispering and gossip were rife. 'The village people thought of city people like me as coming from a different race . . .' She would trip up the muddy lane in her colourful hat and full-skirted frock to withering looks from the neighbours:

> I was frowned on by the way I used to dress. The village women were dowdy, you know. They didn't have fashion, they just wore clothes. And they'd look you up and down as you walked past them.

But it wasn't just her fashion sense that set her apart from the static, insular community she had entered. Dot was taken aback by the village morality that glossed over sexual responsibility. If she imagined that the pretty thatched cottages of Rodmell housed a pastoral bevy of innocent milkmaids, she was to be quickly disillusioned. Ignorance prevailed in deepest Sussex, à la *Cold Comfort Farm*. Fifteen-year-old lasses fell pregnant with distressing regularity. Nobody knew which young yokels had led them astray through the sukebind, though gossip over the garden hedge gave rise to many a guess. The baby would be brought up by the girl's family, unless she was old enough and the father could be traced and made to marry her.

The sex divide in rural England seemed set in stone. But Dot was determined to retain her own interests and opinions:

> Ron was surprised that I liked reading books for example. He'd say, 'Haven't you got anything better to do?' He didn't see reading as useful.
>
> It was a bit stormy when we were first married. He was brought up that the husband ruled the house. Their wives did as the men wanted them to do. But it didn't always work in my case. If I didn't want to do things then I didn't do them. He wasn't used to that. It came as a bit of a shock to him.

But Dot was shocked in her turn when election time came. She had joined the Labour Party youth branch at the age of fifteen,

and had grown up with the presumption that women were entitled to a say:

> The village women were very accepting of their lot in life. I
> remember during the General Election, talking to some of them
> about politics, which I was very interested in, and I'd ask them,
> 'How are you going to vote?' And they'd all say, 'Well, I'll have
> to ask my husband.'
>
> I remember asking one of the men what he would be voting,
> and he said, 'Oh, we've got to vote for the Conservative candi-
> date,' and I said, 'Why've you got to?' and he said, 'Well, the
> boss said to us – "You *do* know how to vote, don't you?"' So I
> said, 'You know you can please yourself how you vote, it's a
> secret ballot.' And he said, 'No, no, he'll find out, 'cos he's a
> magistrate. We've got to vote the way he wants us to.' And the
> wives couldn't do anything without asking their husbands, and
> then they just did what they said. It was like the Middle Ages.

For Dot, whose proud working-class mum had brought her up
to take everyone of whatever background at face value, unfairness was built into the village system. There at her own back
door was the evidence of entrenched social inequality. The
workers were creating the wealth out of their sweat and toil and
being paid a pittance, while the bosses 'who are supposed to
know better' were protecting their political interests and getting all the money.

And yet despite her clear-eyed view of the injustices and
narrow-mindedness of her adopted community, Dot Medhurst
never questioned the fundamental divide in which men and
women ruled over opposing power bases:

> Women were the mainstay of the family. That was their domain.
> That was where they had the power – in the home. I wouldn't
> have wanted to not have my family, or to be a career woman . . .

Like her mother before her, Dot channelled her intelligence inwards, gaining her ends with cunning, not conflict. Over the years Ron was persuaded to read books and talked into voting Labour, while being flattered into believing he was master of his own house:

> I run our finances. I'm the one who runs things here.
> But don't tell Ron, he thinks he does.

*

Modernity had barely touched villages like Rodmell. Bogged down by primitive ignorance, they held fast to their feudal traditions, stagnant conservatism, and superstition.

Ancient folklore survived intact in the post-war countryside. Women were not supposed to whistle, and many still believed that it was bad luck to look at the moon through glass. On the night of a new moon you had to stand outside and turn over a silver coin in your pocket. If you opened an umbrella indoors a goblin would fly out, bringing bad luck. Tripping while going upstairs presaged a wedding, and a bird flying into your house or a picture falling off the wall were both omens of death.

Female functions gave rise to innumerable superstitions. Some believed that menstrual bleeding was caused by the Devil getting inside you. Others thought that a menstruating woman shouldn't be in contact with a pig because her touch would turn its meat bad. And she shouldn't walk in long grass because her scent would attract snakes, while touching snow would cause the bleeding to increase. A girl's menarche was no guarantee of her inviolability. The view of the boys in one village was 'If they're old enough to bleed, they're old enough to fuck!' In remote Fenland communities rape – often incestuous – was a hidden, and shameful, fact of life. Shameful to the woman, for nobody reprimanded the men. Explanations for pregnancy ranged from the misguided to the absurd: it could be caused by French kissing, or it could be caused by a Morris dancer inadvisedly placing his flowery feathered hat upon your head. Prophylactic measures against pregnancy also entered the realms of the bizarre. In one family the practice for generations had been for the woman to sit on a chamber pot after intercourse had taken place and sniff pepper from the pepper pot. This would cause all the semen to be sneezed out of her. Others believed it was possible to 'wee it all out'. And if the worst came to the worst an unwanted baby might be aborted by going for a long walk, or sticking a penny coin to your belly button with plaster. 'This will stop the baby breathing.' But few rural girls were censured for having pre-marital sex; in many cases it was regarded as the natural precursor to marriage, which took place as soon as a child was conceived. A working man wanted to be sure his future wife could bear him children before he took her to the altar.

Unless they were well off, women in rural districts also had to contend with the backwardness of basic amenities. In 1952 Elaine Morgan and her family were living in a farmhouse in Radnorshire. 'In many respects it might as well have been the 1850s . . . There was no electricity, no gas, no piped water, no mains drainage . . . we were at the end of the line.' The earth closet was at the bottom of the garden under a plum tree, picturesque enough in blossom time, but not so much fun on a stormy night. A bus to Hereford picked up passengers twice a week from a stop three miles away. Water came from the stream, 'the mountain mists got into everything'. There was an exodus of young women, reluctant to spend the best years of their lives milking cows and scrubbing dung-smeared overalls. London beckoned.

They were sorely missed. A wife is as indispensable to a hill farmer as a horse, and not nearly so easy to find. So news of a young farmer's forthcoming marriage would be greeted with a buzz of excitement and envy. 'Where did he get hold of *her*, then?'

Who would willingly choose the rigours of rural life, as house-wife Winifred Foley did in 1955, transporting her family from an inner-city London slum to the Forest of Dean? The family had no financial slack, and Winifred was not too proud to earn two shillings an hour as a 'casual' on the local farm. There, potato-picking was a back-breaking task, muddy, freezing and laborious. The workers were in thrall to the relentless plough-ing tractor which uprooted the tubers and tumbled them caked in dirt on to the furrows. At the end of the day Winifred was 'on all fours'. Apple-picking was better. But some mornings the apples were frozen to the grass, and windfalls had to be collected from among patches of stinging nettles. Surplus apples went into everything the family ate that autumn.

*

Bottle them, or make them into jam. Surpluses – whether of apples, beans, raspberries or gooseberries – were of defining importance when it came to that glory of British country life, the Women's Institute. The WI movement was founded as a vil-lage federation; by definition, towns and cities could not set up branches. And ever since the 1920s, from Dorset to Derbyshire, Lincolnshire to Lanarkshire, the WI was an essential part of the rural landscape.

Post-war, the Women's Institute, like the Young Conserva-tives, was more popular than it had ever been. We are in an era of 'joiners'; in 1955, 5 per cent of the total population of England belonged to some sort of women's club, from choirs to knitting circles, Townswomen's Guilds to tennis clubs. In 1951 there were 7,710 branches of the WI in villages across the country, and by 1954 membership stood at 467,000. The concerns of members like Mrs Thompson emerge clearly from its members' magazine, *Home and Country*. Mrs Thompson, whose Christian name was not revealed, was the winner of a competition in 1950 to write an essay about a day in the life of a countrywoman. Her published description could have been anchored in any decade since the early years of the organisation, now almost 100 years ago.

It has been another warm, still July day. Somewhere in a remote farmhouse between the Downs and the sea, Mrs Thompson is listening to the wireless; the news tells her about distant events in London. High temperatures have meant crowds at railway stations jostling to escape to the seaside. There are reports of industrial unrest and foreign tensions. 'It all seems very far away.' No urban neon or sodium lights penetrate the velvety half-light of a summer evening in Mrs Thompson's garden. Honeysuckle and stocks release their heady scent into the dusk. A white owl glides from its roost in the branches of an elm tree, and hedgehogs can be heard rootling in the mulch below it.

London, and thoughts of her annual theatre visit to the far-away capital, serve as a welcome distraction next morning as Mrs Thompson washes the dishes after breakfast. For her it has been an early start. The drought-stricken garden must be watered and the hens fed. And once that meal is put away, preparations for the next begin: 'Come what may, meals must be ready on time.' Peas and raspberries must be gathered from the garden, potatoes must be boiled. After lunch blackcurrants must be prepared for bottling before a deputation arrives from the local Women's Institute Committee to discuss arrangements for the village Flower Show. Decisions must be made about the tea tent: what is best, fruit cake or plain cake? – and would it be best to serve tea in pots or cups? How should vegetable marrows be judged – on their size, or their shape? Then it's time to feed the hens again, check the pigs, fill up the water trough for Annabel the nanny goat. Another day passes.

Issues of *Home and Country* may make the activities and aspirations of its members seem quaint and comic: members competed to knit on matchsticks, learnt how to make toys from straw, and how to use a piping bag ('It enables a cook to turn out a homely dish in really slap-up professional style . . .'). Branches undertook communal rug-knitting sessions, and the lucky winner of a gift-making competition was rewarded with the prize of a realistic woolly dog. There were interesting articles on washing woollens, an impassioned debate on the acceptability of knitting in public places, and a tragic reader's letter about the difficulty of finding net collar supports ('Some ladies still wear net collars and are in great distress, not being able to find any alternative supports . . .').

But the same pages betray a campaigning, contemporary side to the WI. These women were starting to look beyond poultry-keeping and meal preparation. The 1950 AGM took issue with hospitals for not allowing parents to visit their sick children, and a few years later started a national drive against the litter louts, still remembered as the KEEP BRITAIN TIDY campaign. In later years there was a discussion of violent American so-called 'comics' which gave negative portrayals of women, and forums about child delinquency, food labelling, vivisection and world peace. While constitutionally bound not to engage in party politics, a progressive wing of the WI was gaining confidence and making its voice heard on controversial internal issues ranging from ecumenical carol services to a kill-joy ban on alcohol at the WI's Coronation Day celebrations. After years of isolation and the sense that their views didn't matter, the Mrs Thompsons were finding like-minded support, and flexing their muscles. At their yearly gatherings in the Albert Hall – to the polite astonishment of the press – thousands of middle-class matrons from the shires voiced a message of female solidarity that in time would become hard to silence.

5. When I Grow Up . . .

Gymslips

Recalling her school teachers in the late 1940s, Joan Rowlands (later the broadcaster Joan Bakewell) wrote:

> Most of my teachers were single women of a generation whose men had been slaughtered in their thousands on the battlefields of the First World War, the missing generation of the men they might have married.* It gave them a curious take on education. They welcomed greater education for their 'gels', but at the same time they had a rather wistful, misty-eyed view of what a woman's destiny might be. On speech days not a single prize, or scholarship, or university entrance was ever announced from the assembly-hall platform without a final aria from the headmistress, Miss Lambrick, that a woman's true calling was to be a wife and mother.

Society had determined that woman's place was in the home. This view was reflected in the education of girls.

Many women like Miss Lambrick had marched proudly into the male-held territory of universities and training colleges. As pioneers of women's education, they took the view that it was a privilege and a matter of great seriousness. But as unmarried women they still felt their loss keenly. After all, they had grown up before the First World War regarding marriage and motherhood as a birthright, denied by fate to millions of them. The

* See Virginia Nicholson, *Singled Out: How Two Million Women Survived Without Men after the First World War* (2007).

majority of teachers were all from that conspicuous (by their numbers) generation, the post-First World War 'Surplus Women'. But now the population had re-balanced. By the 1950s the gap was closing between males and females. There would be husbands for everyone, and women would reclaim their natural destinies. No more struggling to compete in politics, the law, business or industry. Teaching the next generation cookery, embroidery and laundry skills alongside French and Latin was uncontroversial and came naturally. These were the skills that women were believed to need, and these were the attributes that kept them in their domestic ghettoes.

John Newsom was an education theorist who pressed for an ever more traditional syllabus. It seemed to this commentator that girls were being force-fed with unnecessary aptitudes. He quoted Samuel Johnson, saying 'a man is better pleased when he has a good dinner upon his table than when his wife talks Greek'. What was the point in teaching girls foreign languages, sciences and higher mathematics, he argued, when their calling in life demanded quite different skills? Married women living in small houses didn't need to calculate logarithms or construe Racine, they needed to be able to shop, cook, clean, nurse, garden, do needlework and simple accounts. This was the reality of life for the majority of women, and our schools were failing them. Newsom robustly countered the suggestion that women were domestically over-burdened by claiming that this was their choice:

> No woman is compelled to get married and to accept the degra-
> dations involved. Yet she chooses it deliberately as her main
> occupation and a great part of her early womanhood is spent
> trying by one artifice or another to get entangled in the domes-
> tic toils.

Though John Newsom was an extreme advocate of change in girls' education, he seems to have regarded the status quo as immutable where women's role was concerned. They were going to be housewives, *ergo* they must be trained for housework. It was a reductive, results-driven approach, which left no space for the pleasures of the intellect or the joy of ideas.

How did their schooling affect this generation of girls? Their future roles were imbibed from an early age. Many children learnt to read from the *Janet and John* books, in which Janet helps Mother to cook, while John and Father do manly technical things with the car or wheelbarrow. Describing her later educational experience at a provincial girls' grammar school, the social scientist Mary Evans holds a magnifying glass over the ideologies and assumptions of the educational establishment. Socially limited, snobbish, but also imbued with the higher purpose of success in a modern world, Mary's girls-only school in Brentwood, Essex, prioritised Latin and Greek over Spanish ('a language fit only for waiters and the dull-witted'). Girls in the C-stream pursued Domestic Science (shortened to 'Domski'), whereas the A-streamers did this subject for only a year, prior to taking up Classics. For them, ten interminable months were spent smocking a green gingham pinafore. It was stressed that this mind-numbingly pointless task was an exercise in patience and the ability to 'work steadily'.

Poise and deportment were also part of the girls' training in the female perfections, and approval was conveyed through the awarding of 'posture stripes'. School rules were specific about protecting the girls' virtuous image; they were never to go upstairs on buses, as this was the domain of nasty men who smoked cigarettes, and they must never, *ever* eat in the street. The school's sumptuary laws were arcane and convoluted. Skirts were expected to be of a length whereby the hem touched the floor when the wearer was kneeling. Hats were to be worn respectably in the street at all times, Panama in summer, velour in winter. The blanket ban on mirrors, jewellery, coloured underwear and high heels was enforced, but there was no ban on using make-up or ear-piercing: 'It never occurred to anyone that we would do these things.'

Mary Evans comments on an interesting paradox. Her teachers were, in the eyes of her and her classmates, sad spinsters, 'unclaimed treasures', who had evidently failed at the business of being a woman. They flat-shared with other women teachers, and pedalled to school on their heavy-framed push-bikes. They wore blouses and pleated tweed skirts, with stumpy, round-toed shoes and ankle socks. As such, and as representatives of the worth of education and the feminist fight, they seemed to their teenage pupils like Mary to offer a sorry spectacle.

> We associated education for women with ankle socks and bicycles. Our own aspirations ran in the direction of cars, men and fashionable clothes . . . We longed to enter what we saw as the glamorous adult world, an adult world which was peopled by men.

The patriarchal world seemed the only world worth belonging to, and striving for. Mary's spinster teachers had striven and triumphed and yet, ultimately, they had failed. For if getting a good education meant isolation from men and frumpy clothes, who would embrace it? University, and battling for women's rights, were emphatically *not* seen as constituents of 'the good life', while for most working-class women they were essentially an irrelevance. Against a backdrop of incomprehension from the older generation, it took commitment and an unusual thirst for study to induce even grammar school girls to aim for further education.

Uniformity was all in this world, both in clothes and in social class. A bank manager's daughter herself, Mary Evans describes a homogeneous body of pupils drawn from the suburban bourgeoisie. Butler's 1944 Education Act might have provided free education for all, but in effect the working classes could not afford to equip their children with the essential new wardrobe, purchased from an exclusive outfitter, to attend a grammar school like this. Nonetheless, just occasionally, a member of the proletariat slipped under the net.

★

Brenda Nash was growing up in a large purpose-built pre-war council estate about six miles from the city centre of Birmingham. For years she was to be the only girl in her neighbourhood to pass the 11+ and gain a place at grammar school. Equipping her was far beyond the means of Brenda's parents, and she was only able to go because her kind Gran cashed in her Club savings to buy the uniform. But nobody in the family, Brenda least of all, understood what was needed. Gran bought her a blouse, a blazer and a gymslip. Dressed in this gymslip, heavily box-pleated from yoke to hem, Brenda resembled a St Trinian's madcap. It was not exactly the image she had had in mind. Meanwhile all the others in her class were clad in 'up-to-the-minute four-gore pinafore dresses'.

Brenda suffered torments. It was bad enough that her accent was a little coarser than theirs. It was dreadful, too, that she was charged with the humiliating weekly job of taking her father's suit to the pawn shop after school, of evading the prying questions about what her bulky bag contained, and of ducking her classmates' inquisitive gaze as she sidled down Green Lane to 'pop' the offending item for £2 10s – 'without which we couldn't have lived through the rest of the week'. This was all mortifying. But for Brenda the worst aspect of grammar school was enduring, for six years, the ignominy of appearing conspicuously different from everybody else. For years the dire prospect of being taken to task for her oddity hung like a menace over her daily journey to school: 'What detail of my dress or behaviour would be singled out for criticism that day?' Miss Haworth, the Senior Mistress, was her persecutor, incessantly finding fault with her divergent outfits: wrong school tie, bought in a second-hand shop, cardigan knitted by Gran with weird coloured borders, blouse cut down from one of her father's old shirts, hand-me-down *green* blazer . . .

> I sat in school assembly, a patch of alien green in a sea of navy blue, and wanted to die . . .

Brenda Nash would later describe herself as 'a very mediocre student'. And yet she alone among all the local teenagers on her estate remained at school until the age of eighteen, four years longer than any of them. This unusual situation came about because her father wanted his children to have the education he had been denied, but also because her mother unapologetically exploited her. Brenda's mum kept down a series of lowly factory jobs, passing the burden of childcare, cooking, cleaning and shopping on to her oldest daughter. Thus at the age of fifteen Brenda's day would start at the crack of dawn, having to rouse, dress, wash and feed her younger sisters. Then, because her statutory travel allowance was invariably embezzled by her mother, she was always short of money for fares, meaning she could only afford one bus, not two. So she walked over a mile to the bus stop, followed by a short bus journey and another half-mile walk to Waverley Grammar School in Small Heath. In the evening the return bus journey was just long enough for her to do her maths prep. Back home, she was expected to clear up the awful mess left by her slatternly family, clean out the grate, light the fire and prepare her father's evening meal. Unsurprisingly, she was not keen to invite friends home to see the chaos. The family's poverty also denied her the chance of participating in concerts and operas staged by the school's talented choir – 'I couldn't raise the bus fare to attend the many rehearsals necessary.'

Brenda's academic experience mirrored that of Mary Evans. There was the same needlework horror. Ham-fistedly, she struggled over two terms to make an apron. In the third term the students were expected to sew a pair of navy blue knickers. Brenda botched the measurements. Horrible, thick and ill-fitting, her voluminous handmade under-garments ended up collecting mildew in a cupboard. Then there were the same unfathomable choices, with science regarded as an inferior option behind Latin and History, and creative students compelled to choose *either* Art *or* Music. Brenda excelled at English and French, and took 'O' levels in her stride. And if she was only grateful to her ferocious teachers for one thing, it was that they did not discriminate against her, nor did they patronise her, for coming from a 'different' background. Academically, she was expected to come up to the same standards as everybody else:

> I could not under-achieve and blame my family background for my failure: I was expected to do what everyone else did, and I did it. This hard philosophy enabled me to get out of my poor background, go to university, at a time when only one working-class girl in a thousand had a university education, and so to make myself a different life.

It was 1955. Gradually, despite all the trials of being a have-not in a middle-class milieu, the advantages of education were becoming self-evident. Brenda was perceptive, and she had only to look around her at the limited lives, the soul-destroying jobs and the poverty. Girls just as much as boys were staring into the abyss:

> – a couple of years after school working in a factory or a shop, then early marriage and the closing shutters of husband, children and making ends meet.

> What I did envy boys, however, was their unquestioned
> superiority within their society. Even in their teens they were
> superior to their female relations, even to their mother . . .

This gloomy reflection was prompted by Brenda's awareness
that she would *never, ever* be allowed to play in a football team.
For years the unfairness of this would gnaw at her. Football was
the light of her life, Wolverhampton Wanderers her team, and
its star player, Billy Wright, the object of her passion and adoration. If she couldn't play for Wolves and England, she vowed to
do the next best thing, marry their captain.

> After all, girls were supposed to have no other profession but
> marriage, weren't they? . . . [So] I grandly decided that in my
> fantasy life I should have nothing but the best.
>
> At night I lay in the dark, beneath my threadbare army blan-
> kets and dreamt of a different life: a life of glamour and glory
> (of reflected glory, to be sure, but glory all the same) and an end
> to misery and insignificance.

Wife School

What still mattered most was getting your man. Glory might
come, but it would be vicarious. The word 'ambition' remained
incongruous in the feminine lexicon, unless coupled with the
word 'marriage'. A careers-advice book published in the 1940s
laid as much emphasis on achievement within the domestic
sphere as outside it, stressing 'one of woman-kind's most natural and even desirable ambitions, that of trying to look her
best'.

In the post-war world the fuzzy dream of equality and
opportunity was coming into focus, but much still held women
back: discrimination, entrenched prejudice, offensive sexism –

and, not least, nostalgia for the past, and the yearnings, fears and inhibitions of women themselves.

A fascinating survey★ of the aspirations of school leavers conducted in 1956 reported on a girl who told the investigator that 'what she wanted to *have* was a wedding ring, what she wanted to *do* was to get married, what she wanted to *be* was a wife and mother'. The author of the survey, Thelma Veness, commented that this case was somewhat extreme; nevertheless, 'there is little doubt that marriage and maternity is the central objective of the "average" girl and that all other ambitions are ordered round this objective in an entirely rational way'.

One might rephrase Veness's comment, as follows: 'The objective of most *schools* was to educate "average" girls to be wives and mothers. Any ambitions of their own that they might nurture were regarded as subsidiary to this objective.' Secondary modern schools, whose pupils had not passed the 11+, were unambitious for their pupils. Such schools were under-funded, housed in gloomy worn-out buildings, with thirty or more disaffected, uninterested children to a class. But parents were equally to blame. Segregated working-class communities – such as the north-eastern mining villages – tended to see education for girls as wasted: 'They only get married.' Educational deprivation was cyclical; stay-at-home mums lacked the vision or understanding to see how better schooling might advantage daughters otherwise fated to follow in their footsteps.

The teachers colluded with this view, in offering 'vocational' education. It was, inevitably, gendered, often literally, with

★ In Thelma Veness, *School Leavers: Their Aspirations and Expectations* (1962), a sample of 107 girls were asked, 'At what age do you expect to get married?' Seventy-three out of 82 (89 per cent) girls at the secondary modern school predicted that they would get married between the ages of 20 and 25, while 19 out of 25 (76 per cent) of those at the technical or grammar school expected to be married at that age.

girls and boys occupying separate playgrounds, and a strict chaperonage system in place during school hours. Ill-afforded funds were spent on cookers and sewing machines for the girls, woodworking and metalwork facilities for the boys. Lessons for girls might include dairying, horticulture, cookery, dressmaking, mothercraft, nursing, and housecraft. This last might include lessons on how to launder a traycloth, how to place it on the tray, how to lay the tray and serve tea.* While they were occupied on these subjects, the boys took extra English and mathematics. Most female pupils left these schools at the age of fourteen for a few years in employment before marrying. The boundaries between school and work were blurred; as in the case of Valerie Gisborn, it was not unusual for rural education departments to let children out of school for up to two days a week to earn money during harvest or potato-picking time.

Mary Evans and Brenda Nash weren't 'average'. Brenda broke the mould when she found herself making a lengthy daily journey to Waverley Grammar School, but her younger sisters, who didn't make the grade, went to the nearby secondary modern. Brenda could see that, as 'average' girls, they weren't being educated as she was. 'The Secondary Mod saw its role with girls as preparing them to be wives and mothers, nothing else. In my sisters' school, they even had a fully equipped school flat, which the girls were expected to keep clean, and where they were expected to entertain the Headmistress to tea, to prepare the meal, and to wash up afterwards.' Nor was this a one-off; in 1953 a girls' secondary school in West Sussex invited the Pathé Cinemagazine cameras in to film their pupils having a good housewifery lesson. Over a jaunty little theme, the male commentator explained – with Pathé's usual sprinkling of jocose

---

* These skills were also taught at my own grammar school in the late 1960s by a domestic science teacher who stressed the need to perfect them 'in case a duchess came to tea'. But I have never needed to.

witticisms – how the students were being prepared for their inevitable future fate:

COMMENTARY:
What woman *doesn't* dream of a kitchen so lofty and well-lighted as this? These girls are polishing up their domestic science in the County Secondary School at Steyning in Sussex, and given time they'll get a good grip on the subject.

[SHOT OF GIRL LIFTING SAUCEPAN LID]

Mmm, I bet *that* smells good enough to eat!

[SHOT OF GIRL OPENING DOOR OF FLAT]

And this leads to their Holy of Holies! It's the entrance to a school flat which *even* the staff aren't allowed to enter until the girls are satisfied everything's shipshape!

[SHOTS OF GIRLS SWEEPING, POLISHING, ETC.]

It'd probably be more realistic if they had a real live family living in it, and a little of man's untidiness to clear up, but they're getting down to things all right!

[SHOT OF GIRL POURING WATER OUT OF KETTLE INTO COFFEE POT]

It's right that the girls should keep up their standards of taste – and the men too! – but let's hope 14-year-old Pat Willard hasn't forgotten to put the coffee in while taking her screen test! It's just as well that future housewives should learn from the outset the importance of 'elevenses'!

[SHOT OF GIRL CLEANING THE BATH]

June's finished her polishing, Mavis has made the bed, Anne's done the sweeping – *but* – what's a home without a *man* about the house? And that's where the headmaster, Edwin Crawford, comes in!

[SHOT OF HEADMASTER ENTERING AND SITTING AT LAID TABLE]

And trust a man to know the right time to arrive! This is *one* cup of coffee that'll be *right* up to standard – but not unless he comes back for a second will she get top marks!

[SHOT OF HEADMASTER ADDING SUGAR TO HIS COFFEE AND SITTING BACK]*

John Newsom would surely have applauded.

Seen in this context, the answers to Thelma Veness's survey of school leavers were predictable. Her next question to them was, at what age they expected to get married, and what *job* they thought they would have in a few years' time. A large majority imagined themselves at the altar before they were twenty-five, and envisaged their eventual job as being 'Marriage'. How could they think otherwise? She then asked them to write a composition projecting themselves into their own imagined futures. Most of the girls lingered on details of their courtship ('a fair-haired man with a lovely suntan called John') and wedding dress ('I got married in White and He was just superb').

Nevertheless, a minority – around 20 per cent – of these schoolgirls barely mentioned marriage, while a small number confessed to having quite different ambitions: 'I was a career girl and I knew it . . .'. For a girl in the 1950s, running your own life and making your own money was not off-limits. But there were still so many obstacles. From too many of my own interviewees and correspondents, and from memoirs of the period, come anguished cries like these:

* 'These poor girls! I hope they went on to be astronauts and bareback riders . . .' reads a distraught cataloguer's note at the foot of the entry on this Cinemagazine clip in the Pathé archive.

As a girl I wanted to be a lawyer. [But] my headmistress said it wasn't for girls and anyway I wasn't bright enough to do it.

I left school in 1950 [to take up a] place at Birmingham School of Architecture. [But] I was refused a grant on the grounds that I was a girl . . .

I wanted to be a teacher from when I was knee-high. But my mother was bemused by it. She wrote in my autograph album:

> *Be a good girl*
> *Lead a good life*
> *Meet a good husband*
> *And make a good wife*

It took luck, talent and a different kind of ambition to break the mould and fashion your own life, as Flora Calder did in her job with *Woman*.

And yet, the names of women illustrious in their fields were now common currency in the press.* Their numbers make it onerous to list many of the individuals, but throughout the decade women civil servants and politicians like Edith Summerskill and Barbara Castle were making their mark on government, while the views of the public were steered by influential women journalists, commentators and editors like Vera Brittain and Mary Grieve, many of whom kept alive an insistent, if muted, debate about feminism. There were stars of the Bar like Rose Heilbron, while charitable enterprises were buoyed up by the efforts of many great benefactresses like Edwina Mountbatten and Dame Cicely Saunders. Science and academe too saw the extraordinary contributions of Rosalind Franklin, Dame Helen

---

* In her recent book (*Her Brilliant Career: Ten Extraordinary Women of the Fifties* [2013]), Rachel Cooke tells the stories of ten mould-breaking career women of the decade and makes an excellent job of ensuring that they are now better known.

What, women in court? *Punch* magazine, as usual, ensures that its readers get a laugh at the thought of them being engaged in anything so seriously male as the law. 10 November 1954.

Gardner and Dame Veronica Wedgwood. The arts and literature benefited from the imaginative genius of women like Barbara Hepworth, Joan Littlewood and Kathleen Ferrier, to name just a handful. Women like this were making their mark. They could overcome the obstacles in their path. But they were conspicuous for their rarity. Too often they were seen as misfits: women who had succeeded either because of their inability to find a husband, or their unwillingness to conform.

Bluestockings

The view was still widely held that being educated was unwomanly. The cliché was that learned ladies were NOT sexy. They were probably – dread word – spinsters or (whisper it) lesbians. Of owlish appearance, they wore hand-woven skirts, leather sandals and gig-lamp spectacles; their hair was cut à la pudding basin. A woman who could discuss current affairs would be referred to as having 'a masculine mind'. A career in science, the law, finance or industry didn't check the box labelled 'feminine'. If you were clever, but didn't want to be dismissed as a 'witch', a 'blue-stocking' or a 'sexless woman intellectual', there was no option but to play the feminine game. Many a whimsical hat acted as camouflage for its wearer's acute intelligence; Margaret Thatcher, for example, specialised in feathered and frivolous headpieces.

But what about those thwarted castaways whose voices were still to be heard pleading for qualifications, a chance to make their dreams come true? In Carlisle Margaret Forster looked in horror at her mother's and grandmother's lives – the drudgery, the privations, the sacrifices – and knew that she could never submit to that deal in exchange for a husband. Though she had no concrete goal in the form of a career, Margaret was fixated on the idea of getting into university. She was fortunate in having an English teacher who encouraged her, giving her leaflets describing the Oxford and Cambridge colleges: 'I was spellbound by the photographs – they looked like fairy-tale places to me, so beautiful, so utterly desirable . . .' But tantalisingly hard to reach. There were only five women's colleges in Oxford. They did not achieve full collegiate status until 1959, and the university operated a quota system for women that was not abolished until 1957. Until joined by New Hall in 1954 Cambridge had only two undergraduate colleges for women.

Joan Rowlands was possessed by the same yearnings. Her mother, snobbish, under-employed and religious, consumed by inner demons and obsessions, made the family's lives a misery. Perfectionism ruled, the house had to be spotless, her insane cleaning rituals dominated everything and extended to her daughters, who must also be pure and unsullied. Joan felt suffocated:

I needed to be in touch with other sorts of people, people like me interested in ideas . . .

How did you meet those sort of people? The answer, I discovered, was an institution called a university.

From then on, Cambridge became her goal in life.

*

At this time, 1.2 per cent of female school leavers gained places
at university (today, more than 50 per cent go on to higher education, and more women graduate than men). The figures speak
of a tiny minority of young women – like Margaret Forster or
Joan Rowlands – driven by a powerful desire to escape, to learn,
and to forge their own future. But the great majority, many of
whom might have found further education liberating, had little
idea of what it had to offer. Take Hazel,* a privately educated,
well-read middle-class teenager from Torquay, with a hunger
for clothes, shoes, dances, make-up and glossy magazines. Like
any teenager in fact. Her teachers told her she could go to university if she chose to. But if she went away to study, how
would she afford to buy the patent leather shoes and pink lipstick that she loved? Hazel felt she couldn't rely on her frugal,
war-generation parents to keep up the money supply, so in her
ignorance getting a job seemed the better choice:

> A school leaver had several options. She could be a nurse or a
> secretary or a clerk, or she could go on to university or college.
> Absolutely nobody told me what I could expect at college.
> Nobody gave me any pointers at all. I didn't want to do any-
> thing that I thought a college qualification would prepare me to
> do. What I didn't know about . . . was the vast number of things

---

* Hazel's life story appears in an anthology of 1950s oral histories, *Growing
Up in the Fifties* (ed. Terry Jordan, 1990). The interviewees are all known only
by their first names.

I might have done with a degree, and I often regret not going on to further education.

In any case, all the girls in her class talked about was getting married. 'That was the be-all and end-all.' In 1955 Hazel went to work at the Torquay Gas Board as a cost clerk, where her employers instructed her to calculate thirty-three and a third per cent profit and add it on to every estimate that came in. 'I spent all day doing that.' Every day for a year . . .

Ruth Barnet from Merseyside was equally in the dark when it came to making decisions about life-after-school. Coming from a sheltered working-class background, there was nobody to explain what the choices were, no TV, no internet, no window on the world outside:

> You only knew what you saw around you. What would you want a career for anyway? You were only going to get married, have children, and then you would stay at home . . .

Ruth didn't want to stay at home. She was fascinated by the idea of travel, loved gardening and plants, and did well at school. She made the grade into a grammar school, and consistently stayed near the top of the 'A' stream. Nevertheless her big brother gave her to understand that she was too stupid to go to university.

> After all, he was male, and thirteen years older than me – he must be right. I knew nobody who had ever been to university, so how was I to know how clever you needed to be? It sounded very, well . . . 'not for people like me'. These were the days when 'not for people like me' loomed large. We knew our place!

★

Our society is littered with the disappointed hopes and crushed dreams of women over the age of seventy who knew their place, and knew it was not university.

A minority, who did get there, were as cocooned from the perils of the outside world as vestal virgins. When Anne Howarth went to study Geography at Reading University in 1953 it was almost as though she had never left her Nottingham High School. Anne had led a sheltered life in her provincial backwater. Studious and hard-working, she was wrapped in innocence, to a degree almost unimaginable today. 'I knew nothing about sex, little about the world beyond my immediate horizon. I lived in a bubble.' Studying away from home did little to change that. Anne packed her navy blue pleated school skirt and wore it for her first year as an undergraduate. As far as style went, students in those days were barely differentiated from their mothers. Serious-minded young women in twinsets, pleated skirts and discreet strings of pearls were to be seen in lecture theatres and libraries. If you needed a ball gown you borrowed your aunt's. Anne lived, studied, slept and ate a minute's walk from the main campus, which meant that there was barely any need to stray beyond the university boundaries. Her halls of residence were barred to men after 7 p.m. Innocent evenings were spent toasting crumpets over the gas fire. The Student Christian Movement and the Choral Society, both of which she joined, were within easy reach. It was a protected, comfortable environment, not far different from that of a boarding-school. In her three years at Reading Anne suffered nothing more threatening than the once-a-term social ordeal of finding a partner for her hall of residence ball. She had been taught to dance at school – 'It was thought to be something that any young woman ought to be able to do' – but Anne simply had no experience of boys. Eventually she plucked up the courage to ask one of the chaps in her botany group. Nothing

1. Donkey-stoning, Liverpool: a daily spectacle in working-class neighbourhoods in the 1950s.

2 and 3. Over the years, pearls have symbolised unblemished innocence. Wearing them, two optimistic 1950s women, *left*, nurse Eileen Hawe, *right*, Young Conservative wife Liz Monnington.

4. Judith Hubback, the academic who exploded 'the Feminine Mystique' in Britain seven years before Betty Friedan's pivotal work sparked second-wave feminism in the USA.

5. Working girls in Soho, 1956.

6. 'Sitting out' the foxtrot on Saturday night at the Astoria Ballroom, Nottingham, 1952.

7. All eyes are on 'the Dolly Princess' during her tour of Jamaica, 1955. From the rear seat of the Land Rover Margaret's lady-in-waiting, Iris Peake, anchors her mistress's voluminous skirts 'for modesty's sake'.

8. 'I saw a career so marvellous and different to anything I had ever dreamed of.' Valeric Gisborn would wear her policewoman's uniform with pride for the next twenty-six years.

9. 'To be an air hostess was the most sought-after job for a woman at that time.' Angela Austin in 1957, soon after she joined Hunting Clan. The airline equipped her with a hat specially designed not to blow off in windy airports.

10. Post-sales exhaustion in a department store; then as now, the assistants were expected to wear black.

11. The 1951 election campaign. Margaret Roberts tries to persuade a Dartford chimney sweep to vote for her. She lost, but from 1958 her political rise was unstoppable.

12. Glamorous and lighthearted: Ruth Ellis and David Blakely at the Little Club in 1953. His murder by her in 1955 was the *crime passionnel* of the decade.

13. Working-class mothers taking a break from their chores, 1950.

14. 'I had a perfect husband.' Miner Len Alssebrook and his wife Audrey enjoying a day out.

15. Sheila McKenzie on stage at the Gaiety, Butlin's, Clacton-on-Sea, *c.*1957.

'happened' with him. 'I was really a little girl until I was about twenty-two.'

Ann Owen was another young woman who felt that her education infantilised her. She had grown up in a small Welsh village, and in 1950 gained a place at a teacher training college in Barry, Glamorgan. She anticipated a great adventure. But the college was single-sex, ruled over by 'a true martinet of the old school'. At eighteen, the girls were still expected to wear a brown and cream uniform blazer – and ankle socks. No make-up was permitted. Their curfew was strict: girls were to be in their dormitories by 8 p.m. Fearsome Matrons imposed petty rules: no belongings to be kept on the tops of wardrobes, no towels to be hung out of windows to dry. And they were not to go out with boys unless they had met them first in church or chapel. 'I complied with this in every degree.' The girls nicknamed their college 'the nunnery'.

With women in such short supply at universities, one might have imagined they would be welcomed as rarities in the mixed ones. Instead, women students were largely discriminated against and ghettoised. At Reading a male student found with a woman in his room after hours could be expelled for a term, while women transgressors had their university careers terminated. When Joan Rowlands arrived at Cambridge University in 1951 the university was 'irredeemably male'. Women were outnumbered nine to one by men. Newnham College – then as now women-only – took an equally protective attitude to its students. The rules were, no male visitors after ten at night, and any student leaving the college for the evening had to sign out and sign back in again. The girls resorted to complex subterfuge. Joan's ground-floor room, with its easily accessible sash windows, was one of the established routes used by her friends, who risked expulsion creeping in and out from their after-hours assignations. But other rules were harder to circumvent. Despite being a contemporary of the most illustrious 'Footlights' stars of her day – like Jonathan Miller and Frederic Raphael – Joan and all other female students were barred from their exclusive club performances. Nor were women allowed to join the Cambridge Union, so they had no opportunity to gain debating skills. 'It was assumed we wouldn't need them.'

Anthea York was Joan's contemporary at Cambridge, but their backgrounds were worlds apart. At nineteen, Anthea was a clever, rather awkward young woman, lacking confidence and lacking initiative. From their base in the shires her upper middle-class family had groomed her for social success, and at Cambridge she took her place among the posh set that Joan looked up to for having the 'right' clothes and the 'right' accents. Their ringing timbres indicated class, and money. Joan, by contrast, had been born into the respectable working classes. She had a Lancashire accent, and her attempts to imitate the 'posh girls' proved disastrous (though the resulting voice was to prove useful in her later broadcasting career).

Anthea herself never felt she quite fitted in with what was a very narrow group at Cambridge. 'I had no non-public school friends.' But even Anthea and her top-drawer college pals had to contend with the crushing disdain of some of the men. The 'county' sent their sons to Magdalene and Trinity Colleges, bringing with them a recognisable whiff of snobbery. In term time these young squires didn't mind consorting with a few blue-stockings over sherry. After all, women were in such a minority at the university that one had to make do. But when it came to inviting a date to the smartest balls, the upper-class male's fear of 'clever' women kicked in. A London deb carried the status that a college girl didn't. Anthea recalled how one Magdalene chap who had two highly coveted tickets for the Pitt Club Ball was stood up by his debutante date, specially summoned from town. He asked a Girton girl he knew to step into the breach – but it was to be on the absolute understanding that she wouldn't tell anyone she was an undergraduate. A gifted academic, she spent the entire evening passing herself off as a debutante from South Kensington.

It was the same at Oxford, where for a girl to be seen studying was regarded in some circles as grey and frumpy. Though she went on to become a prominent writer and campaigner, Teresa Hayter spent very little time at her books:

> The dominant social element was the careless, public-school, party-going variety. When asked once what they talked about at supposedly intellectual dinner-parties, one of them replied that they didn't need to talk about anything in particular; they 'just glittered'. They had no need to study, although some of them did; their future was in any case assured. Those who did study tended to conceal it, because studying was not socially acceptable.

Teresa reckoned that in her first term at Lady Margaret Hall, Oxford she went to sixty-four parties in fifty-six days.

Reds

For Christine Finch, who went up to Cambridge in 1949, the word party meant something rather different.

Christine grew up in north London, and went to grammar school, but though her home there was comfortable and 'technically middle-class', that status seemed to her superficial. Her mother was fundamentally unschooled; her father was self-made, and the culture and mores of the middle classes had never taken root in her family. Accordingly she was sent to an inadequate fee-paying girls' school, and only transferred to a grammar school at the age of sixteen. There she felt like an outsider.

However, by temperament Christine was bright, serious and questioning. She told me, 'I learnt feminism at my mother's knee.' By this, she did not mean that her mother was committed to the women's cause, rather the reverse. Mrs Finch was an entirely inward-looking woman, socially detached, profoundly repressed and unfulfilled. There was in fact a rebellious streak in her, but she clamped the lid on it, and for the rest of her life it seethed explosively, unexpressed and unadmitted. Mrs Finch was teaching her daughter to be a feminist by counter-example.

In due course Christine's headmistress encouraged her to sit the Oxbridge entrance exam; she promptly won a scholarship to read English at Newnham College, Cambridge. A true intellectual, Christine was in her element. Soon after enrolling she discovered that she could opt for a course in Old English, Norse and Archaeology. The lectures would draw her into a world of abstruse, ancient things: runes, cruciform brooches and alliterative epic poetry. There was no question of 'glittering', and on her state scholarship she couldn't afford it. In any case, her first year was sadly dominated by inexplicable feelings of depression, which (with hindsight) seemed to be related to her family's inescapable unhappiness. Despite pride and pleasure at her academic achievement, a sense of helplessness at her mother's plight nipped lightheartedness in the bud. Despite this, Christine continued to study hard, achieving a high Second in her summer exams. And it was during that year that she joined the student branch of the Communist Party of Great Britain.

Christine was already conversant with the vocabulary of struggle. One of her older sisters had married a journalist on the *Daily Worker*; both of them had influenced her, and while still at school she had attempted to join a young people's peace delegation to Berlin, though this scheme ran up against parental objections.

I gave way, and didn't go, but I hated myself for being a coward and determined that as soon as I got away to university I would live honestly and openly.

Knowing little or nothing about the realities of politics, I strongly believed an ideal society would follow the Communist rubric 'From each according to his ability; to each according to his need.' Soviet Russia had only just stopped being our brave wartime ally, making the biggest sacrifice in blood of any of the allies. People like me knew nothing, as yet, about Stalin's atrocities.

Once at Cambridge, she ordered the *Daily Worker* to be delivered to her at her hall of residence, and gravitated towards a like-minded crowd.

By 1950 approximately one third of the globe was controlled by socialist regimes. The clash of ideologies and superpowers resulted in a terrifying Cold War in which, for some forty years, the world was on permanent suicide-watch. Here in Britain, Communism was not illegal as it was in the USA. But CP members – many of whom were leading intellectuals – could expect their pro-Russian sentiments to contribute to the irreconcilable and antagonistic character of the Cold War. The language of 'isms' was polarising: Americanism, capitalism and materialism were lined up against Communism, collectivism and Marxism. In Britain during the war membership of the Communist Party had tripled, and in the 1945 election the CPGB won two seats in Parliament. That parliamentary success was not to be repeated – in 1950 both MPs lost their seats – but the party's influence remained significant in the Trades Union movement during the first half of the 1950s. In Communist circles dissidence was frowned on, Stalinism was revered, and western democracy disparaged.

Though it espoused no one party line, Christine now joined the Cambridge University Socialist Club. It seemed to her to provide a congenial platform for debate between left-leaning individuals of all persuasions, at a time when dissent was largely discouraged. 'As was my wont, I kept a very low profile . . .' But towards the end of that year, she hesitantly offered her services to edit the CUSC student news-sheet, and it was here that she found herself working alongside a brilliant and attractive American postgraduate, over in England on a Fulbright scholarship, named Jack Margolis.

> Jack was very left-wing, and it felt like a meeting of minds. Class-wise, too, I felt comfortable with him. He was working-class, from a secular Jewish family, intellectual, strongly moral and idealistic. Maths was his subject, but he was hugely into politics. And of course he was handsome and charismatic too . . .

Jack had grown up in the industrial city of Philadelphia, where his father, Sam Margolis, was a trades union leader and card-carrying Communist. Though Jack had never joined the CPUSA he, along with his parents, was a committed left-winger. In the early 1950s such views inevitably placed them on a collision course with the American authorities. This was the McCarthy era – a time of acute paranoia about the Communist 'Red Menace' and the 'enemy within'. A combination of Russian nuclear testing, Chinese instability, and increased spying had heightened fears in Washington. The case of Ethel and Julius Rosenberg – arrested on charges of espionage for the Soviet Union in 1950 – intensified the Reds-under-the-beds panic. The Cold War was getting colder. In Jack's rooms on Trinity Great Court, and at the Socialist Club where they were both members, he and Christine followed the Rosenberg trial as closely as they could, knowing that it was likely to be a matter of time before the FBI caught up with his father. Sam Margolis would have little defence if he too were to be held and questioned about 'un-American activities'. The atmosphere was fearful and overwrought.

Though her relationship with Jack Margolis was starting to look as if it might outlast their time at Cambridge, Christine's membership of the student Communist Party branch endured barely a year and a half. The more she and Jack saw of the CP faithful, the less impressed either of them was with their dogmatic inflexibility. It was a bond between them.

> Jack and I realised that the CP-ers were only interested in ramming through their own ideas by any means available. They paid lip service to democracy but in the event couldn't brook dissent.
>
> We each independently realised this mindset wasn't for us. I had meanwhile let my membership lapse. I doubt they even noticed – I had been such an ineffectual member . . .
>
> I never made a great stand, or any public renunciation. I just left.

But Christine's brief allegiance to Communism would change the direction of her life, and cost her dear.

In summer 1952 Jack's Fulbright scholarship came to an end. Though Christine had no idea at this point whether he would ever return, she had her own plans. Having sat her finals, and graduated with a first-class Honours degree, she naturally hoped this would ensure she received a British Council scholarship to fund further studies. Full of hope and a renewed thirst for learning, her project now was to apply for a British Council Scholarship which would fund a trip to Iceland. There she would undertake research for a thesis that would in some way bridge the language of Norse and archaeology. It would lead, she trusted, to the award of a doctorate, and eventually to eminence in her chosen field. With her top degree the interview was clearly a simple formality; and she eagerly awaited the letter which would confirm her travel and support grant. But weeks passed. Then more weeks. 'I heard nothing.' Eventually she picked up the telephone and got put through to the grants office. When she explained her business there was a long, and very embarrassed silence. She had, it appeared, been turned down. No, there was nothing they could do. And no, there was no official apology or explanation.

'It was clearly political.' Somehow, the British Council had determined that Christine Finch's brief and inglorious sojourn with the student Communist Party was sufficient to disqualify her from the scholarly investigation of ancient Icelandic culture. The witch-hunt that she had followed so fearfully on the other side of the Atlantic was now in full cry in pursuit of a studious Cambridge graduate. And in case this seems improbable, Christine was not alone in being persecuted. As David Kynaston tersely puts it,* at that time 'to be a Communist, or even merely a "fellow-traveller", was not (in the short term at least) an astute career move'. CP membership made one ineligible for the Civil Service; party adherents were rooted out from the executive of the National Union of Teachers and there were cases of schoolteachers being dismissed from their jobs. Applicants for university posts were vetted and jobs given to non-party members, and certain corporations demanded that their employees sign anti-Communist declarations. Of course none of this prevented the upper echelons of the Foreign Office from being infiltrated at this time by some of the most ingenious traitors in British history.

Defeated, Christine enrolled to do a two-year MA course in Archaeology at London University. Her Icelandic dreams were in pieces. It was back to north London. Meanwhile in America, the Communist witch-hunt was approaching frenzy. Thousands of suspected Communist sympathisers were investigated, blacklisted and harassed; some were imprisoned. At sundown

* In *Austerity Britain: Smoke in the Valley*, Part One, Chapter 3, p. 341.

on 19 June 1953 the Rosenbergs were both executed in the electric chair.

But happily for Christine and Jack the relationship kindled over the CUSC news-sheet back in 1951–2 survived his year-long absence in the USA. Not long after his return in 1953 they were married. The early period of Christine's and Jack's marriage – a time of study and excited intellectual inquiry for both of them – should have been full of promise. But by now the McCarthyite spotlight had fallen heavily upon Jack, and their daily lives were blighted by the uncertainty and risk that hung over them. 'Sympathisers' could expect to be penalised by the system; Jack came from a prominent left-wing family, and it was unlikely that he would be spared. 'At that time the knock on the door at midnight was a very real fear.' In the autumn of 1954 the Margolises moved to Durham, where, having been awarded his doctorate, Jack was now given a post as Research Fellow.

They had been married a year when the blow fell. Jack got a letter instructing him to report to the American Consulate in Liverpool. Here, he listened while an official solemnly confiscated his passport and informed him that it was to be exchanged for a one-way passport. Effectively, Jack could now be regarded as stateless. If he were to travel to America, he would be eligible for military conscription and unable to return to England, nor would Christine – as a 'red' – be granted a visa to join him. He was not informed of the charges against him.

Oddly, however, it appeared that the official wished Jack to know what those charges were, since immediately after this declaration he pointedly left the room, leaving a document lying open on the desk in full view. There, Jack read the fabricated charges against him. He had never joined the Communist Party of the USA, and yet there it was in black and white, complete with false membership number, written down as one of a list of lies. In among the lies were the correct statements that at the age of fourteen he had attended Russian language classes, and that he 'had consorted with communists'. True or false, the document was enough to have him damned by the American authorities.

*

Getting the most out of a university education was a matter of self-belief, and good role models. Sarah Myers from Preston grew up with a healthy dose of both.

> I remember when I was in my first term at school, talking after lights-out in the freezing dormitory of our girls' boarding school in Keswick, about what we were going to be when we grew up. And I said firmly, 'Prime Minister.' And they all laughed at me. They just said, 'You *can't*, because you're a girl.' And I remember actually thinking, 'That's stupid. Why?'

Sarah had clever parents, and clever sisters. Her father was a doctor; her mother, a beautiful, moody and unpredictable woman, was much more taken up with politics and human rights than she was with domesticity. Though Mrs Myers's financial extravagance ensured that Sarah and her sisters grew up without luxuries, they were always encouraged to think, work and achieve. At fourteen she was a pacifist. At fifteen she won her school's essay-writing competition with a denunciation of the South African policy of Apartheid. Nothing could hold her back, and going to St Hugh's College Oxford in 1954 was the realization of her dreams. But studying Greek tragedy and Latin epics was low down on her to-do list. Oxford seemed to Sarah to have so much more to offer than dead languages.

> For one thing, being one woman to every seven men was extraordinary. And I'd never seen a boy before! So I went out with someone different every evening.

Oxford was teeming with glamorous politicians. Michael Heseltine was President of the Union when she first arrived in Oxford. 'We all thought he was *so* dim, and his views were *awful* – but I cannot tell you how good-looking he was! I can still remember him walking in the door, so tall and golden-haired. We were wobbly at the knees at the sight of him!' The Liberals' pin-up boy was Jo Grimond, devastatingly sexy with his stray forelock. In Michaelmas term 1956 Sarah was made President of the Liberal Club, and straight away increased its membership by organising to have Grimond's sultry features plastered across the campaign posters.

Just a year earlier, the Principal of St Hugh's College, Miss Evelyn Procter, had issued a gloomy warning to her girls:

> I am convinced that undergraduates try to do too much and provide themselves with too many distractions. Dances are far too numerous and there is far too much amateur acting.

She went on to lament the inexorable proliferation of clubs and societies that were taking the students away from their books:

> Our undergraduates tend to lay less emphasis on the pursuit of learning and more on making contacts, meeting people, enlarging their outlook and experience, on gaining a wide but sometimes superficial culture.

Miss Procter might as well have tried to hold back the incoming tide. Despite the persistence of academic gowns, scouts, bedders and Formal Halls, the old order was passing. The spinsters still took their coffee in the Senior Common Room while talking of nothing more controversial than ornithology or Jane Austen, the food was still terrible (baked beans and lentil roast), and Professor Wrenn still insisted that all students wear black scholars' caps to his lectures on *Beowulf*. But even among the dreaming medieval spires of Oxford times were changing. The Popina was a cool coffee bar that had opened in the Cornmarket. If you couldn't stand the lentils in Hall, you could get a curry with pilau rice at the Taj Mahal in the Turl. St Hugh's girls were to be seen pedalling down the Banbury Road in fluttering nylon petticoats – or sometimes even jeans – below Marks and Spencer's Orlon cardigans. One even scorched around Oxford on a Vespa motor-scooter: 'I remember adorning it with a black velvet bow as "sub-fusc" when it served to transport me to the Finals.' And though hugely frowned on, some girls were going 'over the top' into sexual relationships. Sarah Myers didn't dare to take the plunge, as her mother had told her that sleeping with a man inevitably led to pregnancy, but her friend Jean was caught in bed with a boyfriend from Trinity. Jean was penalised by being sent down for a term. Nothing happened to the boy.

The old view that being clever also meant being a nun was melting away. For Sarah Myers vistas were opening. Her three years at Oxford were 'a liberation': a time of earnest gatherings over tea, of mind-altering intellectual conversations, outings to the cinema, furious campaigns, intense passions and friendships, and party politics.

Joan Rowlands, too, blossomed under the stimulating influ-ence of talk, drama, lectures and Fitzbillies' cream cakes. In her first few weeks at Newnham she joined as many societies as she reasonably could, and threw herself into new friendships. 'I wanted to feast on everything, do everything, meet everyone, study hard, go to parties and, above all, to be perpetually in love.' In the summer after her second year at Cambridge Joan concocted a series of elaborate alibis to persuade her mother that she was spending a chaste holiday with a girlfriend in Rome. Instead, once in Italy, she and Michael Bakewell, a handsome, floppy-haired undergraduate actor and leading light of the Cambridge poetry scene, met clandestinely and took off for Florence, where they 'rapidly and thoroughly fell in love'. For

the remainder of their time as undergraduates they were inseparable. So, when the time came to find grown-up jobs and live in
London, there seemed no alternative but to get married: 'No
landlady would rent a flat, no hotel would let a room to a couple
who hadn't evidence of marriage.' In May 1955 Joan climbed
into a full-length white bridal gown, fixed a floating white veil
decked with blossoms to her head and, clutching a trailing bou-
quet of roses and lilies, knelt at the altar of her parents' church
and became Mrs Joan Bakewell.

> I . . . plunged into all the old entanglements of a traditional
> marriage. I had never known what it was to be on my own.

Wasted Women

The overwhelming majority of women who set their sights on
further education in the 1950s did so because they planned to
follow a career. Mary Evans was absolutely dead-set on becoming a writer. Anne Howarth was determined to teach, and
ultimately to become a headmistress. Sarah Myers wanted to go
into politics, or perhaps journalism. Joan Rowlands was single-
minded about going to university, having some vague notion
that it would transform her into 'a Bernard Shaw heroine'. But
like her contemporaries, she listened spellbound to the Third
Programme, 'speculating about what golden creatures, blessed
by knowledge and opportunity, must work for the BBC'.
Brenda Nash from Birmingham just wanted what so many of
her deprived contemporaries were denied: a chance.

But when it came to marriage, women were still firmly 'on
the programme'. Like Joan Rowlands, Sarah Myers's contemporaries at St Hugh's submitted all too quickly and willingly to the
inevitable:

They either didn't get married at all, or they acquired boyfriends
while they were there and got married very soon after leaving
the university. After all, the men wanted very much to get married too. Many of them had been on their National Service. And
of course they were afraid of extra-marital pregnancy . . .

Years later, in 1984, when Sarah (by this time Sarah Curtis) conducted a survey among St Hugh's graduates, she recorded that
80 per cent of the 1950s alumnae like her had married (in the
1920s that figure had been just 55 per cent). All those legions of
spinster dons were becoming a thing of the past. Women with
Firsts in French and Seconds in Science were closing the doors
behind them in leafy suburbs, turning their backs on the kind of
jobs where their degrees qualified them to compete with men,
and to contribute to the society that had formed them.

So what did this mean for all those bright hopes and ambitions? In 1953, Judith Hubback, a woman whose own frustrations
were to give her special insights into her chosen field, sent out
questionnaires to 2,000 women graduates, asking them what
they had done with their lives. Her three small children helped
to stuff the envelopes. The resulting response was the remarkable and controversial book, *Wives Who Went to College*,★ in
which Hubback explored the contradictions of emancipation in
a way still highly relevant to us today.

Judith Hubback was born Judith Fisher-Williams. She was a
gentle, thoughtful person: nervous, vulnerable to strong passions and with a latent spirituality that did not emerge until her
middle years; she was also a poet who intensely valued nature
and her own inner life. Born in 1917, she was a pre-war student
and studied history at Newnham, graduating with first-class

★ Hubback's mother-in-law, Eva Hubback, had initiated the research. After
her death in 1949 Judith expanded the data. A pamphlet, *Graduate Wives*,
appeared in 1953; *Wives Who Went to College* followed in 1957.

honours in 1936.* Three years later she married her Cambridge
boyfriend David Hubback. Their first baby was born in wartime, followed by two more soon after it was over. Despite
being able to afford help, Judith was left struggling with the
feeling that her intellect and skills were being wasted as a housewife. 'It was a juggling job, and an unremitting one. I had to be
a kind of chameleon, inside which there was the next potential
version of me. I discovered that I had committed myself to a far
more demanding and complicated series of tasks, and pleasures,
than I had imagined beforehand.' The satisfactions of domesticity were also eroded by the sense that she had to live up to an
unrealistic ideal of wifehood: that, surely, she had no right to
complain at always being on duty, that she should be cheerful
and undemanding. Instead, she was desperate for intellectual
stimulus, she envied David's rewarding work as a senior civil
servant, and she longed to be able to contribute financially. 'The
idea of embarking on research into various aspects of the lives
and views of married women graduates came to me in a flash,
one evening, in the bath.'

In the introduction to *Wives Who Went to College* Judith Hubback confesses that she might have treated the subject with more
academic detachment, had she not herself been one of them.
The book is a story told from the inside.

Judith's opening premise was as follows:

> It is that to be as happy and useful as possible, women as well as
> men should use all their capacities to the full.

Pursuing this theme among the sector of educated women
whom she had chosen to study, Judith Hubback addressed the
themes of motherhood, marriage, domesticity, over-tiredness,

---

* At the time when Judith left Newnham, women were only granted a graduation certificate. Full degrees were withheld until 1948.

time-management, multi-tasking, money, modern feminism, career breaks and the future of education for girls. And despite the occasional omission characteristic of the 1950s – she never, for example, queries the non-participation of husbands in childcare – much of her material would not be out of place in an early twenty-first-century discussion of the gender and work-life balance. Today, expectations have shifted, and a woman with a degree will most likely expect to do the kind of work for which she is qualified. But once she becomes a mother she will surely, also, recognise her fortune in not necessarily being subjected to enforced domesticity, as happened to her mother or her grandmother, two or three generations earlier. And when it comes to making decisions about whether to care for her child or return to work, the responses sent to Judith Hubback back in 1952 still have value.

Before listening to some of their voices, take note of a few of the statistics that emerged from her survey. Judith's questionnaire asked women graduates whether they had planned a career before they went to college. The vast majority – 72 per cent – were young women who, like Joan Rowlands, Mary Evans, Anne Howarth and Brenda Nash, had been determined to channel their education into a profession. And yet their answers to Judith's other questions show how badly that hope had been derailed. The war had ended or delayed the careers of 17 per cent; marriage had caused another 23 per cent to resign from their jobs and become housewives. But for those who hadn't already stopped work, the birth of their children was the most interrupting factor: a further 26 per cent put their professional lives on hold when they had babies. Along with their careers, their earning power collapsed. Fifty-four per cent of the graduate sample were entirely dependent on their husbands' earnings. But it appeared that most of them kept hope of outside fulfilment alive. Only 15 per cent declared that they did not hope to work again at some point in the future.

Society had educated these women, but for what? Historically, Judith Hubback identified a discouraging flaw in the process of emancipation. In the nineteenth century, and the early part of the twentieth century, the futility of a spinster's life, followed by the wave of post-war 'surplus' women, had contributed to the granting of the franchise and an explosion in rights, education and access to male preserves. By the post-war period, more women were qualified to compete with men than ever before. And yet, by 1953, here they were, wielding degrees and diplomas – reduced to becoming nappy-changers and cooks. Was that a full use of their capacities? Judith saw marriage 'straight from university' as the culprit:

> The crux of the matter lies in whether a woman graduate has become established in her profession before she marries.

If she could achieve professional standing *before* she sank into the swamp of domesticity, there was a good chance she could and would claw her way back out again. The urgency of this message underlay a situation in which more and more women would be facing the work-life dilemma: qualified and eager to seek fulfilment through work, but reined in by maternal responsibilities. There would come a time when men might well exceed women in the population, meaning that even fewer would remain unmarried; at the same time education would surely become more widespread.

There was, it is true, a minority of educated women in the survey who rejoiced in stepping off the career ladder, but much more typical of Judith's numerous respondents were the woman graduates who bitterly regretted the waste of their potential:

> I certainly think it is a pity that so many women, because they want a family, are more or less forced to spend a large part of their time in domestic work, when they might be doing something more useful and satisfying.

Another respondent felt that more money could have been the key to alleviating her difficulties:

> I think the question of not being able to afford domestic help is by far the most serious problem . . . I personally feel I am 'rotting away on a Kentish hillside', though I admit it is a very lovely one . . .

There was resentment, too, at the unfairness imposed by selfish husbands:

> The hardest of all my tasks is attending to children at night and in the early morning; my husband will not help because he is so sure he needs more sleep than I do, and I think this is only part of the general attitude of 'the children are the woman's concern . . .'

And a final, pessimistic conclusion:

> Brains are a distinct handicap to a woman's prospects of happiness and contentment.

The qualities needed to see any woman through were a combination of the intellectual, mixed in with physical stamina, patience and a sense of proportion, Judith asserted. But she herself found the combination unachievable. By the mid-1950s she was stretched on all fronts. She had a teenager and two younger children. Her own research work was starting to generate controversy. Involvement in David's world was closed off to her; she felt excluded by its high-level secrecy, and envious of his professional fulfilment and status. There seemed to be a void in her life, something 'irrevocably lost'. At the same time she was ashamed to be feeling such things. In 1956 David was due to travel abroad for a series of high-level meetings. On the morning of his departure she walked with him to Golders Green tube station, where they said goodbye. With a sense of dreadful helplessness she turned and climbed the hill ahead of her, back to their empty house, engulfed by a wave of depression.

★

Meanwhile her survey, *Wives Who Went to College*, moderately expressed and reasonably argued as it was, stirred up a hornets' nest in the press. Columnists wrote angrily that it proved taxpayers' money was being squandered on teaching women irrelevant disciplines. The mere existence of frustrated, lonely, yet educated wives seemed to reinforce the belief that their university years had been a waste of time and money. 'Plato is being thrown away with the potato peelings and nuclear physics with the nappies,' wrote one journalist. 'This is throwing education into the family dustbin with a vengeance.'

Marjorie Proops in the *Daily Mirror* was more considered. She read Judith's book, then went off and conducted her own survey. She asked a few men what they thought about having educated wives. For Proops's male sample, it seemed that marrying a graduate held no allure. The majority were emphatically opposed to the idea of being shackled to a highbrow housewife. One man offered up the example of Marilyn Monroe, at that time still seemingly happily wedded to the 'egg-head' playwright Arthur Miller. 'He seems very happy indeed married to Miss Monroe, who is noted for many attributes, none of which includes higher education.' (Was *she* happy too? In reality, this was a tempestuous marriage that was to founder on their incompatibility just a few years later.) But was it really impossible for a 'bluestocking' to be glamorous and sexy? asked Proops. Regretfully, she concluded that it was: 'Intelligent girls who spend their youth getting themselves highly educated have little time to devote to the art of making themselves delectable for the opposite sex.'

Marjorie Proops LECTURES ON THE... **LOVE LIFE of a female EGG HEAD!**

Meanwhile, the correspondence pages filled up with recriminations triggered by Judith's survey. Mr S. J. Rogers, writing from his manor house in the home counties, was of the view that four out of ten girls at universities were wasting everybody's time husband-hunting, 'pleasing Daddy', or 'amusing themselves'. 'Of the other six, two will fail any examination they take, two will be married within two years of graduation, and one will take a job which does not use her qualifications. The remaining girl will prove of some use.' All but this one were, he claimed, 'keeping nine men out of university'. The patrician diplomat and cousin of Winston Churchill, Sir Shane Leslie, was of the same opinion, if milder in his expression. Perhaps, he suggested, the Oxbridge women's colleges like New Hall might specialise in courses on food, cooking, childcare, dressmaking and offer classes in Charm – 'all of which would help to re-balance our topsy-turvy times'.

'Women with MINDS are a bad marriage bet.' *Daily Mirror* columnist Marjorie Proops airs opinions on *Wives Who Went to College.*

Today it may seem astonishing that such comments were given column space. Editors gave as much coverage, however, to the misogynists as to a few incensed women, who wrote protesting against such antediluvian attitudes:

> 'Back to the sink and the nursery, you silly trivial creatures, you
> are wasting our time and worse, our precious money at the uni-
> versities,' bleats the English dodo . . .

wrote Hilda Stowell from Southampton, while Hilda Derrick
of Stroud channelled her scorn towards Shane Leslie: so, women
being educated in the domestic arts was all well and good if you
were a man, wasn't it? Then go ahead, keep women in their
kitchens, then men needn't fear competition:

> Secure in their academic superiority [they] can go with clear
> consciences to their clubs to escape the uninteresting conversa-
> tion of their wives.
>   And Britain will still be short of scientists, technologists, and
> teachers.

There was also a letter from Jenifer Hart, Judith Hubback's
sister, published in the same column, drily taking issue with
Rogers's assertion that two out of ten female graduates would
fail in any examination. He had his facts wrong, she said. The
previous year only two out of 310 (0.6 per cent) of women taking Oxford Finals had failed. The comparable figures for men
were considerably higher: 75 out of 1,700 (4.5 per cent).

The row rumbled on.

*

Seriously depressed, Judith Hubback took the step of approaching a friend who put her in touch with a Jungian analyst; it was
the first step on a road that would ultimately lead to a new career
as a highly respected analytical psychologist. But David Hubback was unsympathetic. What was all the fuss about? He took
a brisk, rational view of life. How could she possibly be depressed
when she had a good husband, a good home and three nice children, all doing well at school? Complaining in these circumstances

was pure self-indulgence. The paraphernalia of analysis – dreams, images and symbols – was either taboo or held no interest for him. As their paths diverged in their mid-years, Judith realised with a sinking heart that she and her husband were changed people from the young adults who had got married with such high hopes in a different, pre-war world.

★

At the height of McCarthyism, Christine Margolis – with her record as a member of the student branch of the Communist Party – would never have been permitted to travel to the USA with Jack, her American husband, and in any case, though he was not excluded from his own country, he could not go there with any expectation of being allowed to return to England. Moreover, he now had responsibilities that would keep him here.

For by autumn 1955 Christine was pregnant. The prospect of a baby was exciting. But it was insufficient. Armed with her University of London MA, Christine was not yet ready to let go of the hopes she had had of intellectual fulfilment and an academic career. Unfortunately for her, she soon found that the archaeological disciplines in the catchment area of Hadrian's Wall diverged from those of the London 'school' in which she'd trained. Her guiding academic precepts turned out to be held in contempt by the reigning stars of the north-east, and that ruled out a PhD. Did they also examine her political record?

Looking for stimulus, she sought companionship with the other university wives. It didn't work out. Few of them had been to university; of those who had, a proportion had left without taking a degree. To them she seemed too 'clever', too ambitious, and her friendly overtures were rejected. She tried joining the University Ladies' Tea Club but felt like a misfit among its more privileged attendees:

I strongly felt that they couldn't imagine the life of an academic wife whose parents didn't have money, who didn't have access to domestic help, and who wanted to pursue her own career.

At such social events, she remembered, even wives who worked in the university were categorised via their husbands' attainments. 'A wife who turned up at a university social event was not asked who and what *she* was, but which Department her husband belonged to.' It was thought helpful to wear a badge, and regardless of what *you* might be, if your husband was a scientist you spent the evening with 'Chemistry' or 'Physics' pinned to your breast.

Christine felt frozen out, crushed, demoralised. 'Society had sent me to Cambridge and given me all these goals, and now didn't have any use for me.' In 1955 the world of academe was far from ready for a wife and mother to double as an intellectual. It was either one, or the other.

6. Queen of Her Castle

Renunciation

Within six months of her Coronation, Queen Elizabeth II embarked on the first extended overseas tour of her reign. It was to be a great undertaking: a six-month progress to greet her Commonwealth subjects, starting in the Caribbean, finishing in New Zealand. In 1953 global travel still held terrors, and a journey of this magnitude seemed to many to be a step into the unknown. As she set forth to visit jungles and deserts inhabited by unfamiliar peoples, there was a feeling among the Queen's subjects that they – like her own small son and daughter – were about to be abandoned by their mother, left in the care of substitutes. But as she kissed her younger sister goodbye and climbed on board the shining Stratocruiser at Heathrow airport, the young Queen may well have felt some relief at leaving Britain behind, and with it that bothersome business of the curtailed romance with Group Captain Peter Townsend.

In Kingston, Jamaica, crowds were there to greet her. One of them, Phyllis Dennis, still has vivid memories of that day:

> She came to Jamaica, you know? And we all went to see her!
>
> You could only see her from afar though, because so many bodyguards were around her. And she was *so* tiny, but she was *so* pretty! And it made me feel real good to go and see the Queen.
>
> And when we were coming back home we sang the 'Rule Britannia', you know?

But Vilma Owen's family stayed at home that day. As a strict Seventh-day Adventist it was not Mrs Owen's way to indulge in flag-waving and royal hoopla. However, Jamaica at this time was drawing closer to the Mother Country. Faced by poverty and lack of opportunity in their islands, more and more Afro-Caribbeans were setting sail for Britain. In 1951 there were 5,000 Caribbean immigrants to the UK. Another 2,000 emigrated from the West Indies in 1953. In 1954, following the Queen's visit, that figure would rise to 11,000, and in 1955 27,500 left home for England's shores. From Vilma's extended family, Aunt Ivy was the first to go.

But if the pretty Queen hoped that the problem of her sister's entanglement would go away while she was touring the world, she was to be disappointed. As one friend said, the couple remained 'terribly in love'.

At the start of 1955 Princess Margaret's duties also took her – and her faithful lady-in-waiting Iris Peake – to the Caribbean. A foreign trip to sunny climes meant new clothes: straw hats, sandals and sunglasses, and Iris shopped carefully for her island-hopping wardrobe. Always a few respectful steps behind, Iris tended to her Princess's every need; there were ribbons to cut, trees to plant, bouquets to accept, gloved hands to shake.

> She always travelled in an open-topped Land Rover, standing up for public appearances, and of course it was a time when full skirts were in fashion. Well, if there was a breeze, it would blow her skirt up, so I sat in the back clutching onto her skirt for modesty's sake.

The younger royal seems to have charmed everyone; among the West Indian press her petite beauty and willing smile soon earned her the name of 'the Dolly Princess'.

For Iris and her mistress, the royal yacht *Britannia* was a refuge from the exhausting round of duties. What a relief it was to stop living out of a suitcase:

It was nice, because you could relax and unpack, and you'd have
all your clothes in one place . . .

But for Princess Margaret, royal relaxation didn't extend to bar-
ing her heart. On the tour, Iris never once heard her speak about
Peter Townsend.

In her turn, the Princess was entranced by the Caribbean. Festive and friendly, that string of sun-kissed islands found a lifelong
place in her heart. On 3 March she landed back in London.
'BRAVO! MARGARET – YOU DID A GRAND JOB,'
shouted the *Mirror* headline next day. But only three days later
their front page was running a different story. Blazoned beside
the masthead the line 'Princess Margaret marriage sensation' was
eclipsed by the main headline: PETER TOWNSEND TALKS
TO THE 'MIRROR'. The reality was that Townsend, ostracised
by the Palace, was now being hounded by an indefatigable pack
of reporters who besieged his apartment intent on getting either
a confirmation or denial of the persistent marriage rumours.

Though the couple had still not met since 1953, there was to
be no let-up as month after month the press probed their relationship. Would they? Wouldn't they? The 21st of August
– Princess Margaret's twenty-fifth birthday, when she would be
able to decide for herself whether to marry him – came and
went. The family celebrations at Balmoral were held against the
backdrop of a restive pack of newspapermen and photographers
baying for another bleeding royal morsel.

From a distance of sixty years, the ensuing events and the
controversy surrounding them have an air of unreality, even
lunacy. British women, on the whole, supported their favourite
Princess's right to marry whomsoever she chose. Reporters
taking vox pops got emphatic reactions:

Well, I married the man of my choice, and I'd like to think she
could do the same.

If she was likely to be Queen then it would be a different situation, but I think she should be left alone now to enjoy herself.

Even the reticent Iris Peake conceded that she 'liked Peter very much, and had hoped it would work out . . .' The *Daily Mirror*, having secured the exclusive with Townsend, took a proprietorial stance on the story. As the crisis grew to fever pitch, it conducted a poll of its readers. Ninety-seven per cent responded that the Princess *should* marry Townsend for love.

The Establishment took a very different view, however, and the Establishment was male. The official government attitude was one of implacable opposition to the union. Meanwhile, from their pulpits, Anglican vicars denounced the relationship:

If Princess Margaret marries Group Captain Peter Townsend she will deliberately be sinning against the express command of our Lord . . .

with Catholics joining the chorus:

The holiness of marriage seems at the present day to be held ever more and more lightly and example even in the highest quarters does not help those who wish to preserve in our society, still nominally Christian, the ideal of Christ that marriage is an indissoluble union.

The advocates of that profoundly held faith now called the Princess to account.

Meanwhile, in superbly ringing prose, the *Times* Leader, voice of the Establishment, urged the Princess to step back from the brink:

There is no escape from the logic of the situation. The QUEEN'S sister married to a divorced man (even though the innocent party) would be irrevocably disqualified from playing her part in the essential royal function . . .

> Happiness in the full sense is a spiritual state, and . . . its most
> precious element may be the sense of duty done.

On Thursday 27 October Iris Peake accompanied her royal
mistress to Lambeth Palace to speak with the Archbishop of
Canterbury. By this time, as Townsend himself recalled, 'the
smile had vanished from her face, her happiness and confidence
had evaporated'. It was impossible to ignore the pain she was in.
There, while Iris made small talk to 'Mrs Archbishop', Princess
Margaret made her intentions clear to Dr Fisher:

> I am not going to marry Peter Townsend. I wanted you to know
> first.

At last, on 31 October 1955, a statement drafted by them both
was broadcast to the world:

> I would like it to be known that I have decided not to marry
> Group Captain Townsend . . . I have reached this decision entirely
> alone . . .

The Establishment had prevailed.

The royal announcement: a culminating moment of press hypocrisy? 'I
hope that . . . they had the sense to hop into bed a couple of times, but this I
doubt,' reflected Noel Coward in his diary.

Feed Him, Love Him — or Lose Him . . .

But had it? The clerics and leader writers who so brutally crushed the Princess's long-nurtured hopes were behaving like a wounded animal in its death spasms, ferociously mauling its attacker. And they were a vanishing breed. Change was imminent. In a very short number of years, divorce in royal circles would come to seem regrettable, but uncontroversial. The vehemence of the anti-divorce rhetoric during this episode can be read as symptoms of a real fear among those with much invested in the status quo, that the institution of marriage was on the slippery slope.

In truth, the statistics gave plenty of cause for nervousness. Between 1936 and 1940, an average of just 6,029 divorce decrees were granted yearly. By 1950 the proportion of marriages terminated by divorce in England and Wales had risen nearly fivefold to 30,870, prompting the Attlee government to set up a Royal Commission on Marriage and Divorce in 1951. The RCMD probed the question of why marriage break-ups were on the increase, and noted that the laws had been gradually liberalised, making divorce easier, while many hastily contracted wartime marriages had foundered. But the post-war blip seemed to have become permanent, and the lawyers on the RCMD were forced to ask why. In their report, they pointed the finger at women's emancipation:

> Women are no longer content to endure the treatment which in past times their inferior position obliged them to suffer. They expect of marriage that it shall be an equal partnership, and rightly so.

So far, so good. Marriage was becoming not a hierarchy, but a collaborative enterprise. On housing estates the pram-pushing, dog-walking husband and father was starting to make his appearance. Social scientists like Ferdynand Zweig commented on the disappearance of the tyrannical bully model, and the emergence of the devoted father who gave time to his children. The phenomenon of the working wife was jolting her husband out of his complacency: 'he is no longer contemptuous of women's ideas as he used to be'. For the most part, Zweig and his ilk looked on such developments as a new dawn for the family:

> [This] is one of the great transformations of our time. There is now a new approach to equality between the sexes and, though each has its peculiar role, its boundaries are no longer so rigidly defined, nor performed without consultation . . . Man and wife are partners.

Could a marriage really be a democracy in the new, post-war era? When *Woman's Realm* published 'Recipes for a Happy Marriage' their exemplary newly-weds, Pam and Peter Osborne, described the caring, sharing deal they had forged:

> 'Shared lives, individual interests . . . That's what we believe in. There's none of this "that is my job, this one yours" business. We share everything, chores, cooking and especially money.
>
> 'We are determined not to get jealous or possessive,' continued Pam. 'Once a week I go to my dramatic society and Peter to his motor cycle club – *and* he washes his own muddy clothes when he gets back!'

But therein lay the seeds of disagreement. To put it bluntly, equality was a threat to stability. The RCMD report was very doubtful whether partnerships like this were the way forward:

> The working out of this ideal exposes marriage to new strains. Some husbands find it difficult to accept the changed position of women; some wives do not appreciate that their new rights do not release them from the obligations arising out of marriage itself and, indeed, bring in their train certain new responsibilities.

In other words, the Osbornes' democratic marriage was a high-risk gamble. Peter would start to resent having to wash his muddy bike gear and would insist that Pam should do it instead of gadding off to her AmDram sessions; Pam would take umbrage. It would all end in tears, not to say the divorce courts.

A leaflet published by the National Marriage Guidance Council also sounded a warning note:

> In truth it is the new equality of women with men that has led inevitably to the disruption, for the present, of stable marriage and family life.

And indeed, following on from the royal gossip, mothering advice and recipes, the problem pages of *Woman*, *Woman's Own*, *Woman's Realm* and so on were packed full of laments from correspondents about infidelities, desertions and affairs.

★

But who was to blame for the divorce explosion?

If the architecture of marriage had always stood upon a foundation of female subordination, by the 1950s that was beginning to look a little shaky. The stakes were high. Fearing collapse, society's commentators looked to women as the bedrock guardians of marriage and the family. If they were to hold up, it was wives who must bear responsibility for the stability of the edifice.

Agony aunts and authors of advice manuals stressed that wives were in debt to their husbands. He's the one who buys your security – rates, taxes, insurance, a roof over your head. But that laid a different responsibility upon the wife. She must live up to expectations. The message was, 'Nothing less than perfection will suffice':

> If [a man] wants to have the cleverest, the prettiest, the wittiest, the sweetest or the best-dressed wife in the world, that is what

she had better see to it that she is in his eyes, or he will be unsatisfied.

Every husband expects his wife to be a kind and loyal mate to
him and a good mother to his children. If he is a working man
he will want her to be able to cook and make his money go as far
as possible. If he occupies an important executive position it is
easier if his wife is accustomed to society and knows how to be
a gracious hostess. If he is a clergyman he wants someone who
can help him with his parish work . . .

Love him, feed him, sympathise with him, stimulate him, admire
him. There you have the recipe for married happiness.

Investigators were hearing the same message from their interviewees. In 1956 psychiatrist Eustace Chesser surveyed 1,400
married women, who agreed unanimously that as wives they
ought to be able to run the home well, cook well, and continue
to look attractive after marriage. The indefatigable social anthropologist Geoffrey Gorer surveyed a cross-section of men to find
out what they most wanted from their wives. Topping the list,
29 per cent looked primarily for a good housekeeper. Love came
fourth. Good cook came sixth. Respondents return repeatedly
to the theme of mealtime punctuality. A married man who
worked at the Vickers factory in Leeds told an interviewer that
he was 'the old-fashioned type. My dinner had to be on the table
at 12 o'clock and my tea at 5.18.' This precision reflected the
time it took for him to ride home from Vickers on his motorbike. One of Stephanie Spencer's* interviewees recalled her
own exertions when it came to pleasing her husband:

I'd start the day in old clothes, and then, it sounds ever so old
fashioned, at half past four I'd go and change into something

---

* Stephanie Spencer, *Gender, Work and Education in Britain in the 1950s* (2005).

respectable because he was coming home and then the minute he walked in the door, the dinner would be in front of him.

Geoffrey Gorer also confirmed that women themselves were complicit in stacking up expectations when he spoke to a twenty-eight-year-old middle-class housewife from Tiverton:

> After marriage it's harder to keep a man than before because really you should try to be as attractive as the day he married you . . . Always have his meals *ready*, nice clean house and home, listen to all his troubles about what a horrid day he's had, even if yours has been dreadful . . . Above all, look clean and attractive yourself.

Keeping the home together entailed ticking off a daunting checklist of absolutes. Socks must be mended, buttons sewn back on to shirts – and not forgetting those unfailingly punctual meals.

The magazine *Good Housekeeping*, which by 1957 had a circulation of over 200,000, opens a window on to the imperatives of the 1950s homemaker. Leafing through 1950s copies of *Good Housekeeping* is to enter a world peopled by women with radiant smiles, clean pinafores and gleaming coiffures. One senses a slight ache of nostalgia at the aspirations of these beatific wives. Does some part of us wish to be like them? The accompanying text guides us round a promised land of batch-baking and the latest in home technology, brightly-hued plastics and man-made fibres that simplify life and save time. Queens in their kitchens, these lovely ladies are always conscious of how best to support their husbands in their professions and help them get ahead in their career. They have much invested in that key promotion.

And their kitchens are indeed delightful: 'the gayest room in the house', with cheery red coal-scuttles, yellow enamelled storage jars and matching casseroles. They are modern, too.

'Is your Kitchen a happy place? Think what a difference "FORMICA" would make . . .' And they are spotless. The sinks are disinfected and the dishcloths boiled. The store cupboards are full of jams, jellies and bottled beans, and free of weevils too, because *Good Housekeeping* wives are careful to keep cereals in closed jars and mop up spills immediately. They are clever cooks, who know the secret of success with yeast dough; they have wonderful ways with mince and they can set a junket.

They are *so* organised. They can bring up their children and cope without a cook. They have always made nutritious packed lunches the night before and wrapped them in polythene bags, and they never fuss when it comes to arranging a party. They have ordered doilies, cocktail sticks and paper dish covers in advance. The table is laid ahead, but covered to protect it from dust, and a crumb brush is laid out ready. So that everything will run like clockwork, they have halved oranges with zigzag edges, scooped out the insides, refilled them with jelly and Bird's custard, and decorated them with maraschino cherries before the visitors arrive; they have prepared fancy ice-cubes by putting small pieces of fruit into their freezing trays. The hot things are hot, and the crisp things are crisp. Their good manners, easy etiquette and talent for conversation are to the fore, so guests will be entertained with games and amusing chat. At the end of the evening they will remember to empty the ashtrays and plump the cushions before slipping out of their luxury-feeling wool velour hostess dresses ('a blessing to any wardrobe') and retiring for the night.

Their clothes are always correct for the occasion, summing up 'elegance imparted by a deceptive simplicity'. In spring they hand-make a rose of snowy white piqué, starch it and pin it on to their lapels. They may also make a ruffled white piqué umbrella case to match. They are accomplished needlewomen and quite capable of sewing a Viyella shortie nightdress and a pair of stripy Tyrolean bib shorts in Super-Tremendo cotton from a 'Simplicity' pattern. Their summer straws are hand-trimmed with swansdown and chiffon. Nor are they defeated by simple DIY jobs. They know how to give their old clawfoot bath-tubs a facelift with clever boxed-out panels cut to measure, or construct a telephone shelf out of three-ply.

They are, above all, 'perfect in every detail', impeccable, assured, timeless and vivacious. Their exercise routines keep a lilt in their walk, keep them slender, and keep them 'young, young, young.'

They would have only themselves to blame if their husbands looked elsewhere. As Geoffrey Gorer commented drily, 'For some reason, which I confess to finding obscure, a permanent wave is considered particularly efficacious in bringing a straying husband back to the fold.' But the demands didn't stop there. Barbara Cartland warned:

> Make-up . . . should be as much a discipline and a habit as cleaning one's teeth . . .

So beware the consequences of being the kind of fat slovenly wife who lies in bed with their hair still in pins, and a greasy nose:

> They are astonished when their husbands, who see them looking so unpleasant, fall out of love and run away with another woman.

But if serenity, taste and a perfectly powdered nose eluded her, there was no better opportunity for a woman to display her perfections than by sallying forth with an immaculately groomed and turned-out baby in the latest model of pram. Miner's wife Audrey Alssebrook bought two prams, one for each of her two babies, before they were born:

> We sent away for the first one months before Frieda came. It
> were a brand new pram, navy blue.
>   And then we had Malcolm, he'd got to have a new pram too.
> Cream. I felt right posh with that pram.

This represented considerable financial outlay.

And in the 1950s a pram was *not* a buggy. They took up a lot
of space on the pavement (in 1956 Harlow New Town's traffic
problems were caused by 'pram-jams'); coach-built and sprung,
complete with elaborate folding hoods and drop-down seats,
these elevated, status-enhancing, baby-transporting vehicles
had a certain capacious magnificence. Nothing less would do.

> And you had to wash their things out didn't you? And iron them
> up, even the children's little knickers and things, and their little
> romper suits. I'd iron these here frills on her pram pillow per-
> fectly. Then every Friday I used to doll up and go down to
> Shirebrook to t'market . . .

In church halls and marquees nationwide, the annual village
Baby Show was the biggest public opportunity to parade your
pride and joy and, potentially, bask in a glow of maternal triumph. Unfortunately it wasn't so much fun for the celebrity
judges wheeled in to rank the infants. Lady Isobel Barnett grew
to dread these events: stuffy tents full of pink-faced, insuffi-
ciently-winded, fractious babies, and hot harassed mums glaring
at their fellow-competitors in scorn and derision. 'How that
Mrs Bodkin dares enter that scrawny baby of hers when she
knew my Trevor were going in for the competition, I don't
know?' Fixed smile pinned to her face, Lady Isobel would pick
her way between the prams, prodding and appreciating, amid a
storm of grisly howls and catty taunts. No, never again.

Still, a bonny baby, poise and good cooking could do wonders to cement a marriage. But if you really wanted to keep his
interest and stop him wandering, astute wives knew that they

had to arouse their husband's desire in the bedroom. Here was yet another duty to add to the lengthening list of marriage essentials, without which the perfect partnership would soon hit the rocks.

★

Ten years earlier, this topic would have been taboo. But in 1948 the lid came off with the publication of the first Kinsey Report, *Sexual Behavior in the Human Male*, followed in 1953 by a sequel, *Sexual Behavior in the Human Female*. In the second of these weighty works, Dr Alfred Kinsey (a zoologist at Indiana University) interviewed 6,000 American women with the thoroughness and scientific precision he might have applied to a field survey of a chimpanzee colony. But Kinsey also recognised that human beings had progressed from the chimpanzee model observed in the jungle, in which each primate family was 'dominated by the physical brawn of its male head':

> Until half a century ago, many human females in Europe and in this country were as nearly male-dominated as the primate family is in the wild. But with the emergence of the female as a significant force in the political, industrial and intellectual life of our Western culture, marriage is increasingly becoming a partnership in which the duties, responsibilities and privileges are more equally shared by or divided between the two spouses . . .

In this context, Kinsey took data across the sexual spectrum, ranging from Incidence of Nocturnal Sex Dreams to Animal Contacts, from Frequency of Masturbation to Frequency to Orgasm.

The publication of the Kinsey Report was a sensational event. Many of its findings subverted the moral position of the day; for example, it emerged that 50 per cent of college girls were not

'I see they've invited Dr Kinsey to come and take a look at us.' *Punch*, July 1954, is straying onto unusually risqué territory, but stays safe by implying that there wouldn't be much to look at in this bedroom.

virgins when they married. Homosexuality came under its scrutiny too – apparently 13 per cent of women had experienced orgasm from lesbian acts; and other hitherto unmentionable acts such as fellatio and masturbation appeared to be widely practised. Several newspapers refused to publish Kinsey's findings, but the 'K-Bomb' inevitably raised the bar for women. With so much information now in the public domain, it was becoming harder to plead ignorance of sex. With Kinsey's promotion of orgasm as a measure of sexual fulfilment, it was now up to women to provide mutual and simultaneous satisfaction, resulting in all-round fulfilment.

'[Girls] need to get married to enjoy themselves properly,' Nicholas said, 'for sexual reasons . . .'

– a comment which, surely, could only have been written (in this case, by Muriel Spark★) post-Kinsey:

> [He] added, 'Heaps of sex. Every night for a month, then every other night for two months, then three times a week for a year. After that, once a week.'

Could a married couple in the mid-50s achieve this kind of happy outcome? Yes, but not easily. Letters to agony aunts, responses to surveys, interviews and oral history memories continue to suggest a high level of ignorance and unhappiness about sex. The National Marriage Guidance Council reported bewilderment in the bedroom: 'Many happily married women have never had an orgasm. Most of them would have done had their husbands known how to help them.' When Eustace Chesser interviewed 712 young wives aged between twenty-one and thirty in 1956, half of them claimed to be sexually satisfied, 235 of them were fairly satisfied, while 114 had no satisfaction at all. But satisfaction fell steeply from then on:

Degree of Sexual Satisfaction (% of total in each group)

	Age 21–30	31–40	41–50	51+
A lot	51	41	35	27
A fair amount	33	39	37	38
Little or none	16	20	28	35
Total number of cases (100%)	712	797	419	121

Less scientifically, now listen to a range of real-life wives talking about what it felt like for them. Here are three women from rural Lincolnshire:

> I had intercourse for the first time on my wedding night. I got undressed in the bathroom. I was very shy. When I came out of

★ In *The Girls of Slender Means*, set in 1945, but written and published in 1963.

the bathroom, he was already in bed. After it had happened, I felt nothing, I couldn't believe it . . . The hotel was nice and the food was good, but that wasn't what I was looking forward to!

I've never enjoyed sex, I don't know what an orgasm is! I've just put up with it all my married life.

My old man got it every night for years. That's why I'm so exhausted. The only pleasure I got out of it was the kids. How could you tell him he wasn't doing it right?

Janet Lee, a housewife from Leicester, who got married in 1955 at the age of nineteen, shared her wedding night memories with another oral history interviewer:

First night? Oh dear, oh dear! I said to John, 'Let me go to bed, and then you come in a bit.' So I went upstairs and got undressed quick and lay in bed with the covers right up to me neck. And I lay there and I lay there – and I thought, 'Where is he?' He was ages and ages. Anyway, finally he come upstairs.

So I said to him, 'Where have you been?' And he said, 'I got talking.' And he stood there, and he got undressed as if he'd been doing it for years. But it wasn't . . . what I thought it was going to be. I suppose we – you know. We all expect more than we get.

A widow from Gloucestershire, Dolly, recalled how her enthusiasm for the act fell a long way short of her late husband's:

He came up to bed like a young colt. ''Ow about a bit then?' he said when he got into bed. I can tell you I wasn't interested, but anything for a quiet life, so I opened me legs and said help your bloody self and he did . . .

An unplanned pregnancy at the age of forty-four was the result. And Geoffrey Gorer's respondents (interviewed for *Exploring English Character*) were equally disillusioned. A thirty-seven-year-old woman from south-east London was typical:

> My husband made such a mess of it, we ceased relations after the
> first year . . .

– as was this thirty-five-year-old mother of four from Berkshire,
who had separated from her husband:

> A wife should be entitled to say no if she wants to, and not be
> forced . . .

– and this forty-six-year-old married woman from Kent:

> I really loathe sexual experience. This has only happened since
> my marriage, as my husband was almost a sexual maniac.

Gorer cited many more along similar lines. Indoctrinated from
adolescence with the idea that it wasn't feminine to like sex,
these wives' voices seem to be expressing their own uneasiness
about giving in to enjoyment.

Loathe it or not, many women like Mrs Lester from
Scunthorpe put up with sex as just another thoroughly dis-
agreeable but unavoidable marital chore:

> He'd be home around ten to eleven . . . I'd pretend to be
> asleep. He would come home full of beer and start mauling
> me . . . There was no affection with it, no love, they just
> wanted sex. It was a duty, a horrible duty to me, I didn't like
> it. A woman didn't get satisfaction from sex then, she was just
> disgusted with it, if she was owt like me. And you'd lie there
> and you'd be looking at the cracks in the ceiling thinking, 'Oh
> that crack could do with filling in, that could do with a bit of
> whitewashing.'

And finally, a specimen quote produced by *Woman's Own*'s
much-loved agony aunt Leonora Eyles, who produced the following as a typical example of at least 60 per cent of her weekly
postbag:

I love my husband, and we have a charming home and three
wonderful children. But it is all spoilt for me because I do so
hate bedtime and all it implies.

Eyles took a briskly sympathetic attitude to the problem, which
she broadly believed could be relieved by home decorating.
Newly-weds who rolled up their sleeves, mixed up some paint
and wallpaper paste, and got busy 'making their nest' would
find physical love blossomed through physical activity. 'Night
will approach and a happy mating with it.' For the more jaded
long-married couple, she advised the woman to build up her
sense of gratitude to the husband who worked so hard to finance
their joint lives: 'He is doing this for us, to keep going this home
we share, to buy things for me, to pay our rent . . . to give me
treats . . . I love him so much!' Sex was that: a transaction. The
man got what he wanted. The woman got a roof over her head.

Three years after the Kinsey Report, Eyles was preaching the
idea that sex difficulties could be resolved on a material level.
She meant well, but as a moral mentor, she found it impossible
to endorse one of the Report's most morally unpalatable, but
fundamental, findings: that women who had sex *before* marriage
had a two to three times higher chance of a better sex life *after*
marriage. Five years later (in her book *Sex for the Engaged*) Eyles
was still advocating pre-marital virginity. Just wait it out, she
pleaded to engaged couples. You know in your heart promiscu-
ity is a mistake. So get rid of your sex urge by swimming, joining
a hiking club or a choir.

The literature of sex was on the increase. Eyles and the other
women's magazine columnists felt able to refer (if only
obliquely) to physical relationships in a way that, twenty years
earlier, would not have got past their editors. '[Not] every girl
understands completely the responsibility she accepts with her
wedding ring . . .' wrote *Woman*'s Evelyn Home in 'An open
letter to a young bride' in 1953. 'If you were my daughter and I

came to talk to you on the night before your marriage, I would tell you to love your husband with all your heart, give yourself to him completely – and fear nothing.' A 'Sex in Marriage' pamphlet issued by the National Marriage Guidance Council was less evasive: 'A wife who refuses to give her husband the sex life he needs causes him to be irritable and difficult to live with.' Generally, the implication was clear that the woman bore a duty to her husband. One self-help author cited the case of an unhappy woman who complained that her husband was too tired to make love to her. The sex doctor she consulted pressed her to come up with some titillating novelties in the bedroom. '"Desire requires imagination," he said, "and stimulation! Women get into bed, talk about the price of potatoes and then are surprised when their husbands turn over and go to sleep!"' Though sex toys or pornographic magazines were not specified, it was plainly the wife's responsibility to come up with something new, something 'unusual or original to excite his interest'.

What emerges? Attitudes to sex in the 1950s remained entrenched. Ignorance, shame and squeamishness inhibited the well-intended efforts of scientists, doctors, writers, therapists and counsellors to alleviate a source of extensive misery. Progressives were still pitted against an unyielding majority of moral conservatives unwilling to countenance a change to the status quo. Geoffrey Gorer, the social anthropologist and author of *Exploring English Character* (1955), wearily but restrainedly commented on what seemed to him the elephant in the room:

> What seems to me most noteworthy is the high seriousness with which the great majority of English people approach and regard marriage . . . The high valuation put on virginity for both sexes is remarkable and, I should suspect, specifically English.

Three Marriages

Real life is peculiar, complicated, messy and unaccountable. In social history, there is no substitute for case histories. Here are the stories of three actual marriages.

Nineteen-year-old Liz Jones and David Monnington became engaged in 1952. Liz was steeped in sexual ignorance and fear. 'I didn't even know that sex could and should be fun for women.' Without entirely understanding why, she knew she had to remain a virgin until marriage. Her own mother was member of a committee for 'Moral Welfare', an organisation that helped unmarried mothers. Was it the hushed, conspiratorial tones of the meetings that took place in Mrs Jones's drawing room that deterred Liz from doing anything so implicitly prohibited, with its dire, dreadful, but unspoken-about links to a rescue 'home' for these unfortunates, somewhere in Tunbridge Wells? There but for the Grace of God . . . No, one didn't dare risk the shame. Today, Liz admits that there's much to be said for a 'try-out' period. 'I don't think many people are virgins now when they're married. I've known several friends who've said if they'd lived with their husband before they were married, they would never have married them.' But Liz was impatient, and so was David.

Unfortunately old Mr Monnington, David's rigidly Victorian father, was opposed to the match. The fact that Liz did not come from farming stock ought to have disqualified her – in the eyes of her future father-in-law – from membership of the Monnington clan. 'This is a blow,' he pronounced, when the news of their engagement was broken to him. 'I *am* disappointed.' Liz felt crushed. But somewhere inside she was made of steel.

Well, I sort of gritted my teeth. I thought, I will have lots of children, and I'm going to make a success of the farm office and

the house, and I'm going to get the garden nice, and I'll jolly
well show him!

As soon as she and David were married, Liz Monnington set out
to do everything a wife could do. In their first home, a primitive, isolated farmhouse on the Pevensey levels, she buckled
down to work. There was no heating apart from open fires, and
few carpets. 'The garden was so neglected I could have spent
twenty-four hours a day on that alone . . .' At the age of nineteen, Liz was now discovering what it meant to be a full-time
housewife, and it was unremittingly tough. She had many new
duties, and found she had to grow up quickly. David naturally
wanted his lunch on the table at twelve sharp ('Woe betide if it
was later than that!'), she had no car, no help, and the house was
un-modernised and shabby. At the same time David expected
her to accompany him to socialise with other local landowners
and pillars of the Conservative Association. By 1956 she had two
babies; four more were to follow.

Proving to her father-in-law that she could be a capable farmer's wife was one thing, but keeping her husband's approval was
another. David was genuinely fond of his sparkly young wife.
However, it now turned out that he had inherited something of
a controlling streak from his father: he was an alpha male primate. Liz had nothing to gain from conflict in her marriage. For
all her steely determination, she opted to go down the 'patient,
tolerant' route, rather than stir things up. Industriously, she
applied herself to her tasks. She put the right food at the right
time on the table, and kept herself looking youthful. She also
complied with his conditions – laid down on the occasion when
he had proposed to her up on the racecourse – that she stop (as
he put it) wasting time on frivolities. Liz enjoyed music, and
would have loved to go to the opera at Glyndebourne, which
was nearby. But David had no interest in the arts, regarding an
opera house as an expensive place to go to sleep. So she ceased to

go to the opera. He could be inflexible. There was no negotiation when it came to family decisions, whether on mealtimes, holiday destinations, or the children's education. Liz was expected to submit, or face the consequences. And there were strict boundaries. For example, David couldn't abide swearing in women. On one occasion, Liz became incensed by some trivial annoyance and let rip with a vehement '*bloody . . .*', at which David turned on her with a chilly severity. 'Take your pearls off,' he said. Tearfully, Liz unfastened her treasured necklace and handed it to him. 'Right,' he said, 'I'm confiscating this – until you learn not to swear.' Liz wept, but the pearls disappeared and she didn't get them back again for several years.

> It mattered terribly to me – I remember being very upset at the time. In those days, I really had to watch my Ps and Qs.

David was competitive too. Liz's sportive talents put her easily in his league when it came to holiday activities. 'If I swam, he always had to swim further. I remember beating him skiing downhill; that didn't go down at all well.' He couldn't bear to lose a race.

In the end, Liz's stoicism and natural optimism prevailed; she proved to her husband, and to her father-in-law, that she was capable of running a home, a large family and a farm office. Though this demanded almost complete subservience to an uncompromising husband, and cost her her youthful ambition to be a journalist, Liz would nevertheless come to see her married life as 'charmed'. Over a marriage of nearly half a century, her discreet, unassertive perseverance paid off, for David Monnington eventually came to recognise how much he owed her. 'In his last few years, he told me he did not know what he would have done without me, which was reward enough for me. I do feel I have had a completely fulfilling life.'

Today, she looks back at her marriage and remembers the fun

and happiness over the travails and tribulations. A product of her era, she took a robust view of her choice of husband. Divorce wasn't an option: 'In my day, if anything went wrong in your marriage the only thing to do was to go home to Mother. That would have been the ultimate shame. Anything better than that.' Widowhood at sixty-seven would offer other, unexpected rewards. Liz was freer to indulge her loves of riding and tennis; more importantly, she took over the complex business, arranging conversions, sales and commercial lets of the farm properties. 'And that was when I think I really grew up.'

★

The story of the Mooney marriage is a 1950s morality tale. Eileen Hawe hadn't been looking to get married at twenty-four; she'd have liked to travel, work and have a bit of fun. But at her wedding in December 1952 she was four months pregnant. As a nurse, she admits she should have known what she was doing before she slept with George Mooney, her first and only lover. 'I'd *never* have let him get that far if I wasn't drunk!' After that, the Catholic culture in which she'd been raised gave her little alternative. She had sinned, and conceived a child. Marriage must put that right, but the priesthood made it clear that she had to bear a burden of guilt. It didn't help when George added, wryly, 'I made an honest woman of you by marrying you.'

And so the Mooney marriage started on a punitive note. Their daughter Marie Therese was born in May 1954, followed by two more babies in 1955 and 1959. In those early days the Mooneys were young and passionately in love, and George was doing his best to keep the family afloat. But his job as a travelling salesman was a trap. It didn't bring in much money, he was away from home for long stretches of time, and the undignified nature of his employment eroded an already fragile sense of self-worth. This was a man with a passion for literature and the theatre. What was he doing on the road in a Ford Anglia selling greetings cards? Depression kicked in at regular intervals. 'He'd get withdrawn, he'd get snappy . . . You could see it descending on him. He'd sit in his chair and you could see him age . . .' Depression wasn't recognised as an illness. The doctor would put 'influenza' on his medical certificate, but taking to his bed, refusing to speak, refusing to get up, George lost job after job. When he emerged it would be to re-apply for a new one through the *Telegraph*'s 'Situations Vacant' columns, and yet again, the family would up stakes and move house.

The insecurity left Eileen shouldering much of the burden of their joint lives. Money was painfully short; even when he was in work, George found it hard to part with. 'We had nothing to spare, you know? Sometimes for my meals I'd just have whatever Marie Therese didn't eat from her little tins of Heinz baby food . . .' But as a trained nurse, Eileen found it easy to get temporary and flexible hospital work.

> I'd jump on the bus, get my few hours done, and back in time for tea . . . I had it down to a fine art how many hours I had to do to meet the bills. I got very good at managing. I'd walk to the bus instead of getting a ticket and all that.
>
> God, there were times . . . When I was nursing I got paid on a Friday, in cash in a brown envelope. But sometimes by Thursday I wouldn't have any money. I'd often have to borrow eightpence from the children's money-boxes, just for a tin of something to give them for their tea.

All too often supper was a can of Heinz baked beans.

Eileen's upbringing, with three live-in servants in her parents' Kilkenny home, hadn't prepared her for the daily rigours of housekeeping, and it was to be a learning curve:

I hadn't a clue about anything. I was in a flat in Cardiff, on my own, husband away Monday to Friday, and you don't want the baby to cry too much in case they throw you out of the flat. It was the bin men in Cardiff who taught me how to run a home. They'd see me throwing out a burnt milk saucepan and they'd say, 'Missus, why are you throwing out these saucepans?' and I'd say, 'They're all burnt,' and they'd say, 'You can clean that off!' I'd have just gone down to Woolworths and bought a new one! But I learnt . . . And with all those nappies . . . I didn't have a washing machine. I boiled them in a bucket on the gas stove.

I don't know how I coped. I just did!

But Eileen's public face was a different matter. High standards of presentation were second nature to a nurse accustomed to keeping a ward spotless with Lysol and carbolic. Undeterred by her lack of knowledge, she soon learnt to shine her floor tiles and scrub her doorstep with the best. And Eileen too yearned for the picture-perfect pram. 'I kept begging George to let me buy a new pram on the Hire Purchase . . .' But George would have nothing to do with it. Somehow, Eileen managed to save ten pounds. 'And then, at last, he let me have it. And, oh God, I was as proud as Punch in the park with my new pram, with a drop-down seat too!'

There was a moment each day when she let herself unwind. As the lilting signature tune of *Mrs Dale's Diary* took to the airwaves, Eileen, along with thousands of British housewives, settled into an easy chair, slipped off her shoes, and lit the first of her daily ration of two cigarettes. 'It's what kept me going!'

Like Liz Monnington, Eileen Mooney learnt the hard way that life was what she made of it. The charm and personality that had so bowled her over back in those early Dublin days were to prove George's undoing. Travelling for a living gave him opportunities to womanise, and lacking willpower he gave in to them. Over time his ability to swim against life's stream dwindled while his depressions grew more severe, and Eileen's valiant attempts to create a happy home were no defence against the encroachments of mental ill-health. Nevertheless she atoned for her sin, sticking by him and soldiering on for twenty-seven years before they finally divorced in 1979:

> What experience has taught me is that you're on your own no matter what. Today I don't owe anybody anything. You have to rely on yourself, and you have to be self-sufficient. But no, I would never get married again.

*

To this day, Marion Turnbull mourns the untimely death of her husband Sir George Turnbull. The couple met when Marion was employed in the drawing office of the Standard Motor Company, where her father worked. The job would never be a career; the idea was that it would plug the gap before she inevitably married. Meanwhile it brought her money, fun and a supply of admirers. Until George Turnbull arrived on the scene, Marion had a nice long-standing boyfriend named Bob. Today, she is willing to admit that with Bob their relationship had crossed the boundary and become a physical one. Which made it all the more unfortunate when George joined Standard on an apprenticeship. Marion found him completely irresistible. He was forceful, passionate and self-confident. He was also captain of Warwickshire's rugby team and looked a bit like Clark Gable. It was a Midlands motor industry romance. A horrible episode ensued in which she forced herself to break off with Bob. 'It was very nasty. His mother rang me at work and cried over the phone . . . It was a ghastly parting, but I did it. I just had to, because I'd met George.'

Deeply and passionately in love as they were, she and George abstained when it came to going the whole way. Marion quickly came to respect that she was dealing with a man who wanted to be in control of his own life:

> George had formed his own ideas of what he was going to do, he'd sorted out an apprenticeship and got a scholarship to go to university. And if I got pregnant it would interfere with all of that. It would be a problem. It would mess things up. And he would NOT do that. So he was prepared to wait.
>
> Yes, there was a bit of heavy petting . . . but he wasn't one to take a chance, I'm certain of that.
>
> It's true that when, inevitably, he found out about Bob and me he wasn't very pleased that I'd already done it. But once he'd got used to the idea it was all right. He just didn't want to talk about it again. 'Just don't remind me,' was his line.

In 1950 Marion and George got married. And from that day on Marion never ceased to adore him. George repaid her lifelong devotion with comfort, security and the knowledge that in all circumstances she could count on him.

George Turnbull's unstoppable rise to become one of Britain's most powerful executives, eventually knighted for services to the motor industry, was built not only on the explosion of car purchase that happened between 1945 and 1956, but on the foundation of an entirely traditional marriage:

> A strong character – that's what I go for in men. You know, I had a strong father, and I had a strong husband – I don't like weak men. I felt that whatever happened George would always take care of things. Because he made the decisions and that was it. I think I probably do – still – compare all other men with George. No one else has that strength of character, and I still think everyone else falls short.

Where did that leave his wife? Marion was a confident, open-minded woman with a sunny and warm-hearted temperament.

In her twenties she was radiantly pretty. George Turnbull had chosen well. But Marion too knew that she had found the man who most suited her, both emotionally and financially.

The Turnbulls had started their married life in a two-room flat in Leamington Spa; within four years George was earning enough at Standard-Triumph to move his wife and two baby daughters into Holly Hill, an eight-bedroom house with a staff cottage sitting in five acres of grounds, at Balsall Common outside Coventry. Here, Marion led the kind of life that many women of her generation could only dream of – and she knew it.

> I was living a very, very comfortable life, in a lovely home. We had more money than most people. It was a very nice life and I appreciated it.

The Turnbull marriage perfectly exemplified how wives and husbands could live entirely compartmentalised lives. Marion spent her day attending to the children's needs, supervising the refurbishment of Holly Hill, gardening, shopping, playing golf or seeing her friends. Mrs Fisher came in from the cottage to do most of the housework.

George meanwhile was based at Standard-Triumph's vast sprawling headquarters in Banner Lane near Coventry. By 1954 he was in charge of the experimental department; two years later he became manager of the car section but would soon be promoted to general manager. He spent his working day focused on production lines, the technicalities of engine manufacture, and industrial negotiations. This was a man's world, and one he never brought home with him. It was not George's way to talk shop under the domestic roof, so Marion had no idea what deals he was brokering, nor what troubles might be brewing on his management watch. At Holly Hill, that part of his life, along with his jacket and tie, was discarded as he came through the front door.

A well-spent evening for him consisted of an hour before the television in company with the *Daily Telegraph* crossword and a glass of scotch. Then wine with dinner. Small talk was not his thing, and Marion knew better than to divert him with the petty details of her own day's doings. From time to time they dressed up and sallied out for a dinner dance with friends at the Leofric Hotel in Coventry. Women were charmed by George, who was attractive, broad-minded and forthright; but the reality was that he much preferred the company of men. A sociable weekend, a game of chess, a jocular exchange with the lads about rugger teams or golf handicaps was how he preferred to relax.

> He always had respect for me. And yes, he must have loved me. But I think the job must have filled a lot of his thoughts. I think he just assumed I was happy. Which I was.

The transaction worked. A simple, unspoken bargain decreed the course of their marriage, and their lives. George's high-pressure job meant that Marion made no demands on him when he came back from work. But George in his turn did not trespass on her power base, trusting her judgements where the home was concerned. Marion felt needed, and lucky to have a husband who didn't question the decisions she made. In all the houses they ever lived in, Marion chose every stick of furniture, every picture, every lampshade. George simply took care of the bills. He didn't share with her their financial situation, any more than she shared her domestic problems with him, but if she did, as a gifted executive, he would provide a solution:

> I remember saying to George, 'Oh, I'm fed up with doing all this cooking at the weekend.' Well, he had an answer for everything of course, and it always seemed so simple to him, so he said, 'Well, get a cook.' So I did, and Mabel came along and stayed with us for a few years, and did all the cooking at the weekend.

Because she loved him, Marion never took advantage of his generosity. Expensive clothes weren't important to her; nor did she yearn for grand jewellery. But he rewarded her love anyway. George bought her two mink coats, 'one long and one short . . .'

And I never even knew he was a millionaire until he died . . .

Marion Turnbull had learnt the secret of contentment. And when she remembers how close she got to settling for Bob, she still counts her blessings. 'If I'd married Bob – oh, dear, dear! When I think about it – oh my God! Think what my life would have been . . . I'm *so* lucky to have married George.'

My Own Front Door

Liz Monnington, Eileen Mooney and Marion Turnbull shared one thing. All three of them – and many thousands of other women across this country – were as emotionally connected to their homes as they were to their husbands, if not more. Liz's triumph over her domestic circumstances permitted her to gain territory in a complex marriage. As she wrestled the garden and interiors into submission, she felt able to claim victory. Meanwhile Eileen, scrubbing burnt saucepans in a shared flat in Cardiff, was dreaming of a day when she would live in her dream cottage with fruit trees and roses round the door, away from the blight of poverty and depression. It would come true – but not until after she and George Mooney divorced. Holly Hill (and the many subsequent houses she was to live in as Sir George Turnbull's work took him around the world) was Marion Turnbull's private domain, her power base, her channel for self-expression.

The psychological dramas of so many women's everyday lives – happy and unhappy marriages, discontents, frustrations and small triumphs – were played out not on a visible or public stage, but beside the washing line, bustling around the stove, at the sink. As Nella Last wrote, '[Home is] my real "core" of life and living.' By the 1950s Nella's husband Will Last was in a bad way, clinically depressed, brooding and unwell. As she busied herself turning out her kitchen cupboards, worrying about the lack of space to dry a pair of curtains and two blankets that needed washing, baking bread and economically using up the scraggy remains of the weekend's cold mutton to make a nourishing soup, her mind was preoccupied with worries about Mr Last's incapacity. Could he be persuaded to go to the cinema? No, a film would over-stimulate him. He'd be better off reading a library book. Make sure it's one with a happy ending. Look at him ageing. Look at him 'letting go of so much . . .' How could she prop him up? When would the letter come with an appointment for him to see the psychiatrist? 'By tea time today I could have climbed the wall. My hands shook – I sliced tomatoes for a salad to eat with cheese, and I cut my finger.' A neighbour dropped by for a chat. 'I breathed a heartfelt sigh of relief . . .' Nella's own mood swings and moments of elation happen against the unremittingly domestic backdrop of 9 Ilkley Road, Barrow-in-Furness: topping up her stockpot, boiling up lights for the cats, stitching her rag dolls by the fire.

In another domestic 'day in the life', contentment and aspiration go hand-in-hand. Here is Jean Metcalfe, blissfully married to her *Two-Way Family Favourites* co-presenter Cliff Michelmore. Their joint memoir (*Two-Way Story*, 1986) records a perfect 'companionate' partnership of equals, on air but also in the home. On 6 October 1952 the happy young couple went shopping together in Reigate. With rationing still in force, they spent four shillings on pork chops and pre-emptively bought nylon stockings for Jean in case they became unavailable again. Then Cliff went home to catch up on the housework (dusting and polishing), while Jean, in her capacity as radio celebrity, opened a church 'Fayre' at St Luke's. Cliff's apron-wearing was not a front – he was fanatically houseproud and always happy with a tin of Mansion polish or a carpet beater – but the division of labour ended there; Jean did all the washing, starching and ironing without a spin dryer or washing machine, and she cooked.

> Home to make coffee walnut and ginger meringues. C. planted bulbs . . . Tea by fire . . . Finished red/white curtains for kitchen. To bed with two hot water bottles and Eartha Kitt on the record player. A lovely day.

'Home, Sweet Home' – ornately embroidered on framed samplers, or notched in fancy pokerwork on a chimney-breast icon – was the repository of deep emotion. The academic Richard Hoggart drew on his own 'Dickensian' roots in Leeds when he described the 'inalienable quality' of the working-class home, but his portrait holds good thirty years on, in 1950s back-to-backs, prefabs and council houses. Hoggart tells of the importance of privacy ('keeping y'self to y'self . . .'); of the half-length lace curtains and scrubbed doorsteps reinforcing each family's respectability. Windows with leaded lights and coloured panes, their sills adorned with showy geraniums or nasturtiums, added to the overall cheerfulness. Inside, the notorious aspidistra, focus of the 1920s living room, was now replaced by jaunty images of cute big-eyed infants with puppies or baskets of cherries. Furniture, once mahogany, had been jettisoned in favour of 'chain-store modernismus, all bad veneer and sprayed-on-varnish-stain'. The sideboard also bore its cargo of newfangleness: plastic and chrome biscuit barrels, bird-cages complete with budgies, and a radio, often a television – but 'no telephone to ring'. The family gathering-place was a 'cluttered and congested burrow . . .', with the hearth at its centre, and still, in some homes, that emblem of economy, thrift and skill, the clip-rug. Colourful, snug and patterned, these rugs represented months of devoted toil by 'our Mam', in assembling hundreds of snippets from worn-out woollies, remnants and old blankets, prodding or hooking them through hessian to form cheery diamond or circle designs. Hoggart conjures the timeless cosiness and intimacy of these rooms:

> The iron thumps on the table, the dog scratches and yawns or the cat miaows to be let out; the son drying himself on the family towel near the fire whistles, or rustles the communal letter from his brother in the army which has been lying on the mantelpiece behind the photo of his sister's wedding; the little girl bursts into a whine because she is too tired to be up at all, the budgerigar twitters.

This was 'a good and comely life . . . [with] a strong sense of what a home is for'. A place to 'stay in', to sit by the fire, behind closed doors. And at its heart, 'Mam'. She is the benchmark of womanhood to her daughters and granddaughters, and 'the pivot of the home . . .'

Hoggart's picture of the working-class matriarch may be seen through the rose-spectacled eyes of one who was orphaned at the age of eight, but his observation is sharp. At bottom, Mother's job was to make ends meet, to stave off penury. Despite not being the breadwinner, it was her job to budget for the family; most northern husbands handed their pay packets to their wives. She would then return a portion of it to him, for beer, cigarettes and perhaps a bet on the horses. Her husband and family relied on her skill to 'fadge', to contrive with the housekeeping money. Being able to do this spelt the difference between misery and contentment; a reasonable life depended on her ability to calculate. He appeals to us to examine the face of an old working-class woman, wrinkled and ingrained, with forceful clefts running from the nose to the pinched mouth, so expressive of her deepest concerns. 'They tell of years of "calculating".' Or watch her, listen to her as she taps her fingers, smooths the upholstered arm of her chair, rocks in her seat, mumbles with her mouth. No, these were not symptoms of derangement, but voiceless testimony to the constant process of interior calculation.

*

A few words here about mining communities: in 1950 the National Coal Board employed more than 700,000 people, but the industry had peaked in the 1920s and had begun its long, slow decline. Beyond the colliers themselves, hundreds of thousands of families in this country remained reliant on the industry for sustenance and a way of life – one which was the subject of a revealing study, *Coal is Our Life* (1956), by three social anthropologists* who chose as their field the Yorkshire mining town of Featherstone near Wakefield (re-named 'Ashton' in the book).

In 'Ashton' in the early 1950s, the family model seemed like an almost bestial throwback, with sex relationships reduced to their primitive essence. As if corralled by long custom, males and females lived almost entirely separate lives. Home, their only intersecting space, was for the husband a space for leisure, for his wife a space for unremitting labour.

A young woman growing up had little prospect of being other than a housewife. Until marriage, she gave time to clothes and appearance, but once that purpose was achieved, and with a home to look after, she quickly gave up bothering. 'One notes, in Ashton, as in other mining areas, the rapid decline in physical beauty among young married women.' They developed ailments, anaemia and prolapsed wombs.

Territory was as defined as if the genders were different species.

* Norman Dennis, Fernando Henriques and Clifford Slaughter.

A married woman who stepped beyond her domestic boundaries – into the workplace or the pub – was frowned upon, while rare was the husband who spent any time under his own roof beyond the essentials of eating, resting and cleaning. His 'real' life was spent down the mine, at the club, playing darts, having a drink and talking about work and politics. The woman's 'real' life was expected to be her kitchen and the homes of her immediate neighbourhood, where she and her friends would gather daily over cups of tea to 'have five' (minutes, generally stretched to an hour or more), and talk over family and domestic matters. In anticipation of her husband's return, she was expected to clean and produce punctual, hot, well-cooked meals. Any inferior offering could expect short shrift from the weary husband, back from the pit, who would feel within his rights to 'throw it to t'back o' fire'. The economic deal was paramount. An Ashton wife expected a steady housekeeping income from her husband; as in Hoggart's working-class household, it was the man's job to earn the money, and the woman's job to control the household finances. Storms over money brewed up regularly, but subsided quickly. Women's low, almost negligible status was reinforced by the men's bawdy and indiscriminate language, most of which the study team regarded as unquotable, apart from 'A woman's only good for two things – looking after the house and lying on the bed.'

Little likelihood, here among the coal dust and the slag heaps, of caring, sharing companionship, with the result that –

> – as the years go by, and any original sexual attraction fades, this rigid division between the activities of husband and wife cannot but make for an empty and uninspiring relationship.

Love was scant; sex peremptory and business-like. On marriage generally, the team concluded that couples were generally happiest in the early years, when 'most problems were solved by going to bed'. Subsequently, it was a question of sticking it out – just 'carrying on'. In just one regard did men display any profound reverence or attachment for women, and that was for their mothers, whose strength, courage and sacrifice were spoken of with unstinting and often tearful emotion.

The Ashton survey makes for depressing reading. But Audrey Alssebrook's relationship with her husband, miner Len Alssebrook, tells a different story.

In most respects, Audrey fitted into the mould of housebound miner's wife. At sixteen she was put into service with a gentleman's family in Nottingham, at twenty she was married, by the age of twenty-three she had two children. 'I never had a chance to have a career . . .' In the early years they lived with Len's parents, and Audrey learnt from his mum how to feed a hard-working miner:

> She used to have a big iron pan over the open coal fire, and she used to do onion pudding, boiled, in a cloth all tied up. The men'd been at work and they'd got to have a piled-up plate. And they could eat it!
>
> I can cook any blummin' thing. Len had to have a hot meal every _every_ day. When he were on day shifts up at Worksop Main he used to go out at half past five in the morning, back home about half past three. His dinner'd got to be done when he walked in the door. Meat, stewpot and all them sort of things, you know? And he used to like a rice pudding done in t'oven, with t'skin on top, all creamy . . .

When it came to talking about his work, Len was as reticent as other miners.

> He wouldn't ever talk about it in company. He said when I'm at home I'm at home and when I'm at work I'm at work . . .

leaving Audrey prey to dreadful fears for his safety. Shafts collapsed, explosions happened, men became trapped underground,

breathing noxious gases. Between 1950 and 1959 there were fifteen serious pit accidents in Britain, killing a total of 283 men.
No matter what, the sight of Len walking down the path came
as a daily relief. She now remembers the day that he finally finished at Worksop Main pit as the happiest day of her life next to
the day she married him.

Almost twenty years since his death, Audrey still has nothing
but praise for her husband:

> Len wouldn't go out drinking and get drunk. And he wouldn't
> tell anyone how he voted either, or mention politics – no way.
> We never fell out over money. He used to say, 'Help yourself,
> take what you've got to take.' There were no one in charge in
> our house. We shared.
>
> You know to be honest, when I had my children, Frieda and
> Malcolm, unless Len was on nights, I never, ever made a baby's
> bottle at night. Len did it. And something else – neither our
> Malcolm, nor our Frieda, would ever let their dad go out to
> work without they had a kiss. If his dad were going on nights,
> our Malcolm used to run across and say, 'Eh up, Dad, just a min-
> ute . . .', and he would give him a kiss before he went to work.
> And our Frieda did too.
>
> It's as true as God's my judge, Len never grumbled. And he
> were quiet, he weren't a mouthy man. You know, we were t'first
> in our street to have television. Because that's how Len were –
> he were all for his family you see?
>
> He were ever so good. I had a perfect husband.

The Alssebrook marriage, with its new television set and affec-
tionate family framework, tells of a gentle shift in the
mid-century landscape. Not feminism, but feminisation, and
the individual, were in the ascendant. Miners and their families would continue to fight tooth and nail for their industry
and traditions; the macro structures and imperatives of trade

unionism would remain dominant. But in their clean stone cottage in Scarcliffe, Derbyshire, what Len and Audrey Alssebrook wanted most was better lives – not for the proletarian masses or the British miners, not for the workers of the world, but for themselves and their family.

*

The sweat, dirt and toil of life in the pits stamped themselves indelibly on mining communities. Audrey Alssebrook could 'smell t'coal on our Len, even when he'd had a bath'. In 1996 Len died of pneumoconiosis brought on by breathing coal dust. The investment of lifetimes of labour and suffering meant that many found it impossible to accept the decline of their industry.

A generation earlier Charlie Mason was supporting his family by working as a miner in Lightmoor colliery in the Forest of Dean. His wife, Margaret, struggled in the Depression era to feed them all on the little money he could earn. A lifelong love of books, along with a deep-rooted political idealism, was transmitted by Charlie to his younger daughter Winifred. She grew up well versed in the vocabulary of H. G. Wells, Lenin, redistribution, the working-class struggle. After leaving school at fourteen, she was in service until she met Syd Foley at an anti-Nazi rally and married him in 1938.

After the war Winifred and Syd were living in rented rooms in a slummy tenement in Lisson Grove, Paddington. Here, the task of making ends meet dominated Winifred's days. She, Syd and their three little boys occupied two rooms and a kitchen with one cold-water tap, up three flights of stairs. The building itself accommodated six tenancies, including Meg from the valleys, purveyor of scandal, and unofficial tenement loaner of shillings when the money wouldn't stretch – for all too often 'the week was longer than the housekeeping money . . .' Then there was Lally the nymphomaniac, a source of wondrous enlightenment on sexual matters, and Mr and Mrs B, who weren't *really* married. 'We shared two landing lavatories, the front door, the stairs, and most of the ins and outs and ups and downs of each other's lives.' Winifred's work was cut out. Washing day meant a half-mile trip to the municipal wash-house with two prams – one for the baby, another for the dirty washing – then home again carrying the clean washing, in time to dish up Syd's tea of casserole and rice pudding punctually. Once a week Winifred supplemented the Foley family income by charring at a mansion block round the corner, while keeping an eye on baby Richard sitting up in his pram on the pavement, being happily fed chips, orange segments and chocolate biscuits by friendly passers-by. The young wives who lived in the mansions were friendly, and Syd's sister lived round the corner, too, a benign family presence.

In 1949 Winifred had her fourth child. This time it was the longed-for girl, and they named her Jennifer Fleur. Two rooms and an external toilet were not enough for a family of six. The Foleys put their names down on the council housing list. It took two years, but one day in 1951 a letter arrived announcing that the family were to be rehoused three streets away in a three-bedroom flat with hot water, fully equipped kitchen, built-in wardrobes, and an internal bathroom and toilet on the second floor of a brand new apartment block. 'I would bet that Aladdin felt no more gratified when the Genie opened the door to his treasure cave than I did.'

Winifred's joy at this outcome was replicated by thousands of women across the nation, as inexorably their names shifted to the top of council lists. Like Hilda Price in Glamorgan:

People do not realise the sheer joy it was for a family in the post-war years to move into a council house with all its 'mod cons'. We were so excited . . .

or Mr and Mrs Cousins and their four little daughters, who moved from shared accommodation with a backyard toilet in north London, to a three-bedroom council house at Bedwell near Stevenage:

> Never before had we had the luxury of a bath, hot water on tap and best of all in the children's eyes, our own stairs. They ran up and down them on that first day calling out 'these are our stairs!' and they all kept flushing the toilet.

Meanwhile Mrs Newman was fêted for being the 1,000th Bletchley council-house tenant:

> 'It's just like being a film star . . .'

– Mrs Brace felt as though she'd won a lottery:

> When I walked through my own front door, it was just like I'd been given a million pounds . . .

and a Liverpool woman remembered:

> I felt like the Queen.

Like these, Winifred Foley was delirious with gratitude. Undeterred by the higher rent, and by ominous warnings from housing department officials that the downstairs tenant was 'difficult', the family moved in.

And now Winifred was in her element. At last, she had a place over which she could truly assume command. All her life she had been poor, and ashamed of her poverty. All her life she had felt herself to be a slave, not a master. Working in service had convinced her that she was 'a second-class citizen'. Here, for the first time, she was Queen of her castle. In a dream of domination, she cleaned and polished her new territory into submission. The floors shone, the windows gleamed, and the sparkling white refrigerator purred.

I became that most unsuitable creature, an over-house-proud
mother. That flat had gone to my head and partly covered my
heart . . . Not a speck or spot of dirt or dust, not any sort of
muddle would I tolerate.

She turned her back on the cosy clutter of their old way of life.
The old mahogany sticks and shabby clip-rugs were outclassed
by her sparkly new lounge-diner.

One objective filled my thoughts, the purple patterned carpet in
Jordan's window.

Nine guineas, this beauty cost. And it would be money well-
spent to deaden the noise made by her rowdy offspring thudding
about above the cantankerous witch living below, who otherwise threatened to oust them from their new-found paradise.
Every moment she could find, Winifred was out on hands and
knees, scrubbing and polishing at half-a-crown an hour, to
afford that wonderful factory-fresh purple carpet. Calculating.
Every five shillings she earned went straight to top up her
advance payment, until at last the lovely, longed-for carpet was
hers.

But as time went by, Winifred began to realise how much the
family had lost by moving to the new apartment. The old
dropping-in-and-out days had passed. Syd's sister had moved.
Meg would visit, and occasionally she ran into Lally in the market, but 'something had been destroyed and would not revive'.

We had left a community. Nobody was bringing a cup of tea to
my door, nobody was having a chat on the landing, there was no
smiling face in the opposite window . . .
    On these new big clean stairways there was no fellow
feeling . . . These fine new glossy doors were always shut.

And still the family was struggling. A moment's extravagance –
another rug, or new shoes for the children – could leave the

Foleys having to borrow from Meg, or else with nothing to eat for three days. Life was precarious and beset with perils. 'My nerve-ends [were] in tatters.' The Foleys seemed to have made a terrible mistake.

Standing at her new sink, hands immersed in greasy suds, Winifred felt herself cracking under the strain. A saucepan slipped from her grasp and clattered on to the echoing tiles; she felt her body start to tremble spasmodically. Her ears rang with the relentless tinnitus of workmen in the street drilling up the pavement with a pneumatic drill. In the yard the dust-cart thundered and clanged.

> Was I going mad? I wanted to scream my own neuroses into the din.

The letter-box snapped open and shut again. On the mat lay a picture postcard. Still shuddering, she picked it up. It showed a tranquil sylvan scene with ferns and foxgloves, dappled light falling through the canopy of oak branches on to a woodland glade in the Forest of Dean:

> The pent-up tears broke; I sobbed and sobbed for the green peaceful aura of my childhood years.

It was summer 1955. A month later, the entire family and their worldly possessions were crammed into a removal van as it trundled past Cirencester, struggling in low gear down Birdlip Hill's giddying descent, below which, stretched out like a pilgrim's vision, lay the Forest – and the cottage where the Foleys would pick up the next chapter of their lives.

The Grand Plan

Between 1945 and 1964 local authorities built 866,000 permanent dwellings in the United Kingdom. Winifred Foley's moment of crisis in the kitchen of her new flat hints at a greater shift in women's lives at this time. The post-war housing short-age was the catalyst for a building boom. Families were relocated to council estates in suburbia, or to entirely new towns like Corby, Stevenage, Basildon, Hemel Hempstead or Harlow. Social scientists looked on in fascinated dismay as East Enders from Bethnal Green were uprooted from bombed-out or fester-ing slums and tenements and transposed to new fully plumbed accommodation with front doors and garden plots.

Perfect, planned homes, for perfect wives. It was easy to equate the rebuilding of the family with post-war reconstruction. In the 1950s crowds flocked to the *Daily Mail* Ideal Home Exhibition, the yearly showcase for housing innovation, the intensity of their interest reflecting an irrepressible public passion for dream houses. In 1950, bungalows were the theme. The 1951 Exhibition hosted the Women's Institute House – the result of 400,000 WI members pooling their suggestions. One hundred and forty thousand peo-ple visited it, and were delighted by its 'ample and well designed outhouses', and the electric drying machine installed for wet coats. The following year saw 'The Old People's Home'. In 1955 C.O.S.M.I.T.H. (the Council Of Scientific Management In The Home) exhibited plans for 'A House with a Separate Meals Room' (86 square feet of dining space in addition to a large kitchen and living room), and 1957's top exhibit was 'The Frostproof Home'. That year Pathé's cameras visited Olympia and filmed a wealth of gadgets and gender-targeted modern trends, from cedar cladding and up-and-over garage doors for the men, to a telephone-cabinet-and-combined-seat and eye-level wall-mounted oven ('And about time too, eh girls?') for the ladies. Only from *Woman's Hour* presenter Jean Metcalfe's diary entry for March 1956 came a dissenting voice:

> 'House of the Future' perfectly frightful. Food treated with gamma rays keeps indefinitely ... Heating under floors!

Transparent walls! *Remote* control for TV! Even a machine which records telephone messages when you're out!! Can you imagine living with all that?

But for most the Exhibition was a fantasy world of aspiration; in 1957 it broke its own record with 1.5 million visitors. 'How much we all pine for the Ideal Home . . .' sighed Pathé's commentator.

Post-war development and its associated 'Grand Plan' mentality is much discussed today. Were those suburban closes with their hot-and-cold running appliances a new Utopia, or soulless, inhuman wildernesses? Could the comforts of an Ideal Home ever be sufficient substitute for those cheery burrows with their outside taps and tin baths, so lovingly described by Richard Hoggart?

When Maureen Johnson moved to a tiny box-like detached modern house, recently built in Codsall in the hinterland of Wolverhampton, she began to feel that she had lost not only her sense of direction, but also that inner life which she had so painstakingly worked to sustain.

'If I'd been born ten years later I would have had a proper education, maybe I'd even have tried for university.' Nevertheless Maureen's sharp, argumentative wit and rebellious political streak placed her on an intellectual level with her college-educated boyfriend and fellow Labour Party supporter Brian Nicol. It was a meeting of minds. In 1952 they married, she became Maureen Nicol, and in 1956 the couple started a family. Brian's job with the Coal Board now took him to the Midlands. Uprooted from the home counties where she had grown up, Maureen found herself marooned with a noisy and active baby to look after, no car, no telephone, and no social life:

> I was isolated, geographically and mentally. And I was miserable, separated from friends and family.

Lack of money hampered everything, even more after a second baby appeared. The Nicols couldn't afford childcare; though Brian was still able to attend political meetings, one of them had to babysit, and it was usually Maureen. She began to feel brain-dead.

> I wanted to get out and do things and I couldn't. I guess frustration was the key word. There was this expectation that I would stay at home – at least while the children were under school age – and that this was my life.
>
> I remember once, I'd had such a day of it, dealing with the kids, and I just thought, Oh God, there must be more to life than this! Well, I went down to the bus stop with both the children, and as Brian got off the bus from work I handed them over and said, 'Right, I'm off, I'm going – anywhere – the theatre, the cinema, anywhere! I'm off. Just take the kids!'

But despite her isolation, Maureen Nicol started to sense that she was not alone:

> It just seemed so stupid that there were probably so many women out there like me . . . who had moved to areas where they knew not a soul, and who were really going round the bend . . .

At that time, Maureen felt powerless. But as she was to find, modern suburbia did indeed conceal a huge substratum of unhappiness: young intelligent women, uprooted from friends and family, spending their days with only babies to talk to, shut in by four walls. The discovery was to give meaning to her own life – and to that of many others.

*

Maureen Nicol's very real frustration in the hostile desert of Wolverhampton plays into an equally real preconception – particularly among left-leaning, collectivist intellectuals – that suburbia, Metroland, the new towns, Council developments and purpose-built estates were not only culture-free zones, but also breeding-grounds for narrow-mindedness, conformism and neurosis. The politician Edith Summerskill described the London suburban housewife as 'one of the loneliest people in the country'; her only regular point of contact being the doctor's waiting room, where she patiently waits to pick up her prescription for phenobarbitone tablets, to ward off 'nerves'.

The Ideal Home mentality, with its cocktail cabinets and three-piece suites, seemed to many to mask isolation, along with triviality and petty respectability. The flip-side of this was a tendency to romanticise old-fashioned proletarian communities: that world of turbaned women gossiping over picket fences, corner shops, and grubby urchins playing in the street. We are all familiar with the argument that the East End's legendary neighbourliness and comradely spirit got lost in the transposition to planned, aseptic developments like Codsall.

But we need to remember the strains that so many people were living under, post-war. One study showed that in the decade from 1945 around 40 per cent of couples were cohabiting with their in-laws, for periods of up to five or even fifteen years. Close relatives could be, well, just too close. And another story emerges when we examine individual cases. Look at the dysfunctional Nash family in suburban Birmingham, whose chaotic unravelling is much more typical of the complexity of real life. In fact, many working-class wives like Mrs Nash simply couldn't wait to pull up stakes and put as much distance as possible between themselves and 'Mam' and their other poisonous relatives.*

* The topic of the planning mentality is fascinatingly aired in Mark Clapson, *Invincible Green Suburbs, Brave New Towns: Social Change and Urban Dispersal in Postwar England* (1998).

Before moving to Westcott Road in Sheldon, Birmingham, the family – Brenda, Mom, Dad, Brenda's brother Reggie and her baby sister Pamela – shared a dingy three-bedroom 1930s semi in nearby Stancroft Grove with Aunt Doll, Uncle Reg and their son Buster. The eight family members who lived, slept and ate under this roof shared a kitchen so small that only two of them could fit into it at once. In this claustrophobic cul-de-sac, the community consisted predominantly of other people to whom Brenda was related. Three doors down lived Gran, Grandad and Aunt Maud. Uncle Reg's brother and sister lived next door with their widowed mum. Aunt Lizzie lived opposite with Uncle Sam, and their married children lived nearby with their families.

The overcrowding wore everyone's patience thin. It didn't help that Doll and Reg were 'selfish and malicious people', who made it very clear that they wanted their house back and behaved as badly as they dared in the attempt to force Brenda's family out. Relationships became strained, and the Nashes were equally keen to move – but where? Hope was kindled when they heard about a local disused army camp being taken over by squatters who were setting up home there with chemical toilets and orange boxes. The corrugated iron huts stood in a compound surrounded by barbed wire. Brenda's desperate parents took themselves off to see if there was one going free, but – to the children's intense relief – the camp was already fully occupied.

They applied for a council house. Officials came to assess their needs. At long last, the postman handed over a brown envelope with the words, 'This is what you're waiting for, I think.' They had been allocated a brand new house, just built on what had recently been farmland, only a few streets away. As the day approached when the family was finally due to move out, stress levels rose alarmingly:

My parents began to treat Aunt Doll and Uncle Reg with something of the same malevolence that we had had to endure for so
long from them. It was no longer necessary to placate them, to
pander to their most unreasonable whims, to bite our tongues
when an angry retort rose to our lips, and the last few weeks
before we moved were a strange mixture of unbearable tension
and exhilaration.

Like refugees, the Nashes transported their belongings piece-
meal in handcarts and prams. But the long-awaited arrival in
Westcott Road was an anti-climax. Clutching the remainder of
their possessions, the family escaped up the gully behind Aunt
Doll's house, walked the short distance to the adjacent estate,
and up the front path of their new home, to find two dead rats
lying on the doorstep.

Once inside, the family found space they had never known
before. So the first problem was lack of furniture to fill its
cavernous emptiness. Gran donated some chairs, and Mom
scrounged three ill-assorted sideboards and a monumental chest-
of-drawers. Then there was the challenge of decorating the
bland, clinical wastes of its institutional cream-distempered
walls. Under Mom's baleful command the family covered them
with peach distemper and 'ragged' over it with scrunched-up
balls of string dipped in red and green paint. Everyone agreed
the effect might just be mistaken, at a distance, for aspirational
wallpaper (which they couldn't afford).

Here in Westcott Road the stifling network of malevolent
aunts and garrulous grannies was replaced by a more heteroge-
neous community: the Butlers, whose explosive rows were the
talk of the neighbourhood; the hated Mr Batchelor, surly and
ever-reluctant to return balls kicked into his garden. Next door
to the left lived a fascinating family with undisclosed connections to the stage and theatre, while next door to the right was
inhabited by Phoebe Cook, aka 'the honourable Feeb', so-called

for her pretensions to gentility. Opposite lived a dysfunctional couple of drunks with their neglected children, a family of incomprehensible Glaswegians whose ever-increasing brood were packed off one by one to join a Scottish army regiment, and the Winns, with their massive Staffordshire bull-terrier, Bruce.

For Brenda's mother, moving house to a new estate didn't bring an end to the calculating. If anything it now got worse. Food appeared on the Nash table courtesy of Mr Gee and his grocery store, which gave credit, the bill to be settled each Friday. Brenda was sent begging round the neighbourhood for her mother's cigarettes. Sometimes when funds gave out the family shared a hearty stew of leftovers with the Butlers over the road. The pawn shop produced £2 10s weekly in return for Mr Nash's suit, redeemed on pay-day, to be popped again on Monday. Clothing could be paid for by a kind of hire purchase scheme: £20 worth at five shillings a week, an easy way to run up unpayable debt. Often when the rent collector came, the family skulked in the pantry or hid under the stairs, 'hardly daring to breathe lest he should suspect our presence . . .', until they heard his receding steps.

> Dad never knew, or cared, about our money worries. He simply handed over the housekeeping money on Friday and believed that his duty was done. He then repaired to the pub, leaving us with the perennial headache of just who to pay before the money was quite used up. It was always a question of robbing Peter to pay Paul . . .
>
> My father remained oblivious . . .

*

When it comes to tackling the contrariness of real life, social engineering and planning fell miles short. Mr Nash worked hard, did what he saw to be his duty, and opted out. But Mrs Nash, too, failed to conform to expectations on every front. She was wasteful, scatterbrained, incompetent, argumentative. When it came to 'cooking and making his money go as far as possible', she was an abject failure. The marital home objectified the flimsiness of their relationship. 'In a very real sense,' Brenda Nash would later write, 'Westcott Road was to be the catalyst that caused the irrevocable unravelling of the family.'

In Aunt Doll's cramped semi, jammed in at close quarters with their hellish relatives, Mom and Dad had stood shoulder-to-shoulder against adversity. But once they had a home of their own, forced into intimacy with each other, it was impossible to ignore the dire incompatibility on which their terrible relationship was founded. As the cement of their long-ago attraction crumbled, the very house seemed to participate in the destruction of the Nash marriage. And yet Dad spent little time under its roof. He would return from work only to eat his dinner, before repairing to the local. He took no responsibility for the children. From Monday to Friday the volcano of resentment rumbled away. Then at weekends it erupted 'into violence of nightmare proportions . . .' Dad would return late from the pub, insisting on his conjugal rights. There was no pleasure for Mrs Nash in the loveless mauling which ensued, but she wasn't the type to lie passively looking at the cracks in the ceiling. She let rip. Brenda and her sisters cowered, too frightened to cry out, listening to the shrieks, the sound of breakages, and 'other, more unmentionable and sinister noises'.

Ten years after the move to Westcott Road, Mrs Nash decided she'd had enough. She packed her bags, abandoned her children, and walked out of her suburban front door for the last time.

7. What's My Line?

Clocking On

In 1954 Rose Hendon left her school in the dusty urban wastes of North Kensington. She was fifteen, and she was expected to contribute to the family budget.

> My first job was with McVities Biscuits. As they came down the belts you had to pick out the broken packets. It gave me a headache, so I walked out and came home. My mum said, 'You don't walk out of your job!' So she took me all the way back!
>
> Next one after McVities was Heinz's. And it was the same there, if the labels on the cans were torn you'd have to pull them out, you know?
>
> From there I went to a chewing gum factory. It was piecework. The more of them you wrapped the more money you got. Then I went to Askew and made cornets for ice creams, and from there I went to the drug house, where they made tablets. And after that I went to a record factory. And when I had a bit of overtime I worked in a potato crisp factory.
>
> I was never out of work.

In 1955, unemployment in this country was the lowest it had been for forty years, and large numbers of young women like Rose Hendon were steadily adding to the labour force. In 1951, nearly 85 per cent of women aged between fourteen and twenty-four were working. And in the decade between 1951 and 1961, the percentage of women in employment rose from 35 per cent to 37.5 per cent, while in the same period the number of part-time workers rose from 779,000 to 1,851,000, a 58 per cent increase. But a glance down the columns of figures gives a topsy-turvy picture. The top professions were dominated by men, with women under 10 per cent; while high proportions of women were working in jobs which required their subservience to a male majority:

	Per cent
Higher professionals	8.3
Clerks	60.2
Shop assistants	51.6
Semi-skilled manual workers	38.1
Unskilled manual workers	20.3

No great mystery there, given their education. Remember that 98.8 per cent of female school leavers had no prospect of university. Their expectations, as described by Brenda Nash, were directed towards pairing off with a boyfriend, steady courting, and early marriage:

> Girls like my sisters went to a secondary modern school and left at fifteen. Then they worked for a couple of years in a shop or a factory, and then they'd marry. And working-class girls had to be married.
>
> The thing was that no girls could earn enough money to keep themselves because they worked in low-paid employment, and they certainly couldn't keep any children on that kind of pay. So if somebody asked you to get married, you said yes. Like Mrs Butler across our road: she married at nineteen to the first man who asked her because she thought she was on the shelf, and her life turned out to be miserable. So many of the men were completely boorish. Why would anyone want to marry them? But they had to.
>
> The idea that working-class people wanted education is wrong. They did not want education. School was alien. It was a

place where you were shoved until you could leave and do something else.

'Something else' might have been any of the low-skilled factory jobs mentioned by Rose Hendon above. Rose's experience is mirrored in interviews carried out by the social researcher Pearl Jephcott, who set out in the early 1950s to build up a picture of young people's everyday lives. Eileen, Gladys, Elsie and a range of other working-class teenagers in London and Nottingham talked to Jephcott's researchers about money, boyfriends and work. A few years later the left-leaning social scientist Mark Abrams conducted a survey of British teenagers and their spending habits. The composite young working woman that emerges from these two reports is one whose life revolved around entertainments and boys. Jobs – easy to get and easy to leave – were a means to an end, no more, no less. The girls' attitude was lackadaisical: they were unambitious, unwilling to progress in their work, and lacked pride in it. With an average forty-four-hour week, a high proportion of each day might be spent 'putting silver paper on cardboard', packing chocolates or aspirins, folding cartons or magnetising cycle hubs; others might be semi-skilled machinists, over-lockers or cutters, but few of them were trained. There was nothing much to learn. Work was often local, and these adolescents went home for their midday meal. In her teens Margaret Forster had a holiday job in a Carlisle laundry. Her description of it makes a compelling case for jacking in this kind of work at the earliest opportunity: the working environment was horrible, deafeningly noisy, with a suffocating stench of disinfectant. Margaret was put to sorting the dirty clothes:

> I could hardly bear to lift some of the filthier items. My fingers plucked at blood-stained knickers disdainfully . . .

The laundry's toilets were swimming in foul scum and overflowing with soiled sanitary towels; the job was cold, repulsive and ill-paid. Margaret providently saved what she could for her going-to-university fund. But the general view was that such employees were doomed, at seventeen, to remain in this kind of work for the foreseeable future. In other words, until they got married.

Meanwhile, that goal dominated their out-of-work behaviour. As Mark Abrams commented:

> Teenagers more than any other section of the community are looking for goods and services which are highly charged emotionally.

They spent what they could afford on clothes, on romantic magazines like *Mirabelle* or *Valentine* ('Brings you Love Stories in Pictures . . .'), on cafés and dance halls. But with earnings between £2 5s and £5 – more for piece work – these girls would hand most of their pay packet to their mothers, who took responsibility for food, fares and most other essentials and non-essentials.

The remainder was pocket money. Much of it went on sweets and cigarettes. Everybody smoked, men and women alike, their chosen brands loaded with glamorous associations. A woman smoking Kensitas would be ribbed mercilessly for her posh aspirations: 'What favours you doin' for the boss?' while cheap Woodbines were for the old. Their appearance was of absorbing interest. Of Abrams's sample, 96 per cent used cosmetics, above all face powder and lipstick: 'Pink Passion' from Woolworths. His survey also showed that 40 per cent used nail varnish, 35 per cent mascara, and 25 per cent eye shadow. 'Leisure to [Eileen] means spending money, and work earning it.' Gladys went to the pictures three times a week and always went roller-skating on a Saturday night. This was a high figure – but even so 60 per cent of teenagers went to the cinema once a week.

Many teenagers coupled up at the age of thirteen or fourteen.

Just a few years later they would be planning to 'get engaged at Christmas', and then saving for their wedding. Grand 'white' weddings were the fashion now, 'with all the trimmings'. One survey claimed that 58 per cent of skilled workers, and 45 per cent of unskilled workers, were married 'in the grand manner'. Midwife Jennifer Worth describes one ostentatious East End wedding at which the guests were ferried 100 yards in a fleet of eighteen Rolls-Royces, and plied with slices of cake from a seven-tier extravaganza complete with mini bride and groom. The Liverpool shop assistant Joyce Kearney had a church wedding at St Benedict's, followed by a 'do'. The neighbours in her Everton community were both guests and providers, bringing in quantities of food and casks of beer, before settling in for a lengthy feast. Once they'd eaten, the men all exited en masse to go to the football match; but returned for more beer once it was over. Though the happy couple were booked on to the coach leaving that night for a caravan honeymoon in Wales, the do looked like it had a lot more life in it:

> It was going down a bomb – dancing, food, drink . . . running out of bottled beer so the men had to get crates from the pub . . .

– so Joyce and her husband missed the bus and decided to stay. Bedtime approached. Seeing as the plan was to live with Joyce's parents anyway, the newlyweds had their own room in the attic, but here they found the bed littered with unconscious bodies; the wedding night was spent with one on the settee, the other on the chair. The following morning they came downstairs to find the do still going on.

> It went on all day Sunday. And again we didn't want to go. And we finished up leaving on a coach on the Monday for our honeymoon.

★

Though they might return to wage-earning at a later stage in their lives (Joyce Kearney did), the workplace, for most young women like her, represented only a brief interlude between school and marriage. According to Pearl Jephcott, those who raised their sights beyond the production line or conveyor belt and imagined themselves into a 'career' were in a tiny minority. 'Their friends regarded them as odd fish . . .'

In 1957 Valerie Gisborn gave in her notice to the knitwear factory where she worked in Leicester. Valerie was now twenty-two, reserved, timid, and young-looking for her age. In the eight years that she had worked in the garment trade her wage had risen from £1 5s a week, to a little over £5; but though this was reasonably good money, satisfaction continued to elude her. 'I knew I was capable of better things . . . But what . . . ?'

Valerie had been accepted as a police recruit. Reactions among her colleagues were mixed. She was given the 'odd fish' treatment, and subjected to a great deal of ribbing. 'Where did *you* get the idea you could be a police officer?' said one of the older women on the production line. 'You're only a factory girl.' Few believed that such a little mouse could direct traffic or catch criminals. ' "I'll show them," I thought.'

For at last, one Saturday afternoon in October 1957, the answer had come to her. Each weekend, Valerie helped her mother by taking the bus into Leicester to shop for vegetables in the central market. Bearing her basket-load of carrots and onions, she was caught that day by a downpour near the historic Clock Tower, and dived for shelter under the overhang of a convenient shop doorway. There, entranced, she found herself sharing the small dry space with a woman who seemed to personify her yearnings. Cool, confident, impeccable and efficient, her neat navy-blue uniform, with its buttoned and belted jacket, peaked cap and collar and tie gave this female an unchallengeable air of authority. From time to time as she stood there shoppers or traders would accost her with questions or demands; polite and assured, she gave them information or advice and sent them on their way.

I was lost in admiration.

A policewoman was a rare sight on the streets of Leicester, and the small band of female officers I had seen were very much respected.

I began to wonder if I could do such a job.

In a kind of trance, Valerie carried the vegetables home. That afternoon she thought and thought about whether she could make the leap. Once lodged in her mind, the idea refused to detach. Secretly, her mind was made up to apply for the police force.

A week later she called at her local station to inquire about the application process. At her initial interview a woman sergeant did her best to deter her with alarming stories of anti-social hours, shift work and the sordid underworld of crime. Next came the examination – 'my brain had gone to sleep during those eight years . . . I struggled through, praying I was giving the right answers . . .' – followed by a surprisingly cursory medical. The time had come to tell her family, for before she could be accepted, they too would have to be vetted. To her great relief, they supported her decision.

But Mrs Gisborn was flabbergasted a few days later to receive a visitation from a high-up female police officer, making searching enquiries about her daughter's personal life. Did she have a boyfriend? Was she engaged? Was she involved with, or had she recently broken up with any man? 'Mother was shocked and worried sick.' What on earth had been going on? Maybe her daughter had been up to something behind her back? But no, it emerged that assurances were needed that female recruits were not looking to join the police force for the purpose of husband-hunting. As

Valerie was twenty-three and unmarried, it appeared that she might be 'man mad', flighty, or 'looking for a good time . . .' The officer was gradually convinced that Valerie's motives were solely to pursue a career.

Once this matter had been cleared up, she was invited back to the police station, and told she had been accepted.

> I did not regret for one moment the step I was taking . . . I felt free. To begin a new life away from the humdrum boring days in the factory, a chance to be away from home for the first time in my life and be independent, to accept responsibilities and achieve something with my life gave me a great feeling of satisfaction.
>
> I felt like a pioneer. It was still in the early days for women to be accepted into male dominated professions, and I knew there would be many prejudices to overcome.

Once her notice had expired, Valerie wiped away a tear, waved goodbye to her family; then, equipped with all the necessities for three months away, and kitted out in regulation navy-blue, she climbed into the shabby van that was to transport her sixty miles away, to the police training school in Staffordshire, and a new life.

*

As a teenager, Valerie Gisborn had accepted factory work because it seemed like the only available occupation and she could see no alternative. Joyce Kearney was one of the few who outfaced the peer pressure to enter a factory in the first place. Most of Joyce's friends in the Everton area of Liverpool simply signed up to work at Barker & Dobson's sweet factory, or Ogden's tobacco factory.

> But I didn't want that. And I loved shops – shops and smells and that. So I went down town, and I went to the Bon.

Lewis's Bon Marché was a Liverpool icon, housed, since 1951, in a magnificent new five-storey building, with four passenger lifts. Joyce knew that shop work differed from factory work in requiring a certain level of polish and manners. Punctuality was all-important. And appearance mattered; you had to be tidy, in skirt and blouse, un-made-up, hair neat and fingernails clean. Beyond that, she had no idea what to expect, and didn't know where she would end up working.

> The Bon in those days was so posh. They had a commissionaire on the door. Well, I'd always loved maths – so they said, all right, you can start in the tube room.

Two heavy doors opened on to the lugubrious underground cavern where Joyce was now required to spend her working day. Lewis's new building had a sophisticated built-in pneumatic tube system to deal with payments, nearly all of which were in cash. Instead of tills, the assistants in their various departments placed each payment, along with the paper bill, into a small brass canister and screwed the lid on. Then the canister was loaded into a tube, to be vacuum-sucked all the way down to the basement. Windowless, dark and noisy, this basement room was like a scene from Hell. Here Joyce and a secret army of other women (the sole man was a – largely absent – supervisor) sat all day before a monstrous machine which vomited out the innumerable clanking canisters arriving from every department in the building through row upon row of metal spouts, and deposited them in compartments in front of the operators. Their job was then to unscrew each one, take out the money and the bill, check it, put the change back in, lift the flap and push it back up the corresponding chute to be vacuum-sucked all the way back up to the Menswear department – or wherever.

The noise was deafening, and Joyce and her co-workers had

to move fast to ensure that their fingers didn't get trapped by the descending flaps.

> Of course you were sometimes too quick and you sent it to the wrong department and somebody got it upstairs and had to throw it down again, and it would do the full circle again . . .

On twenty-one shillings a week (with seven-and-sixpence deducted for lunch) she stuck it out for little over a month before decamping to a rival store where tube technology was being phased out. This store, Owen Owens, was less posh than the Bon. There were no fancy commissionaires on the door, instead their market was solid working class, market traders, on-shore seamen, and vast hordes of Welsh customers, who travelled up from North Wales every Thursday to do their shopping in the Liverpool metropolis.

Here, to her joy, Joyce was put on junior staff training in the baby linen department, starting on twenty-five shillings a week, no deductions. Menial as it was, she learnt on the job; polishing the glass counters, running errands for the buyer, writing out bills, learning how to wrap awkwardly shaped parcels with string and brown paper, looking after little children and taking toddlers to the toilet. In time she was entrusted with creating product displays. These had to be strictly symmetrical, with a focal point.

> It was a fabulous training . . .

Joyce quickly grew to appreciate not only the qualities of the merchandise, but also the interaction with customers:

> They sold these little double-breasted coats in velour and that, with velvet collars and muffs and hats, you know, like the Royal Family have.
>
> And they had these drums for the children to stand on – so sometimes we'd be asked to dress the children.

The staff themselves were expected to wear an unvarying uniform. Black was de rigueur: shoes and dress. During the 1950s the code gradually relaxed and a white collar was permitted. Of vital importance was how to treat the customers:

> They were always Sir and Madam – without exception. And they were *always* right, regardless of what happened, one hundred per cent.

At the age of seventeen, after a year in baby linen, Joyce graduated to the corsetry department.

> I trained as a corsetière/fitter. There were six members of staff on the corsetry department, four on corsets and two on bras – and we'd get the fish ladies from the market and they'd come in saying, 'Oh I want a good corset luv, those boxes are getting heavy!' And they'd want real lace-up corsets – but even they expected to be called Madam – and we'd be saying 'Yes Madam, no Madam.' And they'd say 'I'm sorry luv, I stink, I've been lifting fish boxes all day.'

It was a happy life in corsetry. Many customers arrived fearful and vulnerable, reliant on the discretion and tolerance of Joyce and her fellow fitters. The human rewards of treating them tactfully were great, on both sides. A snooty mum might arrive with her twelve-year-old to be fitted for her first bra. Even if Joyce could see she didn't need one, it was her job to allay the child's embarrassment while placating the demanding mother. Then there was the memorable occasion when the ballet came to town, and two of its principal male dancers arrived on Joyce's floor looking for some way to deal with the unsightly visible bulges under their tights:

> We sold them panty girdles you know . . . I don't know what damage it did!

Nuns were treated with special respect in this department. Owing to an unspoken reservation regarding the other two corsetry assistants, one of whom was a Northern Irish Protestant and the other a Northern Irish Catholic, it always fell to Joyce to accompany the nuns into the fitting rooms. Joyce modestly tweaked bra straps and adjusted cups for each of the holy sisters in turn, while the Sister Superior would sit patiently in the adjoining fitting room awaiting hers.

> Working in shops – there's so many people you come into contact with. It broadens your horizons and you learn so much . . .

Joyce's charity and broadmindedness were particularly appreciated by certain nice Liverpool businessmen who liked to visit the ladies' underwear department and make their purchases incognito. These gentlemen, regular customers who were well known to Joyce and the girls, always took the precaution of ringing up beforehand to check whether the department was likely to be busy. If it was, they'd call back half an hour later and drop by when it was quiet. Then their requirements were attended to with the utmost prudence and discretion.

> We knew who they were and we could sell them what was suitable for them – in other words, something not too ridiculous. It didn't bother us at all. We had so many nice men that used to come in.
>
> After all, they were customers – and the customer is always right.

★

Joyce Kearney worked for Owen Owens for nearly ten years. By 1959 she was promoted to assistant department manager and only left, eventually, because she had the opportunity to realise an ambition, and become a buyer for Littlewood's. Unusually, she continued in this job after her marriage in 1960, until the birth of her second child.

More typical was the experience of north Londoner Patricia Saville, whose post-school, pre-marriage years – 1948 to 1955 – were spent as an employee of the Central Telegraph Office. This was the clearing-house for national and international telegrams. Today, communications have been so transformed that it is hard to imagine how labour-intensive it was in the 1950s to send information, greetings or news at high speed. From a birthday wish to an urgent embassy dispatch, telegrams had to be hand-written or dictated over the telephone, then rendered into Morse code. At the other end, teletypewriters decoded them, typed them on to ticker-tape, the strips of which were then glued on to a blank form for delivery. They were charged by the word (giving telegraphic prose a uniquely abbreviated and almost poetic style) and mainly transported to their final destination via bicycle or motorbike, by perky young men in peaked caps.

In Patricia's eyes, the job carried status. She secured it at the age of fourteen having scraped through her school certificate and gained a good headmaster's report. The girls were the indoor equivalent of the delivery boys, taking telegrams around the building to be sent to their destinations. For two years she ran around the huge, maze-like CTO headquarters, which stood proudly a short step from the majestic landmark of St Paul's Cathedral. They issued her with regulation green overalls ('wrapover granny ones that did absolutely nothing for one's image . . .'), and she was paid £1 a week. But there was a promotional ladder. At sixteen, Patricia could choose to become either a telephonist or a telegraphist. She chose the latter, and attended an intensive three-month course to learn all aspects of telegraphy.

We were not allowed to pass out of the school until we could send at least 100 telegrams in an hour with a maximum of three mistakes . . . We also had to be able to take telegrams over the phone direct from the public; this could be tricky as any unknown or strange words had to be spelt out phonetically and repeated letter for letter. This could be quite difficult, especially when dealing with foreign customers.

Transferred to a district office at Staples Corner on the North Circular, Patricia joined a staff of 200, working intensive shifts from 8 a.m. to 7 p.m. The office had nationwide links; Patricia and the other telegraphists were bombarded with messages.

No mention of 'Repetitive Strain Injury' in those days. The worst job was the phones; members of the public and the Press could ring in direct with their telegrams. I had one once that was two thousand words long. The poor old ears would be burning after a two hour stint on them, with the big heavy headsets we had to use then.

But this was my early working life, and I loved it . . .

Fully qualified, she was posted to a variety of sub-offices, and at various points on her shift was given authority over the messenger boys. Inevitably, there was a sexual frisson around the teleprinter consoles, with plenty of saucy teenage banter and backchat. One reason why Patricia loved her work was that – in contrast to the largely feminine world of the corsetry department – fraternisation with the messenger boys was half the fun. 'It was forbidden – but this didn't stop us of course . . .' She had caught sight of Roy while still on probation at the CTO. 'I fancied him like mad . . .' After she was sent up to north London, Roy reappeared, and overwhelmed her by confessing that he found her Titian hair and freckles irresistible.

Gradually we all seemed to pair off. The Post Office was a real mating ground. There always seemed to be a collection for someone who was getting married . . .

And that was the end of Patricia's seven-year spell with the Post Office. After a brief courtship – much of it spent careering helmetless around the North Circular on Roy's 250cc motorbike – they married in August 1955. And as Patricia's family expanded (she would have four babies) she, like thousands of other new mums, jettisoned any thought of a career for the duration.

A Little Extra

> However helpful the extra money may be, however successful her career, I am always against married women working. There cannot really be any compromise in the dispute of home versus work where a wife is concerned. And the best women and the happy wives find it a sweet sacrifice to yield up their economic independence.

Barbara Cartland – writing, above, in *Marriage for Moderns* (1955) – was far from being the only stern advocate of staying at home. During the war, few people questioned whether it was reasonable to expect women conscripts to keep up with the chores while making barrage balloons, high explosives or sewing service uniforms. The men were away at the war. Who else was going to get meals on the table, if not the womenfolk? Ten years after its end, the fundamental assumption that their role was primarily a domestic one remained largely unchallenged, but the 1950s would see a surge in married women's employment, and a corresponding crescendo in the home-versus-work debate. Since then the clamour has barely died down.

Between 1951 and 1961, the proportion of 20–30-year-old married women in work rose from under 25 per cent to nearly 30 per cent. The number of married 35–45-year-olds in work rose during the same period from 25 per cent to 36 per cent.

Despite the assumption enshrined in Beveridge's Welfare State, that wives should remain, unpaid, at home, more and more married women across the age spectrum were deserting their posts at the kitchen sink in favour of days spent in front of a conveyor belt, a shop counter, or a typewriter.

A woman who might have invested a year of her life in gaining secretarial skills, shorthand and typing, was less likely to throw away her hard-earned qualifications after marriage. Margery Hurst, founder of the Brook Street Bureau, was herself a committed working wife; she didn't distinguish between the single and married women who in the 1950s flocked to her branches hoping for secretarial placements. Hurst's business expanded rapidly at this time, on the back of a competitive market for temporary office workers. Looking for top-quality staff, she could take her pick from women who had excellent typing speeds and were equally willing to buy socks for the boss, all for £4 and ten shillings a week (£100 today).

Though wages were far from equal (the average female wage was 59 per cent of the average man's wage), a measure of spending power could give wives like Eileen Mooney her picture-perfect pram, or Winifred Foley her longed-for purple carpet. It felt good and boosted the ego to save and buy things for oneself. However, the sociologist Ferdynand Zweig stressed that real economic need did not top the list of motives for married women to work outside the home. 'Many women go out to work rather under the emotional pressure of loneliness than under the economic pressure of low wages ...' he wrote, an assertion borne out by the working Lancashire mums from whose interviews he quoted:

I come out because I get bored at home, not because of money.

The work outside keeps you in touch with the world and makes you feel younger.

When the boy went to school, life became unbearable within four walls.

You don't get so morbid and you feel younger. When my husband and I have a bit of an argument, I can say to him, 'You don't keep me.'

Pay-packet power was playing its part in eroding male authority. But as their numbers rose, so did the concerns that such women were deserting their posts. Shift work meant dereliction of duty on other fronts. What would become of the children of dual-earner families, whose mothers weren't at home to get them properly fed, clean, tidy and ready for school? 'If the mother is not at home when the child returns from school, he often has to stay out in the streets until she returns, and this may lead to undesirable conduct . . .' lamented Mary Macaulay in *The Art of Marriage* (1952).

Her fears echoed those of the psychiatrist and mental health consultant John Bowlby, whose influential writings on childhood trauma were to have a double-edged effect. Bowlby was a caring and humane man, who argued strongly against disrupting the intimacy of a child with its mother, especially during the early years. The stakes were high, as he described them, for it was only through the devoted provision of constant attention, 'night and day, seven days a week and 365 days in the year' that one might reap the reward of seeing one's child grow to mature independence.

Bowlby's 'attachment theory' views were to change practices in hospitals and institutions. But the middle classes leapt on his arguments with enthusiasm. His book *Child Care and the Growth of Love* (though it was a study of institutionalised children) gave a boost to the stay-at-home argument. The concept of 'maternal deprivation' was a decider for many women. Perfect mothers were supposed to stay put in their ideal homes.

Bowlby's theories were harnessed to demonstrate that children with absentee or working mums grew up to become juvenile delinquents, neurotics, and emotional cripples. What kind of choice did that leave them with?

Three years into her marriage with Michael Bakewell, Joan Bakewell was working as an advertising copywriter for McCann Erickson. But the job was short-lived. Once a baby was on the way, any thoughts she might have had of pursuing a career were shelved. Motherhood was a serious commitment – even if the casual approach to pre-natal health seems shocking today. Despite drinking whatever alcohol she felt like, and smoking forty cigarettes a day throughout two pregnancies, Joan did not for a minute contemplate working once she was a mum.

> My generation was beginning to take parenting seriously to a degree that hadn't happened before. As well we might. There was no maternity leave from jobs: no jobs were held open. You simply left employment. There was no maternity pay: you stopped earning.

The Bowlby effect was part of this. Educated women like Joan Bakewell were well versed in his Freudian theories:

> We applied his ideas to ourselves, seeing it as our duty to stay close to our babies' development . . . It became central to our lives and brooked no argument about careers and part-time work.

As Mary Stott (woman's editor, from 1957, of the *Manchester Guardian*) drily commented in her memoirs, 'the name Bowlby became synonymous . . . with guilt feelings about the risk to children of deprivation of constant maternal care'. Stott was clear, however, that the guilt was mainly experienced in middle-class circles. Educated women like Joan Bakewell were living out the dilemma described by Judith Hubback in *Wives Who Went to College*: changing nappies and wheeling prams while allowing their minds to stagnate, for fear of the consequences to their children. Meanwhile the mass of women gladly sought jobs that would bring in a little extra – maybe even enough to pay for a washing machine, a vacuum cleaner, or a holiday. Their children, parked with aunties or grannies (for most day-nursery provision had been closed down since the war), were, they believed, the happier for it.

Does this to some extent explain the extraordinarily narrow range of jobs on offer to women at that time? Lesser-educated women were resigned to the fact that they could not compete in the professional sphere, banking or industry. Meanwhile, many of those educated women who might have pushed for better nursery provision, or greater employment opportunities for their sex, had put themselves out of the running, sacrificing their economic independence along with any dreams of self-fulfilment, and meekly donning their aprons in the noble cause of their children's sanity and well-being. Far too many women like this lacked any sense of entitlement – let alone the choice – to stand alongside men in the greater world, society or the workplace.

*

When economic demands became pressing, the options were indeed limited. Lorna Rainbow married her American husband Bob Arnold in 1949. She gave up her job at the Family Planning Association, and soon had two babies. Much of the time she led a solitary life with the children. Those early days were spent 'baking, cooking and taking the boys to the park'. The pioneering diplomat now found herself in an enclosed world, wheeling a pram, immobilised by her shaky health and the burdens of motherhood. That summer Lorna was told by her doctors that a hysterectomy would be necessary. Her stalwart Auntie Phyll moved in to care for the boys, and the operation was carried out

in hospital at Northwood. But soon after she fell seriously ill
with an infection; it was touch and go, and weeks passed before
she was well enough to return home, frail and battered. Back in
Kilburn, Bob seemed more troubled than ever.

> I remember him coming back from a recording trip. We were in
> the sitting room, and the children were upstairs asleep in bed,
> and he kept on and on saying, 'I don't want to go, but I have to,
> there's no way I can stay.' He was in a terrible state of distress;
> he was more or less talking to himself . . .

Soon after, the bombshell dropped:

> One day, when Bob was away on what I thought was a business
> trip, I received a letter from him, saying he was on a ship on his
> way back to America. It was a very sad letter, but a loving one.
> He told me he could not cope with life in England any more.
>
> Bob had longed for a home and family, but his homosexu-
> ality pulled him in a different direction. It was not, as he had
> hoped, a passing phase, but a part of his identity.

Would Bob Arnold have abandoned his wife and family if he
had thought that Lorna couldn't cope on her own? He had
married a woman of extraordinary capacities: clever, versatile,
attractive. But Bob cracked under the strain of reconciling his
sexuality with his role as husband and provider. Though views
were slowly starting to shift in more enlightened quarters,
homosexuality remained a criminal offence. Gay men were har-
ried mercilessly by the Vice squads. Prosecutions and the public
stigmatising of homosexuals peaked in 1953. Bob would have
been justified in feeling frightened at this time, and desperate to
flee from his 'false' life. But from now on, Lorna would have
to demonstrate that as a woman she could cope, providing for
herself and the two boys. Becoming a single parent couldn't
have come at a worse time; her children were tiny, she was in

poor health, she had no income. Bob Arnold had broken his side
of the marital bargain.

> For all practical purposes, he was gone, leaving me a single par-
> ent, wholly responsible for my family, and without any income.
> I would have to get a job.

Lorna was highly qualified. But for three years now she had
done little but cook, shop and baby-mind. Faithful Auntie Phyll
would help to look after the boys, but what could Lorna do that
would feed her family without carrying her far from home?
Quarter of a mile from her front door in north-west London
stood a biscuit factory.

> There was a notice on the gate saying HANDS WANTED, so I
> went in. The receptionist was a pleasant woman, polite but
> suspicious.
>
> 'Are you a journalist?' she asked me.
>
> 'I need a job,' I replied, 'close to home. And I need it now. I
> may not stay very long.'
>
> 'Not many do,' she replied, and I was in.

For the next two months, Lorna worked on the packing line:

> The arrangement was, you stood on the side of a long conveyor
> belt, with the biscuits tumbling down in masses, and everybody
> had one of those big square biscuit tins in front of them. Then,
> as the conveyor belt went round, you picked them up as fast as
> possible. You were told how to arrange them – and you fitted in
> as many as you could. And then your tin moved on.
>
> Some of the girls who'd been there a long time were marvel-
> lous – they were like conjurors, you know – you saw their hands
> flying around!
>
> I had to concentrate *so* hard to get these biscuits in their boxes,
> and it was all so novel, that I didn't have time to feel either bored
> or mindless or anything. It was just a *huge* challenge.

During her time at the biscuit factory, Lorna's dexterity improved, and her pay rates with it. She also enjoyed the company of her co-workers, when they got the chance to chat at tea breaks. The factory was mainly staffed by young married women who were there to earn enough money for a little car, or a three-piece suite. One woman was saving to buy a house; she and her husband had come over from Ireland, having left their young children with her grandmother, and between them the couple held down four jobs.

> My biscuit job really did open my eyes, and I didn't feel it was time wasted.

Lorna Arnold's inquisitive, adaptable nature would stand her in good stead in years to come. But at this point in her long life, her priority was survival. The biscuit factory helped her get food – including broken biscuits – on the table for her little boys. Over the next five years Lorna had an assortment of jobs – manual, clerical and secretarial – all of which failed to stretch her enthusiasm, interest, intellect, or professional abilities. Lorna could feed her family. But psychically she felt directionless and adrift.

> There were times when I felt very alone.

You Might Be a Secretary

At this time, there was a substantial readership of career novels for girls.* Under the cover of fiction, these publications contained much sound advice about qualifications, training and hints

---

* In her authoritative *Gender, Work and Education in Britain in the 1950s* (2005), Stephanie Spencer fascinatingly probes the brief flourishing of the Career Novels, discussing their authors, their readership and the phenomenon of their publication, and convincingly demonstrating their value as social history source material.

about the types of personality which might be appropriate for particular jobs.

Nursing – but not doctoring – features in Noel Streatfeild's round-up of careers for girls, as a job that drew on 'feminine', subsidiary qualities, but also offered intimate titillations.

Few of the careers discussed strayed from the 'feminine' orthodoxy. One might read of Sheila who wanted to become a dental assistant but not a dentist; of Ann who would become an air hostess but not a pilot. There was a heavy bias in favour of modelling, hairdressing, nursing, cooking, secretarial work and teaching. *Margaret Becomes a Doctor* (1957) and *Anne in Electronics* (1960) stand out for their rarity.

None of the mothers in the career stories worked, but though their daughters would ultimately marry, their choice of career was largely presented as having lifelong value. Books like *Social Work for Jill* (1954) and *Joanna in Advertising* (1958) were directed at the first generation of girls for whom employment was taken for granted. Jill, the aspirant social worker who loves small children, experiences casework and group work in a Welfare Office, while Joanna works her way up to become an advertising copywriter via retail and the publicity department of a big store. However, Jill's caring qualities don't go unnoticed by her friend Bill. In the final chapter, when she's all set to opt for casework, Bill takes her out to a dinner dance, tells her how stunning she looks, and gently suggests that they have a future together in which *he* will take care of *her* . . . Similarly, Joanna's commitment to the Dawnmist Stockings and Lanaire Cosmetics accounts is rewarded in the final pages when her boss promotes her to a post where she will be thrown into contact with a devoted boyfriend:

> 'We're not married, you know,' she laughed.
> 'You will be.'
> 'But he hasn't asked me!'
> 'He will.'

The implication in nearly all of the books is that work was never wasted, but that a walk up the aisle was the more desirable outcome for any young woman.

As in so many respects, the dominant voices of society were conflicted when it came to women in the workplace. After the war, it had become hard to deny that women had the capacity to take on 'male' jobs. But now those who did so ran the risk of being made fun of, regarded as freaks. Pathé's Cinemagazine producers were always on the look-out for anomalies like the 'three little girls' employed at a service station in Wembley to fill

tanks and wipe windscreens, thereby adding 'a touch of feminine glamour' to a predominantly masculine business. In 1953
Pathé took a film crew to record sixty-six-year-old Madge Tart
'manning' the Dungeness lifeboat; women like her didn't go on
board, but helped pull the launch ropes; and in 1954 cameras followed Southampton housewife Violet Robinson, who had
started a chimney-sweeping business 'as a cure for nerves'.
Meanwhile Mrs Smith and Mrs Donovan from Enfield – next-
door neighbours who shared a crumbling wall – had their
moment of glory being filmed for a Cinemagazine: 'Yes, the
two housewives find time in between their normal chores to
tackle the man-sized job of bricklaying! And the only difference
between mixing pastry and mixing cement is that you need a
heavier touch!' The jovial tone masked a dismissiveness – or
maybe it was fear? – of women trespassing on male territory.
How hilarious to watch a housewife sweeping a chimney or
carrying a load of bricks on to a building site! With growing
numbers of women employed in engineering, manufacture,
technological and chemical industries, the printing and clothing
trades, laughter helped to neutralise the threat that they presented.

This was the reality. And as we know, the walls built by men,
to keep the weaker sex out of politics, the Civil Service, journalism and the arts, sport, science, medicine, the law and
academe were themselves collapsing. In the post-war world,
there was little – except a residual belief in her own incapacity
– to stop a young woman from training to become an architect,
a biologist or a lawyer. The opportunities were there. But, in
fear of a deluge, traditionalists shored up the defences with
restrictions and propaganda. The Women's Engineering Society
opened its doors wide to girls – but the girls themselves felt it
was not their world: '[they] thought that in engineering their
fingernails would be broken, their stockings would be laddered,

their hair would be covered in grease and their faces would be black with smuts'. Across the board, women at this time were paid an average 59 per cent of a man's wage for the same job. The 'glass ceiling' overhung women at a lamentably low level, with career obstacles placed in front of women in business, administration, the Church and universities.

In *The Art of Being a Woman* (1951) Amabel Williams-Ellis described the obstacles an ambitious girl might encounter on her journey to seek her fortune, and put her finger on the problem. It was passive aggression:

> The world will not believe the poor girl for a moment when she modestly hopes that she might one day have something to contribute to human knowledge or human achievement. She will not, today, actually be told, as was the great Marie Curie (when as a child she wanted to learn chemistry), that her name has been put down for the cookery class. No! She will be allowed to train. The big dose of discouragement will be given her a little later, when some prize in science or the arts, some really influential post in administration or in business, seems nearly within her reach . . .
>
> At every stage, in trifles and in big things, [she will] find that her ways are made harder, for the odd reason (so it is said) that she belongs to the weaker sex.
>
> We are at last equal before the law, and equal as citizens. But the girl is never, in the way of pay, promotion, or public consideration, given the same chance as her brother.

Few young women were likely to find encouragement to compete for the same jobs as their brothers. The City? Business? A captain of industry? The Bar? A pilot, soldier, engine driver, mechanic, engineer? None of the above featured in the career novels, or in Noel Streatfeild's line-up of careers in her 1950 advice book for girls, *The Years of Grace*.

> The best career for every woman is, of course, taking care of her
> husband and home . . .

wrote Streatfeild – wistfully, perhaps, having never married
herself. But she had been lucky. Having chosen to train for the
stage, she switched mid-stream to become a children's writer.
The success of *Ballet Shoes* (1936), which would nurture many a
young girl's dreams of stardom à la Margot Fonteyn, would
eliminate all money worries for the rest of her life. Those thes-
pian and bookish experiences probably influenced the distinctly
feminine slant of her collected careers wisdom:

- Ballet as a Career
- Making Music
- Careers in Films
- Who'd Be a School-Marm?
- 'On His Majesty's Service'
- You Might Be a Secretary
- Shop-Keeping
- Let's Take a Look at Nursing
- Cecilia Colledge – Skating Star

And even within those confines the discouragement persisted.
With at most five ballet companies in Europe the would-be
ballerina must not expect to be employed. Women trying for
the film industry must assume that camera work and art direction
were largely the preserve of men. The achievements of film
director Muriel Box and producer Betty Box were the excep-
tion not the rule; they still are. The Civil Service was freely
open to women – but they should anticipate being vastly outnumbered by men. As for the prospect of becoming a skating
star like Cecilia Colledge, few young girls could hope to have
the privileges and advantages that she had grown up with: a
well-to-do father who paid for his daughter's extra-curricular

interests, winter sports holidays, club memberships and top tuition under a Swiss coach.

'You Might Be a Secretary'. Every reader of women's 'Cinderella' fiction knew that the rich boss often married the poor secretary. But the route to secretary-dom was via the typing pool, or a clerical job, and the working day of a female clerk was laborious and often thankless.

Jean Hart, who was a junior insurance clerk, gives a picture of her working life in central London. At the age of sixteen, and kitted out with a maroon overall, Jean started organising files in a basement off Hyde Park Corner. Later she graduated to a noisy upper office, where a strict hierarchy of clerks, ledger clerks and clattering audio typists was maintained. Her duties increased; Jean was assigned to policy endorsements and calculating premium changes, but at £15 a month the salary stayed low. 'These were the days when one was paid according to one's age and sex, never mind how responsible the work.' The job involved dictating documentation on to a cumbersome portable recording device called an 'Emidicta', a cross between a record player and a small fridge on wheels, whose technology comprised batteries, a microphone, a Bakelite cylinder and a moving stylus. But more indelibly printed on Jean's memory were her lunch hours: spring interludes spent strolling along Knightsbridge or Constitution Hill; glimpses of Prince Charles out walking, accompanied by his Nanny, and even Winston Churchill on his way to the Hyde Park Hotel in a limousine. 'We gave a wave and were thrilled when he smiled and waved back.' Such were the perks for a cooped-up city clerk and, with the choices so narrow, many thousands of young women like Jean were grateful not to be consigned to factory work.

But a junior filing clerk only stood a chance of secretarial promotion if she had shorthand typing qualifications. Not only that, but she had to qualify in other ways. *He* (for your boss will inevitably be male) has additional requirements:

Your employer will have to look at you all day! Remember that. He will wish you to be smart, neat and radiantly clean – hair well-brushed, teeth well cared for, nails short and quietly shining.

But, be warned: 'She may not marry . . .' John Betjeman's 1954 poem 'Business Girls' evokes the sadness, narrowness and stress of the female wage-slave's everyday commute:

> Rest you there, poor unbelov'd ones,
> Lap your loneliness in heat.
> All too soon the tiny breakfast,
> Trolley-bus and windy street!

Flight Paths

That didn't stop some girls from chasing their high-flying dreams – even if those dreams were bounded by the parameters of 1950s femininity. 'When I became an air hostess, in 1957, it was considered a very glamorous job and was probably the most sought-after job for a woman at that time . . .' recalls Angela Waller – Angela Austin as she then was. In 1950 Angela had passed out of her shorthand and typing course top of her class. Since then she had been working as a secretary. Now twenty-four, she was unmarried and living at home, and she had itchy feet:

I had a yen to travel. I wanted to see the world – and there's an awful lot of world to see.

There was so much glamour attached to air-hostessing. To go to a *foreign* place – to go to the Costa del Whatever – and to go to the Mediterranean! People just hadn't been to these places. The opening up of foreign travel was a *huge* change!

And everybody knew that lots and lots of people applied for the job, but only very few were chosen. I didn't fill in an application form. I spent a year writing to lots of airlines. Some replied, some didn't. The job I finally got was with Hunting-Clan Air Transport.

And I was one of just four girls they took on, out of five thousand applicants.

Straight away, the new girls were sent off to be measured for their uniform. Distinctive, and status-enhancing, the fitted black suit with company lapel badge, characteristically jaunty little hat and pristine white shirt gave off messages of authority with a hint of sex appeal. It was impressed upon the hostesses that, having obtained such a sought-after job, they were special – and must look the part. Attractiveness was a necessary qualification, and Angela unquestioningly signed a contract that stipulated 'automatic resignation' on her thirtieth birthday, after which (it was assumed) her looks would have passed their sell-by date. During her time with the airline this rule was amended, but only so far as to allow the hostesses to renew their employment on a year-by-year basis. Every twelve months, Angela and her friends were checked over 'to see if [we] still looked "presentable"'. If not, you were out.

'You were aware that people were looking at you. Laddered stockings? No fear. You certainly wouldn't let your shoes ever be anything but highly-polished; you would never get down-at-heel.' And those heels were expected to be high ones. No flats, despite being on your feet all day. Rules were strict. Wheels <u>on</u> the ground, hats *on*; wheels <u>off</u> the ground, hats *off*. Black gloves in winter, white gloves in spring. Tropical uniform to be worn south of the Mediterranean. And if hair grew below the collar, it had to be 'put up', never just tied back.

Expensive and reserved for the privileged as they were, each flight in the 1950s was loaded with the sense that it was a special occasion. Complementing the hostesses who served them, most air travellers dressed and behaved with respectful formality. Only occasionally were they obnoxious, and when they were it was the air hostess in charge of the cabin who was in the firing line. One former Prime Minister, normally famed for his courtesy, was renowned among airline staff for his rudeness. He clearly considered the hostess to be so lowly that he couldn't address her directly, and when offered a drink would only accept it via his assistant: 'Tell the girl I'll have a whisky and soda.' One hostess was reduced to tears.

It was Angela's job to wait on thirty-two passengers, plus the crew, whom she was expected to serve with their coffee. She had no trolley, but carried all drinks and meals out on trays, two at a time. Hunting-Clan flew Vikings – refurbished Valletta aircraft – whose 'spar' (where the wings joined the fuselage) ran across the aisle. This meant negotiating two steps up and two steps down with every journey from galley to cockpit – not easy carrying a tray of drinks on a turbulent flight, but the girls were trained to walk with knees slightly bent to absorb bumps and shocks as the aircraft lurched among the clouds. Feminine qualities were to the fore: smiles, conversational charm, reassurances to nervous passengers, and motherly attention to small children.

Angela's dream of travel was coming true. She flew to Ireland and Scandinavia, Paris, Athens, Madrid, Africa. Yes, the Mediterranean really was azure, and the magical realms of the Alps seen through fleecy clouds were breathtakingly white. Africa's deserts and waterfalls captured her heart. 'The job was as wonderful as I'd hoped ...' But it could also be gruelling and stressful. The Vikings in those days were non-pressurised, so normally didn't fly over 10,000 feet. Occasionally a passenger would succumb to the altitude; Angela had to attend to one lady who completely stopped breathing. For about a quarter of an hour, she administered oxygen, fearing the worst: ' "Where do I put a dead body? We have a full load and there's no space anywhere." Our training had not covered such an eventuality.' Suddenly the 'dead' woman came back to life, demanding lunch. 'I've never served any passenger a meal more gladly!'

The cabin crew might be on duty for up to thirty-six hours, and on choppy flights, their work was a misery:

> I have every sympathy with anyone who is airsick. I have actually propped up a sick bag in the galley, round the corner so you couldn't see. There is only you, and there are thirty people out there, and they all want a drink before lunch.
>
> And there I am pouring out the gin and tonics ready to take out – and then being sick – before taking the gin and tonics out – and then rushing back and being sick again. And saying to myself all the while, 'Oh God, I've got to take these drinks out, I can't not, it's part of what these people have paid for. It's their holiday – Just do it! Do the next lot of drinks before you're sick again!'
>
> I have knelt on the floor of the lavatory with my head resting on the cool seat praying, 'Please God, get me off this aeroplane and I promise I'll never fly again!'

Undeterred, Angela would turn around and be on the next flight out of Heathrow. Life on the flight paths remained intoxicating. As the planes headed south, breaking through the clouds into brilliant sunshine at cruising altitude, spirits rose. Mundane concerns were left behind in that grey corner of the planet called England, to be swapped for palm-fringed beaches, volcanoes, safaris and shooting-star nights. Inevitably, romance came with the territory.

Early in her flying career, Angela found herself off-duty at the Phoenicia Hotel in Valletta, Malta. She was naïvely charmed to be invited out by the Captain of another crew, whose chat-up over dinner, as he talked amiably about the domestic

responsibilities awaiting him at home, revealed him to be a deb-
onair opportunist. Angela didn't understand. Why on earth was
he talking about mowing the lawn? He couldn't possibly have
asked her on a date if he wasn't single. Ah – presumably he lived
with his parents, and they expected him to help out? Angela
inquired about his domestic arrangements, only to be told, to
her horror – and quite impenitently – that he was married with
children. 'Yes! I certainly *was* naïve!' Later they took a stroll
round the town before heading back to the hotel, where the
suave Captain continued to run rings round his innocent prey.
As they were saying goodnight he apologetically explained that
he had come out on the trip without a comb. 'I'm so sorry.
Please may I come into your room and borrow yours?'

> It never occurred to me what he was up to! So I said, Yes, I've
> got a comb, of course, come in! But I had a little problem get-
> ting him out.
>
> How stupid can you be? Why didn't I say, 'It's quarter past
> eleven, why do you want to comb your hair *now*?'

Angela held out against this particular Airline Romeo, but the
flying culture militated against chastity. A week with nothing
much to do in a tropical paradise, a high percentage of men to
women, a few too many ouzos and one would have had to be a
nun to resist the pressure. The air hostesses weren't nuns, according to Angela:

> Of course – there were affairs and goings-on all the time!

Hunting-Clan's staff manual carried an instruction that caused
many giggles, but was often taken literally: 'At all times, the air
hostess comes directly beneath the captain.'

> All my group of girls were doing it. Virgins? Well, they might
> have been when they joined the airline. But I'd have given them
> three months . . .

We were in our twenties, mostly attractive women, and the men were almost all ex-wartime pilots, thirty-somethings. You'd often be away for over a fortnight, and nobody would know who you were with, or what you were doing . . . It was all too easy. Say you were in the hotel in Benghazi on a Sunday night:

'Oh, when do you leave?'

'Oh, not till Wednesday – you know.'

It was inevitable. And it was a lot of fun. Though funnily enough I never knew a girl get pregnant!

Just as well, since in her case, Angela lost her virtue and heart not to a member of the flight crew, but to a very wealthy married man whose business interests involved regular travel. It was a trifle for him to pay the rent on a chic London flat on the route out to Heathrow airport, just three minutes' walk from Harrods in Knightsbridge, and a conveniently placed stop-off for them to conduct their affair when both were in town. Illicit as it was, Angela was persuaded to believe that the situation was temporary. He would leave his wife, get a divorce and – if she would only be patient and keep their secret – they would be married. Until then, she was having the time of her life.

★

Everything to do with flying was saturated in glamour. During the London Season, the smart set would dance till dawn, then pile into a cavalcade of sports cars and head out to Heathrow airport for breakfast. In the holidays, dissatisfied teenager Brenda Nash used to trek to the perimeter of Birmingham airport just to watch the planes taking off, and imagine their exotic destinations. But air-hostessing was something she could never have aspired to.

The job carried such kudos, it was not even thought necessary to reward the female crew with proper rates. Angela Austin's last secretarial post had paid £12 12s a week; at Hunting-Clan she took a substantial drop in salary. They paid £5 15s a week, and provided her uniform. Angela explained that for many of her colleagues, pay wasn't really an issue. Nearly half of the air hostesses she worked with came from well-off titled or old-fashioned aristocratic families. They were 'nice gels' from the top drawer. Their cut-glass accents and swanky social life raised the tone of the airline, and gave them a sense of class entitlement. If you were the daughter of an Earl – as indeed some of them were – a well-bred put-down to the plebeian passenger who behaved objectionably came naturally.

Angela Austin was not the daughter of an Earl; she was the daughter of a middle-class professional. Even for advantaged women in the 1950s, their rise to promotion was often obstructed, the boundaries between 'men's' careers and 'women's' jobs were strict, and they were hampered by the pressure to jettison their employment once babies appeared on the scene. For most women, the sexual status quo continued invisibly to define the kind of jobs for which they felt qualified.

At the age of twenty-four, Dilys Hughes was a typically unconfrontational young woman, one who never sought to stray from the path of middle-class maidenliness. Her father was a vicar in suburban London; her mother 'kept the home fires burning'. Until she was sixteen, Girl Guide camp was Dilys's idea of an adventure. A proper education was taken for granted, and she graduated from Edinburgh University in 1949.

> If you'd got a calling you'd have a career. But I didn't have any particular urge . . . So I did the shortest secretarial course I could find.

So far so good. Dilys started her working life as a secretary in London, then put her first foot on the social ladder by working for a high-ranking army couple who needed a glorified babysitter to help out while they were attending the Coronation. This was a world in which word of mouth and personal recommendation meant everything. And it was through their circle of thoroughbred contacts that Dilys found herself being interviewed by Lady Berthoud, wife of the British Ambassador to Denmark, who was looking for a social secretary to work in the Embassy in Copenhagen. Soon afterwards, the job was hers. The ensuing two years were to be the highlight of Dilys Hughes's working life. She very quickly became immersed in a world of arcane etiquette, flying the flag for British-Danish interests in the way her paymasters knew best – by enabling their professional social life, and by supporting 'Lady B' to support her husband. Dilys was based at the residence in the city centre – an imposing building hung with gilt mirrors, sombre portraits and the usual complement of British emblems: lions and unicorns, photographs of the royal family, and Union Jacks. There was a large staff of maids and cooks to attend to the endless flow of visitors. Such guests came to Dilys to make their social arrangements, send their telegrams, or for guidance on Embassy proprieties.

But her main job was arranging parties. There were endless invitations to write, in her best, most legible copperplate: '*Their Highnesses Count and Countess Fleming of Rosenborg – for lunch to meet Sir Edmund Hillary . . . RSVP Social Secretary.*' Table seating plans dominated her day. Who was to sit next to whom? Dilys was fascinated – though daunted – by the cryptic niceties of the diplomatic pecking order. There were political considerations as well as factors of social status. What kind of risks were you running if you put the Russian Ambassador next to a US military attaché? Then, too, the French had the longest-established Embassy in Copenhagen, and their representatives might take offence at being placed next to some wealthy but arriviste Dane who just happened to own vast estates in the Baltic. But she was helped in this by 'a marvellous thing called The Blue Book which explained the seniority of ministers and so on from abroad'.

Dilys herself attended most of the receptions, chatting politely and handing round cigarettes; the Queen's birthday was a particularly important date in the Embassy calendar. From time to time she was asked to dinner. Her own social calling card was that her father had been Field Marshal Montgomery's personal chaplain during the North Africa campaign, so if the couples at table didn't add up neatly, she might well be required to brush up, climb into her evening dress and make up numbers.

In this way Dilys encountered a range of political and cultural celebrities, from Haile Selassie to Hugh Gaitskell, Sir Edmund Hillary to the entire cast of *Hamlet*, including Richard Burton and Claire Bloom, who were visiting Denmark to perform the play at Kronborg Castle in Elsinore:

> They came for lunch at the Embassy and they were late and His Excellency was furious. He said, 'Lateness is simple rudeness. You just think that your time is more important than other people's.' There was a terrible atmosphere.

Much more fun in Dilys's eyes were the occasions of naval visits. RN officers who had spent weeks at sea were invited ashore by the Ambassador and plied with supper and dancing. That included laying on (as it were) a few dozen nicely brought-up Foreign Office or expatriate girls, or others like Dilys on the Embassy staff, to provide innocent entertainment for the lieutenants – 'We were expected to be very correct and polite. And of course we would never have behaved badly because we were working for the Embassy . . .'

Living in the residence, Dilys became attuned to Lady Berthoud's peculiarities. 'Lady B' never shirked her duties, but there was nevertheless a hint of the rebel about her. Her day was taken up unveiling statues, cutting ribbons, greeting dignitaries; her evenings entertaining them at table. Being on show all the time was exhausting: ' – she was really happiest stomping about in English tweeds . . .' But she was also a thoughtful and questioning woman. Her deepest interest was in psychoanalysis and whenever she could, she liked to gather like-minded friends around her to discuss Jungian theories. Being married to H. E., and all the Embassy 'pomp and circumstance' that entailed, was a very mixed blessing.

After two years Dilys Hughes returned to England. For all the splendour of Embassy life, she would have observed that – for women – the diplomatic service was a club from which they were largely excluded. As table-arrangers, invitation-writers, and decorative additions to naval gatherings, most women in embassies were as much superficial embellishments as the gilt candelabras and urns of chrysanthemums that adorned their state rooms. Few intrepid women worked as emissaries. Those who did gain postings – like Cecily Mayhew, who was assigned to Belgrade in 1947 – were discriminated against. In 1949 Mayhew's short diplomatic career came to an end when she accepted a proposal of marriage from a dashing young Foreign Office Minister. The marriage bar remained strictly in force in the diplomatic service until 1973. In 1976, more than twenty years after Dilys Hughes's time working for Sir Eric Berthoud, his Copenhagen post would at last be occupied by Britain's first female Ambassador, Dame Anne Warburton.

Two years later, after a spot of temping, and a spell working in the secretariat of the Society of Authors, Dilys Hughes met a respectable solicitor named Ralph Thompson at a friend's wedding. He was very correct, wore a bowler hat to travel to his city office from his home in Beckenham, and in due course asked the Reverend Hughes for his daughter's hand in marriage. The wedding took place in Ripon Cathedral in 1956. Dilys describes it as 'very Trollope . . .' Soon after the wedding she was pregnant. The Thompsons moved to a pretty coastal village in Sussex. With a long commute, Ralph was out of the house for twelve hours a day, leaving Dilys red-tiling the floor, polishing her furniture and pushing her pram round the village.

> Being a mum and a wife seemed to be the thing to do. Very nice. True, there were long days in the winter when I felt I wasn't getting anywhere – a bit shut in – when I felt, I'd like to get out of this house and be doing something. 'This also shall pass . . .' Hm.

But after 1956 Dilys never worked again.

What did feminists have to say about this situation? Contrary to popular belief, feminism did not die after the war.* A wife and mother herself, the talented star politician Edith Summerskill devoted much of her career with the Labour Party to improving women's lot, and campaigned long and hard for them to have a fairer deal within marriage (for disaffection with the institution itself had not yet set in). Writing to her student daughter Shirley in the early fifties, Summerskill squarely blamed the selfishness – and envy – of

---

* As mentioned earlier, women's clubs and organisations thrived at this time, many of them adopting a campaigning agenda: the National Federation of Women's Institutes, the British Federation of University Women, the British Federation of Business and Professional Women, the National Women Citizens' Association, the Married Women's Association, the Women's Group on Public Welfare, the National Federation of Townswomen's Guilds, the Young Women's Christian Association, the National Union of Women Teachers, the British Housewives' League, the Soroptimists, and more, gave voice to women's concerns then and now.

attention-craving husbands, for deterring their clever wives from re-entering the workplace.

> This is morally wrong, socially indefensible and economically stupid.
>
> Everybody loses – the children, the husband, and the country – from keeping an intelligent, industrious, energetic woman chained to the sink.

A few years later, two feminist intellectuals, Alva Myrdal and Viola Klein, published what now seems like a rather modest analysis of the work-life dilemma, entitled *Women's Two Roles: Home and Work*. In their book, Myrdal and Klein gently challenged the idea that the workplace had no further use for women like Dilys Thompson once she had handed in her cards. They unpicked the idea that mothers were a round-the-clock necessity for their babies after the age of twelve months, while advising devoted mothers to remain at home until the children were three years old. Next, they demonstrated that in a woman's life span, the 'family phase' normally ran from the early twenties to the late thirties, after which point most women had two useful decades ahead of them in which to earn, replenish their own sense of themselves and contribute to society. They then tentatively suggested that housewives should be spared from the guilt attached to using convenience foods or spending time away from their children, and made some sprightly recommendations to help working women, such as adjusting the opening hours of shops, hairdressers and launderettes to accommodate the woman's working day. At no point did the authors argue that the burden of shopping, cooking and housework might be shared by husbands. Nevertheless, Myrdal and Klein offered a way forward, in which women might 'have it all', and which, for its time, was radical. In all this they were characteristic of many of their other feminist contemporaries who focused

'I'd love to join, but I'd have to ask my husband' (*Punch*, June 1953). There were still insurmountable contradictions built in to the feminist position.

their concerns on marriage and motherhood, while (as has been persuasively argued*) tending to cloak challenges to the patriarchy in a polite, 'feminine' guise.

But in 1956 Dilys Thompson wasn't open to such messages. Vaguely, she was aware that some great-aunts on her mother's side had worn the purple and green of the suffrage movement, and had 'tied themselves to railings a bit' for women's rights. But their courage, and their victories, seemed to have no bearing on her own life.

> Feminism had no impact on me. I don't think I was ever really bothered about equality. None of my friends had permanent jobs after they were married. It didn't really worry me.
>
> Do you think I should have been jumping up and down more? I don't really think I thought much about it. Isn't that awful?

Despite being the foundation and rationale of her job with the British Embassy, politics – for Dilys – was 'for the chaps . . .' Her vote went to the Tories because in her family 'it always had', just as, since childhood, her Sunday prayers had always been offered up to the God of the Anglican Church.

> I didn't question my life. I didn't want to rock the boat. I suppose I've always felt that the boat was better going on as it was.

Playing at Working

In *Women's Two Roles*, Myrdal and Klein explore the ideal of the 'Lady of Leisure':

---

* See *Feminism as Femininity in the Nineteen-fifties?* by the Birmingham Feminist History Group, *Feminist Review* No. 80 (2005); also Joyce Freeguard, *It's Time for Women of the 1950s to Stand Up and Be Counted*, D. Phil thesis, University of Sussex (2004).

> This ideal, cultivated more in the [nineteenth] century than the
> present one . . . put parasitism of women at a premium. The task
> of an upper-middle-class wife was chiefly to be an ornament to
> her husband's home and a living testimony to his wealth.

Delving into her history, Myrdal and Klein showed how the
pointlessness of the well-off woman's existence – with its reli-
ance on servants, and each day frittered away feeding the canary,
paying calls and stitching embroidered wool piano-backs – had
itself given rise to the emancipation movement of the late nineteenth and early twentieth centuries. Those clamouring for
women's education and for the right to work were reacting to
economics, but also to an unnatural state of affairs.

They then proceeded to show how, in 1950s Britain, the
mythic 'lady of leisure' was still alive, perfectly coiffed with her
beautiful manicured hands, a by-product of the new affluence.
The Queens of their kitchens whom we admired in the pages of
Good Housekeeping were not racing home from their offices or
shop-floors to lay out iced fancies for their guests. They were far
more likely, as Myrdal and Klein point out, to have been shopping or at the hairdresser. Or, indeed, having slimming
treatments – for the figures of well-off women who could afford
labour-saving electrical gadgetry were more liable to betray the
effects of excessive leisure.

Though Myrdal and Klein accepted that, for many, marriage
represented an escape from the factory, they pointed out that
the existence of this gentlewomanly ideal – side by side with
that of the hard-working, much-loved and all-providing 'Mam'
and housewife – did much to thwart and devalue the ambitions
of innumerable women. Professional opportunities were there,
but it took unusual confidence and self-belief to pursue them;
to sidestep the class-ridden claim that being a 'lady' meant not
working, and to disregard the insistent images of those perfect
wives in their ideal homes.

Incarnate in white satin, pearls and ostrich feathers, the 1950s debutante was the archetypal lady of leisure of her day – a parasite worthy of her nineteenth-century forebears. But she was a dying breed.

In her memoir of debutante life in the 1950s, Fiona MacCarthy explains that it was acceptable for debs like her to have a job, on the understanding that it was not the done thing to be earning a living, and was therefore largely frivolous. You could be a model – 'approved of since it was not only extremely lowly paid but was regarded (incorrectly) as somehow rather jolly, an extension of the Berkeley Debutante Dress Show'. Floristry and working in an antique furniture shop were also tolerated, as the skills acquired would be bound to come in useful once the deb had been whisked off to her rightful stately home by Mr – or, rather, Lord – Right. MacCarthy also notes sardonically that the Fortnum & Mason's Soda Fountain 'was at that time almost wholly staffed by ex-debutantes . . .' It was fine to spend your day cutting sandwiches, just so long as they were thin, cucumber and crustless. Unpaid work like helping out with tombolas or rattling a tin in the street for the King George's Fund for Sailors was also well thought-of by the parents of debs. Qualifications were not thought necessary. The Hon. Emma Tennant left school at fifteen, worked briefly as an assistant in the fashion room of a glossy magazine, and duly 'came out', before marrying at twenty. Nothing in her upbringing had prepared her for any alternative, and fear drove her into the embrace of the first young nobleman who offered. Emerging from the church as a child bride, she felt 'the panic of class, the trap of marriage: am I to be a housewife? An upper-class lady of leisure?'

Once married, it was all right for the deb to take on a little charitable work on committees. Or, like Laura Charteris, who later became the Duchess of Marlborough, she might go one step further, and use her connections and social base to experience some retail therapy from the other side of the counter. In 1956 Laura opened a chain of seven shops selling interior decor, dress materials and furnishing fabric. She named them 'Contessa'.

> [I knew] that people of those north and north-west suburbs of London were likely to be fascinated by the idea of a Countess running a shop, which did me no harm at all and indeed was a useful and simple way to success.

Contessa was more of a tax-deductible toy than an occupation. Laura employed manageresses, while she dropped in occasionally to dress the windows, interfere with the buying and give customers the wrong change; she was playing at working. The shops were also useful security when she wanted to borrow money from the bank to buy a lovely Georgian house in Hertfordshire, where she continued to employ a butler, maid and gardener, and run her Alfa Romeo. But her real career was marrying. Her first marriage, to Viscount Long, didn't last. Her second marriage, to the third Earl of Dudley, also ended in divorce. Soon after Laura married her third husband, an American publisher and well-connected playboy, Contessa was sidelined.

In her sixties, Laura Duchess of Marlborough wrote in her autobiography, *Laughter from a Cloud* (1980), 'I believe life to be a game.' Her life story encompassed four tumultuous marriages. After the American publisher died she married the Duke of Marlborough, whom she outlived. But there were also numerous dramatic entanglements, and a glittering array of weekend parties, ball gowns, tiaras and exotic travel. Laura's only child – by her first marriage to Viscount Long – was a daughter, Sara. As her mother's love-life ran off the rails, Sara's early life was spent being batted like a ball from nursemaid to grandmother, from governess to boarding school. Sara did the season, and in 1954 married a wealthy and good-looking landowner, Sir Charles Morrison.

But the similarity with her mother's life ends there. Sara Morrison's adult career is a catalogue of laudable achievements. She was to become the Deputy Chairman of Edward Heath's Conservative government in the early 1970s, and later a trusted confidante of Margaret Thatcher. She joined the General Electric Company in 1975 and was appointed as a director in 1980. She has sat on the boards and committees of charitable and educational organisations, participated in think tanks, been conferred with fellowships and doctorates, and – as Chairman of both the National Council for Voluntary Organisations and the National Council of Social Service – has been an eloquent advocate for the voluntary sector. In her memoir, Laura wrote:

> A great sadness to me is the way that as mother and daughter Sara and I have grown apart . . .

This is the voice of regret, the uncomprehending voice of an ageing woman who sees her bright summer fading to a wistful autumn. Sara, as her mother could see, had contributed much to make the world a better place, but she found it hard to come to terms with the gulf between that world and her own.

> In some ways she disapproves of me, which makes me unhappy as I don't know why. Sometimes a year can go by with scarcely a talk on the telephone let alone a meeting. Sara has grown into a woman of considerable capabilities . . . She is a good citizen. [She] will probably end up a peeress in her own right or a Dame.
>
> I think that perhaps one of the fundamental differences between us is that I believe life to be a game and here my darling daughter would not agree.

I love and admire much in her character. I wish that we could pull back from the chasm that separates us.

Depression accompanied Laura's decline. Now, set against her daughter's modern accomplishments, Laura's 'star-spangled years . . . with wonderful sparkling moments' – the lifestyle of the lady of leisure – appeared fruitless, irrelevant and obsolete.

8. On Parade

The Regiment

Sheila McKenzie left school at the age of fifteen. At sixteen, in 1953, she was working as a cashier at Lewis's, a Liverpool department store. That summer, in company with a small troop of friends from the office, she travelled to Ayr for a week's holiday. It was a time of never-to-be-forgotten freedom. The girls stayed in chalets at the recently opened Butlin's Holiday Camp. Here, diversions and entertainments of every kind were laid on: a funfair, covered and open-air swimming pools, tennis courts, an amusement arcade, shops, sports facilities, a theatre and a ballroom. Boredom or opting out were firmly discouraged by Butlin's staff, the irrepressibly jolly regiment of redcoats in their cheery uniform blazers, whose duty it was to rouse the campers from their slumbers with a commanding breakfast-time reveille, and to ensure that everyone enjoyed themselves to the full.

Butlin's was the brainchild of rags-to-riches entrepreneur Billy Butlin, who had risen from running hoopla stalls in fairgrounds to starting up his own self-contained holiday and entertainment complex, the first one being at Skegness in 1936. When war broke out Butlin used it to his advantage. The Ministry of Defence contracted him to build a naval training camp on the Ayr headland overlooking the Firth of Clyde; Butlin built a buy-back clause into the deal and designed it, as far as possible, to convert easily into a holiday camp post-war. In 1946, after some hasty reconstruction, the ratings' and midshipmen's accommodation was reassigned to happy families and fun-seekers. The old parade ground was made over to donkey Derbys and egg-and-spoon races. Here, in 1953, Sheila and her friends had the time of their lives.

> It was just fantastic. For everyone who went to Butlin's at that time it was wonderful, because there were so many different things to do – so many different people to meet, so many friends to make and activities to take part in . . .
>
> Butlin's brought out the best in people.

Sociable and gregarious by nature, Sheila loved to laugh, and she loved to make friends. Her mother had been a revue dancer with the Bluebell Girls; light-hearted entertainment and a desire to please ran in the family. The Butlin's holiday at Ayr struck chords which continued to chime.

The following year Sheila's father, who was a Regimental Sergeant Major with the Royal Artillery, removed his family from the Lancashire countryside where they lived, and flew them to Egypt where he was due to be based. Sheila was now seventeen.

From Port Said on the Mediterranean to Ismailia, from Fayed to Suez on the Red Sea, the road along the canal covers over 100 miles of desert. But in the early 1950s you couldn't travel far along that dusty route without passing through the camps and settlements erected by the British army to house approaching 100,000 military personnel and, in many cases, their families. The installation at Suez alone held 80,000, there to protect British influence and interests in the trade-bearing Canal; in 1956, 80 per cent of western Europe's oil was transported via this key route. At Weston Camp, Hodgson's Camp, Spinney Wood Camp and Gordon Camp regiments of British soldiers and airmen were billeted in compounds spread across the sand, serviced by innumerable additional contractors and civilians across the area. Behind the barbed wire fences and searchlight mounts, they had clubs, messes, canteens, and shops where you could buy an English language newspaper, Ty-Phoo tea, and Scott's Porage Oats. There were churches, the NAAFI, barbers, and hospitals. There were bungalows for married couples, with room for the children. If you took a bus ride or a jeep into Ismailia or Fayed there were open-air movie theatres, restaurants and ice-cream parlours. For the expatriates, here – as in a holiday camp – was everything you could need and more, all in one place.

About forty miles south of Ismailia, the McKenzies were allocated a comfortable bungalow within the perimeter of the Geneifa army camp. Its windows, heavily netted against mosquitoes, looked on to a garden of banana palms. Sheila soon found a job helping out in a NAAFI store a few miles away, selling English groceries to army wives. But for a pretty teenager who loved sport and dancing there was lots of fun to be had too. However, by now, the relationship between the Egyptian population and the resident British army was growing tense; violent outbreaks were frequent, and women were provided with military escorts to go about their daily business. Sheila's undisguised delight at being forced to go everywhere with a compulsory retinue of tanned soldiers perplexed her strictly protective father. But he didn't stand in her way when she found herself a talented partner, named James, to accompany her to westernised ballrooms. The pair soon found themselves much in demand to lead off at social dances, or to give waltz demonstrations.

Sheila found other aspects of Egypt less entertaining. Abroad was 'creepy-crawly-land'. Insects got everywhere. When a friend from England sent her a gift portion of wedding cake, she left it, wrapped, in her bedroom drawer; within hours, ants had invaded. 'When I went to go and get my cake, there was a line of ants going up to this drawer and in, and another line coming out and going away. And that was my cake gone!' The sacks of flour and rice she sold in her store were alive with weevils, and the netting on the bungalow doors didn't seem to deter giant beetles and cockroaches from getting into the family lounge. A rare sortie into the Fayed souk exposed Sheila to the unhygienic realities of Middle Eastern food retail: 'It just horrified me to see the way they had the meat hanging up – just swarming with flies. The meat was covered with them! And then they cut that same meat off, for people to take home and eat!'

The ways of the locals were strange and exotic. Women clothed from head to foot in black robes waded fully clothed into the river to do their washing. And, inexplicably to her, the people appeared to indulge in idolatrous practices, scavenging discarded tin cans from the camps, which they then placed, like a totem atop a small pyramid of sand, before prostrating themselves in prayer before it. 'I could never understand why that was . . . why an old rusty tin? – and why would they be down on their knees?'*

The McKenzies had gone to Egypt expecting to be there for a year or more. But that year, 1954, Anthony Eden (then Foreign Secretary under Churchill) reached an agreement with Egypt's new President, General Nasser, on military withdrawal from Suez. By 1955 the red, white and black of the Egyptian flag was flying over the Canal Zone, and the McKenzie family was back in rural Lancashire. For Sheila, now nearly eighteen and lacking direction, the curtailment of their Egyptian adventure left her restless and disenchanted. She chafed at her father's impositions: a strict 8.30 p.m. curfew seemed unreasonable, but couldn't be argued with. As a soldier, he was a man who saw male threats around every corner, from which his pretty daughter must be

---

*Most mosques contain a semi-circular niche known as the mihrab, to denote which direction is East – or Mecca – the focus of the worshippers' prayers. Sheila probably noticed a Muslim who, unable to get to a mosque, had built himself a makeshift 'mihrab' in the sand.

protected. She loved him, but his sternness took the joy out of life.

Sheila craved glamour, fun, but above all escape. Never had she forgotten the one time in her life when she had tasted the pure and heady pleasure of liberty. Butlin's still held her in its spell. And so, soon after she got back from Egypt, a plan for her future life started to take shape. In the spring of 1955, she wrote and posted a letter of application to be a redcoat at Butlin's, Clacton-on-Sea, for £3 a week, May to September. Sheila's working life was going to be one long holiday.

The Canal

On 4 April 1955, about the same time that Sheila posted off her letter to Butlin's, Winston Churchill resigned. It was the end of an era. His successor, Sir Anthony Eden, walked into number 10 Downing Street soon after.

One of Eden's more committed admirers was Margaret Thatcher; his position on 'foreign dictators' was one she felt able to respect (and would uphold in her own later career). Having lost against Labour in Dartford in the 1951 election, she had married, given birth to twins, and in February 1954 was called to the Bar. But Mrs Thatcher's husband, her home, her children and a busy career as a tax lawyer didn't prevent her from standing for selection for the safe seat of Orpington. Though defeated, the discouragement didn't last long.

The General Election was held in May 1955. During their campaign the Tories called in support from women who appreciated rising living standards and the upsurge in ownership of cars and washing machines. The Conservative victory was a foregone conclusion.

By 1956 relations between Egypt and Britain had polarised.

The military withdrawal was proceeding slowly, and Egyptian nationalists increasingly resented and resisted the British presence in the Canal Zone. President Nasser was becoming a thorn in an enraged Anthony Eden's side. On 26 July, Nasser commanded his forces to seize and nationalise the Suez Canal.

Among the first to react publicly to the seizure of the Canal was the holiday camp king Billy Butlin. Since 1953 he had sponsored and organised a high-profile international 'Butlin's Cross-Channel Swim', with a 1,000-guinea prize. In 1954 and 1955 swimmers from Egypt came in as runner-up and winner. These ex-army Egyptians fuelled their prowess with boiled beans, and were doggedly determined to win. 'If this goes on,' a Pathé news commentator grumbled in 1955, 'we'll have to start calling it the Egyptian Channel.' But in August 1956 Butlin banned Egyptian competitors from his race. 'They've got the Suez Canal, I'm not going to let them have the English Channel!' he was quoted as saying.

Arrangements were immediately made to airlift British families out of the Suez Canal Zone, while behind closed government doors politicians were now preparing to protect their interests by military force. Diplomacy proved ineffectual. In October a task force sailed from Malta to Port Said. In secret, Israel colluded with an infamous Anglo-French conspiracy to let them off the hook of appearing to be the aggressors, by being the first to invade Egypt. Their involvement could then be seen as a peacemaking intervention. In October Nasser rejected an ultimatum to withdraw his troops from the Canal Zone, and Anglo-French forces immediately began a bombing campaign followed by the landing of forces.

In her diary the pacifist Frances Partridge reacted with bewilderment and shock at the 'unbelievable step'.

Eden must be raving mad . . . America, even our colonies repudiate us. I feel extremely fatalistic about the whole thing – only a sort of contempt for anyone who holds the belief that you can solve problems by killing people.

The Suez crisis left the moral authority of the British government in tatters when it came to condemning another violent invasion, this time by Soviet forces suppressing a vast popular uprising in Budapest and other Hungarian cities. The timing was not coincidental. With the eyes of the world on the Middle East, Khrushchev's soldiers were unsparing to the rebellious civilians, thousands of whom were imprisoned, deported or executed. Two hundred thousand refugees fled the country. Rosamund Essex immediately joined a team from the World Council of Churches to bring them relief. The suffering she encountered filled her with enraged pity: dispossessed and traumatised families, dreadful injuries, blood, filth and misery. As a journalist, Rosamund felt herself to be a voice for these helpless Hungarians, forgotten by a Western world which 'looked on and did not care'.

On 5 November, as on so many other occasions in her long life, Violet Bonham Carter picked up her pen to write to the Editor of *The Times*:

> Sir, – I am one of millions who watching the martyrdom of Hungary and listening yesterday to the transmission of her agonised appeals for help (immediately followed by the description of our 'successful bombing' of Egyptian 'targets') have felt a humiliation, shame and anger which are beyond expression . . .

A loyal Liberal to the core, Lady Violet was in many ways a paradigm of 1950s female achievement: privileged, gracious, clever and passionate, a champion of women's causes – yet always repudiating feminism.

On 4 November the MP Edith Summerskill called a mass rally in Trafalgar Square where she addressed an audience estimated at over 30,000.

Never before had I seen such a colossal crowd as that which assembled as a protest against the 'Suez' act of aggression. [They] overflowed into Whitehall, up the Strand and into Cockspur Street.

Afterwards, 10,000 people bearing banners reading LAW NOT WAR surged down Whitehall to Downing Street, where terrifying scenes broke out; demonstrators were charged by mounted police, and members of the crowd fell beneath the horses' hooves. Twenty-seven arrests followed.

Sarah Myers, newly elected President of the Oxford Liberal Club, ached to take the stand at the Oxford Union and condemn the government:

The idea that we could just take over – invade, do this colonial thing . . . I just thought it was monstrous, and to me it showed the Tory party in their true colours . . .

– but as a woman in a male citadel she did not qualify for membership, so was unable to speak at debates. 'We should have chained ourselves to the railings, which we didn't do . . .' But she did the next best thing by successfully inviting Bertrand Russell to the platform and acting as chairman as he denounced the government on her behalf in front of a huge audience.

In 1956 Cambridge-educated Anthea York was working in a solicitor's office. For her, the Suez crisis enhanced an already acute sense that she was a displaced person, both where her sexuality and her establishment background were concerned.

I had been brought up to think we were The Great Nation – that everyone in the world would want to be English if they had the chance. My father was true Blue, and just assumed that people from other countries were lesser breeds. I took the opposite view, that the Suez invasion was being conducted on behalf of a minority – 'Not in my name.'

> Of course this was partly a revolt against my family. I began
> to see things from the other end of the spectrum . . .

The Mass Observation diarists were also, for the most part, predictably anti-government. Sixty-four-year-old Betty Hodge
from Lancashire felt the even tenor of her life jolted by their
action:

> *Thursday 1st November*
> The Middle East situation gets more serious for us . . . I think
> our government has acted very wrongly – & I'm frightened of
> the consequences.

The following day fifty-six-year-old Janice Harrison from
Otley in Yorkshire recorded a shopping trip into Leeds, where
she got a ringside view of a student demonstration:

> [They were] carrying lots of scruffy placards with 'Hands Off
> Egypt', and 'Eden Must Go' . . . Whatever the papers say tomor-
> row there is no doubt that 90% of the demonstrators were
> pro-Egypt – or anti the action of the British & French & Israel.
> The whole affair was so ragged & somehow pathetic . . .

But Mollie Panter-Downes told her American readers that the
British reaction was largely one of passive bewilderment. People in
'little backstreet shops', she wrote, seemed worried and uncomprehending. 'Don't know what to make of it,' they would say,
wagging their heads. '[They] want, above all, England to be right.'

But the world thought England was wrong. On 7 November,
under pressure from the United Nations, and realising that the
economy could not sustain a war without American support,
Sir Anthony Eden called a ceasefire, followed by a withdrawal.
On 9 January 1957 he resigned. Even before his departure, Harold Macmillan was lobbying to succeed him.

The women who stood on platforms, joined demonstrations,
and wrote letters to the editor of *The Times* were in a minority.

I know it were a serious thing . . .

– remembers Vera Brydon, a wife and factory worker from Sunderland.

> . . . but it was so far away that it didn't seem to touch us as much as it probably should have.

And in rural Sussex, cowman's wife Dot Medhurst just dismissed the shenanigans as being the usual antics of 'stupid politicians':

> Something happens to men once they get mixed up in the machine . . . It's power, isn't it?

It wasn't just under-privileged women who paid little attention to the unfolding crisis. True, the introduction of emergency petrol rationing worried Dilys Hughes, whose wedding was fast approaching. It looked as if Ralph Thompson's best man might have to hoard fuel for the bridal car. But Dilys's main preoccupation was getting her home-made wedding dress to fit:

> I took over the spare bedroom to cut it out. It had to be right for a winter wedding, which meant long sleeves and a high neckline. Nobody in those days had wedding dresses with – you know – bare tops . . . And the pattern was for short sleeves, and I got in a terrible temper trying to adjust it. Still I muddled through in the end . . .

The society diarist Betty Kenward also referenced the petrol shortage, though not its cause, deferentially applauding the Queen's splendid example in downsizing to a small car, at least for non-official occasions, and giving instructions that 'the use of oil and petrol throughout her estates be kept to a minimum'. But Jennifer's diary was too full of the social whirl to spare a thought for the Trafalgar Square protest or the travails of Sir Anthony Eden.

The Rose Bowl

Assuredly in post-war Britain the days of Empire were waning. The austerity years had seen the country weak and poor, its ancient might overshadowed by new powers, and the sinister terminology of the Cold War gaining currency. In his magisterial account of the 1950s, *Having It So Good* (2006), Peter Hennessy makes an authoritative claim:

> Those few days at the end of October and the beginning of November 1956 really do merit the over-used description of a 'turning-point . . .' Everything that could have been in flux *was* in flux . . .

For many, Suez represented a national identity crisis. Hennessy's analysis of the fallout cites trauma, shame, and a crippling awareness that Britain's greatness lay in the past. Military men, political men, and alpha males across the nation felt their authority and potency crumble. Lord Franks, post-war Ambassador to the USA, recalled:

> [Suez lit] up an unfamiliar landscape. It was a landscape in which the two superpowers and principally the United States had told us to stop and we'd had to stop. And this was different. This was not being a world power.

British men in positions of leadership were unfamiliar with this sensation of emasculation. Over centuries, their sex had been accustomed to the dominant role, not only under their own roofs, but institutionally and globally. They were accustomed to have 'the lesser breeds' do their bidding, to hold unquestioned sway over cities, ports, deserts and jungles, to being masters over an Empire where 'the sun never sets'. Suez removed that certainty for ever. The armour of male supremacy was starting to show chinks; through a fantasy world of spies, enemy agents and UFOs the popular press and fiction alike played on readers' vulnerabilities. Though it would take several more decades for the patriarchy to feel genuinely threatened, its defences were weakening.

But humiliation by the United Nations failed to quench the male urge to compete and conquer; the 1950s were signally an age of great physical and sporting achievement, epitomised in 1953 by Sir Edmund Hillary's ascent of Everest which, from the extraordinary height of 29,000 feet, told a public in need of reassurance that the Commonwealth was still on top. But while mountaineers, runners and racing drivers waved banners for Britain on peaks, racecourses and in the arena,[*] women looked around for other opportunities to dazzle a watching world.

> I gave myself a deadline. I was going to win Miss Great Britain by the third attempt.

Leila Williams had begun her career as a beauty queen by winning the *Sunday Mercury* Girl contest in Coronation year. By the time she was eighteen, in 1955, although she was still working at the Wheatsheaf, her mother's Walsall pub, titles were starting to drop into her lap, and Miss Great Britain seemed to be within her sights. The contest was jointly sponsored by the *Sunday Dispatch*, Mecca Ballrooms, Morecambe Corporation and (predictably) Butlin's Holiday Camps. Heats were held at venues nationwide; Leila's mother pushed her to enter a heat at the Birmingham Mecca dance hall. 'Worryingly, I would have to wear a swimsuit.' Quaking with nerves and the agony of

[*] In 1954 Roger Bannister broke world records by running a mile in under four minutes. Donald Campbell's attempts to top his own water speed and land speed records continued through the decade, winning prize money sponsored by the ubiquitous Billy Butlin. Other 1950s sporting heroes included Formula 1 drivers like Mike Hawthorn and Peter Collins, jockeys like Gordon Richards and Lester Piggott, footballers like Stanley Matthews and Billy Wright, and cricketers like the paragon batsman Denis Compton, who held British audiences across the social spectrum spellbound.

exposure, Leila tottered past the judges. It was no good. A late-comer with a broad Brummie accent took the crown. 'You didn't try hard enough,' Leila's mother told her. Undeterred, she entered her daughter for the photographic section of the Miss England, Ireland, Scotland and Wales contest. A swimsuit shoot was organised, and the pictures were mailed to the newspaper. After months of waiting a representative from the *Sunday Dispatch* arrived on the doorstep to verify that the photographs were genuine, and later that day the phone call came; Leila had been chosen as the photographic Miss England. The award brought in modelling and photographic work – 'My earnings were now enough to keep me, but not enough to be able to leave the Wheatsheaf.' A lot of her money now had to go on expensive maintenance and flashy swimsuits; a red and green beaded halter-neck costume came to £40 – worth nearly £900 today. Her small stature too was a handicap. Every day for two years Leila lay on the floor with her feet a couple of inches from the skirting board, stretching hard with her legs to try and touch it. She grew two inches. Putting on weight was the next target; at that time everyone wanted to look like screen idols Marilyn Monroe and Jane Russell, whose curvaceous figures offered a spectacle of lus-cious well-rounded flesh. Leila's mother insisted she drink a pint of milk a day; she hated it, but it seemed to do the trick, and in 1955 she was a Miss Great Britain finalist, coming third.

Leila Williams's rise to beauty queen success came at a cost. John, her boyfriend, a Wheatsheaf regular, was ten years older than her, and making a comfortable living from the iron foundry which he owned. Gorgeous, charming and wealthy, he show-ered her with gifts and attention. They fell for each other – and yet the only unmentionable subject between them was her com-petition career. Shortly before the Miss Great Britain final John fixed a lunch date; Leila arrived to meet him at the factory, and as she crossed the courtyard the workers – already on their break

– subjected her to a barrage of wolf-whistles. John appeared, and whisked her away.

> A couple of days later John arranged to take me to dinner. He had seemed serious for a few days, not his usual light-hearted self. Over dinner he said, if I gave up taking part in the competitions, we would become engaged. Why was it necessary for me to give it all up? He had never mentioned that it was a problem before. He said, he could not have his workmen ogling at me in the newspapers.

John suggested she take twenty-four hours to think things over. That night Leila paced her room, tearful and sleepless. She loved John. Becoming his wife, giving everything up, accepting his offer to live with him in the lap of luxury would, she believed, bring her security and contentment. But who was this man, that he could ask her to turn her back on success? Why couldn't he support her ambitions, be there for her while she worked her way up, wait for her till she got it out of her system? What about 'that thing called trust . . .'? Four years into her career, she was now about to scale the summit. How many times had she heard the girls in the dressing rooms say, that – had they not got married – they might have been a winner?

> The following day the decision was clear in my mind. When John phoned and asked the question, I had to say there was no giving up.
>
> He just slammed the phone down. Oh how I cried and cried. My heart was broken.

John's phone calls ceased, as did his visits to the Wheatsheaf. 'It was all like some horrible nightmare.' Leila fought to come to terms with his cruelty. Despite tears and renewed weight loss, the betrayal sharpened her determination to win the longed-for title. It helped, too, that by now she was channelling her ambitions towards a future beyond that; with an eye to a career in front of movie cameras she enrolled at the Birmingham Theatre School, paying for it with her winnings. The 1956 Miss Great Britain contest saw her come in as runner-up.

As ever, the 1957 final took place at the Morecambe Bay Holiday Camp. Wrapped in a headscarf, her nose red and streaming from a summer cold, Leila strolled the pier with her mother in the teeth of a wet gale. There was nothing to do so they went to have their fortunes told. 'Put out your right hand,' said the gypsy. She glanced at it, but something was wrong, and she asked for the left one. It was all mumbo-jumbo, wasn't it? But Leila sensed that the gypsy had something of import to communicate. 'The life you have been born into will change completely,' said the fortune-teller. And then, to her surprise, she added, 'You are here for the competition, aren't you?' How ever could she have told, from Leila's muffled-up appearance and inflamed face? But there was more to come:

> She must have read my thoughts, as she said, 'You think I tell all the girls who come to see me that they will win. Well, you WILL win. You will look up at the clock above where the judges sit, and it will say twenty minutes past four. Then you will know that you have won, and that I have told you the truth.'

Miss Great Britain stood to win a splendid trophy rose bowl, and prize money of £1,000.* But as Leila saw it, this was money well earned:

> They're not going to give you £1,000 for nothing, are they? You have to earn that money.
>
> All the competitions I'd been in had taught me how to work an audience. I learned that you have to take your time, smile right at them, and make contact. If you've got the crowd with you, you're halfway there.

---

* Worth £20,429 in 2013.

But smiling and looking glossy on the day wasn't enough:

> What people don't realise when they watch a beauty competition is that it is not only about the event itself.
>
> The judging actually starts the whole week running up to the contest, and this was a thing many of the contestants never realised. But I did. During that time we stayed in the wing of the local Butlin's holiday camp hotel, so we had three meals a day with the public. And I spotted what was going on very quickly. So – I came down to breakfast looking as you would expect a beauty queen to look – to the best of my ability. My clothes had to be pressed, hair done, and nails manicured. And I never ever turned up not looking that way. There were some girls – they turned up with rollers in their hair, safety pins in their clothes, and then they'd put their swimsuits on and their make-up, and comb their hair out and they'd look entirely different. And then they wondered why they didn't win.
>
> The night before the final, Morecambe Corporation hosted a dinner. You had a councillor either side of you, and you were judged on how you presented yourself, on how you behaved at the table, on your conversation, and on whether you got drunk – the wine was there, oh yes!
>
> As well as that you had to be able to do after-dinner speaking. You were expected to stand up – if you were one of the first three – and make a speech. And I wasn't prepared for it. Well, I just did it. It was self-preservation really.

The day of the final dawned bright and sunny, but though her cold was better, Leila's confidence was now waning. A fellow-competitor drained her of hope by bragging of her own conviction of winning – and yes, she looked lovely. It would take all Leila's self-belief and ambition to retrieve the positive attitude she now sorely needed to be crowned Miss Great Britain.

After lunch the contestants got ready. There were strict rules about aids to the girls' appearance. Their swimsuits had to be free of boning, wiring or artificial padding of any sort, and there was a nurse at hand to make careful double-checks. Then each one was given a number to carry in the shape of a heart, before stepping out on to the walkway around the gigantic swimming pool. As they did so Leila caught a glimpse of the magnificent rose bowl. It fired her up. 'I *wanted* that title – and that rose bowl! The only fear I felt was not winning.' The girls now filed out in numerical order before the packed audience and the judges, who, that year, included comedian Bob Monkhouse, B-movie film actress Lisa Gastoni, the editor of the *Sunday Dispatch* Charles Eades, crooner Dickie Valentine and – crucially – the Miss World entrepreneur Eric Morley. Leila was Number 30. They made a second circuit of the pool, individually this time, and as they reached the desk of judges they were asked to stop. Then to face them. Then to turn profile-on to them, and finally to face away, so that the selectors could assess their rear view. And smile. That was the hardest thing. 'Your lips begin to stick to your teeth, and they quiver. No one wants to see a sour face, do they?'

But now the hours Leila had practised posing, stripped to her underwear in front of her bedroom mirror, played to her advantage. It had been time well spent. She had taught herself to see her own body as the judges would see it, to assess how to stand attractively, which shoes to wear to flatter her knees, what colours to choose to make the most of her skin. She knew that a white suit would light up her flesh tones against the blue of the outdoor pool, she knew how to *feel* when her pose was right.

Judging proceeded. Leila wasn't surprised to be in the final ten. It was her third time, and she had come third and second already. Surely, this must be her time to come first? Posing beside Number 31, her chief competitor, the current Miss England and finalist in Miss Universe Sonia Hamilton, Leila hoped that Sonia's choice of a white swimsuit beaded in silver would militate against her chances. 'Under the lights it would have looked spectacular, but this was outside, and despite the sun, not a good colour scheme. I knew she had got it wrong. The overall effect was like looking at a grey blob.'

Leila caught Eric Morley's eye. He appeared to be nodding towards Sonia. A wave of disappointment flooded through her. Then she looked up – and saw the clock. It was twenty past four. Time seemed to be running at half speed – and was that a disagreement among the judges? The Master of Ceremonies came to the microphone, but his face gave nothing away; he announced the final three in reverse order. Third place and runner-up were named; Leila was holding her breath, convinced by now that her rival, Sonia – Number 31 – was the winner, and heard the word 'Thirty . . .'

> . . . and I was waiting for the 'One' that didn't come. It took a good few seconds for it all to register. When it did sink in that it was my number being announced, my knees gave way . . .
>
> Relief. Just relief. I was ecstatic.

Leila had achieved her ambition and won the Miss Great Britain title by the time she was twenty. She was now among the celebrities, and within reach of her childhood dream of TV stardom. But in 1957 Leila Williams was not the most beautiful woman in Britain and she knew it.

> I've never thought I was beautiful. It's an illusion you create. If you make up, and you do your hair, and you present yourself, and you win a beauty competition, then people think you're beautiful even if you're not.

In other words, wit, observation and tenacity, rather than physical perfections, had been the tools of Leila's trade. Ambition and perseverance had paid off. Pulling pints in a pub and marrying the first man who offered were insufficiently tempting prospects for a girl who, from an early age, had dreamed of glamour, and escape from an unloving family. Her pretty face and curvy figure were commodities, no better or worse than those possessed by thousands of other attractive teenagers, but when Leila made it to the top of her tree it was because she had played the system, and acted as a professional.

> Everyone wants a piece of you.
>
> And I saw it as a business – a way of making money. Being a beauty queen was easier and better paid than most 9-to-5 jobs. You didn't even have to win – even if you just took part in the final they gave you £10, which was more than a week's wages for most girls in the 1950s. And if you did win, as I did – well, you just do whatever they ask you to do.
>
> I was thrilled by it all. It got me out of my shyness. I'm really very grateful to the competitions, and truly I don't regret any of it.

Good Morning Campers

Sheila McKenzie looked appealing in a swimsuit too, and as a keen sportswoman (badminton was her passion) she never had any hesitation about displaying her athletic limbs. When she applied to be a redcoat at Butlin's Clacton-on-Sea holiday camp, her looks, confidence, energy and sense of fun impressed the interviewers. And in spring of 1956, the job was hers.

> I was going to give it one hundred per cent. Being able to get on well with people helped right from the start. I was introduced to the entertainments manager and various other people, and then I was given my uniform and shown which chalet I'd be living in. And I hit it off straight away with Shirley, the girl I was going to be sharing it with.

To start with I worked as a children's auntie. I took four- and five-year-olds on the beach with buckets and spades, catching crabs and worms and so on. But although I enjoyed it I really wanted to be a redcoat working with adults and soon after I was moved up . . .

Redcoats wore their uniform with pride. Each morning Sheila put on her white pleated skirt, white blouse, red blazer edged in blue with the Butlin's badge on it and high-heeled white peep-toe shoes. A hectic daily timetable meant frequent dashes back to the chalet for quick changes into her sports gear: white shorts, so brief that the hem of the blazer barely skimmed them, and plimsolls. But the overall impression was more fresh-faced and wholesome than sexy; redcoats were expected, above all, to be attractive, jolly and to work hard. Sheila's starting pay was £3 a week (£61 today) with board and lodging.

The site was like a magic seaside kingdom. For the guests, once you'd unpacked and had a welcome cup of tea, there was no need to step beyond it. There were shops, hairdressers, dining rooms, bars, boating lakes, sports fields, a sun terrace, TV rooms, launderettes and a chapel. The ballroom was the camp's epicentre – for next to cinema-going, ballroom dancing was still the nation's favourite pastime. Butlin's was modern, bright, floral and colourful, with rose gardens and row upon row of pastel-painted chalets flanking a huge blue swimming pool. Excluding the camp's huge back-up staff there were about thirty redcoats to 3,000 campers, who paid an average £7 for a week's stay – an all-in-one cost that encompassed food, accommodation and entertainment. Saturdays – changeover day – were hectic for the redcoats, with meeting and greeting, answering of endless questions, and acting as sheepdog to flocks of new arrivals. Each sixteen-hour day started for Sheila in the dining hall at eight o'clock, where she and the others had to be ready to greet the campers with a cheery 'Good morning'.

Her range of duties was huge. She might be handing out games equipment, supervising netball, hockey or rounders teams, organising rambles, keep-fit sessions, swimming galas, tombolas, sing-songs, yo-yo demonstrations and whist drives, or monitoring contests. Most popular of these were the Talent contests, the Bathing Beauties, Miss SHE, the Bonny Babies, the Glamorous Grandmothers, the Fancy Dress, Miss Venus and Tarzan, and the Knobbly Knees competitions. Butlin's prided itself on their wackiness. Prizes were also offered for the best Marilyn Monroe lookalike, Snorer of the Week, Fastest Cigarette-roller, Shiniest Bald Pate, Ugliest Face or Speediest Eater of a plate of spaghetti. Team spirit, 'happy rivalry' and solidarity were encouraged via a system of boarding-school-style houses, based on the different dining rooms on site.

Fraternisation was the point. Sheila was expected to join campers at their table – different ones every day – and could expect trouble from the entertainments manager if she spent too long talking to any one group, or if she wasn't smiling. Problems arose when families became possessive, and Sheila learnt to detach herself tactfully from people who wanted to monopolise her. This included the lovesick youths who mooned around after her, sending photos and cards inscribed to Darling Sheila 'and all that sort of thing . . .' – or the Mr Clever who flattered her with an attentive acrostic:

S agacious
H ilarious
E bullient
I ndecorous
L udicrous
A morous

She didn't go out with this one, but she kept his card.

Dewy-eyed teenage girls were even more likely to develop crushes on the handsome and often very athletic male redcoats, for whom they would have been potential easy pickings. But the male redcoats were strictly enjoined not to make approaches to the younger girls, particularly on the dance floor. Nobody could stop the smitten boys and girls from hopefully booking up for the following season, but redcoats who encouraged holiday romances or gossiped about 'scoreboards' were frowned on by Butlin's management, who steadfastly guarded the camp's image of 'clean family fun'.

> If you upset that image they wouldn't employ you. If you were known to be philandering as far as some of the girls were concerned, you were out. And it was the same with the girls. If you got a reputation for being a bit of a floozy you got the sack.

Boyfriends or girlfriends had to be saved for when you were out of uniform. Sheila only ever heard of one redcoat girl who got pregnant; on this occasion the bosses showed latitude. She was a talented entertainer, so once she'd had the baby and parked it with her mother, they allowed her back.

Entertainment was at the heart of the Butlin's experience and Clacton, like all the other camps, had a fully equipped theatre: the Gaiety. Here, in the evenings, Sheila was often working front-of-house, showing audiences to their seats. But her gift for dancing made her a more natural participant onstage than off, taking part in the redcoats' shows – popular revue-style song-and-dance performances which complemented the programme of high-end professional entertainment. At Clacton Sheila's theatrical co-stars included Tommy Steele and Roy Hudd ('We still get Christmas cards from him!'), Cliff Richard (or Harry Webb as he then was) and the Drifters, and the famous skiffle combination of the Chris Barber Band and

Lonnie Donegan singing 'Rock Island Line'. She found herself a favourite too with Irish crooner Val Doonican, who sent her a pair of white court shoes with an accompanying note 'from an admirer'. But for a star-struck twenty-year-old her most memorable meeting was with her screen idol, the American singer and star of *Seven Brides for Seven Brothers*, Howard Keel. 'Oh, dear, I could have melted when I saw him! None of the others ever came near . . .'

Sheila herself had no ambitions to make the grade as a performer, unlike the many singers and comedians who used Butlin's talent contests as a career launch pad. But when the resident revue company was televised she was thrilled to appear in front of the cameras in a red satin corset with studs and lace frills, five-gallon hat and fringed white cowgirl boots. On this occasion the show required her to lead on a donkey. Unfortunately she chose to ignore the common wisdom that counselled against acting with animals, and coaxed it forward with sugar. Accordingly, just as the cameras rolled, the donkey lifted its tail, and wetted copiously all over the ballroom floor. It could have been worse, and Sheila took the blame for adulterating its normal diet. But the donkey episode has joined Sheila's catalogue of laughs amid the non-stop happy memories of her time at Butlin's.

For Sheila it was the camaraderie that gave Butlin's its magic.

> The redcoats all had a tremendous friendship and respect for one another. And I can't even remember any terrible campers. Butlin's seemed to bring out the best in people, and you got the spin-off from the enjoyment they were having.
>
> And even though it must often have rained and been cloudy, in my memory it's always sunny.

But Butlin's would never be so sunny, so happy, so friendly, so full of laughs again.

Holiday camps peaked in the 1950s. By 1958 Butlin's was catering for around 48,000 campers a week in the season, half a million over a summer. What was it about the camps that made them so inviting to the families – and to the women – who flocked there at that time? Pre-war, a generation had grown up expecting little more than the annual Sunday school outing, or a charabanc trip to the seaside with a meat-tea. Up to 1952 the majority of blue-collar workers had one week's vacation a year, which for many was spent hop-picking on Kentish farms or, for those who could afford it, a bucket-and-spade, whelks-on-the-pier holiday in the kind of lugubrious boarding-house where, rain or shine, the sour-faced landlady chased you out after breakfast and didn't let you back in till teatime. The middle classes might run to a week in a hotel with gardens, clock golf and a 'dinner band', which would scrape and tinkle its way through the three-course meal, from melon boat to sweet trolley. But after 1952 the holiday entitlement was increased to a fortnight.

And now, as wartime memories faded, and weary ex-servicemen and women looked for a well-earned rest, holiday camps came to represent a dream of escape. Above all for housewives and working women, they offered release from the everyday, the mundane, and the domestic drudgery that dominated so many of their lives. Picture the existence of one of the Bermondsey wives surveyed in Pearl Jephcott's late-1950s sample of biscuit factory workers.* For fifty weeks of the year these women barely left the borough, and saw few human beings outside their neighbourhood. Their high-rise homes were without gardens, cramped and dark. One interviewer noted that even in midsummer their Victorian tenements needed the light on at midday. They might be confined with small children or invalid

* Pearl Jephcott (with Nancy Seear and John H. Smith, under the direction of Professor Richard Titmuss), *Married Women Working* (1962).

dependants. And with such physical limitations came a narrow-
ing of mental horizons. Daily life consisted of chores
accompanied by boredom. 'Nothing to look at but these four
walls . . .'; 'I used to turn the room round just for something to
do.' One woman told an interviewer that her chief hobby was
'nagging the old man'; another, that she passed the time by
checking her husband's pools for him. Religion, the arts and
intellectual occupations meant nothing to them.

For women like this holidays were a dazzling novelty, worth
saving up for, a treat to remember all year round. Excitement
mounted in the run-up to the annual summer departure. Of
those who took them (and in 1954, 36 per cent of the biscuit factory workers did not), one in five opted to spend their fortnight
at a Thames estuary or Essex resort like Clacton-on-Sea.

For Butlin's spelt freedom. Your cleaning was done, you were
served with four meals a day; your children were cared for and
your crying babies cuddled. You might sit in a deckchair and
knit, have your hair done, or go for a Babycham in the Jolly
Roger. Plus, the sparkling modernity of the Butlin's site tapped
into the aspirations of thousands of ideal-homers who yearned
for chandeliers, wall-to-wall carpets, mirror-glass and picture
windows to bring sunshine into their lives.

In 1958 Billy Butlin wrote in the Clacton-on-Sea Camp programme: 'Your holiday is my holiday.' Though the activities at
Clacton took place on grounds that had been surrounded by a
barbed wire perimeter fence and used to imprison wartime
internees, military similarities ended there. Butlin's was the
opposite of a boot camp. Nothing was compulsory or enforced,
and though free-for-all individuality and 'doing your own
thing' was still in the future, regimentation was decidedly not in
the spirit of the age.

What did prevail was a spirit of participation and democracy.
For example, entrants to the Miss SHE contest ranged in age

from eighteen to eighty. The contest was sponsored by *SHE* magazine, the glossiest and most dynamic of the affordable fashion weeklies. '*You needn't be a raving beauty . . .*' ran the advert in Clacton's entertainment programme. 'Miss SHE must have charm, personality, dress sense and faultless grooming. There's no age limit . . .' Those contests at Butlin's gave every woman the chance to feel that she could be somebody special. Months ahead were spent planning the matching shoes, gloves and bag that would favour one's chances in Miss SHE. 'You gave us a dream . . .' wrote one lady. And that dream was a potent one. Crowned on the podium, a woman could feel acknowledged and applauded for all the qualities that her own mother had taught her to hold dear: poise, taste and femininity. 'You gave us the glamour, with the hope that we too could perhaps become models and wear fantastic clothes. And, who knows, maybe next time become Miss SHE.'

Swanky Ladies

No social history of women in the 1950s would be complete without a discussion of clothes. I have an early but distinct memory of leafing through issues of my mother's style bible, *Vogue*. She was a keen follower of fashion through its pages, and already at the age of four or five I was awestruck by its dramatic photographic images. Graceful of posture and haughty of mien, gloved and often veiled, impossibly slender yet spectacularly proportioned in their swishing gowns, swagger coats, sack dresses, stiletto-heeled shoes and picture hats, *Vogue* models seemed to embody nothing less than perfection. My mother and I pored covetously over these unattainably beautiful women and their flawless clothes, and together we named them 'the Swanky Ladies', in a vain hope, perhaps, that the rather presumptuous term might somehow bring them within our reach. At this time, *Vogue*'s photographic models were – as described in Chapter 2 – 'Belgravia ladies', and the clothes they displayed were suitably exquisite, polished and high-maintenance.

Christian Dior's New Look, which in 1947 exploded over austerity Britain, had tapped into post-war women's buried longings for femininity. Dior's dresses, with their waspy waists and surging skirts made from up to forty yards of material, were a romantic throwback to an age of hooped petticoats and lace fichus. It would be hard to describe the wearers of these gar-ments, who were so hampered by oceans of fabric that they could hardly board a bus, as opting into emancipation.* And in 1950 Dior was more in demand than ever before. In April of that year the great man arrived in person with an entourage of man-nequins, packers, seamstresses and fitters for a charity fashion show at the Savoy Hotel. Two-guinea tickets for this event were sold on the black market for eight guineas, 'so keen was the ele-gant jostle to view M. Dior's fine clothes . . .', as Mollie Panter-Downes reported in the *New Yorker*. On the day, crowds of well-heeled females, 'giddily hatted and all atwitter', jammed into the sumptuous reception rooms to feast their eyes on his collection of evening gowns with names like 'Saphir' and 'Romantique', in silk, chiffon and lace. The dresses were not even for sale.

This, then, was Fashion: expensive, deluxe and out of reach for all but the wealthy and grown-up. And foreign. The early 1950s had no equivalent of affordable chic, no teenage trends. And normal, 'serious' middle-class girls, like Mary Evans, were discouraged by their academic schoolmarms from taking such trivia seriously; they were assumed to be too high-minded to stoop so low:

---

* Though some have tried: see Angela Partington, 'The Days of the New Look', in Jim Firth (ed.), *Labour's Promised Land?* (1995).

'Good' girls were expected to have little interest in clothes, no personal narcissism and no interest in self-expression in dress . . . Admitting to caring about the matter was about the same as saying that you were in favour of sin.

Virginia Ironside, recalling her upbringing by a dysfunctional but brilliantly talented mother who nurtured a lifelong obsession with clothes, also commented on the sterile fashion environment she had to contend with:

Fashion was not taken seriously in Britain in the late fifties. Men – and many women – sneered at women who were fashionable and called them stupid sheep.

But for Virginia's mother Janey Ironside, who in 1956 was appointed the Royal College of Art's first Professor of Fashion, 'good design and fashion . . . were moral imperatives. [They] were her reason for living.' Barbara Hulanicki, another infatuated fashionista (later the founder of Biba), had her eyes opened to the glamorous side of life in 1954, when at the age of eighteen she was sent to the Côte d'Azur to learn French. She set out wearing a Donegal tweed suit, and appeared on the beach in a draped one-piece black swimsuit. Four months later the local girls' chic had transformed her vision. She returned to England with a bikini suntan, her suitcase full of pastel-coloured T-shirts and matching shorts, wearing Brigitte Bardot ballet slippers. 'My aunt would have said they were bad for my arches.'

Typically, the fifties fourteen-year-old dressed as a thirty-year-old, rather than the other way round, her clothes chosen for her by Mum. As so often, Pathé Cinemagazines are a peep-show on to the world of the 1950s. A coy clip from 1953 presents the rite of passage of Janette, a demure fourteen-year-old, who passes from giggling pigtailed schoolgirl to fully-fledged matron with no intermediate stage. Here, we explore a secret world of fascination with 'adult' clothes. Janette's father has bought her

her first evening dress. She discards her blazer, hair-ribbons, short socks and buckle-up shoes, scrapes her hair into a tidy bun and then dons the shiny brocaded white gown. Though fussy and flouncy, it's also a strikingly modest garment, high-necked, buttoned from collar to waist, puff-sleeved and decked out with insipid silk blossoms. The full skirt reaches almost to the floor and the waistline is constricted by a massive bow like a Christmas gift. The (male, as ever) commentator has the last word on Janette's initiation ceremony into womanhood:

> Flat ballet slippers in matching brocade will complete the transformation scene – for Janette must postpone one thrill for a few more months. Not until she's fifteen will she wear high heels! And so – on tiptoe – a daughter grows up . . .

Puberty, sexuality and their associated messages and challenges were, it would seem from this, still best concealed under layers of taffeta and tulle. Disguised from top to toe, this young/old female poses no threat, and makes no claim. She is a cipher for her father's equivocal fantasy of a spotless and submissive maiden – or maybe a maiden aunt?

When it came to conventions on the wearing of trousers, purity and femininity were also at issue. The war had made a level of unisex dressing acceptable – on parade grounds, railway platforms and in the factories – and to some extent there was no going back. Recalling her teenage years in a small Welsh community in the 1950s, the academic Lorna Sage skilfully unpacks the feminine conformism of its sumptuary laws:

> Girls could wear trousers, for instance – but not generic trousers, not mere pants . . . Instead, the glossy clothes catalogues offered slacks, trews, toreador pants, Capri pants, ski pants, pedal-pushers . . . all in bright boiled-sweetie colours, tartans, checks, stripes and spots, announcing loudly that girls wore trousers only in play, in order to look more girly than ever.

Note Sage's emphasis on colour and pattern. Wartime shades of unrelieved grey, khaki and black were giving way to a kaleidoscope of cheerful hues and brazen geometrics.

Maybe it was because fashionable trousers were unequivocally sexy that 'serious' girls – university students like Sarah Myers at Oxford – were prohibited from wearing them at tutorials or lectures. The prurient powers-that-be saw them as incompatible with a sober approach to academic work. By the same token, what was permissible in a time of national emergency was unacceptable at – of all places – a Warwickshire horticultural college, which specified that 'slacks, shorts or other trousers will not be permitted'. They were also seen as transgressive in offices. An unwritten rule prevailed that women must not wear trousers to work. 'You just didn't. You wore a suit,' remembers Janet Bourne, who joined the staff of *Vogue* in 1956. Janet was overjoyed to secure this prestigious and well-paid job. In addition to £17 a week (good money, worth £360 in 2013) she was given a clothes allowance and told to spend it on looking as smart and formal as possible:

> The first outfit I bought was a suit. And I bought a silk blouse from Liberty for £7, which was terribly expensive. And you had to wear stockings, and decent shoes. And I had two or three pairs of washable white cotton gloves which I wore to work. It was an unspoken law that handbags and shoes matched – a question of living up to our own magazine's features, one of which was, 'What to Wear with What.'

Women's relationship with footwear was as dysfunctional then as now. High-heeled shoes were, as we noticed in the case of Janette, equated with sexual maturity. Steel-capped stiletto heels made their first appearance in 1954, when Dior's shoe designer, Roger Vivier, introduced a slender shoe with a heel tapering to a width of barely quarter of an inch, to complement the frou-frou of Dior's New Look petticoats. They were a common sight for the rest of the decade. Often five inches high, these pronging heels carried a blatant symbolism, at the same time as distorting their wearers' posture, forcing them to throw their pelvises forward simply in order to balance. Vertigo-inducing and killing as these impossible shoes were, midwife Jennifer Worth was one of those who wouldn't have been seen dead in flats off-duty and, as we have seen, on-duty air hostesses were expected to wear heels all day long. The pointed toes, too, were excruciating. Jennifer Worth had even heard a rumour that the top model Barbara Goalen had had her little toes amputated in order to squeeze her feet into them.

Regarding accessories, this was also a time of hats, when – as Isobel Barnett recollected – to attend a Women's Luncheon Club was to feel one had strayed into the parrot house at the zoo. As feminine signifiers went, these feathered, ribboned, petalled and ruffled confections could hardly be bettered. Perky or picture-wide, fur or net, lampshades, turbans or berets, they were every woman's crowning glory, speaking eloquently of folly, frivolity and femininity. These filmy, diaphanous creations were, like their wearers, impossible to take seriously. For Barbara Cartland they were a trademark; she made her platform talks special by appearing decked out in crimson roses or floating eau-de-nil feathers – 'exhilarat[ing] every woman in the audience'. Hats in general were a non-negotiable item of apparel, and people kept them firmly on their heads – at lunch, in church, during radio interviews, in concert halls. When Gracie Fields gave a 1954 Christmas concert to a packed Festival Hall audience of Lambeth pensioners, not a single elderly woman in the auditorium appeared bareheaded, as if their very identity depended on their pudding-basin headgear. One memoirist of the period, John Lucas, also declares the impossibility of any woman appearing hatless in the 1950s. Easter was the time for bonnets, and

Tiny ornamental aprons were a 1950s signifier of asexuality, domestic subservience and frivolous femininity.

every Easter, with a terrible inevitability, Lucas's mother succumbed to the hat-buying impulse. Her trips to purchase millinery were accompanied by a sense of grim urgency, experience having shown that whatever hat she bought 'after hours of traipsing about', would almost certainly prove to be awful . . .

> Home again, tired, down-in-the-mouth, she would reluctantly unwrap the hat from its clouds of tissue paper and we'd see that what she had bought was indeed a disaster . . .

An equally skimpy and impractical badge of female bondage was the apron. *Good Housekeeping*'s model wives took on the cooking, the washing-up and the entertaining not in protective, heavy-duty pinafores or overalls, but in sprigged and frilled squares of dainty cotton, whose modesty and delicacy speak volumes about their wearers' status in the home. Never let it be thought that household chores were in any way the equal of 'real' work, paid work, or men's work.

Many women also suffered torments from underwear. The Hollywood screen idol contours that women craved didn't come naturally; the Lana Turner 'sweater girl' look, or the Jane Russell hourglass, could only be created by heavily structured 'corselettes', 'controlettes', and conically stitched bras. Sheila McKenzie had one of these: 'You could point the way you were going,' she recalls. The Glaswegian graphic designer Flora Calder saw herself as liberated and bohemian but, in love with her velvets and chiffons as she was, she succumbed to the necessity of rigid foundation garments:

> Playtex did bras, but I had one of their rubberised roll-ons – it had little perforated breathing holes all over, so that when you wrenched it off, the areas where the holes had been stood up on your skin like pimples. As for the bras – they were like something out of science fiction – and men thought you were that shape I suppose – until they got them off.

Fiona MacCarthy hazards that the 'horribly complex' girdles and bras she and her fellow debutantes were forced into – 'more like a suit of armour than mere underclothes' – were actually deliberately designed to discourage would-be seducers. Getting inside them was a challenge only the most determined persisted

Feel Uplifted!

with. To add to the complexity, slips were not really optional, and few women dispensed with them. Then there was the precarious, intricate and uncomfortable system for attaching your stockings to your 'pantie-belt' with wire-looped suspenders. Those stockings were ideally made from the coveted new synthetic, nylon, replacing the expensive silk or droopy cotton lisle, the colour of dirty rainwater, of a bygone age. '"Are my seams straight?" was a girl's constant worried whisper to her friends,' remembered Jennifer Worth. When they laddered you didn't throw them away, you mended them. Valerie Gisborn was given her first pair of nylons for her sixteenth birthday –

An advertisement for 'Mystic' bras and girdles.

another rite of passage:

> They were wonderful, so fine and cobweb thin. They could not be bought in Leicester shops . . . I cried with joy to be in possession of such a prize.

Valerie wore them only on special occasions, hand-washed them and only ever dried them over a clean tea-towel. They lasted two years. There were terrible tears when they were ripped and laddered during a rumbustious Christmas party game of musical chairs.

They were totally ruined and had to be thrown away. It broke my heart at the time.

At her Vogue offices, Janet Bourne recalled, she always kept a needle and thread in her drawer to rescue laddered stockings. Or else she took them to a kiosk in Shaftesbury Avenue where a woman crouched all day repairing them with a special machine: 'It cost sixpence. Better than paying fifteen shillings for a new pair.' Tights were for ballet dancers, and were not marketed to the public until the mid-1960s.

Manmade fibres were gaining ground. A writer in the Women's Institute magazine *Home and Country* celebrated the wonders of rayon and nylon among other 'beautiful fabrics' now substituting for silk, linen and wool. 'It's a new age in Nylon . . .' claimed the advertisements, emphasising the extraordinary durability of the new wonder-fabric, while a Mass Observation diarist recorded her joy at hearing that finally the ultimate status symbol might be within her reach:

> In Eye-Witness on the air yesterday, we heard of nylon fur coats, will never wear out (the fur trade will surely be in a panic), moths won't touch them, and at a reasonable price, but not on the civilian market for a few years yet. Sounds wonderful.

The democratisation of women's clothing was also hugely boosted by the increasing outreach of retailers Marks & Spencer, which by 1957 had twenty-three stores across Britain and was fast becoming a national institution. The name behind the brand was that of Sir Simon Marks, who deliberately set out to blur the distinction between rich and poor. His philosophy was:

> Shop girls were going to expect to look like duchesses . . . and feel just as comfortable . . .

One chronicler of the fifties saw M & S as revolutionary: 'British women of limited income were by 1960 certainly the best dressed in the world. The famous "St Michael" label appeared on millions of well-made, cheap, attractive garments, and foreign visitors to Britain hastened to "Marks" to buy clothes.' Anecdotally, debutantes were indeed as enamoured of the store's lingerie department as their working-class counterparts, and between 1948 and 1958 Marks & Spencer's profits quadrupled.

Ultimately, inexpensive chain store clothing would spell the virtual end of home dressmaking. But in the 1950s knitting was still an indispensable female skill. One memoirist describes how balaclavas, scarves, pullovers and egg-cosies seemed to 'cascade' from the knitting needles of his mother and grandmother. Few mums would stoop to *bought* layettes for their newborns; they had their pride, and that emphatically meant the knitting of little garments. Most women were thrifty and skilful with a needle. They took pride in running up a skirt or party dress in their choice of fabric, and at half the price, for sixty years ago Marks & Spencer shared the high street with a plethora of drapers and haberdashery shops. It's also worth mentioning, as Vera Brittain does in *Lady into Woman*, her account of twentieth-century emancipation, that by the postwar period such relative novelties as zip fasteners and press studs were easily available.

I still have some tiny nightdresses made from the finest nuns' veiling, smocked and hand-embroidered round the neck by my mother for her babies. Many of my earliest memories are of her seated at her ornately embellished black-and-gold Frister & Rossman hand-operated sewing machine, deftly removing the colourful glass-headed pins from a French seam as she joined left front to back of a bodice, posting them temporarily in her concentrated mouth as she turned the handle. Her inlaid work-box would be open beside her, brimming with colourful cotton reels, papers of hooks-and-eyes, and assorted mother-of-pearl buttons. The room would be strewn with pattern pieces. Later she would sit in an armchair hand-embroidering excellent buttonholes. Capitalising on the appetite for dressmaking, Mary Grieve, the prescient editor of *Woman*, instituted a cut-out dress offer scheme, which made a fortune for the magazine. Readers sent off for the ready-cut pattern pieces for a specially designed garment in the size and colourway of their choice; then they made it up at home. It was hugely popular, as Mary recalled:

> I could stand on the promenade of a summer resort and see more of *Woman*'s cut-out summer dresses walking by than any other dress . . . I have seen women change seats in a London underground to sit beside each other because they thought it fun to be wearing the same dress, and be readers of the same magazine. I think they also shared a sense of achievement in having made up the cut-out garment themselves.

On a tight budget, Terry Jordan's interviewee Hazel yearned for pretty clothes. The family didn't even own a sewing machine, so she put together the dresses and blouses she craved by hand, long-stitch. Hazel was another avid reader of *SHE* magazine, which fed the growing market for youthful fashion. This was also fuelled by full employment and increasing affluence. Hazel and her contemporaries could afford a 'look'. For her it was circle skirts, paper nylon petticoats, kitten heels, and pony-tails. For others it might be the coffee bar look described in a 1955 issue of *Woman's Own* – 'the new meeting place for all the bright young people . . . Lounge and chat to your friends with a frothy coffee, wearing full skirts in nubbly tweeds, simple clean-cut lines, and neat, good fit . . .' More rebellious was the moody Gallic sophisticate look of black polo necks, tight black trousers and black pumps; Gauloise and paperback *Bonjour Tristesse* in hand, your cool credentials were sealed. American influences – movies and music – also contributed to a sense of style autonomy for thousands of young women like Hazel. 'We dreamt of

America . . .' remembered fashion designer Mary Quant, whose style would influence a generation.

In the 1950s the teenager was born: rebellious, irresponsible and modern. Chewing-gum, rock'n'roll, juke boxes and all, it was a cultural event significant enough in itself to reserve to a later chapter.

9. Keeping Up with the Joneses

How to Get On in Society

In 1950s Britain, 5 per cent of Britain's population still owned 75 per cent of its total wealth, much of it tied to ancestral estates. Fiona MacCarthy's memoir of her debutante days, *Last Curtsey* (2006), brings the world of the chatelaines vividly to life. This caste felt profound ties to the soil – but their fingers were rarely in contact with anything so muddy as a pig or a potato. What mattered across those parklands with their venerable stands of oak and beech was land, and lineage. Night after night before dinner these ladies retired to their dressing rooms to change out of their tweeds, ablute in a stained claw-foot bath and put on a floor-length gown, before descending for 'a lukewarm gin and tonic'. In due course the dinner gong would echo across minstrels' galleries and unheated hallways. Afterwards the ladies retired to the drawing room while their husbands remained in the dining room, stretched their legs and passed the port. The formalities seemed timeless, ineradicable; like part of a dying Brideshead world.

In the post-war era such a way of life was becoming ever more anomalous. But it was all too familiar to Anthea York.

Anthea's privileged country background served only to magnify her feeling of being a misfit. Coronation Day had left her (literally) cold, while the Suez Crisis reminded her how little she had in common with the Establishment. Throughout the 1950s, the deep waters of selfhood and sexuality were to prove, for her, unusually hard to navigate.

16. Every summer throughout the decade, thousands of holiday-makers arrived at Filey station during 'Wakes Weeks' — a fixture in northern industrial towns until paid annual leave was implemented in the 1950s.

17. Putting the price on victory — Leila Williams wins Miss Great Britain 1957.

18. A photograph of Lorna Arnold (née Rainbow), taken during her time working as the only British woman diplomat in Washington DC. 'I lacked confidence. Society at large did not encourage girls to be confident.'

19. Deluged: Maureen Nicol answering correspondence from housebound wives who, like her, suffered from mental isolation in post-war suburbs.

20. A magnificent perambulator told the world that you were an adequate wife and mother.

21. 'How different our national policies might be if only all our men paid more heed to the values and demands of women.' Dora Russell in 1958, setting off in her battered charabanc on the Women's Caravan of Peace.

22. Brenda Nash, *centre*, the only girl from her working-class neighbourhood to get to university. 'It was a very wet Rag day in 1959. We were wearing university scarves sewn together.'

23. A bar scene, 1958. Everybody smoked. Loaded with class aspiration and sexual meaning, cigarettes were a social passport and made contact permissible, while a twenty- or thirty-a-day habit went unquestioned.

24. Summer 1959, Vilma Owen and a small cousin outside her aunt's home in Clapham.

25. Though it was forbidden, Florence Fell was photographed holding her baby just a week before Avril was taken away from her.

26. The last Palace presentation was held in 1958; four debutantes smilingly offer themselves up as upper-class wife material.

27. For many years after Ken Russell photographed them, his pictures of the west London Teddy girls lay undiscovered. Recently, they were exhibited as 'The Bombsite Boudiccas'.

28. Planning a party? *Good Housekeeping* magazine, 1953, shows how it's done. Make soufflés and jellies the day before. Heat up patties and bouchées on the day. Wear 'a slim dress in kitten soft charcoal angora'.

29. A lost ritual, 1952. On village greens, on sunny Saturdays across the nation, proud mums – and the occasional dad – place their babies before the judges. Thanks to the NHS these babies look the picture of health.

30, 31, 32, 33. Poise, grace, grooming, perfection. The Four Ages of Woman, *Good Housekeeping* magazine, 1959, epitomise fifties-style femininity.

From their base in the shires Anthea's upper-middle-class family had groomed her for social success. Home was a country residence near Wells in Somerset. Anthea and her sister understood that they must not play with the village children. They were cared for by nannies and maids, and food was prepared by Ivy, the much-loved cook, on the other side of a green baize door. Outside, the large garden was tended by a man known simply to his employers as Warble. Even as a child, Anthea was puzzled by this: 'That seemed wrong to me, and I always called him *Mr* Warble.' Every evening after five o'clock Anthea and her sister descended the stairs to spend an hour or two with their parents. Mrs York's 'county' credentials in Somerset were impeccable. She was true-Blue, dynamic, energetic and committed to public service. She presided over her home, and ensured that her daughters attended the requisite parties and dances.

> We were a very entrenched, Establishment family. I learned to behave according to proper standards, and how to behave with my peer group. But as a family we didn't open up about things, one of those being that my father had been an alcoholic from the 1930s onward . . .

Dysfunction was something that was never spoken of.

In 1950, at the age of eighteen, Anthea was presented at court, which if anything increased her inhibitions. She didn't 'do' the Season, but waited with a sense of aimlessness to take up a place at Cambridge University. Equipped as she was with all the attributes of society's élite, Anthea felt unqualified to embrace upper-class life:

> My mother expected me to 'land' a nice young man. But marriage didn't figure in my mind, I didn't even think about it.
>
> The problem was, society was overwhelmingly heterosexual, and you had to have a man to go boating, to go dancing, to go to the theatre. You couldn't do anything without a <u>man</u>.

One man wanted to marry me. But when it came to the point something inside me panicked, and I thought, 'I'll lose my independence. I'll be "the wife of . . ." somebody or other. I won't be *me* any more.'

But I didn't know who *I* was.

Lacking encouragement, her suitor soon gave up the chase. But where did that leave Anthea?

Although I didn't realise it, I was living a lie. I was in denial and confusion, and I was lonely. I couldn't confess my feelings about women to anyone, not even to myself.

And I never talked about this to anybody.

The story of so many women in the 1950s is a story of a search for identity, of the conflict between superimposed roles and self-realisation. Anthea's predicament was made more acute by an inheritance of suffocating social rules and practices.

*

Many of these were complex, arcane and pointless. It was considered correct to live in a house (not a 'home') whose postal address was no longer than three words: 'Shirwell Hall, Salop' for example. By contrast, the more hyphenated the surname, the classier the family – as in Twistleton-Wykeham-Fiennes, or Heathcote-Drummond-Willoughby. And girl was pronounced 'gel'. Constantly aware that the upwardly mobile bourgeoisie was closing in on them, the gatekeepers of privilege clung tenaciously to such signifiers.

Thus when Nancy Mitford published an essay on 'The English Aristocracy' in the September 1955 issue of *Encounter* magazine, it sold out in days. Mitford's witty piece on the verbal distinctions to be teased out of the English class system – Non-U (for non-Upper-class) and U (for Upper-class) – was actually a rehash of work done by a learned linguistics professor named Alan Ross. He created the definitions; Mitford popularised them as only she could. Before long, uppers, upper-middles and middles alike were familiarising themselves with a range of social code words that had previously been ring-fenced for a tiny minority. Reading her essay, it quickly becomes clear that the unwary speaker is walking through a minefield of enough potential misunderstandings and embarrassments to drive them mental (or 'mad', as the U person would say). At dinner (which, please note, is an evening meal), the U person will use a napkin, not a serviette. In the land of U people go to the lavatory not the toilet, send each other telegrams not wires, wear scent not perfume, say 'What?' not 'Pardon?' and eventually die, not pass on. As Mitford has it:

> It is true that one U-speaker recognises another U-speaker almost as soon as he opens his mouth . . .

Mitford's sense of mischief was certainly at work here, her catalogue of the linguistic intricacies of social stratification being effectively a bluffers' guide. The public dissemination of the upper-class code both laid it open to ridicule while making it accessible to the determined social climber.

Petty snobbery of this kind was prevalent. Many a teenage Eliza Doolittle was made to recite 'My Wife had the Time of her Life', or 'How Now Brown Cow', in order to soften and homogenise her lower-class or regional vowels. Leila Williams's ambitious mother took no chances on her attractive daughter qualifying for the Miss Britain contests, and sent her for elocution lessons to iron out her Brummie accent, while the same happened to Joan Rowlands (later Bakewell), whose mother went to some lengths to ensure that her pronounced Lancashire diction would in no way betray her as a non-U northerner.

Thus exclusion worked against itself. The U way of life was under threat. Listen, for example, to Betty Kenward writing indignantly about the prospect of the unentitled masses buying their way into court:

> I had been horrified back in the autumn of 1956 to learn that mothers' lunches for 1957 debutantes had already started. This really was ridiculous. In my humble opinion the season was becoming rather a racket! . . . Ladies who had an entrée at court – in that they themselves had been presented as debutantes – were taking a fee for presenting girls who had no mother, or whose mother did not qualify, possibly by not having been presented herself, to present her daughter . . .

From this we understand that entrée to court was upheld by its guardians as almost a divine right, God-ordained. To sell it was as heretical as selling a religious relic. But pedigree depended on it. By marrying 'well', daughters played a key role in upholding dynastic influences and protecting exclusivity. And so the mysterious initiation of debutantes was pursued more hectically than ever (as demonstrated by statistics which show the numbers of presentations rising steadily between 1950 and 1958 – from 877 to a peak of 1,441).

This includes the aforementioned mothers' lunches. For an insider view of the cat-eats-cat world of the debutante's mother, a thinly fictionalised book entitled *How to Be a Deb's Mum* (1957), written by Lady Flavia Anderson under the pseudonym Petronella Portobello, has the last word. Reviewing the book in *The Sunday Times*, Betty Kenward vouched for its fidelity to the facts. The mothers' lunches depicted in its pages took place, as Kenward had already disapprovingly commented, in the autumn preceding the girls' débuts in March. These were 'hush-hush' gatherings of upper-crust females, held in the debs' mums' homes (a hotel would have been non-U): the innermost sanctum of high society's female power base. These occasions were polite, proprietorial, and ruthless, the aim of each mother being to grab the best dance date for her girl. Once claimed, the date would be announced in *The Times* – unless someone else got there first. Coronation chicken was served. The lunches were also opportunities to barter over guest lists, and to acquire eligible and suitable *'jeunes hommes'* for one's own list. Here, some acronyms came in useful, such as NSIT – Not Safe In Taxis, MTF – Must Touch Flesh, and VVSITPQ – Very Very Safe In Taxis Probably Queer.

'Petronella's' book also goes into detail about the outlay required. 'A girl should have five to six evening dresses . . .' Then there were the expensive but essential preambles to Debbery: finding and staffing a house for the season, organising curtseying lessons with 'Madame Toccata', and booking a studio photograph for the *Tatler*. In the case of balls, many debs' mums paired up to save money, but you still had to fork out for an announcer and a cocktail barman.

So much for the debutante's mother. What about the debutantes themselves? Philippa Pullar was one deb who made the most of it. She did two Seasons, 1953 and 1955, both catalogues of empty-headed silliness. High jinks and slapstick à la Bertie Wooster were part of the upper-class mystique. She remembered one party held at Albany where the host's bath was entirely filled with caviar. Philippa and her friends gatecrashed private parties, raided Hawaiian glades where champagne was served, and helped themselves to gulls' eggs and strawberries laid out on gilded marquee tables. At one Belgrave Square ball Philippa witnessed the entry of a social-climbing debutante who descended into the throng by sliding down the banisters. At a dance in Dublin the crème de la crème fought duels with sticks of rhubarb while their posh pals poured champagne on them from the minstrels' gallery above. Philippa's ballgown, which quickly became puckered and grubby, was pink chiffon covered with rose petals. However, her own bloom and curvaceous figure gained her a sheaf of admirers, one of whom wrote to her in the upper-class babytalk of the time – 'I hear that your dance was a tremendous success and you looked absolute blissikins. I was misikins because I couldn't come . . .' Like all good debutantes Philippa got engaged to a country landowner, contemplating with satisfaction a future as Lady Bountiful.

However, far more of the debs who tell their stories appear distraught about the whole rigmarole:

> I never really forgave my mother for making me do it and we still have rows if we talk about it . . .

> The whole operation is monstrous, cruel, terrifying – and I wouldn't go through it again for anything.

For Fiona MacCarthy the ever-present fear was sexual rejection, complicated by mortification at the thought of failing in one's duty to parents who had gone to great lengths and expense to secure you a husband. Philippa Pullar remembered how '. . . there were stories of girls spending all night crying in the lavatory'. Fiona's memory corroborates this, describing the sad huddle of partnerless, brave but desperate debs to be seen at most dances, brazening out their wallflower status in the ladies', before heading home at the earliest opportunity. But for those like Fiona who stayed on – often till 4 or 5 a.m. – permanent exhaustion was a condition of the Season.

> Why was I not driven mad by [the Season's] vacuity? One reason was sheer tiredness. I was, we all were, automatons, drifting mindlessly from party to party.

The Season was becoming a bit of a joke. While continuing to guard their patch against the riff-raff, the smiling double-barrelled Hons in their crumpled pastel taffeta were starting to resemble the fading flowers at the end of the party, a dying breed. After the Princess Margaret–Captain Peter Townsend debacle, insider marriages were starting to seem, at the least, less inevitable, while certain debs blithely broke the rules by eloping or making déclassé marriages.

In 1958 the 'Last Curtsey', with all its accompanying ritual, was made to the Queen at Buckingham Palace. All Betty Kenward's fears seemed to be coming true. Social cachet was becoming devalued, with plutocracy treating the Season as a commercial racket. The consumer boom was making inroads into this last aristocratic preserve; all anybody could talk about was how much the parties, dresses, food, flowers and bands were costing. And anybody could buy their entrée.

> The Season is here. A thousand debutantes with a million pounds to spend are coming to London . . . If you don't know anyone who is eligible to present you at Court, you can buy a sponsor – from a duchess downwards – for a couple of thousand . . . Cash is the key . . .

wrote Nancy Banks-Smith in the *Daily Herald*.

Princess Margaret expressed herself even more bluntly: 'We had to put a stop to it. Every tart in London was getting in.'

Housewives' Choice

There was another world. Pushing her pram up the Hornsey Road on a dull winter morning, Mrs Mary Kennon might have wistfully imagined herself decked in taffeta and pearls at a society ball. She could have read about such glittering occasions in the gossip columns. Some of the names – 1957's Deb of the Year Henrietta Tiarks or the scandalous Tessa Kennedy – might even have been familiar to her. But today, dressed in a skimpily cut button-up overcoat, and hatless in lace-up flats, Mrs Kennon has other things on her mind.

Her first stop is the fishmongers', where before an open shop-front a jumble of similar housewives elbow each other for attention from the fishsellers in their white overalls. Mrs Kennon waits her turn before buying one herring for the evening meal. Wrapped in newspaper it goes into the wicker basket attached to her pram handle. Next, she joins the queue at Edmunds greengrocers'. Apples, cabbages and beetroots are piled loose in boxes outside the shop; the assistant weighs out several pounds of potatoes and tips them from the scale, unwrapped, mud and all, into Mary's bag. The baby protests. Off now to the baker's, where the line of housewives trails out of the door and into the street. When her turn comes, Mary Kennon counts her change and departs with a white loaf.

The time-consuming chore of shopping dominated the lives of women like her. Food-poisoning outbreaks were common in the summer months, before home refrigerators and freezers became common, and the wise housewife shopped daily. In 1951 a Mass Observation survey indicated that a working-class woman like Mary Kennon would spend an average fifty-seven minutes a day shopping for necessities.

Grocery stores, for example, weighed their goods individually for each customer. A request for half a pound of prunes meant scooping the fruit from an open sack sitting on the floor. Cheese was deftly sliced off the block with a wire, butter moulded with wooden paddles into rounds, half a pound at a time. Biscuits were sold unbroken, or broken – which was cheaper. Assistants, skilled at arithmetic, scrawled prices on a tear-off jotter, and reckoned them up at lightning speed. 'Thank *you*, Mrs B——!' they would exclaim, striking the keys of the upright metal till, before with a magician-like flourish bringing down the lever to open its drawer with a resounding '*Ker-Ching*!' 'That's one penny, ninepence, two shillings, Mrs B——!' they would cry, producing the change from a florin for one and sevenpence-halfpenny. At the butcher's, the entire carcases of cows hung from hooks; pigs' heads with oranges stuck in their mouths stared balefully from behind the counter, and the floor was strewn with sawdust to absorb the blood. You chose the cut of meat you wanted and, if the price was too high when they weighed it, you had it cut down to the size you required and not an ounce more. People still relished offal; it was easy to get a cheap meal from chitterlings, liver or hearts. Chicken was a luxury, but every housewife knew the difference between a boiling fowl and a roasting fowl. In the country markets she might buy one live for one-and-ninepence; but it cost threepence extra if she wanted its neck wrung before taking it home. Cabbage, cauliflower and Brussels sprouts were preferred to spinach or pumpkins, which were rarely available; avocados and fruit-flavoured yoghurt were unknown. Chemists' shops had bottles of coloured water in the window. An aroma of oilcloth and polish pervaded the draper's, while at the confectioner's loose sherbet lemons rattled into the scales. Two-and-a-half ounces, twisted up in a paper bag to take home.

Dolly Scannell, who ran a grocery shop in London post-war, felt that 'supermarkets and chain stores do not possess the magic of those small, dark, lovely smelling shops . . .' that she had grown up with. Becoming a 'shop lady' was her dream. When she and her husband Chas took over a grubby corner shop in 1953 rationing was still in force; but as abundance returned to the shops from 1954 – chocolate biscuits, tinned ham, dried fruit and best butter – Dolly was kept busy boning out sides of bacon and skinning cheeses for her customers. It was their privilege to demand as much rindless Cheddar or lean bacon as they desired, correctly sliced, weighed out and wrapped in shiny greaseproof. Competition for custom was fierce, for there were three other grocery stores within a minute's walk. The parade of shops was a community: greengrocer, butcher, baker, dairy, newsagency and tobacconist, confectioner, draper, chemist. Dolly and Chas kept two shop cats, and lived above their business. Once a week, in common with most other town centre shops, they had an 'early closing' afternoon. This was often on Saturdays. But everything – *everything* – was shut on Sundays.

Today, cold storage, the weekly or fortnightly dash to the supermarket, or (just as likely) the weekly online delivery, plus prolonged opening hours, have changed women's lives almost out of recognition. But even in the early 1950s, there were signs of what shopping as we know it today was to become. 'We're Buying More Now', proclaimed the *News Chronicle* in August 1953. Two years later Mollie Panter-Downes was writing in the *New Yorker*:

> The national economy is booming and bounding . . . Prosperity is visible here at every turn, with full employment and expanding businesses . . . People [are] making and spending more money than ever before and a lot of new people [are] suddenly doing the same thing and wanting to own television sets, refrigerators, cars, washing machines and other glossy extras that were only dreams in the lean years after the war.

In 1947 supermarkets, modelled on American chains, with their accompanying trolleys and pre-packaged products, made their first appearance in Britain. And, despite the social loss – no more tittle-tattle over the cheese counter, no more free caramels for an impatient toddler – they met a need. As the decade progressed, and the trend towards shopping in the multiples crept upward, traditional stores began to look nervously at their profits. By 1956 up to fifty 'self-service shops' were opening a month, and by 1958 had gained a 17 per cent share of the grocery market.

Inexorably, it was women themselves who contributed to the demise of the high street. The new supermarkets offered more and more part-time employment to greater numbers of wives, whose increased earnings, in their turn, poured back into the coffers of Sainsbury's, Tesco and the Co-operative stores. The post-war gods of Convenience and Consumption were at this time unquestioningly revered, incarnated in the development of ever more wondrous time-saving products, made newly available in the aisles of such commercial temples. Their advent was a threat to traditional cooking skills, while offering the working wife the promise of liberation: why soak porridge oats overnight when you could buy Cornflakes, or Ready Brek – The Hot Cereal Breakfast Made in the Plate? Perfection beckoned. 'Young Housewives ... know that they can make a perfect sponge sandwich <u>in only twelve minutes</u> with Green's Sponge Mixture.' As for an easy evening meal, why not try Birds Eye Quick-frozen Chicken Pie – Ready for the Oven, followed by Lyons Ready-Mix Suet Puddings – All you Do is Add Water? For a 'dessert sweet with a difference' why not try 'Carmelle'? Sunblest sliced bread was by now becoming a household staple, making it easy to put together a packed lunch with Kraft De Luxe cheese: 'LOOK! It's actually made in slices!' Tea bags were slowly but surely creeping on to the market, and Nescafé Instant Coffee was now in hot competition with Maxwell House. None of this impressed Nella Last. Tins and packets were uneconomical; one should bake, make homemade soup, and cook porridge, as she firmly told her cleaner Mrs Salisbury, who could ill-afford convenience foods. Nella was proud of her own frugality; her diary entries often record her pleasure at the thought of her own home-baked bread, or a hearty soup simmering on the stove: 'such good bone stock with a sliced kidney added to the mixed vegetables'.

It is worth a short digression here to comment on the culinary aspirations of a generation – which could be embodied in the baroque creations of the BBC's first (from 1952) TV chef,

Fanny Cradock. With her arrival on our screens, half a century of suspicion and hostility around nasty foreign food began to slide into history – though traditions died hard. For a number of oral history interviewees, the very mention of such alien foods as yoghurt, curries or pizza prompted disgusted reactions:

> I've tried it when I've been abroad but it's nasty. I tried a bloody fish and I spat it out, anchovies! I just like basic, simple foods, me. It was just corn beef hash, scouse, meat and potato pies, roasts on Sunday and that were it. Just the same as it is now.

But for many a middle-class home cook, weary of shortages and accustomed to making starchy fill-ups like faggots or plum duff, the elaboration of Fanny Cradock's post-rationing cream-filled Frenchified gâteaux and spun-sugar confections was spellbinding. Viewers who had perhaps experienced a continental holiday for the first time since the war were gratified to watch a home-grown version of their culinary experiences, albeit more frilly than the original. Cradock specialised in novelty garnishes. A Pathé Cinemagazine filmed her with her trusty piping bag turning butter whorls into carnations, oranges into serrated baskets, and even hard-boiled eggs into swans, the wings stuck on with duchesse potato – 'an illustration of how a most uninspiring subject can be turned into a romantic work of art by a little ingenuity!' But one biographer writes, 'She was a poor cook . . .' Cradock's trademark pencil-thin eyebrows, ostentatiously drawn in at a dizzying height above her lids, were the dramatic final touch applied to her eccentric adoption – in the kitchen – of velvet hair bows, gossamer ball gowns and costume jewellery, while (unknown to anyone) the bizarre extravagance of her recipes was echoed in her personal life. For Cradock was a double bigamist, name-changer and age-falsifier. Her rudeness and pretension were legendary. But her books sold in record numbers.

Kitchen Magic told its viewers what they wanted to hear: that

'I still can't believe it's true – a washing machine in MY kitchen!' The family is enraptured, and the neighbour peers enviously from behind Mum's kitchen curtains.

fine dining, Radish Whirls and Honeycomb Creams were within their reach – provided they had nothing else to do.

Meanwhile, the tin-opener and packet had their uses, and the feminist writers Myrdal and Klein sympathised readily with the working wife whose recourse to a 'Ready-Mix' provoked tut-tutting from Nella Last. At the same time they unravelled the complex social forces that tugged so unforgivingly at this generation of women. They pointed out that the post-war economy was founded on consumption: not just of Ready Brek and instant custard, but of refrigerators and vacuum cleaners. 'The dream of every woman . . .', wrote Mrs H. Matthews to the Women's Institute magazine *Home and Country*, is 'an electric washing machine complete with wringer . . .'; closely followed by a motorised sewing machine. Women were propelled into jobs that would enable them to afford this wish-list of home appliances. Thus, liberated by their food mixers and twin tubs from domestic slavery, more women found time in the day for paid work. But now, they became ever more dependent on machines to run their homes while they were out all day in their offices and factories, pumping hard-earned cash into a mass-production economy. Already in mid-1950s Britain we are moving into the consumption-oriented society – embryonic but recognisable – that so entirely governs our lives in the West today.

So it was, too, that the inexorable slide began, away from shopping as a chore in the Hornsey Road, and towards the twin concepts of instant acquisition, and shopping for leisure and pleasure. The other great excitement was choice. Once upon a time if you wanted to buy a towel you could have one in white, pale blue or peach. In the late 1950s primrose yellow towels suddenly appeared in the shops. When Janet Bourne got married in 1959 she went on a joyful spree buying primrose bath towels 'because they hadn't been available before'.

Pearl Jephcott's survey of Bermondsey biscuit factory workers went into more detail. The women spent their earnings on labour-saving devices, but also on better furniture and bedding, children's clothes and shoes, entertainment and holidays. A little extra money coming in made all the difference. 'You buy what tempts you . . .' Like new curtains, tinned salmon, oranges *and* apples, or a down payment on a bedroom suite. But the aforesaid washing machines, refrigerators, televisions and cars remained most popular. To own one was to be envied.

'My wife is always getting on to me. She says, "I see the so-and-so's have got a car. Why don't *you* get a car?"'

'As soon as next door knew we'd got a washing-machine,' said a husband, 'they got one too. Then a few months later we got a fridge, so they got a fridge as well. I thought all this stuff about keeping up with the Joneses was just talk until I saw it happening right next door.'

These suburban London neighbours were interviewed by the sociologists Peter Willmott and Michael Young. London itself, observed diarist Frances Partridge after a visit to the capital in March 1955, was now hideously tainted with the vulgar marks of avarice. 'A greedy appetite for material things is on every other face . . .' But not everybody was permanently dissatisfied. Another chronicler of the decade quoted the thirty-three-year-old wife of a Newcastle man as saying, 'We've got everything we want now. I'm satisfied. I've a fridge, a washer and a television set, and that's all I want in life . . .' – a consummation often achieved via a Faustian bargain with the demon of credit: Provident cheques, £20 Clubs, or hire-purchase – the 'never-never'. As a teenager the author Margaret Forster acquired a longed-for bicycle over many months by this method. 'It's wicked. You should be ashamed . . .' scolded her mother, more attuned to the financial ethics of a bygone age. But, with a down payment of

'Just think, darling, seven more payments to the Merrydew nursing home and she's our very own.' *Punch*, October 1954, pokes fun at the newly popular credit schemes.

£2 10s 'the dastardly deed was done'. From then on it was five shillings a week until she'd paid it off. Restrictions on this last form of borrowing were lifted in 1958. Buying through the tallyman was also a no-questions-asked way of obtaining poor-quality goods – until the tallyman came calling the following week, demanding his money.

And now, as more and more covetable durables appeared in the shops, demand, productivity and earnings spiralled, and active expenditure acquired a momentum of its own. With the new televisions came TV accessories. 'All set for TV – the cosiest corner in the house . . .' *Woman's Own* rallied its readers. 'As the evenings draw in, we will all be spending more time round our television sets . . .' All manner of associated non-essential novelties were flooding the market: easy-to-assemble television table kits for just three guineas, one-guinea side tables, rose-shaped TV lights, and – a sign of the times – special trays with compartments for TV dinners, just ten shillings and sixpence. No price tag, however, came with the most expensive item: a lurex-covered easy chair 'whose silver threads glimmer softly in the subdued light from the Marconiphone TV set . . .'

Advertising was having a boom time. Mary Grieve, editor of *Woman*, told how the magazine was hard-pressed to keep up with the agencies' clamour for 'more and more colour to advertise consumer goods'. And from the moment when commercial television arrived in 1955, people on buses could be heard humming the jingles – 'Murray Mints, Murray Mints, the Too-Good-to-Hurry Mints!'; or 'All the Family Love CAR-NATION, 'cos it's Double-Rich!' Daily life seemed touched by modernity's magic wand. Spangles! Colgate! Fish Fingers! Ribena! Camay! All seemed essential to happiness.

So Different, So Appealing

Memories of the war years, the ensuing housing shortage and austerity also lent a Utopian glow to home ownership, and home beautification. We have seen how back-breakingly Winifred Foley laboured to buy her beautiful purple nine-guinea carpet from Jordan's. Satin bedspreads, ivy-leaved mirrors, framed pictures, easy chairs, mirrored cocktail cabinets, hostess trolleys and three-piece suites carried the same freight of fantasy and emotion, achingly conjured up in Richard Hamilton's 1956 pop art dreamscape of contemporary affluence, *Just what is it that makes today's homes so different, so appealing?* Here, brash furnishings and floor coverings, a vacuum cleaner, a tape recorder, a

TV and a cheese plant, alongside the kitsch imagery of romance magazines, present a supernormal background to a male body-builder and a burlesque nude in a lampshade hat posing on the settee. Is this a 1950s Adam and Eve, and is this their Eden?

Such interiors, as Hamilton recognised, were modern conduits for emotion: avarice, excitement, anxiety and love. Collectible porcelain figurines and fragile commemorative teapots were adoringly placed in glass-fronted display cabinets and kept for best. Domestic aesthetics were woman's domain, taste being seen as fundamentally unmanly.★ 'A lovely home', however non-U it might be, was a priority for the Bermondsey wives, for whom a weekend family spree to Blue Anchor Lane in Southwark would invariably result in 'something new for the house'. New wall plaques, new ding-dong bells, new smoker stands, new matching toilet sets and new fancy cushions would be carried home with much rejoicing. In Harlow, a branch of Sheraton's furniture sellers made record profits selling new matching suites to the relatively affluent inhabitants of the New Town. 'It was beautiful . . . solid and very, very comfortable,' remembered one nostalgic customer of her new couch. 'Green, uncut moquette with a sort of Alexandra rose pattern on it in beige . . .' For another Harlow housewife, the purchase of new fittings for her modern home induced a kind of delirium:

> Nobody else had a refrigerator round here . . . I felt sick with the excitement of it. I had a refrigerator coming! And there it was – splendid in its packaging and ice-blue inside. It looked beautiful. I'd really arrived.

Going out to spend one's hard-earned money was taking on a new and glamorous dimension. Having paid a premium for two shiny new prams, blue and cream, one for each successive baby,

---

★ The prejudice prevails today that to be interested in interior decoration is somehow compromising of a man's sexuality.

miner's wife Audrey Alssebrook was not going to lose out on the chance of having them properly admired:

> Every Friday, I used to wheel the pram down to t'market and shop. *Every* Friday! You were dressed up on a Friday, all starched frills and that, with your lipstick on to go shopping. Ooh yes. And Len's mum used to go down with me, all dressed up too!

Nan Marshallsay was another woman of working-class origins who took shopping seriously. Pre-war, a woman like Mrs Marshallsay in a working-class context could hardly have been imagined. She would have been on her knees, donkey-stoning with the rest. But Margaret Forster, her niece, portrays her as an arriviste lady of leisure, spending her well-off husband's plentiful income on making the most of herself:

> Nan did virtually nothing . . . She got up about ten, after lolling in bed having her breakfast, brought to her on a tray by Jack before he left for work, and then she had a bath. Then she dressed and did her face . . . After [lunch], the highlight of the day . . . shopping. For clothes, for herself. People told her she looked like a mannequin, to her delighted gratification.

*

Thus affluence and consumerism contributed to the erosion of Britain's entrenched class system. We have already explored how the 'Lady of Leisure' – manicured and coiffed – became a prototype for the decade. The war had played its part in equalising mistress and maid. Then, as the 1950s progressed, creeping prosperity created aspirational, leisured women like Nan, with time to devote to themselves and their homes. Money was making it possible for many such women to spend the day in idleness, aping society's fashionable debs and duchesses.

This account of the 'never-had-it-so-good' boom risks

presenting women as terminally gullible and frivolous. But the growth spurt of 1950s consumerism went hand-in-hand with an approach to shopping that was more measured. Literally.

Surrounded as we are today by comparison websites and customer ratings, it is hard to imagine how completely unassailable manufacturers were until the 1950s. Advertising claims went uncontested, customers had little redress against cheating salesmen. But in 1951 parliament brought in Weights and Measures legislation, prompting a shift in focus on to the quality of household and mass-produced goods. At this time a number of pioneering women were in the vanguard of consumer activism. One of them was the reluctant debutante Anthea York, who in 1957 got a job as a researcher in the consumer movement:

> It was an era when shoppers – for the first time really – began to realise that they were entitled to send back faulty goods, question them and argue with the manufacturers.
>
> It was a huge education, and it politicised me. I found my feet in the world of consumer activism, and I realised I was cut out for work in pressure groups.

At this time new publications were starting to pitch for the housewife's attention. The chatty and homely *Shoppers' Guide*, edited by the redoubtable Elizabeth Gundrey, was aimed squarely at Mrs Jones-next-door. It was the first publication to take manufacturers and retailers to task for shoddy practices and commercial betrayals, as well as educating customers to choose, to 'watch the scale', and to complain. Its birth coincided with the formation in 1957 of the Consumers' Association, whose famous magazine, *Which?*, was also edited by a woman, Eirlys Roberts. From the start, *Which?* subscriptions took off, and by 1958 there were 47,000. Its investigations are telling: among its more predictable public service reports on washing machines and electric kettles, the magazine tested nylon stockings, bird-seed for budgerigars, and – in 1958 – slimming aids. That particular enquiry demonstrated their complete lack of efficacy. Eirlys Roberts's courage, clarity of thought and professionalism made her a much-loved champion of the underdog consumer. Though the Consumers' Association was not intended to be a campaigning organisation, under her probing and rigorous leadership *Which?* led the way in attacking sharp practices and changing the laws on standards, while offering popular 'Best Buy' advice to housewives. Less rigorously, but no less earnestly, the Women's Institute magazine *Home and Country* advised its readers to check for deceptive labelling, the BBC began the programme *Look and Choose*, fronted by Lady Isobel Barnett, while *Woman* editor Mary Grieve took up the cause of the woman consumer:

> A whole new world of commodities flowed in on the flood-tide of the nineteen-fifties. Younger women had never known such joys, few older women had been able to afford them pre-war . . .
>
> The fifties were undoubtedly a seller's market. And we did an important job in preventing women from being taken for a ride by manufacturers only too keen to rush in and sell on indifferent standards of production.

Mad and Bad

The generation gap that Mary Grieve refers to was becoming ever wider. In 1958 there were approximately 3 million women aged sixteen to twenty-five, most of them earning. And it was through her buying power that the newly autonomous teenager found self-expression and identity: 'We're not kids – but you bet we don't want to be grown-ups either.'

Rose Hendon was one of those younger women who 'had never known such joys'. She had grown up as one of eight children living in a North Kensington slum. 'We slept four in a bed – two at the bottom, two at the top . . . It was "Get your feet out of the way!"' With such a large family, her parents couldn't afford extras for their children. At fifteen, Rose would have to earn her own money if she wanted to dress well or go out. Both of which she did.

> Me and my friends used to go to the Black Ace Club in the Harrow Road. They had a juke box, and we'd all meet up there for coffee. Or we'd go down the Seven Feathers Club, and there'd be music, and you'd do your dancing. That was where I used to go with my boyfriend, Jimmy. He was one of the Teddy boys.
>
> They were smart. And it was because of them that us girls started getting into that look. They had these suede shoes and velvet collars. And then there was the way they were walking – all flash with their haircuts and so on, in their suits from Burtons in the Harrow Road. Honestly, we weren't getting a look in. I liked them! But to get them, we had to get them to look at us.
>
> So we decided to be like them too, and that's how we did it.

Rose always had a wage coming in. And now she knew what to spend it on.

> We started wearing the turned-up drainpipe jeans. Plastic belts round them. And blouses buttoned up with a wing collar. Then we added in cameo brooches, and a scarf, tailored jackets with wide lapels and velvet collars, white ankle socks and flat black shoes with a little bow on the front. Envelope bag. We didn't wear high heels then. But us girls, we were always smart. There was a whole group of us, and the main thing was to be the same as the others. It was *our* fashion – that we made up!
>
> And *then* they started to look at us!

Like the Teddy boys, their chosen look was subversive, and mutinous; the girls had attitude, captured on camera by a hip but unknown young photographer called Ken Russell who would later make his mark as an innovative film director. But the feminine touches – discreet Victorian brooches and ballet pumps – tell another story. 'We weren't bad girls,' says Rose. 'We were all right. We never broke the law. We weren't drinkers and we didn't go to pubs . . .'

So important was it to Rose to wear the right look that she put much of her spare time into sourcing it. Jeans, not readily available in those days, had first to be found, then turned up to the right length. The blouses came second-hand from a man named Dick in the Portobello Market. A Ted hairdo didn't come cheap either, so Rose and her sister did home perms on each other, or spent hours back-combing their hair to get the desired bouffant effect. Rose was on a tight budget. Over half of everything she earned went to her mum. Going out was cheap, because the fellow you were with always paid. But the Teddy girl clothes were starting to get expensive. So when money was short Rose availed herself of the credit system of Provident cheques; the debt cost a shilling in every £ to service, but you got your new things at once without having to wait. By this time Rose was trying to save up – but the money just slipped through her fingers:

> The thing I spent most money on was an Astrakhan coat. It was £25. It came from Debenhams in the Harrow Road, and buying it just felt really good. I felt – I just don't know how to describe it – glamorous.

Jimmy Shine was a Paddington boy – a stranger in her part of Kensington. And his look, as Rose had noticed, was smart. He wore a drape jacket and crêpe-soled shoes. His hair was styled with a quiff and DA – or Duck's Arse – swept back and parted to the nape of the neck. Just one year older than Rose, and endowed (as she describes him) with the suave but rugged looks of a

young Rock Hudson, he'd joined a gang of Teddy boys who
hung around the traffic-free Southam Street blocks where she
lived. There was nothing much to do there, and aimless teenagers like Rose – hair in curlers as often as not, bandaged up
inside a colourful turban – would dawdle on the pavements,
playing cards and chatting. A more energetic game was to lasso
the crossbar of a lamppost with a length of rope and use it as a
swing. And so that evening, there she was, drainpipe jeans,
curlers and all, twirling round the post like a suspended maypole dancer, when Jimmy walked past.

> Well, he just looked over, and he said, 'Do you want to come out?'
>
> Well, I do like a chap who dresses up smart. And I like a chap
> with a nice little bum! I knew when he said that he didn't really
> mean 'out'. All he meant was – did I want to hang around with
> him?
>
> So I did.

The rock'n'roll of Bill Haley and Elvis Presley is commonly
credited with being the music of the Teddy boys; but Rose,
Jimmy and their friends were young to an earlier beat. Down at
the Seven Feathers or the Hammersmith Palais they danced to
the Big Band sounds of Ted Heath, Joe Lewis or the lazy, sexy
thrum of Ken Mackintosh's orchestra playing The Creep, a hyp-
notic, shuffling, swinging jazz rhythm that captivated Rose.

> The Creep was a slow one – but it was the movement that I
> loved . . .
>
> You put your arms around the boy's neck, and they put their
> arms around yours. And one of your legs was in between their
> legs, and you kind of 'creep' like that . . .
>
> Jimmy was a great dancer – we did smooching and all that
> type of thing too!

★

'Suez, and the coming of rock-and-roll divide twentieth-century British history,' the historian Eric Hobsbawm told his fellow-historian Peter Hennessy. For many lesser mortals the memories of that moment remain intense:

Rock and roll burst about my ears . . .

It's easy to see why our age group grasped Rock and Roll with a frenzy and claimed it as its own . . .

The music, so wild compared with what had gone before, permeated our ears and refused to go away . . .

Most agree that the real turning-point came with the arrival on these shores in autumn 1955 of Bill Haley's compulsively syncopated and catchy number, *(We're Gonna) Rock Around the Clock*. By November it was at Number 1, and remained there well into the new year, being the first record ever to sell a million copies.

One, Two, Three o'clock, Four o'clock rock,
Five, Six, Seven o'clock, Eight o'clock rock.
Nine, Ten, Eleven o'clock, Twelve o'clock rock,
We're gonna rock around the clock tonight . . .

Crazed with the beat, teens and Teds swarmed into dance halls. The strobing light of a thousand mirror-glass balls swept over red spotty circle skirts buoyed up by layer upon layer of sugared net frills. In 1956 Haley and his band starred in a spin-off movie of their hit, after which fans danced in the cinemas too. From somewhere came the belief that seeing their idol on screen must arouse an uncontrollable urge to scream; or, more understandably, to jive in the aisles. 'I remember going to the picture house . . .' says Rose. 'And I got slung out of it. The film was on and we went into the aisle and us girls were rock-and-rolling to Bill Haley. And I got a tap on the shoulder, and I was sent out . . .' Rose Hendon remained more or less law-abiding, but by the summer of 1956, the film was setting off riots in the Harrow Road, where the Teddy boys nightly ripped up cinema seats, causing some managements to ban it.

Today, when Rose thinks back to her teenage years in the 1950s, her happiest memories are of those evenings showing off to the boys swaggering past the bomb site, or sitting on the front step in Southam Street playing cards and listening to Elvis Presley singing on her Dansette record player –

> Well it's Saturday night and I just got paid –
> A fool about my money, don't try to save.
> My heart says go, go,
> Have a time,
> 'Cause it's Saturday night babe
> And I'm feelin' fine . . .

– sharing a peach melba, or a juice and a cupcake with her twin sister Elsie, or jiving with Jimmy Shine:

> Elvis Presley, he was just terrific. So – picture me dancing, and really enjoying it, diving, and twisting around, and loving it . . . And it was so exciting: the moves, and the underneaths and the throwing over – we used to do all that . . . Rock'n'roll just got you in the spirit. It made you want to get up and dance. I just loved it, you know?
>
> There was something about that music, it just made you feel alive.

★

We have come a long way from the demure little maiden of 1953 – Janette, with her pigtails and prematurely ageing evening dress. A long way too from curtseys, cocktail parties and debs' delights.

Rose protests that she and Jimmy were innocent, but for many the sexual agenda of rock'n'roll was disturbingly, dizzyingly exciting, its insistent thudding rhythm a heartbeat, a pulsing of blood, the thrusting soundtrack of desire. Elvis Presley made sex as explicit as it had ever been:

> I feel it in my leg.
> I feel it in my shoe.
> Tell me pretty baby
> If you think you feel it too . . .

Modelling themselves on Elvis's mean, cool narcissism, with their challenging looks, their hands thrust suggestively across hips, combs in their back pockets all at the ready to slick down an unruly quiff, the Teddy boys seemed equally dangerous, bad, and unattainable. They were every mother's nightmare, but, secretly, many a girl's dream: like Joan Hilditch, the daughter of a small-town policeman, who met Dan when she was sixteen at a weekend dance near Cardiff in South Wales, where she grew up.

Dan was drunk when he tripped over into Joan's lap at a dance and there and then made a date with her. For a week she was palpitating, hot and cold with nerves. When the evening came she put on her bopper slippers, a felt circle skirt with flouncy petticoats, and pinched her mum's perfume. Dan showed up in tight jeans and a black leather jacket. 'Dad would definitely not approve . . . The evening was a great success.' The following Sunday evening Joan was lounging at home wearing her scruffiest rejects when there was a knock at the door. Her Mum got up to answer it.

In walked . . . Dan in the full dress of a Teddy Boy, the brothel creepers, DA hairstyle, midnight blue drapes with navy velvet collar and cuffs, pink shirt, shoelace tie. My mouth dropped – I

hadn't even known he was a Teddy Boy. Then I flew upstairs
and in five minutes flat was down again dressed in red, skin-tight
sweater, black pencil skirt and the boppers, hair back-combed
and mouth pink and shining. Dad still had his mouth open . . .

Fleeing her parents' gimlet gaze, Joan and Dan made for outdoors. He handed her a stick of chewing gum, and they walked
silently. The moon was shining over the Rhymney Valley,
silvering the mountains.

'Are you a virgin?' he suddenly asked out of the blue. I nearly
choked on [my] gum.
    'Yes,' I whispered . . .

Though Joan would willingly have parted with her virginity
there and then, Dan, for all his mad, bad act, had other ideas.
They were going to wait till they got married. Until then they
walked out, went to the pictures, danced, cheek-to-cheek, and
jived.

I opened my mouth to bumping, passionate kisses and my body
arched to hands which moved like spiders beneath my jumper
and stirred strange feelings of delight within . . .

On mountain walks Dan begged to see her breasts and, full of
pride, Joan offered them to his caresses. He'd kiss them, then
firmly pull down her sweater. 'Not yet . . .' But one day when
Joan was seventeen she lifted up her dress to him on the dry leaf-
strewn floor of a golden woodland, slid her pants down over her
grown-up, pointy-toed high-heeled shoes, and gave him what
they both longed for.

Society's fears of unlicensed sex took on a new shape and
form with the Teddy boy and his dancing. His smouldering,
moody restlessness; his unconventional, sultry, un-English preoccupation with his appearance; his brazen rebelliousness and
sparky defiance all threatened to blaze up out of control, setting

fire to the flimsy façade of femininity and all its paltry orna-
ments: petticoats, puff sleeves, poise. Not surprisingly, the Teds
and their girls were targets for appalled disapproval. The writer
and journalist Ethel Mannin, who seemed to have forgotten her
own bohemian youth back in the 1920s, was repelled and baffled
when she went to see an Elvis Presley film. What could possibly
be the attraction? 'The boys and girls ... scream and shriek
with pleasure at the very sight of his moon face and writhing
belly ...' Later, horrified and fascinated, she went to watch
them dancing at the Lyceum:

> The boys fling themselves backward, bending their knees and
> lowering themselves almost to the floor in a series of acrobatics,
> and [the] girls let themselves go, spinning and whirling and
> revealing their briefs – not much more than a *câche-sexe* – and
> getting 'hep', and all of it a kind of orgiastic frenzy, but still joy-
> less, totally lacking in gaiety or fun ...

Another head-wagger was the agony aunt Leonora Eyles, a
woman of sympathy and insight who over a long career had
provided caring advice to many. But she was getting old, and
when it came to rock'n'roll her normal broad-mindedness failed
her:

> I do want to say that the dancing and its accompanying music
> that have come to us from the jungle, the rock and roll and such
> like, are not fit for the British temperament. These dances are
> often accompanied by drugging and in some cases bring people
> of different races (not nations, that is all to the good) too inti-
> mately and provocatively together ... This is all too strong
> meat for the young people of our cold, grey land; their pulse
> rate, their blood pressure can't stand it.

The well-meaning warnings and prophecies grew louder. Over-
stepping society's limits was a threat to marriage, one couldn't

risk it. 'There are two kinds of girl: good girls, and good-time girls . . . Girls who are good-timers are not likely to attract proposals of marriage from the nicest men.' Girls *must* say 'No'; they must understand that boys had no control over their 'glandular processes', and accept their responsibility if things went too far.

Predictably enough, the older generation were censorious; and they tended to blame America, the land of plenty. Bad things that came from the other side of the Atlantic were now readily available to teenagers with money to spend. Teenage consumption was saturated with the American Dream – brash, fast, big, violent and Technicolor. '[America] was the shining El Dorado of all our wishes,' remembered Katharine Whitehorn. The Good Things that came from the USA were movies, snazzy clothes, supermarkets, musicals, frozen custard, cars, sandwiches. The Bad Things also included Elvis Presley, Bill Haley, Fats Domino, blue jeans and jazz, marijuana, tranquillisers, chewing-gum, advertising, hamburgers, Coca-Cola, cosmetics, the H-Bomb, heavy petting and juke boxes. 'Glaringly showy,' fumed Richard Hoggart about the 'nasty' aesthetics of the modernistic teenage hangouts where fourteen-year-olds pushed 'copper after copper into the mechanical record-player'.

And there was the polluting American language. 'Hep cat . . . in the groove . . . dig that crazy beat . . . cool . . . gone . . .' If you didn't talk the language of *Absolute Beginners* you were a 'square'. The <u>very</u> square Hoggart was just one of those* who lamented the degeneration of society via American 'blood-and-guts'

---

* In 1952, the fear that 'American-style Comics' would fall into the hands of children caused the Women's Institute to pass a resolution against their distribution. Nella Last was also horrified by seeing a row of these comics for sale on a Barrow-in-Furness market stall: 'I never imagined such sexy, pornographic pictures and captions, such sadistic grim torture . . . How they got it past the censors who ban books is a mystery.'

sex-novelettes, the garish progenitors of Lara Croft with their cruelly distorted bodies – huge thighs, straining breasts, wasp waists, and smoking guns. Female imagery was changing. Gaudy and erotic, these 'comics' brought a new degradation into news-agencies and into the hands of boys with money to spare. They were just one portent – as Hoggart saw them – in a transatlantic trend towards sadism, amorality and violence.

Disapproval against youth cultures escalated as the spectre of juvenile delinquency loomed. The journalist (and friend of George Orwell) T. R. Fyvel explored the threatening world of under-age criminals in his book *The Insecure Offenders* (1960). But in his study the female camp follower or sexual partner only gets a walk-on role, appearing briefly as a promiscuous hussy. She is the girl who has sex in a back alley after a dance, as easy as a packet of chips. She is the girl who takes on ten fellows who stand in line for her, one after the other. She is the girl on the game who gives her bloke £20 a night. She is the fourteen-year-old who gets pregnant. She is 'dumb, passive . . . crudely painted up, pathetically young, appallingly uneducated'. She gets pregnant at the age of fourteen: 'Her own bloody fault . . . she asked for what she got.'

Fyvel went up to the North Country and met a gang of these reckless fifteen-year-old girls in a café; they were defiantly drift-ing, had all left their families, earned what they could working in shops, and were 'knocking about with a lawless gang of youths in outlandish Teddy boy garb . . .' And yet, by his account, the idea of marriage remained encoded into their female identity. Not one of them had forsaken the powerful cult of marriage, and its Trinity of husband, home and children. '[This] was the driving force even in their life in Teddy boy circles.'

Betty Stucley was another educated observer of disaffected 1950s youth. An ex-debutante and civil servant, she started a youth club for East End tenement-dwelling teenagers. Her hopes that the girls might prove a civilising influence were quickly dashed when she discovered that they were even tougher and more bellicose than the boys, ever eager to stir up a fight. But she couldn't help admiring their clothes, about which they fussed endlessly:

> The tough girls wore blue jeans, with the names of their favourite rave, screen fan, embroidered down the legs, dazzle socks, satin blouses, duffle coats, earrings, and make-up. It was an astonishing costume.

But Betty Stucley was not among the disapproving Puritans. She saw her young Cockneys as inventive and creative, and early on spotted that they had originated the concept of grass-roots street fashion:

> I think Teddy fashions are particularly interesting, because they have originated with the young of the working class, and have spread their influence upwards, so that Dior and Hardy Amies gave Teddy touches to some of their women's clothes. Fashion, until now . . . has come from the top and worked downwards. It is a good sign that the new young have the enterprise to design their own clothes, and the courage to wear them.

One of these chic kids (another Rose) accessorised her look with a knife carried in her stocking. Rose was rude, angry and – like all the rest – boy-mad. Betty and she had frequent rows, but they got on well because she seemed to lack the prim, cloying femininity of her mates. For beneath the glam hairdos and ostentatious cheekiness of this gang of nymphets, the usual 'home-and-family' narrative was as assertive as ever. Betty was well aware that these girls were not as free as their male counterparts; from the age of fourteen or fifteen they were kept busy shopping and child-minding. And following their mothers' example, they learnt to bleat about their health and pick at their food; they had constant ailments. Betty foresaw that they would soon become like the overworked housewives back at the Block: cross, exhausted, afflicted with infants, anaemia, prolapsed wombs and varicose veins. Youth was short. She wanted to help them make the most of it.

Disgrace

Writing in 1969,* and exploring the root causes of the 60s spirit of liberation, the journalist Christopher Booker identified 1956 as a turning point. 'A new spirit was unleashed – a new wind of essentially youthful hostility to every kind of established convention and traditional authority, a wind of moral freedom and rebellion . . .' Moral alarm always accompanies change. As we have seen, the teenage rock'n'roller embodied society's fears of turbulent youth, of illicit sex, disorder and degeneracy, Americanisation, even miscegenation. Booker is right that upheavals were brewing.

In 1956 new arrivals from the Caribbean peaked at 26,000 (just 2,000 had migrated in 1952) and tensions were escalating on the race front. A public tide was starting to rise against the country's defence policies, with the prospect of mass annihilation dragging ordinary middle-class folk from their armchairs and out on to the streets. The cultural fringe too was turning its back on the creative norms in art and literature. The year 1956 saw the genesis of Pop Art, with Richard Hamilton memorably exhibiting his collage of mass-market imagery as a gently pornographic fantasy. Dramatists were starting to wash their dirty linen in public; the same year John Osborne's *Look Back in Anger*

---

* In *The Neophiliacs: A Study of the Revolution in English Life in the Fifties and Sixties*.

simultaneously startled and disgusted a season of theatregoers with its political posturing and misogynistic ranting. Kenneth Tynan's review in the *Observer* praised the play for its fresh, truthful portrayal, acclaiming its realism, and the ferment of rage which was to designate Osborne foremost among the 'angry young men'. But angry at whom? At society, at the class divide, at complacency. But also at women. Anger at their small-mindedness, their racket and gossip, their deceptiveness, their passivity. Jimmy Porter's wife Alison spends most of the first act at the ironing board, most of the second act cooking a meal. In Osborne's world, men have the luxury of anger, women are still there to service them.

For broadly, there remained a deeply conservative consensus on moral issues. Though small warning tremors were starting to rock the structure, still in the late 1950s there was little cause for panic at the prospect of an earthquake. Virginity, fidelity and heterosexuality were all keystones in the arch of public moral-ity, and women were expected to hold them in place. And those who did not often paid a heavy price.

Earlier in this book we have caught glimpses of the Bethnal Green teenager Florence Fell, the innocent sixteen-year-old who in 1953 stood wonderingly on the Embankment watching the royal coach drive past her on Coronation Day, carrying the object of her idolatry, the Duke of Edinburgh:

He waved to me. He spotted me, and he waved to me. To me . . .

Florence Fell was Rose Hendon's near contemporary, just two years older and, like Rose, she had been born and brought up in the narrow compass of a working-class London borough. But the similarities end there. Florence's adolescence held none of the joys that Rose still recalls with such pleasure: dances, milk bars, boyfriends and clothes. Instead, she felt crushed by an angry and resentful mother who had never wanted her, and whose maudlin religious principles were a pretext for leaving her daughter in ignorance. Boyfriends were off limits; Florence grew up 'on a tight rein', having no notion of sex, no notion of what to expect – only that any form of contact was 'wrong'. 'She watched me like a hawk, but she never quite got round to telling me why.'

Florence struggled through her schooling; a tender-hearted young woman, she dreamt of becoming a nurse, but it took three attempts to get through the necessary exams before she could be accepted for training. Towards the end of 1953 she took her first steps towards independence, bravely enrolling on a nursing course based in Southend-on-Sea, Essex. Here she lived in the nurses' home and for the first time began to feel the thrill that comes with autonomy.

> It was the first time away from the family home. We went to classes, and in between Theory and Practical, we went on the wards to do menial tasks. Bed-making, sluices, feeding patients, bathing them . . .
>
> I studied hard and thoroughly enjoyed the freedom of going out with my friends.

On a minimum trainee's pay, she now started to taste some of the pleasures that self-sufficiency had to offer. She made a friend, Sheila, who, with the other nurses, was happy to go shopping with her, happy to help her buy pretty clothes for her off-duty times: the kind of things that – till now – she had lacked the confidence to choose. She also had a bicycle. On her weekends off she gamely pedalled the forty-odd miles from Southend back to Bethnal Green, for her mother still expected her to contribute a proportion of her earnings to the family budget. Those weekends were a glum reminder of everything she was escaping from, with her mother as unloving as ever, school friends dispersed, and nothing to do to pass the time. Trapped in the small flat, Florence found any excuse she could to get out.

I used to take the bike out for a spin round Victoria Park. And that was where I met William.

He picked me up really. He pretended there was something wrong with his car. He said 'Where's the nearest garage?' – stuff like that, you know? And I suppose I told him where there was a garage. And then he said, 'Would you like to go to the pictures?' So we went to the pictures. He was very likeable I suppose – he would be, wouldn't he? Actually he was utterly charming.

He was in the RAF. After a bit he found out that I was nursing at Southend, and he used to come and visit me there. And he took me out in his car – and after a while he even booked a room in a flat, just for the two of us.

And obviously, at eighteen, I was still a virgin. But I didn't feel any sense of guilt when we slept together. It was lovely – because he loved me. Or I thought he loved me. That's what it came down to: I got this closeness with somebody, that I'd never had before. Despite being a nurse I never thought for a moment about pregnancy. I knew nothing about contraception. It was just so lovely to have somebody hold me tight – and buy me things and – you know? – talk to me . . .

He was thirteen years older than me. He knew what he was doing. But he was already married, and he had a child. And I didn't know anything about that.

Florence's ignorance and neediness were her undoing. Back at the Southend training college, in the late summer of 1956, she started to feel unwell. Rising for her early shift at the hospital she wobbled, staggered and threw up. The next morning she was sick again. She started to miss shifts, but suspected nothing. Completely out of her depth, Florence was beside herself when the Matron and Sister summoned her and instructed her, icily, that she had repeatedly neglected her ward duties and must offer her resignation. There was no mention of the all too obvious cause behind her state of health.

Friends rallied round. Together, Florence, Sheila and the others drafted her letter of resignation. 'I had to write it twice. I had no idea what you had to put in a letter like that, and the first one I wrote was rubbish . . .' Then she packed her bags, already anticipating, with terror, the imminent confrontation with her mother.

I told Mum I'd got the sack from the hospital. But I think she worked things out for herself . . .

Well, then there was a conversation, but it was more of an interrogation. Mum, Dad and me, sat in the girls' bedroom, in the flat, with them cross-examining me about how many times I'd slept with William. Where? When? Who with? How often? I had to explain to them that we'd done it in the back of a car, and that we'd booked a room . . . so that was at least twice wasn't it?

And then they said 'So, you've got the sack from the hospital.' But still, no mention at all of the baby, or of being pregnant.

And I was so confused. There were all these people telling me things, asking me silly questions. And on Sunday morning, the Minister at our church beckoned me, and he said to me, out loud in a public space, 'What's all this I hear about you getting the sack from the hospital?' It was very embarrassing, and I was cowering with shame. But I remember Mum standing there and saying, 'Look up to Mr Sim. Look him in the eye when he's talking to you.'

Gradually, the reality behind her situation began to surface. In her slow innocence, Florence had little understanding that she had acted in a way that disgraced and scandalised her God-fearing family. What had she done wrong? Whatever it was, it now emerged that she was to be sent away. Sent – to a Mother and Baby Home.

'Mother and Baby' – 'Mother and Baby' – 'Mother and Baby'. OK, so now I understand. I'm having – a Baby . . . !

At this point, William reappeared. Florence was sure he would be her saviour, and so it indeed appeared, at first. He arrived bearing an engagement ring, and asked her to marry him. Gratefully, Florence presented him to her parents. Surely everything would be all right now? But something went horribly wrong at that meeting. Florence has effaced the memories. It seems there was a dreadful row. William was told to leave the house. Florence's older brother Tom stormed up to her, seized the ring from her finger, and hurled it from the upper-floor balcony after William's departing form.

> 'Now, that's all over – and you won't see <u>him</u> again.' And all I thought was, 'Oh, so I can't get married.' Full stop. A blank . . . Just like that.
>
> And it turned out all the love I thought he felt for me was just a veneer.

But Florence's ordeal had only just begun. The minister was delegated to explain to her how she had been betrayed. Summoned to his house in Blackheath, and placed before him in a public room where again their conversation was audible to all his family, she shrank under the brutal disclosure of William's perfidy.

> He said, 'I've brought you here to tell you that the man you're having the baby with – the man that got you pregnant – has already got a family of his own, and is married.'
>
> Why couldn't Mum tell me? Mum was the pillar of the church, but she was also the sort of person who would have had me put away in a mental institution. Because she was so afraid of the shame that I would bring on the family if anybody knew that I was pregnant. So I was just bombarded with endless questions, and accusations, and being made to feel small. It ground me down. It was awful.
>
> And yes, I was ashamed, but apparently not as ashamed as they wanted me to be. I wasn't driven into the ground . . .

In October 1956 a social worker arrived at Florence's home and, in strictest secrecy, she was escorted to the small town of Yateley in Hampshire. There, at the bottom of a leafy lane, imposing in its extensive garden, stood the gabled Edwardian residence that was to be her home for the next five months: the Haven. Run since 1945 by the Baptist Women's League,* this mother and baby home was now occupied at any one time by twenty-three unmarried mothers, mostly teenagers, and – depending on their birth dates – an assortment of newborn infants awaiting adoption.

'Sin, shame and heartache ... brought them there ...' remembered Ruby Burt, the nursing Sister who cared for Florence and her fellow mothers-to-be at that time. 'How good God has been, and how He has blessed the work!' Florence still had the greater part of her pregnancy to run when she arrived at the Haven. Eaten up with shame, rage and prudery, her mother had ensured she was sent away before there was any chance of the bump becoming visible. Back home in Bethnal Green nobody was to know. Mrs Fell told Florence's friends that she had gone away to Hampshire to pursue her nursing career, and they were all firmly instructed never to talk to her about her time away. Much, much later, Florence would find out that they all knew exactly what was going on. But that October she believed her mother when she told her, 'You can't bring the child home. You will have to have it adopted. Then you can come home again. And everything will be fine because nobody here will know anything about it. And if anyone asks you about it you must tell them that you were away doing your nursing.'

At first it was a relief to settle into a new, temporary life at the Haven. Here at last Florence was among others who were in the

---

* By 1968 there was a total of 172 known mother and baby homes in the UK, most of them run by religious bodies or social service organisations. Like the Haven, most of them were converted from existing residences.

same boat – 'just normal people who'd made mistakes'. The baby was growing, and she felt well. There was companionship and a sense of purpose. All the inmates were expected to do housework; washing-up, bed-making, cooking or scrubbing the floor – seen as a valuable ante-natal exercise. As a long-term resident Florence was put in charge of the home's laundry. Afternoons were for recreation – a stroll in the garden or a walk to the shops, though Yateley's residents were by no means always welcoming to these outcasts from conventional society, and might well cross the road when they saw them coming. From the staff, however, Florence recalls only compassion. They put in time to prepare the inmates for the forthcoming birth, and there was much kind and heartfelt prayer. On Sundays the girls were sent to church in the village. 'It was an awkward excursion. We walked like schoolchildren, in pairs. Maybe it was "punishment time" – or a reminder to the village people that we were doing penance?'

Autumn turned to winter; the stately trees in the Haven's garden dropped their leaves. As the evenings darkened the girls sat in the lounge knitting tiny vests and matinée jackets, chatting and laughing about their predicament. 'I learnt a lot about Americans, and GIs, and all the forces, and the men that had been away and came home . . .'

Christmas arrived, but five months into her pregnancy Florence would not be going home. Matron Finney, Sister Burt and her staff worked hard to make the season festive, and to remind the girls 'what a happy time can be had, celebrating the birth of the Babe of Bethlehem, without the excesses which had been the cause of the downfall of many of them'. Florence's body swelled. The pregnancy was going well; she felt content, and healthy. In January a magical display of snowdrops in the garden heralded a change in the season, and imperceptibly the days lengthened. The bare roses in the flower garden started to put out early leaf buds. At this time Florence was required to sign her name on forms of agreement that when her child was born she would give it up for adoption. Helplessly, she did so.

March passed, and April came. On days of fleeting spring sunshine the sundial in the rose garden cast a crisp shadow. Florence's baby was overdue. By now she had been taught what to expect, and when her labour started Florence submitted to the pains; but the birth was straightforward. At eight o'clock in the evening she bore a healthy girl.

I cannot remember looking at the baby . . .

wrote Florence later. And it would seem that this omission was intended, for – well-meaning as the Haven's staff were – it was important that the young mothers should not grow too attached to their new babies. In a very short time, they would be taken from them. So for now, the little results of their mistakes were impounded in a night nursery and, during the day, placed in prams in the garden. The mums didn't wash them or change them. They didn't learn – as new mothers do – to distinguish their child's cry, nor did they watch wonderingly over the magical newness of their sleeping infants. Nevertheless, they were required to breastfeed them for at least a month.

And so, we must have bonded a little . . .

remembered Florence. She named her child Avril. For seven days after the birth, Florence was compelled to lie in bed. She was physically sore from the badly-done stitches she'd had, and her hormones were in tumult. At that time, and for a further three weeks, six times a day, Avril was laid at her breast to be suckled. It was then, in those short-lived interludes of intimacy, as her baby latched to the nipple and drew in the sweet, sustaining milk, and as she scented the voluptuous fragrance that only a clean newborn can give off, that Florence learnt to love her daughter. Joy and pleasure rose up in her unbidden.

> I remember saying to the girls, 'My baby doesn't have any prob-lem taking the cod liver oil.' I was so pleased that she'd take it off the end of a spoon. And I was so proud of her . . .
> She was lovely. She was all there. And she was beautiful.

Somehow at this time, though it was forbidden, Florence con-trived to have her photograph taken with her baby. ('Some of the girls had cameras . . .'). At three or four weeks old little Avril holds her head almost erect; her pursed mouth is a cherubic but-ton, and her tiny fists salute the world with a blithe welcome. Her mother's tender downward gaze through inelegant plastic-rimmed spectacles is one of adoration.

> I don't know what that smile tells you, but I felt like a queen there . . .

After about a month, as with all the others, the staff helped Florence to wean her baby. For the last week she saw little of Avril; the nurses now fed her with a bottle. In the garden of the Haven the rhododendrons were blooming. And as spring turned to summer, the end came at last.

> One day when she was six weeks old I was simply told that I had to give her layette to the nurse. You know, three of this, three of that. Nappies, nighties and so on. So I handed it over, and laid it out. And then, another nurse came in with the baby.
> So – there was the layette, and there was the baby. It was all very casual – a bit like a conveyor belt. There was no 'Goodbye, darling . . .' or anything like that. Nobody said, 'This is your baby. Say Goodbye.'
> Nurses. Baby. Layette. Here's the layette. Here's the baby. Both go out the door together. Out the other door – to the adoptive parents. And that was it.

And you know, I suppose I was just accepting. Because I didn't go to the window and peer out to see who was taking the baby. In any case, we weren't allowed to, in case we saw cars or vehicles. The sister stayed with me to make sure of that. And I can't remember what happened then. All I can remember was the nurses going out of the door.

A year had turned. In June 1957, a social worker escorted Florence home again.

But let me tell you, for 50 years I have not been able to cry about it. I've never dealt with all those accusations and all that grinding down.

For thirty years I never even spoke about Avril. I just hid her away. Tucked her away. But I thought about her every day. And I didn't even know whether she was alive or dead. I *could* never know. And it was like a cancer, a lump sitting in there, you know? We call it grief I suppose. I was luckier than some. Some of the women went mental with it.

But I watched my baby being carried out of that door. And until you find them again you want to cry about it all the time. But you can't, because otherwise you'd never stop crying would you? So you put it away, you push it far back inside you, where you can't reach it, until it's safe to cry again.

Therefore I've carried this around with me . . . See, the tears are coming now – I've carried that grief in my heart, and in my body, I've carried it around with me all that time, ever since, for <u>fifty-four</u> years.

10. Under the Radar

We Will All Go Together

On 9 October 1957 staff at the Windscale nuclear reactor near Sellafield in Cumbria observed that temperatures were rising abnormally in Pile No. 1. Something appeared to be very wrong.

> When the plug was removed from the access hole, all four channels were seen to be red hot. More plugs were removed, revealing yet more glowing fuel elements, and they were found to be so distorted by heat that they could not be pushed out. Gausden [the pile group manager] gave orders for the extent of the fire to be determined, and then for a fire break to be created by discharging fuel channels all round the burning zone. If the fire could not be prevented from spreading throughout the core, it would have catastrophic results.

For the next thirty-six hours teams of workers at the Windscale nuclear plant at Sellafield in Cumbria worked tirelessly and heroically to contain the raging blaze. On Friday 11 October the works managers were compelled to make a terrifying decision, which was to douse the inferno with water.

> Putting water on burning graphite and metal might cause an explosive mixture of carbon monoxide and hydrogen with air . . . but the risk had to be taken.

Nobody could predict what would happen if CO_2 combined with such a fire, burning at 400° Centigrade. The outcome might bring about environmental catastrophe; an irradiated landscape, and many hundreds or thousands of sick or dying. But there was no alternative. Following meticulous preparations in fearful conditions the hoses were turned on. Water cascaded into the pile. To the men's phenomenal relief, the critical moment passed. The fans were switched off, and very soon the flames started to die down.

> By midday [on Friday the 11th] the immediate danger was past and the situation under control.

The words in this measured and meticulous account of the West's worst nuclear accident are those of the official historian of the British nuclear project, Lorna Arnold.

We last saw Lorna Arnold in 1953. At that time she was a single mother, impoverished, abandoned by her husband and reduced to getting meals on the table by earning a few pounds working on the production line of a biscuit factory in the Edgware Road. Marriage and motherhood had dislodged her hold on the career ladder; and with the departure of her husband she was left with the simple need to provide for her family. What pathway brought her to Windscale?

Lorna moved on from the biscuit factory, and over the next few years managed to find low-grade administrative work in the charitable sector, but at times she felt paralysed by uncertainty, isolation and lack of confidence, with no spare time to improve her job prospects by studying. By 1958 she was forty-two years old, desk-bound in a musty ill-lit premises in Russell Square, unenthusiastically bringing order to the affairs of the Federation of Business and Professional Women's Clubs. It was a dull job, ego-boosting only for its members. 'I felt I was doing nothing useful.'

That summer the sunshine didn't penetrate the recesses of Lorna's office, and the air felt twice-breathed. At lunchtime, Lorna, feeling that she must stretch her cramped limbs, stepped into the square. As she did so, the facia of one of the new Italian coffee bars now springing up all over London tempted her with its alluring modernity. Caffé, it read, and heading towards it, Lorna nearly ran straight into Charles Plumb, a long-forgotten friend from her post-war past in Berlin.

> It is strange that it all depended on a very small event . . .
>
> If I had stayed in the office . . . or if I had walked in another direction, I would not have met my old colleague, and my life would have been utterly different.

Charles Plumb was a benign civil servant, at that time working for the Ministry of Health, and he was a sympathetic listener. His memories of Lorna's expertise while working for the German Control Commission were still fresh, and on hearing of her plight he was determined to help her. This was indeed an era when what mattered was who you knew. And Plumb wasted no time. Though he failed in his attempt to get her recruited within his own Department, new doors swiftly opened. Passed from pillar to post, Lorna was recommended for an interview with the Director of the United Kingdom Atomic Energy Authority, and was promptly appointed to a position on their secretariat.

Less than a year after Windscale, the AEA was in a state of upheaval. In the wake of the accident came a transformation of radiological health and safety directives, requiring a massive increase in staff. The near-disaster of 1957 was for Lorna the opportunity of a lifetime, putting her on a new trajectory at the age of forty-two, bringing her status, the admiration of her peers and profound personal satisfaction.

Lorna, as we may remember, had been listening to the radio in a Berlin officers' club on the day that the bombing of Hiroshima was announced:

> I was horrified . . . The bomb was not only wrong in itself, but it was wrong because it opened the way to a new and terrible world . . .

She and countless other women were bringing up their children under the shadow of that looming mushroom cloud. Today, Lorna Arnold feels it is hard for younger generations to imagine or appreciate the degree to which the science of atomic power dominated people's minds in the 1950s:

> Could it destroy human life on this planet? Could it make future wars impossible? Or could it be used for peaceful ends – give us, in Churchill's words, 'a perennial fountain of world prosperity'? How could it be controlled, and how could it be used safely?

Thus for her, to find work in the AEA felt like taking a place at the world's top table, a place of intellectual excitement, immense significance and hope.

But for a great many others, atomic energy was still new, mysterious and terrifying. The looming threat of total destruction made everyday concerns seem, at times, meaningless. When Nella Last attended a Civil Defence class in Barrow she was overwhelmed with 'sick pity' at the thought of her own powerlessness. If a bomb fell on Barrow, the instructor explained, the town would be destroyed for a five-and-a-half-mile radius.

> A queer 'sooner it's over, sooner to sleep' feeling stole over me. Ordinary people can do so little – only pray.

A few months later Nella was again reflecting on the 'queer and mad world' she felt herself to be living in:

> The only things we seem able to afford as nations are armaments and atom bombs to further destroy and kill, not only peoples, but the gracious lovely things of life.

Frances Partridge found the topic too dreadful to contemplate; when Ralph, her husband, appealed to her to share his alarm, she did so reluctantly:

What use to think when there is nothing we can do? What use
to think when thinking must perforce reduce one to despair?

Yet Ralph is right of course . . . So yes, we must think about
the Atom bomb.

The Mass Observation diarists felt equally helpless. In Lancashire Betty Hodge read in her paper about the nuclear tests
conducted in the Australian desert on 15 October 1953:

Am rather horrified today by the news of the British experimental atomic explosion. Every one of these trials seems to have
more devastating results than the last . . . If they go on like this,
am afraid it <u>will</u> come to blowing the world to pieces – or at
least making it entirely uninhabitable.

In April 1958, Janice Harrison from Yorkshire was taking a fatalistic attitude:

I've come to the conclusion that we drink too much! However with . . . Atom Bombs looming over the world why
worry?

Katharine Whitehorn agreed:

We were, some of the time, seriously worried about the atom
bomb; but it sometimes had the opposite effect of making us
feel that it was eat, drink and be merry for there may not be a
tomorrow . . .

Meanwhile in Leeds, nursing Sister Jennifer Craig was told to
attend a 'study day' whose topic was how the hospital should
cope in the event of a nuclear war. It all felt so senseless that,
again, getting slightly drunk seemed to be the only reasonable
reaction. Instructions were for all the sick patients, along with
their beds and bedding, to be transported to tents beside the
River Wharfe. Jennifer and her colleagues were sceptical:

'What makes them think we will survive a nuclear bomb?'

'What makes them think that the water in the Wharfe won't be radioactive?'

The practicalities seemed insuperable.

We are shown slides of nuclear bombs going off including pictures of survivors of Hiroshima. By the end of the day we are all thoroughly depressed.

The nurses repaired to the Golden Lion, where after a few beers everyone cheered up and started singing verses from a recent hit song by Tom Lehrer:

> When the air becomes uranious
> We will all go simultaneous
> Yes, we all will go together
> When we all go together
> Yes we all will go together when we go . . .

The Cause of Peace

For centuries women's role in society has been, by custom and tradition, that of the peace-lover, the keeper of hearth and home, the nurturer, healer and carer. The history of women's active involvement with the peace movement is a long and honourable one, with over a century of intermittent protest against militarism and pro-disarmament to draw on. But the Second World War had dealt a blow to pacifism, which in the context of Nazism appeared morally compromised.

In the 1950s awareness of the nuclear threat gave renewed urgency to the efforts of female peacemakers. After it was reported from the House of Commons that a nuclear war would vaporise the planet and that a mere five H-Bombs would be sufficient to annihilate this island, there was public shock. The terrors of atomic genocide, and of radiation which caused birth defects, deformities and sterility, jolted many a stay-at-home mother into the realisation that you didn't have to be a combatant in war to suffer its effects. Unfortunately the campaigning channels – the Labour Party, the Six-Point Group, the Women's International League for Peace and Freedom, the British branch of the World Peace Council – were uncoordinated, partisan (often Communist), and divided. Alongside these, individual women scientists like the Quaker pacifist Dame Kathleen Lonsdale and Dr Sheila Jones of the Atomic Scientists' Association struggled to make their voices heard. As Jill Liddington (author of a history of feminism and anti-militarism*) tells us:

> This, then, was the political log-jam early in 1955. The beginnings of moves to unjam it came from a seemingly unlikely quarter: north London Guildswomen.

In her book, Liddington traces a key source of what was to become the Campaign for Nuclear Disarmament (CND) to the Hampstead gatherings of a small group of concerned women from the local branch of the Women's Co-operative Guild in the years 1955–6. The Guild itself (which still exists) was broadly dedicated to the Co-operative movement, but with an organising, lobbying and leftist political focus. Three of the Guild's members – Vera Leff, Marion Clayton and June Simpson – were initially galvanised by attending a London conference on the H-Bomb. Following this, they started to read about what radiation could do to unborn children, and then attended a talk given by visiting Nagasaki survivor Kikue Ihara.

Miss Ihara showed them photographs of the charred corpses she had seen lying on the streets of Hiroshima. She talked to

* Jill Liddington, *The Road to Greenham Common: Feminism and Anti-militarism in Britain Since 1820* (1991).

them of orphaned children crying and lost, of how bomb blast could flay the skin from a person's body, and of human beings who had been vaporised, leaving simply their shadows on the wall.

> Mothers all over the world should make sure there would never be another nuclear war.

'The Golders Green Guildswomen could talk about little else . . .' writes Liddington. Vera Leff now found herself fronting a small but effective campaign group, organising screenings of *Children of Hiroshima,** running committees, securing press coverage, stirring up churches, trade unions and local political parties. Later they were joined by the scrawny but immensely energetic retired civil servant Gertrude ('Jeff') Fishwick – 'rather melancholy looking . . . very frugal in her life style, and deeply devoted to the cause of peace . . .' On 20 June 1955 Leff and Fishwick were united behind the creation of an autonomous body, the 'Local Committee for the Abolition of the H-Bomb'. Gertrude Fishwick was the 'Hon. Secretary'.

> Jeff went off on her bicycle, a tired ageing woman with an unbeatable spirit . . . We really were poor – in support, public-ity, influence, funds of course. We had no idea how rich we were in potential success . . .

wrote Vera Leff later.

By autumn 1955 north London's streets were plastered with slogans reading 'Ban the H-Bomb' and 'Mothers, would you let your sons drop this Bomb?' Like coalescing atoms, the commit-tees clustered, affiliated, re-formed and expanded from Hampstead to Hornsey, Cricklewood to Muswell Hill. The fol-lowing year saw the Suez Crisis and the Hungarian invasion. While Britain dwindled, the Soviet Union appeared to be

---

* *Children of Hiroshima*, directed by Kaneto Shindo (1952).

NATIONAL COUNCIL FOR THE ABOLITION
OF NUCLEAR WEAPON TESTS 29, GT. JAMES ST. W.C.1

WOMEN'S PROTEST MARCH AGAINST
H-BOMB TESTS
SUNDAY, MAY 12th, 3.15 p.m.
Hyde Park to Trafalgar Square

The cover of a 1957 NCANWT leaflet calling on women
to join a 'silent and dignified' protest.

growing in might. Was this the right time for the British government to be conducting H-Bomb tests? asked Gertrude
Fishwick. As fears grew, so did support for the ever-growing
movement. In February 1957 the scientist Dr Sheila Jones took
her place as Secretary of the National Council for the Abolition
of Nuclear Weapon Tests, its cumbersome acronym –
NCANWT – soon to be replaced by the snappier CND. But
though Gertrude Fishwick's fountain of energy was running
dry (she died, exhausted, shortly before the inauguration of
CND), the movement was gathering pace, with branches opening nationwide. 'Two-thirds of [its] support still came from
women . . .' writes Jill Liddington. 'In the average local group,
women activists apparently outnumbered men by two to one.'

One of these was Pat Arrowsmith. In 1958 Pat, the Cheltenham Ladies College-educated daughter of a vicar, was
twenty-eight, with a history of irrepressible rule-breaking and
dissidence both at school and at Cambridge behind her. She had
travelled intrepidly to Africa and America, got caught up in a
racial reconciliation project, adopted atheism and – after a brief
'straight phase' – embraced her gay sexuality with enthusiasm.

In the mid-fifties, having reached the conclusion that her degree in history equipped her to do nothing of use or value, she got part-time work as a cinema usher, and rented a 'dungeon' with a bed in Chalk Farm, where she lived off bacon scraps and bottles of Ribena while writing a series of unpublished novels. With no ties, she was a free agent. In 1956, driven by a strong streak of social conscience, she re-educated herself in Social Sciences at Liverpool University for a year, then worked for a while in a psychiatric hospital in Chester. In the summer of 1957, in the Central Pacific Ocean, a series of thermonuclear explosions were being carried out high in the atmosphere above Christmas Island. The British government hailed the tests as successful, and pronounced that the UK was now a nuclear power alongside the USA and the USSR.

> That time all merges in my memory with getting involved with the campaign against nuclear weapons . . .

remembers Pat . . .

> Around then, the news broke of a Quaker named Harold Steele who was proposing to sail into the British nuclear test area at Christmas Island, which seemed to me a very estimable thing to do, and I thought I should involve myself with it. So I wrote to the organisers. And not long after I met Harold Steele, who was a sort of Old Testament-like prophetic person, in a thunderstorm on a hill in Shropshire, and we talked to each other about the dangers of getting incinerated by the radioactivity of the British bomb tests.
>
> So then I volunteered to join the team that was being set up . . .

Pat promptly began by distributing anti-nuclear-test literature among her colleagues at the psychiatric hospital. It got her the sack, but she was undeterred. In late 1957 she attended a thirty-strong meeting in Gower Street, called by Hugh Brock, editor of *Peace News*. Harold Steele's proto-Greenpeace-style boat protest had stalled, but now Brock and his followers had come up with a new idea:

> Hugh Brock was very interested in trains. And having noticed a rather puzzling place on the line near Reading, he'd done a bit of research and discovered it was where the British atom bomb was being researched and worked on. I refer of course to Aldermaston . . .

Soon after Brock formed CND's Direct Action Committee against Nuclear War, Pat Arrowsmith started organising for the cause. A giant four-day march was planned for Easter 1958, from London to Aldermaston. Arrangements would have to be made to feed and accommodate an unknown number of people. Marquees, loudspeakers, litter collection, toilet facilities and medical aid had to be laid on at stopping points and at the end of the march. Having been sacked from her job, Pat was living in the YWCA in Earl's Court on National Assistance, and she was available:

> I became sort of office factotum for this impending march at Easter. They paid me a modicum of money. I'd never done anything like it in my life. You know, the phone was endlessly ringing with the press being interested, I had to cope with all the practical arrangements, and farming a lot of jobs out. It was always hectic and I felt pretty overworked. But you kept going. You know, it was the drive to stop the world destroying itself with nuclear weapons . . .

In the run-up to the march, CND held a wave of public meetings. Many of these were male-dominated (the most familiar orators on the subject of nuclear destruction being the philosopher Bertrand Russell, Canon Collins, J. B. Priestley,

Michael Foot and A. J. P. Taylor). But women's voices were heard too. Foremost among them was the inexhaustible Peggy Duff, one of the principal organisers of CND and mastermind of Aldermaston, who had quit the Labour Party after its renunciation of the principle of disarmament in 1957. Then there was J. B. Priestley's wife, the fiery and statuesque Jacquetta Hawkes, an eminent archaeologist in her own right and a co-founder of the movement, untiring in her capacity to write letters to the press and stand on platforms. Dr Antoinette Pirie, a biochemist and editor of a book on what nuclear bombs could inflict,* worked to understand and publicise the dangers of radioactivity. Other CND activists included the writer Vera Brittain, who chaired the Peace Pledge Union and the board of *Peace News*, the scientist Charlotte Auerbach, author of *Genetics in the Atomic Age* (1956), which warned of the physical consequences to human beings of radiation, who supported CND from day one, and the pacifist Labour politician Judith Hart, who did her best to initiate parliamentary debate on the Christmas Island tests.

April the 4th 1958 was recorded as the coldest Good Friday for over forty years, and the entire Bank Holiday weekend was the wettest since 1900. The Committee of CND optimistically hoped for 300 marchers. But an estimated 4,000 arrived in Trafalgar Square for the off, and over the four-day, fifty-mile march numbers never dropped below 500. Jacquetta Hawkes was prominent at the front in an impressive hat. Pat Arrowsmith opted for high visibility in a mauve raincoat and scarlet socks. Despite the atrocious weather, spirits were high, with the marchers singing along to Ed McCurdy's 1950 peace anthem.

---

* *Fall Out: Radiation Hazards from Nuclear Explosions*, ed. Dr Antoinette Pirie (1957).

> Last night I had the strangest dream
> I've ever dreamed before
> I dreamed the world had all agreed
> To put an end to war . . .

But Hertfordshire supporter Lindsey Miller emphasised that the march was not primarily a party:

> I remember having a good time but I do feel that the way we were portrayed in the press as just a lot of people having fun, singing and playing guitars was wrong. It was not like that. It was very serious and important for many people. I remember feeling very optimistic about it all, feeling part of a mass movement.

Peggy Duff's memory of the six years of Aldermaston marches (for the event was to become an annual one) also stresses the essential anonymity of the participants:

> When they joined the march, they were lost in it. They became homeless and faceless . . . Like everyone else they had merged into something which was simply 'the march'.

On Easter Monday, as the procession approached Falcon Field outside Aldermaston, its numbers were anything between 5,000 and 10,000. They marched the final solemn mile in complete silence.

The Women's Caravan

Among those thousands who made the first Aldermaston march was a small, dishevelled, bespectacled elderly woman with a characterful, intelligent, almost masculine face, travelling in a battered motor-coach, cheerfully dispensing cups of tea and sausages to the weary marchers walking alongside. In spring 1958 Dora Russell was sixty-four, but although a fifty-mile hike was now beyond her portly capacities, her feminism, her campaigning fervour and her intellectual energy were as strong as they had ever been. And, distinct from the CND rank and file, Dora believed passionately that hope for the future lay primarily with women. She was not alone in this belief, which sustained many fervent women who carried their anti-war banners in the name of progress, socialism and the International.

Russell was Dora's married name and, though divorced, she kept it. Bertrand Russell's fame as a philosopher, journalist and political campaigner would always eclipse hers – but even before she became infected by her first husband's radical and reformist views, Dora was already an idealist, and a brilliant and enthusiastic student of language, philosophy and politics. When she was just twenty-three the Russian Revolution took place, and three years later she made a visit to the Soviet Union which was to cast a spell over her entire life.

> The spirit of the Revolution, abroad in the land, communicating itself, as it were, through the very air one breathed, was not at all of the West. It came from the uprising of an awakening giant, the birth of a new culture, and it was here, in these first days, that my enduring love of the Russian people was born in me . . .

Today, with hindsight, Dora Russell's blindness to the reality of life in Soviet Russia appears naïve. But she was far from alone, and it is important to understand that to twentieth-century feminists like Dora, Communism had a very practical appeal, with its insistence on women playing a full part in society, and its rejection of glamour and frills. In the course of that 1920 visit, Dora met the Marxist activist Alexandra Kollontai, the most prominent woman in the Soviet Union, a powerful Bolshevik and advocate for her sex. Kollontai appeared to her everything a woman should be: elegant, tasteful, but contemptuous of fashion. At that time it was impossible to dress grandly; but clad in raw undyed linen, Kollontai exuded dignity and simplicity. 'She was an unforgettable, graceful, inspired leader of women.' In Russia, from a peasant woman on a plough to a female university professor in a laboratory, women were expected to hold their own, and to be the antithesis of the fake, poised, beauty-queen blondes so adulated in the West. How refreshing that was for intelligent women like Dora who yearned for emancipation, but saw little sign of it. Feminism – and world peace – were, all her life, the causes dearest to her heart.

In spring 1957 Dora bought a second-hand charabanc which had been adapted into a camper-van, and later that year, with disarmament the hot topic at the Labour Party conference, she parked it outside the Brighton venue, its sides blazoned with banners reading 'Women of All Lands Want Peace.' A week later she was distributing leaflets from her charabanc to the Tory supporters in Blackpool. But Dora found that her passion for peace fell all too often on deaf ears. Male ears. The men she talked to seemed fixed on the idea that nuclear weapons were essential to frighten off the Russian Communists who wanted to take over the world. They could not be persuaded that there was any other version of events.

Nor was it easy to get the younger generation of women to hear her message. Dora despaired of their absorption with materialism. She could feel nothing in common with the made-up, stiletto-heeled fashion princesses to be seen on the streets, aping Marilyn Monroe, with their contorted hourglass bodies and 'dressing up like film stars'. Did the younger generation only care about plucked eyebrows and nail polish? 'When you think,' she wrote sadly to a campaigning colleague, 'of the lovely intelligent faces of Russian women and their devotion, and compare it with the false values our women seem to have.'

Dora took comfort from talking to those of her generation – mothers, mature women – who seemed instinctively to understand that the world had everything to gain by combining with Russians and Soviet bloc women on a joint peace initiative. And so it was that an idea started to flicker into life. In April 1958, brewing hot tea from the back of her campaign coach, making common cause with the Aldermaston marchers, Dora realised that her dream could come true.

Dora Russell's idea was to bring together a huge 'caravan' of like-minded women with the aim of making a pilgrimage across Europe, visiting countries behind the Iron Curtain, ending in Moscow, and bearing the message of peace to all nations. It would be a great adventure, risky, potentially costly, fraught with technical and bureaucratic obstacles. But the ideal was lofty, and the goal noble. She was determined to make it happen.

Very rapidly, it became obvious to Dora that her wilder ambitions would have to be scaled back. Financial support stalled; sponsors dematerialised. The dreamt-of cavalcade of banner-draped vehicles was reduced to just Dora's trusty coach and a solid Ford truck owned by David Burke, an old Irish activist friend of hers who agreed to join them on the journey as driver and all-round mechanic and organiser. Fellow travellers joined in dribs and drabs; from a junior of twenty-one to a veteran of seventy-nine. Eventually nineteen women signed up, having each raised £100 to subsidise their three-month journey. Dora herself spent hours at her typewriter mailing introductions and schedules, while the faithful David was given the task of obtaining visas, frontier passes and petrol coupons. Ferry timetables were perused and maps scrutinised. Meanwhile banners were prepared and leaflets printed in three languages explaining the aims of the Women's Caravan of Peace:

> This is a Mission of Peace and Friendship among all nations!
> Women of the West are on this mission of peace and goodwill to
> the women of the East.
>
> We APPEAL to women of all lands to join with us!
> WOMEN must help to create a united world at PEACE!

And finally they were ready.

> The last stores were stowed, the last touches made to the ban-
> ners, and a few of us went North in the coach to the rally in
> Edinburgh, on the 20th May . . .

Dora told the whole story of the women's 1958 adventure in an
unpublished typescript entitled *We Called on Europe: The Story of
the Women's Caravan of Peace*. It now languishes in a basement
archive in Bristol. Dora suspected that its message of love and
female comradeship between nations undermined the dominant
narrative of male belligerence and the necessary myth of Soviet
hostility. That, in her view, made it too hot to handle.

Maybe. But it is hard to read *We Called on Europe* without his-
torical hindsight. It was the height of the Cold War. We know
now that Western visitors to the Soviet Bloc were routinely
subjected to surveillance, that fear and repression within its
boundaries were endemic, and that when it came to KGB bullying and demands, most people had their price. Dora Russell had
no love for Stalin, but revolutionary ideology held her in its
grip, and she could not, would not see him as any worse than a
beleaguered warlord, just like Churchill. Russia was part of her
own identity. And yet it was little more than eighteen months
since the Politburo had sent Russian tanks into Hungary to sup-
press the uprising in Budapest and elsewhere. The death toll was
2,500. Though, following this, British membership of the Communist Party had dropped dramatically, these brutal events
seem not to have dented Dora's convictions.

And so on 20 May 1958 the coach, laden with the faithful

nineteen, took to the road. The travellers started in the north of
Britain. Two days later they crossed the Channel. The summer
weather favoured them. They camped in barns, picnicked on
verges. Often the women were distributed among spare bed-
rooms of local well-wishers, and on many, many occasions they
were feasted and garlanded. They spoke on platforms in city
halls, addressed village gatherings, wept by war memorials.
There were visits to museums and maternity hospitals, schools,
factories and farms. Interpreters leapt to their aid, mechanics
were mustered at short notice to repair the ailing coach, and at
every stop the weary women were greeted with song, dance and
local delicacies. And so their route swept them onwards through
northern Europe and south through the winding passes of
Yugoslavia, a childhood fairyland of goosegirls and piping shepherd boys. Despite the best-laid plans, rendezvous were
complicated. Tyres burst and telephone connections failed.
Dora would resort to the post offices of tiny villages in mountain fastnesses to alert their next hosts to incidents, delays and
bureaucratic hold-ups, battling with local dialects, wrong numbers and the price of telegrams. The coach rumbled on, coping
surprisingly well with hairpin bends, precipices and the ruts
from ox-drawn wagons.

Sadly, in Albania, the poor battered old coach met its nemesis
in the form of mighty boulders strewn across the road. They
abandoned it in the vicinity of Kukës, and well-wishers provided them with a substitute coach; there were warm embraces
for their new anti-militaristic friends and after a peace dance to
the sound of bagpipes they headed for Bulgaria. There a countryside rich in crops and fruit met their eyes; at the great
collective farms crowds of peasants came out to greet them:

> At every stop a woman . . . would step forward and read from a
> scrap of paper an address of welcome telling of their great desire
> for peace and an end to the cold war. When we got out to reply,

they would throw their arms about us, kiss us and hold up their babies for us to kiss also. Older women stood by with tears running down their cheeks . . . They touched our dresses, as if they wanted to see if we were real or almost as if there were some special magic about us. They asked, had we really come all those thousands of miles to speak to them of peace?

There would be about ten such stops in a day . . .

Surrounded by welcoming villagers, the Caravanners felt they had tapped a well of female solidarity: women who, like them, believed that weapons were not the answer, who saw hope for the future in Soviet ideals, and whose generosity and simplicity gave the lie to Western prejudices about the Communist threat.

In Romania Dora and her comrades admired Communist architecture and a state-run orphanage in Cluj, full of contented babies. Then it was onward, to the border . . .

We had only three days in Hungary . . .

At the frontier the Caravan women were given a hearty peasant feast of rye bread, thick slices of ham, sweet cakes and bottles of beer. Their public greeting was delivered by a woman teacher:

Her every word was charged with emotion as she spoke of the great need for peace. At once one became aware of the still present memory of the 1956 rising, for she told how it had even divided the children in the schools, how those who supported the orthodox had battled with the others to overcome their opposition . . .

But we were not there to take sides in the controversy . . .

Perhaps it was just as well that they were not staying long; Dora might have had to confront the plight of families whose young sons had died fighting Soviet troops, or whose loved ones had been imprisoned for dissent, or had fled as refugees. In the bloodshed of November 1956 over half of those killed were civilians. She might even have caught a sense that their enthusiastic hostesses were, perhaps, not all they seemed to be. But it was over a year since all dissent and public opposition had been ruthlessly quashed, so in those brief three days it is unlikely that the Caravanners would have been exposed to the reality of Communist oppression. And, despite being in Hungary barely a month after it took place, Dora was no more aware than the rest of the world that on 16 June 1958 Imre Nagy, the popular leader of Hungary's anti-Soviet revolution, had been executed by hanging following a secret trial in Budapest, and buried face down in an unmarked grave, his hands and feet tied with barbed wire.

Luckily, Dora and her by now deeply exhausted friends were off to Czechoslovakia, then Poland. The journey had taken fourteen weeks. At Krakow, most of the group now turned their wheels west. Dora knew she had to make it to their final destination, so along with a stalwart few she boarded a flight for Moscow. Its golden domes, its broad boulevards, its magnificent Metro – a marvel of mosaic, marble and fluorescent lighting – were all happily familiar to her. The group was given the Politburo-approved tour of agricultural co-operatives and a watch factory in which most of the work was done by women. They met with the Soviet Peace Committee, recorded broadcasts telling their story, and presided over a well-organised Women's Peace meeting in Gorky Park. Three days later they were on a train for East Berlin. By late August the Caravanners were back in London, telling their story to a taciturn crowd of sceptics at Speaker's Corner in Hyde Park.

Today, we have largely forgotten Dora Russell, along with her valiant little troupe of anti-militaristic comrades and their Caravan of Peace. They have been superseded in our communal memory by their far more significant Women's Peace Camp inheritors at Greenham Common over twenty years later. But the Caravanners and their ideals deserve a place in this account of 1950s women, alongside the air hostesses, beauty queens, rock chicks and society belles whose ambitions were more limited. Dora Russell could never have been a perfect wife in an ideal home. At sixty-four – and for the rest of her life – despite her blindness about the Russian regime, she was ahead of her time, driven by an unshakeable belief in her own sex, and an intense love of life and adventure. For her, the bomb had started it. Its burning shock waves accumulated around the feminist position. If men were setting out to mass-murder the children that women bore, it was up to those mothers to stop them:

> The women's cause immediately became my own, and has since inspired my almost every thought and action in a long life.

Fish Out of Water

The task of the Direct Action Committee against Nuclear War was to picket and disrupt the nuclear weapons industry, often through acts of civil disobedience. After Pat Arrowsmith became the DAC's Field Officer, she travelled around the country, talking to the workforce at building sites, haranguing the unions, organising protests, vigils and sit-ins and often colliding with the police. Later, Pat and her team discovered that Thor Missile sites were planned at Polebrook in Northamptonshire. It was while collaborating with the local Peterborough branch of CND to disrupt their construction that she met Wendy Butlin.

For the next fourteen years Pat and Wendy were a couple. Blunt and unpretentious, Pat wasn't unduly worried about acceptance when it came to her sexuality:

> In general I suppose society assumed one was heterosexual. Despite this I didn't feel isolated. At school there was that whole

teenage culture of crushes and pashes and what-have-you. It's
true I did at times feel rather, well, concerned about myself. I
can remember asking a friend who ran one of the family service
units, 'I wonder whether I should be having psychiatric treatment?' And she said, rather wisely I think, 'Well, it depends on
whether you feel this is what you want.' Nobody suggested that
I should be 'cured'. So I just stopped thinking I should get
'cured'.

I think lots of people were aware that Wendy and I were
probably a couple, without perhaps formulating it very specifi-
cally . . .

Pat was unusual in her relaxation about being lesbian, in a world
which regarded female couples as odd and aberrant. But on all
counts, Pat had chosen an aberrant path in life. From Barbara
Cartland to Noel Streatfeild, disabling missile sites wasn't on
anybody's list of womanly achievements. Pat was frank, straightforward and impatient of humbug; she saw no reason to disguise
the fact that she preferred her own sex.

What was life like for lesbians in the 1950s? Crushes and
pashes may have been the norm at top-drawer boarding schools
like Cheltenham Ladies' College. But in her study of her own
grammar school in Brentwood Professor Mary Evans describes
how an almost pathological fear of lesbianism determined the
girls' behaviour. To be 'boyish', or to be too fond of other girls,
was to be sexually suspect. Mary recalled that to be 'normal'
meant to be beyond reproach, with all feelings of affection kept
strictly reined in and directed at the goal of heterosexual
marriage.

We learned that rule number one of the school was never to be
in love with anybody but boys and men.

Anthea York's conventional county upbringing and public
school education, in which 'we didn't talk about things', had

also caused her to internalise this rule. The result for her –
despite being usefully and interestingly employed in the
fledgling consumer movement – was an increasing sense of
alienation and distress.

> I didn't know I was gay till I was thirty. Until then I was living
> a lie, inhibited and repressed. It's such a lonely life. You can
> understand why gays get together, but I didn't know how to. So
> I just never spoke about it.

In her late twenties Anthea watched as friends, colleagues and
flatmates paired up and got married. She had rejected one proposal, panic-stricken at the thought that once married she would
lose her identity. But though she felt no desire to make her life
with a man, in her milieu dating seemed to be the only way of
engaging with society, even of getting a theatre ticket. 'I just
waited to be invited out. One man I went out to dinner with
was a womaniser, and it became clear that he had something in
mind. I was a bit slow on the uptake . . . He never asked me out
again. In any case, he turned out to be married.' All the time, she
lacked the courage, the independence and even the vocabulary
to express her deeper desires, and the loneliness gnawed at her.

Emotionally naïve, Anthea developed intellectually, professionally and politically. Her exciting job made demands on her;
she could hold her own in a radio interview, lobby MPs, influence people. She developed her views about feminism, equality
and racial tolerance, cooked, and entertained her friends. On so
many fronts she was learning to question the class-ridden British world she had grown up in. And yet –

> I felt like a fish out of water . . .

In 1958, it seemed that Anthea York was fated to live her life
wrapped in a suffocating lie.

Had she but known it, though secrecy, subterfuge, prejudice

and discrimination coloured their daily lives, there were many gay women in the 1950s who lived under society's radar.

Lesbians who were asked by oral history projects* to recall their lives in the 1950s were quick to produce memories of injustice and persecution. Legal sex discrimination often hit single women harder than it did married women; for example, no bank would authorise a business loan without a man's guarantee. Vicky, who wanted money to buy a car, clashed with her bank manager, who insisted on her husband's signature and, failing that, demanded the deeds to her house. But their sexuality was even more of a sticking point. Sandie was expelled from her teacher training college when the tutors were informed that she was gay; the information stayed on her file and barred her from ever finding work in education. Janice had a nervous breakdown and ended up in an insane asylum, where she confessed to a psychiatrist that she had feelings for women. The psychiatrist sent her for aversion therapy – 'where you are given injections and made to feel physically ill at the sight of women doing anything . . .' But it didn't make her like men, and it wrecked her for months. Gill and her girlfriend, both police trainees, were interrogated by detectives after one of her colleagues shopped them for 'having unnatural desires on each other and behaving like cows in a field'. They denied everything.

Too often, the search for validation was in vain. Siobhan wrote to agony aunt Marjorie Proops desperate for a word of sympathy regarding her aversion to physical contact with men, only to be told 'Don't worry, dear, you'll grow out of it.' 'I felt like screaming . . .' Josie had to endure the neighbours' prying remarks to her mother: '"How is it your Josie's not getting married? Isn't it time? What is she, some sort of freak?"' Janine's

*Brighton Ourstory Project, *Daring Hearts: Lesbian and Gay Lives of 50s and 60s Brighton*, QueenSpark Books (1992), and Jill Gardiner, *From the Closet to the Screen: Women at the Gateways Club, 1945–85* (2003).

mother read her love letters and had a terrifying fit of hysteria, so bad that she had to be put to bed for a week. When she was sufficiently recovered she summoned Janine and told her 'I have

torn them up and put them down the lavatory.'

But there was another side to this story. At 239 King's Road, Chelsea, proprietor Ted Ware and his exotically attractive wife Gina generated a permissive and welcoming atmosphere amid the smoky artists' murals of the Gateways Club. Here every night was a party, and Gateways offered a haven to countless women for whom it was often their first introduction to an openly gay milieu.

Jessie was a petrol pump attendant, chauffeur and truck driver who had left her home in the north of England to live and work in London in the late 1940s. In a coffee shop in Wardour Street she ran into a gang of Cockney girls – Addie, Gypsy Rose Lee and the Dolly Sisters. 'You look a bit lonely, love,' they said.

Sketches of the clientele at the Gateways Club present an exercise in male/female stereotypes.

'Well, I've just come to London, I don't know anybody.' They asked if I liked fellas, I said no, I wasn't interested. 'Come on, gel, we'll take you down a club . . .' They took me down the Gateways . . . [Addie] said, 'You'll be all right, we'll look after you.' And they did. I got a job, I got my own place and a girlfriend.

Pat Arrowsmith was a Gateways regular. Her anti-militarist activities earned her a prison sentence in 1958 (the first of eleven), but also cemented friendships with fellow-inmates in Holloway who were eager to chat about the lesbian club scene. 'Oh, yes,' she would think, 'Wendy and I must try that one when I get out.' 'Jo', who frequented the Gateways right through the 1950s, was equally relaxed about the social mix of the club – 'lady bank managers . . . school teachers . . . prostitutes . . .'

In time, one would discover remnants of the Gateways clientele pensioned off on the south coast. Brighton was – and remains – a favoured haunt of gay women and men. Its pub and club scene was cosy and welcoming, with a plethora of tiny bars 'like people's lounges' to be discovered down the city's twittens and alleys. 'There was a sort of family feeling . . .', and a sense of private recognition. Codes helped:

> If somebody was out in the gear, you'd give them the glad eye or they'd give you the glad eye. You always had a little finger ring, whether you were butch or fem. Or you'd wear a wedding ring if you were fixed up with somebody, on your other hand.

In the Kemp Town area, word soon got round about an understanding male barber who was prepared to give girls a masculine short-back-and-sides. Soon all the butch girls were on his doorstep, leaving an hour later with identikit haircuts.

Wherever you went in the evening, looking the part was important. Depending on your orientation, you could pick from a range of looks: the dandified dyke, the brassy lipsticked blonde, the butch type in cloak, tie and sombrero, the hefty-handed labourer in oilskins and breeches. Women who liked suits were into severe tailoring, and might often be mistaken for men in their grey flannels, cufflinks, short-back-and-sides. Jessie adopted Teddy boy drapes, string ties and brothel creepers. 'Ricky' bought her suits at Savoy Taylors, her shoes in Bond Street, and was content to be addressed as 'Sir'. There were those who used to bind their breasts with tight elastic, or pad up their crotches to look more like men. But it was not unknown for cross-dressers like this to find themselves spending a night in the cells, especially if they had been accidentally spotted in a gents' toilet. 'Cross-dressing was not against the law, but the police didn't like it.'

Vicky wore a skirt on her first visit to a Brighton club, but was quickly made to feel like an outsider by the short-haired women wearing clean-cut tailored trousers. While outside gay circles trousers were often seen as unfeminine, here, wearing a skirt made you a misfit. So during the week Vicky walked into a menswear shop and asked to try on a pair of trousers. The assistants refused on the basis that she couldn't be permitted to use the male changing rooms, so she had a battle on her hands. After much argy-bargy she won her point, and the following week marched into the club in trousers and a crisp men's shirt. 'I felt much more at ease.' Meanwhile, the femme women were identified by glamour, skirts, high heels and black patent-leather handbags, and never paid for their own drinks.

The oral history interviews offer a fascinating picture of the lesbian community in the 1950s, for against a social backdrop of rigid gender divisions, these bohemian clubbers were oddly in love with sexual stereotypes. The behaviour of lesbian couples mirrored the coupledom of the heterosexual world. The 'butchy' types worked in garages or in transport and brought home their wages. If their femme partners worked, it was as secretaries. But many were housewives, staying at home, minding the pets, and cooking.

> As a butch I sat down at the dinner table and my dinner was put in front of me as my father before me and my grandfather before that. Whereas the femme always took the role on as the house-wife and mother.

Impersonation? Role-play? Whatever it was, this was a kind of sexual conformity. It would appear that the convention of the perfect wife was so locked in the public imagination that – subversive as these women were – they had no vocabulary of transgression through which to express themselves. And yet, many of them – like Sandy – rejected society's overwhelming feminine imperatives:

> I wasn't interested in kids, washing-up powders, the price of butter, knitting patterns and all that crap. I wanted to do what I saw boys doing.
>
> I was also interested in girls and women, sexually. Men weren't encumbered by stockings and suspender belts and corsets and bras and tight skirts. They wore trousers and they could move around freely and run and dance, and that's what I wanted.

Ticket to Freedom

Where the female sex was concerned, Britain in the 1950s remained a world of stereotypes and impossible ideals, where 'deviancy' met with ignorance and hostility. Our society was one which tolerated intolerance, and sanctioned sexism.

Brenda Nash was not sexually interested in girls or women. But the physical liberty of being a man was denied her. Growing up at the bottom of the pile in a Birmingham council house, Brenda chafed daily against the mischance which had decreed her to be a girl not a boy.

> To be born a girl was to be born a second-class citizen. [Boys] were something in [our] world; girls were nothing.

Her Gran, her mother, her sisters were accepting. Brenda wasn't. Embedded in her personality was a chip of steel, a resolve not to remain in the working-class rut fate had decreed for her, and a determination to challenge a world which ordained what kind of woman she would grow up to be. There were so many things women weren't supposed to be or do. One of them was to play football for England.

Post-war, the game took hold in this country as never before. It was the working-class sport par excellence, and one which commanded fierce local loyalties. Look at any 1950s newsreel of a league match or cup final, and the stadium is thick with tiers of mufflered men shouting themselves hoarse for their home team. Gates were enormous. Brenda's team, Wolverhampton Wanderers, could count on support over the 50,000 mark for a big match – but with barely a female face among them. And yet from an early age Brenda nurtured a passion for the game. Every year she burned with disappointment as, unwrapping her relatives' Christmas gifts, the predictable 'home-making' toys emerged – tea-sets, dolls and prams. How happy she was when her brother (who, mysteriously, had no interest in sport) was given a real leather football, which she promptly swooped on 'with whoops of joy'. But dreams were in short supply in the Nash household. Constantly hovering on the brink of destitution, the family were argumentative, dysfunctional and crushed. When Brenda wasn't travelling to and from school, or coping with lessons, she was deputising for her feckless mother at the stove or kitchen sink. It was hard to see any future:

> For girls it would be a couple of years working in a factory, or, at best, a shop, before early marriage, children and the perennial problem of how to make ends meet . . .
>
> This, I promised myself, wasn't going to be my lot. I was going to cross the divide, get out of the rut I seemed destined for: and my first way out, I decided, was to be through the forbidden world of football.

And so she set about trying to break in, not an easy proposition. It was more than Mr Nash's pride could handle to be seen taking his teenage daughter to a match, and it took two years to wear her

father down. Finally in 1955 Brenda attended her first Football
League match, Birmingham v. Lincoln, 3–3, but Wolves and their
glamorous captain Billy Wright soon captured her heart, and
from then on her loyalties were unwavering. There was, she
admitted, something a bit shameful about so risking her 'credibility as a serious football supporter by letting my emotion rule . . .'

> But, then, football is wholly to do with emotion, isn't it, and I
> could hardly ignore mine.

From now on, every penny that came Brenda's way went on her
ticket to freedom – those Saturdays in the Molineux stadium at
Wolverhampton, 'a patch of heaven in a life of infernal misery'.

> I got out of the house as much as possible and dreamt of a new
> life, immersing myself in the camaraderie of football, where, for
> a few precious hours a week, I could dream I was somebody and
> meant something to somebody.

On match days she rose at dawn to complete her chores, before
heading for the station swathed in her black-and-gold team scarf.
After the short train journey there was the thrill of approaching
the ground itself amid the crowd. Threepenny programmes,
black-and-gold rosettes, photographs of the players, team pictures and autograph books were among the tempting souvenirs
on sale; Brenda was an obsessive autograph hunter. Then on,
through the turnstiles, and there below was the vista of the
Molineux – 'laid out before me, the terraces filling up with
expectant fans and the pitch a pristine green, just waiting for the
sounds of "The Happy Wanderer" to boom out from the tannoy
system as a signal for the players to run out on to the field'.

To participate in the moment of a Wolves' win was to know
glory, to become part of the legend, and to carry with you 'the
courage to get through next week . . .' To lose was to contemplate hurling oneself dramatically into the nearest canal.

In 1957–8 Brenda basked in one of the best seasons Wolves had ever played, her joy blighted only by the numbing news that came through late on a chilly February afternoon, that the flight carrying the Manchester United team back from Belgrade had crashed after a refuelling stop-off at Munich airport. Seven members of the squad lost their lives on that bitter day. United were the Wolves' greatest rivals, but Brenda, along with the entire country, grieved for young lives cut short. To her, and to millions of English football fans, their deaths felt like a personal tragedy.

But worse was to come, and this time the news punctured forever her inflated fantasy of football as an escape route. In July, her adored Billy Wright married Joy Beverley, the eldest of the three Beverley Sisters, whose much-loved singles ('I Saw Mommy Kissing Santa Claus' had reached Number 6 in the Hit Parade in 1953) brought them national and international celebrity. Joy Beverley was blonde, curvaceous, talented, glamorous, feminine and rich. When she heard the news, Brenda was – for only the second time in her life – on holiday with her family, camping in Devon. The rain poured down in sheets on their army-surplus tent. Inside, Brenda lay on her clammy groundsheet, and cried, and cried.

My misery was complete.

Football itself was changing. Now television was forcing the clubs to look for new ways to generate income, draughty terraces were being replaced by stands, and the cloth cap and muffler was being superseded by the suit and tie of the corporate client. The game's working-class roots, its love affair with its local supporter base, had meant everything. In 1958, though Brenda's passion for the sport remained undimmed, that door seemed to be closing.

For Brenda Nash, 'football belonged to the people'. It had

given meaning to her pinched, deprived and obscure existence. It had meant something to live for, someone to love, and a door to a different destiny beyond the one usually set aside for working-class women. She could never marry Billy Wright now. Goals on the pitch had meant everything to her. At the age of eighteen, Brenda had to look to goals beyond team autographs, Molineux and a Wolves' win.

Butler's 1944 Education Act had, theoretically, given working-class girls like Brenda access to higher education and the professions. Could exam results open the doors to her dream of a better life? For excitement and stimulus, school had never come close to football for Brenda. 'I hated school . . .' She would willingly have been spared the tedium and mortification of being a working-class girl at a middle-class grammar school, but as the football dream receded she was smart enough to recognise that passing exams offered her the only real escape from her narrow, poverty-stricken background:

> I didn't want my mum's life. I didn't want the ignorance. I didn't know where I was going *to*, but I knew what I was getting out *from*. And I just thought, I'm getting out. And I will do what I have to do to *get out*.

So she soldiered on, kept at her studies by family attrition: Mom needed her at home to be nanny, cook and housekeeper. In autumn 1958, Brenda Nash emerged with a place to read French at Leicester University.

Achieving this had been a hit-and-miss process. There was no UCAS system. She wrote letters of application to Sheffield, Nottingham and Leicester, agonising about how to fund the necessary trips for interviews. She struggled through the subsequent interrogations in torment, hoping that knowledge of her 'A' Level set books would suffice, for with the *Daily Mirror* being the only printed matter in the house, her literary background was nil. Soon after, she was amazed to be offered places at all three universities. Her decision to choose Leicester was influenced by the fact that England player Derek Hogg played outside-left for Leicester City, but an even greater source of satisfaction was the knowledge of being the only young person living on her council estate ever to have gained a university place. And that October, Brenda's life changed overnight.

To begin with, there was the luxury of living in a residential hall. Here, the furniture was new; the bed was comfortable. To her astonishment her laundry was done for her, her room cleaned, and her meals – of a stodgy but wholesome nature – provided. Brenda didn't care.

> I loved it. Cooked meals that I hadn't had to cook myself! It was food of the gods . . . All we had to do was study and pass exams.
> Transformation from domestic drudge to carefree student!

From that moment on, she inhabited a new world, cosy, ordered and civilised. Lectures and tutorials were compulsory, and students were expected to appear at them dressed in academic gowns. All staff were addressed formally, and repaid the courtesy to their students: 'Miss Nash'. But for a working-class girl there was still so much to get used to. Soon she was writing essays on Descartes, Molière and Zola, and attending with earnest absorption to lectures on Linguistics, Dadaism and the Theatre of the Absurd. Intellectual and social horizons were expanding at the speed of light. Her fellow-students had names like Celia and Angela. With the money from her student grant she opened a bank account. She bought iced buns and coffee from a coffee bar. Brenda was nineteen, yet till now her social life had never offered more than the cinema or the local swimming pool. At university, she was spoilt for choice. From AmDram to debating, local history to the film society, there was so much to do, and so many people to do it with. Now, Saturday

nights saw Brenda trying out jive steps at the weekly hop, aston-
ished to discover, too, that the world was full of young men
who found her attractive and wanted to join her on the dance
floor. For this working-class Cinderella, university was a magic
wand; and to crown the transformation scene, she fell in love in
her second year with Peter Bullock, an English major and the
son of a comfortably-off Birmingham accountant.

Their marriage in 1962 relocated Brenda irreversibly among
the educated middle classes. Both would become teachers. Later,
Brenda sat a Masters degree in Linguistics, presenting her dis-
sertation on Taboo and Euphemism with particular reference to
the seventeenth century. In 2012 the Bullocks' Solihull sitting
room was copiously furnished with paintings, objets d'art picked
up on their travels, and walled with shelf upon shelf of poetry
and literature. The transferral seemed complete.

But the British class system had a final revenge to exact on
Brenda.

In his seminal social commentary *The Uses of Literacy* (1957),
Richard Hoggart devoted a deeply heartfelt chapter to discussing the consequences of social displacement. As a working-class
boy growing up in a book-free environment who had risen to
become a highly respected academic (as a student Brenda Nash
was aware of his presence at Leicester University) this had been
his own fate. Hoggart's examination of those like him, alienated
from their roots by their new identities, was also an examination of the new post-war world, which seemed to him to be
peopled with Jude-the-Obscures. This educated proletariat was,
he explained, afflicted by fear, lack of confidence, cynicism,
self-consciousness, anxiety and a sense of loss. He painted a picture of an uprooted individual thrown between two worlds, cut
off from parents, peers and community, enduring detachment
and isolation, and difficulties with friction, incongruity and
adjustment.

> He has moved away from his 'lower' origins, and may move far-
> ther. If so, he is likely to be nagged underneath by a sense of
> how far he has come, by the fear and shame of a possible falling-
> back . . .
>
> He has left his class, at least in spirit, by being in certain ways
> unusual: and he is still unusual in another class, too tense and
> over-wound.

Note the pronoun. The subheading of this chapter is 'Scholarship Boy'. Women, in Hoggart's world, are tender-loving
background figures, attending with sympathy and gentleness to
the needs of the clever son of the family. Hoggart's own compassionate identification with his subject matter blinds him, in a
manner very much of its time, to the same problems besetting
the clever working-class woman. How much worse was it for
the likes of Brenda Nash? For working-class boys, social mobil-
ity meant a choice between claiming their place in the patriarchy,
or betterment. For working-class girls, the choice was much
more extreme. Had Brenda gone to secondary modern school
and left at fifteen like her sisters, her fate would have been a lifetime of domestic drudgery. In 1959, only one in 100 girls went
to university after leaving school. Of those, the vast majority
were middle-class; Brenda was in a tiny minority of council-
house girls to seek higher education. But just like Hoggart's
scholarship boys, that move came at a cost.

Mom, Dad, her Gran and brother and sisters would never
understand what had happened to Brenda. With few regrets, she
had cut loose from her roots. The family was bewildered. But in
some ways Brenda herself remained as lost as they were.

> People don't realise that when you've been brought up to have
> nothing, and to go nowhere, and to be terrified of everybody
> and everything that's new, it makes you into a frightened per-
> son.

My marriage gave me the security that I never had. Peter is a very good man. I couldn't have got by without him.

But people see me as outgoing — and I'm not. It's a cover. I talk a lot — but I sometimes think it's to conceal the fact that really there's nothing there.

And there was no going back.

11. A Living Doll

Sardines in Suburbia

In 1957, in New York, a university-educated mother of three was at home feeding and caring for her family. Feeling restless and without purpose, she set out to survey a number of her Smith College contemporaries about their education and subsequent experiences, much as Judith Hubback had done four years earlier in Britain. But soon after, Betty Friedan started to publish articles based on their responses, probing to identify what she called 'the problem that has no name'. Her conclusions would later (in 1963) be expanded into a world-changing book: *The Feminine Mystique.*

Deep down, a problem was indeed searching for expression. But attempts to name it, or to articulate it, collided with the entrenched stereotype of femininity that we have already encountered so often in this book, a stereotype that was still emphatically alive and well as the decade ended. In a 1959 issue of *Good Housekeeping*, a colour feature demonstrating 'The Four Ages of Woman' presents four images of 1950s female perfection, each one groomed within an inch of their lives.

First, the twenty-year-old: 'The age of sparkle, enthusiasm and experiment.' A strawberry-blonde Barbie-doll in a scarlet shirt-waister dress, perched with her favourite disc ready to place on the turntable of a teak-finish radiogram, encapsulates the younger generation:

> At 20, a girl likes to indulge herself. She plays records over and over again; wears bright, bright red with charming assurance . . .

Good Housekeeping's thirty-year-old is also flawlessly made-up and manicured. She poses in an impeccable jacket-and-skirt suit beside a laden hostess trolley, while a cubist painting on the wall behind her re-affirms her confident modernity:

> She dresses in a discreet, but definitely head-turning way: maintains a home that is remarkable for its combined serenity and vivacity . . .

At the age of forty, the model is divested of all frivolity. She wears a classic, floor-length brocade evening gown. The only prop is a similarly upholstered Louis Quinze-style armchair:

> She has an assuredness that younger women are still striving to attain. She knows that her husband, by now reaching the peak of his career, relies on her to be perfect in every detail . . .

– while the fifty-year-old is also pointedly photographed sitting down, wearing a triple rope of pearls, a trim, dark dress and court shoes, in a set-up of antique furniture. Her spectacles lie on the desk in front of her:

> Her life is at its fullest. Her husband, her family and several social organisations all make heavy demands on her time. Yet she remains enchantingly unruffled . . .

Not one of them is wearing trousers.

The paradigm of the perfect wife in her ideal home was going to take some shifting.

*

Maureen Nicol was thirty in 1959, a mother of two with a good husband and a secure roof over her head. But all was not well.

We last saw Maureen stranded in Codsall, a suburb of Wolverhampton. Here there was no social infrastructure, and forming friendships was 'really hard'. Meanwhile Brian, her husband, had a job with the Coal Board and was out all day; he was also politically active and spent many evenings at Labour Party meetings. Maureen would dearly have loved to join him for these, but by 1959 there were two babies, nobody she could turn to for childcare, and insufficient money to pay for help. Serenity and vivacity eluded her, for even as a homemaker she felt inadequate. An episode with a stuffed marrow with which she had planned to impress her in-laws left her feeling that she would never make the *Good Housekeeping* grade:

> I had absolutely no idea how long it took to cook a stuffed marrow; it was raw as anything. My parents-in-law were sitting there watching, waiting for their lunch for hours . . . and I've never forgotten the humiliation. So I didn't really think of myself as an efficient housewife – because I wasn't.

But finally, after three years in Codsall, Maureen was beginning to find her feet. Then the blow fell. It was a time when the expectation for many young professionals was that they would move every few years, to gain experience in their field. There was no need to make allowances for wives, as it was assumed that their jobs, if any, were subsidiary. They would meekly accept being uprooted and just tag along. In 1959 Brian got a new posting. So the Nicols pulled up their stakes and moved, this time to an enormous council estate at Eastham on the Wirral. It exemplified bad planning. 'There was virtually nothing on it – no buses, no shops . . .'

> For months after we moved there I hardly spoke to anybody. It was just awful really. I felt absolutely murderous.

By now Maureen was beginning to feel she was losing her mind.

It was while she was in this state of fatalistic desperation that Maureen one day picked up a copy of the *Manchester Guardian*.

Leafing though, her eye fell on an article by journalist Betty Jerman headed 'Squeezed in like Sardines in Suburbia'. And this article seemed to be all about her own life. 'Suburbia,' wrote Jerman, 'is an incredibly dull place to live, and I blame the women. Their work kept them alert. Home and child-minding can have a blunting effect on a woman's mind, but only she can sharpen it.'

Maureen's mind was not yet so dulled that she could not feel the prick of this spur. She had never written to a newspaper in her life, but driven by the realisation that she was not alone in her predicament she penned a swift letter to the editor:

> Perhaps housebound wives with liberal interests and a desire to remain individuals could form a national register so that whenever one moves one can contact like-minded friends?

And fortunately, the editor on the receiving end of Maureen's letter was Mary Stott.

Mary Stott's sympathies were readily awakened; she knew from personal experience what it felt like to have one's gifts and intelligence undervalued. Determined from an early age to become a journalist, Stott had faced obstinate sexist discrimination in her rise to the pinnacle of her profession. As a trainee reporter on the *Leicester Mail* she was broken-hearted to be relegated to the women's page – 'I thought my chance of becoming a real journalist was finished . . .' – and as a sub-editor on the *Manchester Evening News* she was fired in 1950 to make way for a man who would pre-empt her promotion to chief sub-editor. But in 1957 she was appointed to the post that would bring her fame, that of women's editor of the *Manchester Guardian*. Here, her remit was to cover 'women's interest' topics – fashion, cookery and children – but, goaded by her own experience of unfairness, Mary soon made the pages her own, expanding their reach to feminist issues of every kind, from playgroup provision to domestic violence, disability to divorce. In the 1960s her pages would become a forum, a community and a voice for women. Maureen Nicol's letter fell into a welcoming in-tray, and – to her astonishment – was promptly published.

She was even more surprised by the response it got. Several dozen letters were forwarded to her by the *Guardian*, all saying the same thing: 'What a good idea, go ahead, do something about it.' With the ball now squarely back in her court, Maureen was initially bewildered:

> I thought, my God! How can I? I've got no car. I didn't have a typewriter. I mean we didn't even have a telephone, and we were really hard up . . .

She talked it through with Brian, and he was gently supportive. In the end, she thought, 'The hell with it, I'll give it a try.' And so she wrote again to the *Guardian*, proposing that she set up a register, divided by region, so that women moving into a new area could get in touch with each other. Over the next few weeks the postman arrived at the semi in Eastham, his sack bulging with desperate letters begging for like-minded human contact. These were from women who, largely, had worked in interesting and fulfilling jobs, who had been uprooted from friends and family by their husbands' work. Some of them were suicidal: 'I tramped around the streets looking for somebody to talk to . . .'; 'I go home and I shut myself in four walls, and I feel they're crowding in on me . . .' One day the Nicols' letterbox fell off with the sheer weight of this correspondence. Maureen realised she had tapped a profound well of loneliness, unhappiness and non-fulfilment. And now, to her own feeling of misery and frustration was added a sense of responsibility to all those women who shared it. She couldn't let them down. With limited support from the *Guardian*, she set to work with a borrowed typewriter and a borrowed duplicator. She recruited regional organisers, forwarded letters to them, maintained a card index. For a year Maureen was permanently exhausted, but over that time 2,500 women joined her register. The cost of stamps and stationery was mounting, and before long it became necessary to charge a membership fee of a shilling. Nobody objected. Over time, the regions would become increasingly self-supporting, but initially Maureen – as national organiser – held sole responsibility for her newly founded network: the Liberal-Minded Housebound Wives' Register.★

Happily for her, a number of the letters came from addresses in nearby streets – 'within walking distance of me . . .' They were from intelligent women, equally stranded and friendless, who were as yet unaware of each other's existence. Suddenly, the Register became meaningful for Maureen herself. The Wirral group started meeting. It was quickly decided that these gatherings should be held in people's homes, and that they should be evening occasions; the atmosphere must remain personal – but it was no good trying to talk with toddlers rampaging around the place. It was also agreed that the sessions would be participatory, conversational and informal. There was no hierarchy, no minutes, no chairman. And there were only two strict rules. First, that you weren't there to talk about your children. And second, that coffee and biscuits only were to be served – 'It was **not** going to be about competitive salmon sandwiches!' They also deliberately eschewed 'feminine' topics: make-up demonstrations, jam-making sessions, sewing bees. The meetings were to be about waking up their minds. Discussions ranged from art to nuclear disarmament, from local issues to world

★ 'Isn't that awful? It sounds dreadful really . . .' remembers Maureen. Within a year the name was changed to the National Housewives' Register and later, when 'housewives became a term which people weren't prepared to accept . . .', it was rechristened with the name by which it is still known today, the National Women's Register.

government. They tried out oil painting and talked about the books they had read. They learnt not to become locked into political differences. Sometimes the group visited an exhibition, occasionally they invited a speaker. The groups also offered warmth and a listening ear. Members came from very different backgrounds, nobody was categorised or expected to conform. But friendships evolved, and with them came common experiences, anticipation, rejoicing and at times, grief. 'And you just think, women are marvellous at supporting each other emotionally, aren't they?'

As for Maureen herself, she never looked back.

> It was a tremendously empowering experience . . . It gave you great confidence at a time when most of us had been fairly battered by leaving work and being at home. You do begin to feel a bit zombie-like after a bit. In fact, I've never felt that isolation since . . .

Fifty years on, settled in Warwickshire and with an OBE to her name, she remains a stalwart of her Kenilworth group:

> I shall be forever grateful to NWR for so many years of friendship, laughter, arguments and real female bonding. I can sometimes hardly believe my luck to have been in the right place at the right time to have given a starting push to an organisation that has benefited so many women and in doing so to have enriched my own life for fifty years.

*

Maureen Nicol had found a way to articulate the 'problem that has no name'. Hindsight tells us that the sprinkling of determined and enterprising individuals like Maureen were soon to be swelled by battalions of women making demands, protests and claims, and using a new language of rights and liberation.

And already in the later 1950s new strong, brave, persuasive voices are to be heard: like that of Jo in Shelagh Delaney's *A Taste of Honey* (1958), or Beatie in Arnold Wesker's *Roots* (1959).

In 1959, the blooms of flower-power and second-wave feminism were still a decade into the future, but their seeds were starting to sprout. The English edition of Simone de Beauvoir's *The Second Sex*, exposing and exploring woman's subjugation, had been published in 1953, though it would take years for its intellectual challenge to the patriarchy to become mainstream. Sex remained a minefield of dislike, ignorance and superstition. But the Kinsey Report, the advice columns and the growth of birth control clinics were increasing the pressure on women to give of their best in the bedroom, and smaller families were becoming the popular choice. Throughout the 1950s, research into the production of a hormonal contraceptive for women had been gaining momentum in America, and in 1957 the US Food and Drug Administration cleared the combined oral contraceptive Enovid to be prescribed for severe menstrual disorders; in the same year in Britain it was made available (though not yet for contraceptive use) through the Family Planning Association. A debate was unfolding about sex, whose pin-up imagery – whether of the bulging busts and cavernous cleavages of Jayne Mansfield, Diana Dors and Marilyn Monroe, or the suggestive quiffs and thrusting pelvises of rock'n'roll stars – was becoming unambiguous and omnipresent as never before. But Brigitte Bardot's kittenish sensuality was starting to overtake Monroe's dumb blonde glamour in the daydream fantasy stakes.

Meanwhile, although the numbers of unmarried mothers were still small in absolute terms, they were increasing steeply: in the under-twenty group, from one in eighty (in 1938), to one in fifty (in 1958), to one in forty (in 1959). 'Is Chastity Outmoded?' queried a booklet published by the British Medical

Association. While sex outside marriage was becoming less frowned on, abortion was still not tolerated by the law. The result was more unwanted babies.

Among pundits, artists, Angry Young Men – and even in parliament – authoritarian moral codes were starting to be questioned, and at times relaxed. In 1959 legislation was passed to allow illegitimate children to be legitimised if their parents married. That same year the Wolfenden Report – briefed to explore the possibilities of legalising homosexuality – recommended the implementation of the Street Offences Act, sending prostitution underground. But the public wasn't yet ready to countenance same-sex relationships, and the legal persecution of homosexuals continued. The 1950s saw the start of a long slide in church attendance; between 1950 and 1960 the number of baptisms dropped by 17 per cent. 'Television masts seem to sprout thicker each day over the suburban housing-estate roofs . . .' wrote Mollie Panter-Downes in her *New Yorker* column. In tandem with home-viewing (in the decade from 1950 the number of TV licences obtained had multiplied from just 382,000 to 10,554,000), cinema attendance was thinning. 'The tellie keeps the family together. None of us ever have to go out now . . .' claimed one proud paterfamilias. By 1960 half the population were watching prime-time television on any given evening, car ownership had rocketed over the decade by 3,343,000 to 5,650,000 in 1960; the number of married women in paid employment had risen nearly 10 per cent from 1950, and racial tension was rising alongside immigration figures.

Though the popularity among teenage girls of air-hostessing as a profession had slid down the scale by 1959 (to be replaced by modelling), work – for married and unmarried women alike – was now a fact of life. Their new spending power offered them new choices, not just in buying refrigerators and vacuum cleaners, soap suds and knitting patterns, but also pop records, eyeliners and clothes. In 1955 Mary Quant made fashion history when she opened Bazaar on the corner of Markham Square, Chelsea. Here, and at her follow-up store, which opened on Knightsbridge Green in 1957, Quant sold liberating mini chemises with kick flared skirts that were 'short, short, short . . .':

The passion for these dresses was amazing . . .

In late 1957, Christian Dior died.

But now the world seemed to have so much more to offer – from contrast wallpapers to Green Shield stamps, motorways to long-playing records, coin-operated laundries, transistor radios, and direct-dial (STD)* telephone calls. Until 1958 anyone who wanted to telephone outside their own area had to be connected manually by an operator (always female) at the telephone exchange. This friendly service was phased out after the introduction of STD on 5 December 1958, when the Queen, warmly clad in a winter coat with cheetah-print shawl collar and matching trimmed hat, visited Bristol Central Telephone Exchange. She dialled a number with care; then, in a carefully scripted conversation, amplified for all present to hear, she listened smilingly as her call was answered:

The Lord Provost of Edinburgh speaking . . .

and replied:

This is the Queen speaking from Bristol. Good afternoon, Lord Provost . . .

And yet the Queen herself was no longer exempt from ridicule and contempt. In 1957 Lord Altrincham publicly launched an attack on the monarch's taste, complacency, snobbery and priggishness. Expressing views that, till then, had been inexpressible, he described her speech-making manner as 'frankly "a pain in the

* Subscriber Trunk Dialling.

neck"'. It took the happy news of the Queen's third pregnancy, announced in spring 1959, to restore a shaken royal equilibrium.

Shortly afterwards, in May, came the news that two monkeys launched into space by the Americans had safely returned. Horizons were widening, even for stay-at-homes. My mother, a

Though peppers and artichokes were still unobtainable in British greengrocers, John Minton's illustrations to Elizabeth David's books fed the dream of Mediterranean cookery and culture.

'university wife' caring for three small children, was among the early adopters of Elizabeth David's cookery books – *Mediterranean Food* (1950), *Italian Food* (1954) and *Summer Cooking* (1955). At a time when most English children were only familiar with tinned spaghetti in glutinous tomato sauce, we were brought up on home-made pasta *al sugo*, while her dinner party guests in Framlington Place, Newcastle-upon-Tyne, were offered brave versions of *Veau Sauté Marengo* and *Saint Émilion au Chocolat*. This was privilege indeed. In 1957 my family were among the 2.5 million passengers who flew abroad on holiday; the figure would rise from half a million to nearly 3.5 million between 1950 and 1960.

Lollipop

In the late summer of 1957 Miss Great Britain, Leila Williams, checked in at Heathrow airport for a flight to Helsinki. The journey, on a twin-engined Dakota which stopped to refuel in Stockholm, took all day. Leila was on the first leg of her triumphal tour, at the behest of the Federation of British Industry, to sell British beauty and goods to the Finns.

In the pages of *Good Housekeeping*, Leila Williams most nearly approximated to the ideal. In part, Leila owed her triumph – taking the Miss Great Britain title in 1957 at the age of twenty – to intensive grooming. Her clothes were immaculate, her nails were manicured, her hair shone with health and shampoo – and she never turned up wearing rollers. But the beauty, the charm and the approachable smile that won her the prize were less the result of overflowing bubble and sparkle, and more to do with ambition, perseverance and sheer hard work. Leila's perfections were a front – and she was soon to find out that their rewards were equally insubstantial.

Nevertheless, that 1957 victory spelt freedom, and her top priority was to leave the Wheatsheaf in Walsall, where she had felt imprisoned by her mother, the pub's landlady, for so many years. But moving to London was a step into the unknown. The only friend to whom she felt able to turn for motherly advice was her mature cousin Frankie, a worldly and warm-hearted woman who kept a pub near Dorking in Surrey. Apart from this she knew almost nobody, and her first attempt at metropolitan independence got off to a shaky start.

Over the ensuing months, Leila was to learn the true cost of becoming a beauty queen. To start with, Helsinki was sheer hard work. Leila was expected to be available eighteen hours a day for fashion shoots, press calls and receptions. On her return she collapsed at Cousin Frankie's pub, and slept for three days non-stop, before throwing herself into the preliminaries for the upcoming Miss World Contest, sponsored and organised by Eric Morley, the pageant's bumptious founder. Groggy with flu and exhaustion Leila left for London for another round of dress fittings, dinners and publicity stunts with the other Miss World contestants. The girls were chaperoned everywhere, and conveyed by coach, accompanied by two of the judges and an oily representative from Mecca. Seated next to Leila one day, this man remarked, 'If you play your cards right, you could be the first British Miss World.' She was disquieted.

But she was less suspicious when a few days later she attended a showy dinner at which a bevy of businessmen had paid to sit next to the contestant of their choice. Leila's date introduced himself as Harvey, a meat wholesaler and, hearing of her search for a flat, he suggested that she would be welcome to take over a basement apartment belonging to associates of his in Mayfair, a proposition that she eagerly – if unwisely – accepted. 'He said he would arrange everything and pick me up at the hotel after Miss World.'

The day before the contest the Mecca representative again buttonholed her, back on his old theme: that if she played her cards right she would win Miss World. Leila told him that, if she did win, she hoped it would be on her merits.

He then said 'Everyone has a price.' That remark sent shivers down my spine.

Back in the hotel the girls were allowed a quiet evening, prior to the big day. Leila retreated to her room. The phone rang. It was Mr Morley himself:

> 'I want to see you.'
> 'But what about the chaperones?'
> 'Walk down the stairs, there will be a car waiting for you.'

With the words about 'playing her cards right' ringing in her head, alarm bells were starting to join the chorus.

> 'Do I go or do I stay?' Then I thought, if I don't go I'll never know what he had in mind.

She picked up her handbag.

Outside the hotel's portals a black limousine was waiting. 'This way, Miss Williams,' said the driver, holding the passenger door open, and she was alone in the car. A short drive, and they arrived at an apartment block where the doorman, primed, directed her to a lift which sped her to the penthouse, and opened directly on to Morley's suite. Leila's feelings were in turmoil. She had no idea what it all meant.

> My mind was turning somersaults.

Morley was standing by the coffee table, with two glasses ready filled. As she stepped from the lift he advanced, and placed one of them in her hand with a greeting. At this last minute, something indefinable stopped her; pride, and self-preservation took over.

> Without hearing what he had to say I put the drink down and ran to the lift which was still there.
> The limousine was still outside, the driver opened the door and drove me back to the hotel.

Afterwards, Leila could never decide whether she was right to 'run like a frightened rabbit'. Maybe she should have felt flattered that the all-powerful Eric Morley had singled her out? Maybe she should have stayed and listened to whatever proposal he wanted to make to her. At the time, she judged it best not to compromise herself, but in the event – though she may have guessed – she was never to find out for certain what it was he had in mind that night.

At the Miss World rehearsal the next day Morley was in a foul temper. He refused to meet her eye. After that Leila knew that, whatever happened, she would not be crowned Miss World. That year the title was won by Marita Lindahl from Finland. 'But my pride and dignity were intact.'

Next morning Harvey the meat merchant arrived in a yellow Rolls-Royce to take Leila to his friend's Mayfair address. As they rolled through the London squares her new admirer pointed out the various hotels which he was proud to supply with fresh products from the abattoir. And the basement flat, when they arrived, was lovely, all she could have hoped for: tastefully furnished, with its own front door. She settled in with delight, and soon after Bertie Green, its owner, telephoned to invite her upstairs to dinner that same evening.

Bertie's party was a ritzy affair. Harvey rolled up in best bib and tucker. All the men were in black tie; the women were dripping with diamonds. Even as Miss Great Britain, Leila was awestruck by their glamour. After dinner the company strolled down to the Astor Club in Berkeley Square. Here, the lustre of chandeliers was reflected by satin drapes and champagne flowed freely; but Leila was drunk on dazzle. 'This was a lifestyle I could become accustomed to!'

Next day Harvey, who continued to play the role of a complete gentleman, reappeared and asked her whether there was anywhere she would like to go. Still conflicted by the Eric Morley episode, Leila longed to confide in Cousin Frankie and get her advice. She begged her new protector to take her down to the Kings Arms at Ockley, near Dorking.

We walked into [the pub] during lunchtime. Frankie smiled –
then glared at me. Without a word she beckoned to me to follow
her. We went into the kitchen.

'Get that man out of my pub now!' she shouted.

'But why?' I asked. 'He is a butcher in London.'

'Yes, and he has butchered most of the bodies that are in the
concrete holding up the bridges on the main roads,' she said.

In the late 1950s the Kray twins and their gang 'the Firm' were
already famous as villains in the East End, with a reputation for
protection rackets, arson and violent assaults. As the Krays
acquired a taste for high-stakes gambling and extravagant living,
their fearsome influence was steadily moving west. Like his
friends Ronnie and Reggie, it seemed that Harvey too had got
rich on cleavers and choppers. And Bertie's dinner party guests
had probably included the infamous pair themselves. Leila listened horrified to Frankie's explanation as to who her glamorous
friends really were. She realised she had to unstitch her new relationship at whatever cost, and quickly. Casting about for a rapid
excuse, she rejoined Harvey and told him that she had had an
argument with Frankie and must leave immediately. She climbed,
quaking, back into the gleaming yellow Roller,* and an hour
later he dropped her off at the flat. Her first attempt at living in
London had come crashing down around her. As soon as Harvey
had left she packed her case, wrote a polite thank you note to
Bertie, called a taxi and took the first train back to Walsall.

When she returned to London early in 1958, Leila had an
uphill struggle to pursue her long-nursed ambition, which was
to act. She found a bedsit in Kensington. This time the landlord
was a bohemian jazz drummer. But the talent game was brutal,
and for months Leila sat by the telephone. One agency was only

* Readers may recall that the über-pimp Gino Messina also ran a yellow
Rolls-Royce – a favoured status symbol among kings of the underworld, it
would seem.

interested in seeing the shape of her legs, while more reputable agents and casting directors cold-shouldered her when they found out she had been a beauty queen. Promised film tests dematerialised at her lack of 'serious' credits, and her prize money was running out. But Leila had proven tenacity. She didn't give up. At last, after trying everything, she landed first an agent and then, through her, a shampoo commercial. The corner had been turned. It was followed by a Cadbury's advert. She lay winsomely on a rug with her hands clasped around a mug of drinking chocolate, but the ad was never screened because the camera angle pointed too far down her cleavage. On another shoot she was required to quaff Babycham from half past eight in the morning till six at night. Small film parts began to come in, and then television work. The BBC hired her to co-host their flagship rock'n'roll programme, *The Six-Five Special*,

Publicity for the BBC's teenage pop music programme, which was co-hosted by Miss Great Britain Leila Williams.

which had launched in 1957. Dressed to kill in skin-tight Lurex pedal-pushers, big belt and fitted top, Leila joined DJ Jim Dale to introduce the hottest bands of the day, from Marty Wilde and Petula Clark to Lonnie Donegan and Tommy Steele. The show, with its live all-dancing studio audience, kicked off weekly with a catchy signature song by Don Lang and his Frantic Five, thrumming over film of a clanking steam train: 'Over-the-points, Over-the-points, The Six-Five Special's comin' down the line, The Six-Five Special's right on time . . .'

In 1958 an addictively syncopated novelty song called 'Lolli-pop' made chart success in America. It crossed the Atlantic, was picked up by a brothers-and-sister band named The Mudlarks and in May that year reached number two. It went:

> Lollipop, Lollipop
> Oooh, Lolli, lolli, lolli
> Lollipop, Lollipop
> POP!
> Call my baby Lollipop
> Tell you why . . .
> Her kiss is sweeter than an apple pie
> And when she does her shaky rockin' dance –
> Man, I haven't got a chance!

Mary, Jeff, and Fred Mudd were accordingly invited to perform their hit song on *The Six-Five Special*. Leila met them, and was instantly won over by vocalist Fred's open-faced good looks and easy ways.

> You know how you meet someone, and you just know . . . The chemistry was there. He was very kind, caring and funny. Everything that you look for actually . . .

Their relationship quickly developed. In the early days Leila couldn't think how to tell him that she was a famous beauty queen. So she didn't. And Fred had no idea. One day a journalist asked him, 'What's it like to be going out with Miss Great Britain?' 'Who's Miss Great Britain?' was his response. Leila felt loved for herself, and in return gave him all her trust.

And 1958 was the year that Leila's career took off too. That autumn she landed a coveted contract, again with the BBC, to present a brand-new magazine-format programme aimed at children. There would be crafts, competitions, cartoons, stories, pets, activities, and one male and one female presenter, appropriately stereotyped. Christopher Trace was hired and allowed to indulge his personal passion for model railways on-screen; Leila would be his feminine sidekick, with dolls and soft toys. The programme's name was *Blue Peter*, and for the next three years it was her world.

1958–9 were good years for Leila Williams. She and Fred Mudd were as inseparable as his rock-star schedule allowed. If she could get away she would join him wherever the band was booked – Blackpool, or Manchester. As a rock couple, they were in demand wherever they went.

> Manchester had an amazing club scene in the 50s. The Cabaret Club was the place where everybody went to after the show and they'd all do a jam session. You'd have the Mudlarks, the Jones Boys, the Dallas Boys, Cliff Richard, Matt Monro, Roy Castle . . . And the atmosphere was quite electric. Everyone was on a high after the performance, and that was their way of unwinding, often till the early hours.

Now, at last, Leila was living her teenage dream. The corners of living rooms around the nation glowed softly with her radiant image. Television had touched her with stardust, she was a household name, she was earning well, and she was in love, as she would be for the rest of their lives together, with Fred Mudd. The teak-finish radiogram was playing their tune.

> Sweeter than candy on a stick
> Huckleberry, cherry or lime
> If you have a choice he'd be your pick
> But Lollipop is mine!

And in 1960 Leila and Fred got married.

The Golden Palace

I loved pop music . . .

The Leila surrogate playing her favourite record in the pages of *Good Housekeeping* exudes the effortless confidence of an advantaged caste: pretty, blonde – and white. For the 'Four Ages of Woman' feature included no black women.

At her school in Kingston, Vilma Owen was a quiet and docile student. But at home in the evenings there was nothing she loved better than listening to the latest sounds on Radio Jamaica, volume turned high. American music crowded the airwaves, and rock'n'roll's infectious rhythms frequently had her jiving round the living room to Elvis Presley, Fats Domino and Chuck Berry. At seventeen years old, this was the nearest she came to the high life Leila Williams was so freely enjoying. And much though she adored her mother, this pretty Jamaican teenager chafed under that watchful maternal eye. In their household, Saturdays were a day for religion, not relaxation. At weekends she could hear the thump-thump of all-night parties in their Kingston neighbourhood – 'I would have loved to join in!' – but she was not allowed to go. The ban also applied to romances:

> I was seventeen in 1959. And in Jamaica, in the 1950s, seventeen
> was a very young age. It wasn't a time for young women to
> think about having boyfriends . . .

She was left ignorant and wondering. In church, demurely hatted, Vilma's attention would stray across the pews to the equally
clean-collared boys opposite, and sometimes eyes would meet,
pulses would quicken. But under her mother's sharp-eyed surveillance it never went any further than that.

Mrs Owen had other ideas for her bright daughter. It was not
her plan to have Vilma marry, as she had, at twenty; to be
reduced to sewing piecework to make a living, struggling to
keep poverty at bay. Despite being separated, both Vilma's parents were prepared to make sacrifices to ensure that their joint
children would prosper more than they had. Vilma was sent to a
fee-paying secondary school. 'Education was the most important thing.' And it was decided that she would train to be a
professional nurse.

Aunt Ivy's letter – with a British stamp, postmarked south
London – arrived in the summer of 1959. 'It had never so much
as crossed my thoughts that I might go over there. My mum was
so protective! She wouldn't even let me go to a dance.' But
something in Aunt Ivy's letter must have persuaded Mrs Owen
that Vilma's future could only be launched in England. Between
them, and leaving Vilma herself largely out of the discussion, it
was decided that she would join her aunt and cousins in London, and train to be a nurse at an English hospital.

Plans were made. She would go for three years, stay with
Aunt Ivy, see Trafalgar Square and Buckingham Palace, get her
nursing qualifications, and then come back to Jamaica to make a
life for herself. Vilma filled in forms. She had her photograph
taken and it was put in her new passport. Her mum took her
shopping for what was needed.

My aunt wrote to say, you must bring a cardigan with you. Well, I didn't know what a cardigan was – we don't wear cardigans in the West Indies. And I'm one of these people – if I don't know what something means, I go and look it up in a dictionary. It still wasn't very clear, but I came to the conclusion that it was something that would keep me warm. And my mum ended up buying me a nice lime-green cardigan, you know?

Her seat on the plane was booked. The Saturday before her departure the family went to church and prayed together for her safe journey. On Thursday Mrs Owen and Grandma came with her to the airport for the evening flight via Shannon to London. Three years. Yes, it was a long, long time. But Vilma knew that everything she was working towards was about coming back home again. And knowing how much she was loved, her tears that evening were as much for the sadness they would feel at missing her, as for her own loss. The forested mountains of her homeland, the citrus and acacias, the shanties and low white colonial houses she had grown up with all seemed so familiar. Now, at Kingston airport under a violet tropical sky, her adventure was about to begin.

Actually, Vilma was very frightened. Of course, she had never been in an aeroplane before, nor had her mother flown, so nobody could tell her what to expect. She had to learn how to fasten her seatbelt. Could you walk about on the plane? Would there be a toilet on board? The prospect of her arrival gnawed at her. She had no notion about what would happen once she alighted from the aircraft. How would she find her luggage? Would somebody make her pay to enter the country, and did she have enough money? There were only Jamaican pounds in her purse. Would immigration officials turn her away? And would anyone be there to meet her? As the plane lifted off the runway and her bright beloved island receded to a black dot in the Caribbean below, Vilma felt nervous anticipation. But she also felt slightly sick.

★

What was waiting for Vilma Owen when she landed at Heathrow airport in the late summer of 1959?

Immigration from the West Indies surged over the decade after the SS *Empire Windrush* docked at Tilbury in 1948, with its 492 Jamaican immigrants all eager to find work in Britain in the firm belief that the Mother Country would look after them. They were followed in the next few years by their wives and girlfriends, and by single black women who also recognised that Great Britain offered employment opportunities denied them in the West Indies. But typically – as described by journalist Joyce Egginton in her 1957 book *They Seek a Living* – the husband secured work and a room before inviting his wife to make the journey. Stella Brown, for example, had dreamed of a green and pleasant land, a warm welcome, cheerful gardens and dainty homes. At its centre would be Buckingham Palace, glittering with golden walls. But from the moment Stella arrived with her young baby, she was disillusioned:

> I have tried my utmost endeavour best to like it, but if I could go home tomorrow I would. I miss the climate of Jamaica; I miss the food; I miss my relatives. I miss the people smiling because here everyone goes about with a straight face . . .
>
> Anything that coloured people does bad, they say it is Jamaicans' fault. They think all coloured people is Jamaicans and they think all Jamaicans is beggars . . . I never had to live so horrible as this before I came to England.

From the time that she made her home in Brixton, south London, Stella could not stop crying. The baby grew sick with bronchitis from the cold. Never before had she had to light fires, or sift the ashes in a grate. At the earliest opportunity she sent her boy home to be brought up by her parents. As the middle-class wife of a grocery store owner, she found it hard to endure the laundry work that now helped pay their bills.

Countless other Caribbean women tell the same tale in interviews and oral histories. It's a story of unfamiliarity and cold, of homesickness and unthinking racism:

> It was strange leaving behind sunshine and calypso to come and see everyone dressed in black, the windows were dark with shutters over them . . . Most places you went to you would see signs saying 'no coloureds'.

> When we come to Waterloo and get on the train and we see all these chimneys we were surprised, because at home when you see chimneys, it's factories or boiling house where they make sugar . . . All the chimneys had smoke and we thought what a lot of factories they have in this place, we didn't know it was houses.

> I clearly remember travelling with my sister on the tube and there were some elderly White people who cried out, 'Look, Jamaicans, run!' and they took off . . .

> It was a cold, cold November day. People were so cold. I wanted to turn around and go back; it had all been a horrible mistake.

> The accent, the strange accent . . .

> There was no fruit: there were only apples and oranges . . .

> The first Monday I took my references from home saying I was a teacher. This woman at the counter said, 'Oh, you were a teacher back home were you? Well, you won't get teaching here!'

> If you went and knocked at the door and you asked for a room they closed the door in your face and told you 'Get away you black bastard', or 'monkey' or something like that.

> I remember once on the street someone asked me where I had put my tail and the person was serious and I looked at him and I said 'the same place where you keep yours'.

For as their numbers increased – between 1952 and 1958, 82,000 West Indian immigrants arrived in Britain – levels of fear and hostility on the part of certain white communities rose with them. Fascist organisations lobbying to 'Keep Britain White' were gaining membership; racist attacks became more frequent. Black communities retaliated, among them the Trinidadian journalist and activist Claudia Jones, who had been deported from America in 1955 for membership of the Communist Party. She came to London and immediately renewed her efforts to combat racism in Britain, founding the *West Indian Gazette* in 1958 as a mouthpiece for her campaign. That summer Nottingham erupted with unrest. A week later the Notting Hill Gate area of west London – in those days a largely working-class neighbourhood of run-down terraces, to which immigrants were drawn because of the cheap rents – broke out in violent clashes between West Indians and Teddy boys. Weaponry included petrol bombs, knives, knuckle-dusters and bicycle chains. Pathé News denounced the riots as 'shameful . . .':

> Opinions differ about Britain's racial problems. But the mentality which tries to solve them with coshes and broken railings has no place in the British way of life. This violence is evil and the law and public opinion must stamp it out.

But though this establishment 'voice' sought to inculpate the attackers, many black men and women felt abandoned by the authorities. They were told by the police that the only way they could avoid such aggression was to go back where they had come from. Helpless, they felt they had no option but to organise. These were the birth throes of the multi-cultural society we now live in. Stella Dadzie, an admired historian of black lives in Britain, describes that time:

> We united and fought back. Black women could be seen standing firm, machetes and bottles in hand, side by side with the men, defending ourselves in the 'riots' which were entirely of the British people's making. To us, it was not merely a question of self-defence, but a struggle for survival.

The Candy Shop

Vilma showed her British passport and the official waved her through. She emerged with her luggage, and there, to her profound relief, was Aunt Ivy.

Vilma's memories of her early months in London echo the testimony of Stella Brown and the oral history interviewees. There was so much to get used to: the dirt, the belching chimney stacks which she too mistook for factories, the hard-to-understand accents, the bland food, the cold, the hostility and the lack of neighbourliness.

And yet. The immigrant experience was a complex one. In Jamaica, for all the sunshine and calypso, Vilma had felt circumscribed. Back in Kingston under her mother's roof, it was a case of no dances, no boyfriends, no fun and laughter on the Sabbath, hats on in church, respect, modesty and sobriety. When she left Jamaica Vilma was low in confidence, timid and mousey. But from the first day of her arrival in England she started, joyfully, to break the rules. Almost as soon as she had settled in, her cousin Gloria announced that she must get ready, as she was taking her out to see Trafalgar Square:

> And she left me in front of her dressing table to use her makeup. And there were her sparkly clip-on earrings, and her

perfume, and her lipstick. And I'd never worn lipstick in my life, because my Mum wouldn't allow me to. Well I put the lipstick on. I didn't even know how to! And I felt so – so – like I was disobeying my Mum. It was as if, at the first test, I just fell!

You know, Mum'd done her best, she'd taught me and instilled these things into me for seventeen years. And they were all over in one second!

Trafalgar Square lived up to Vilma's hopes. There was Nelson's Column, as promised. There was water spraying out of the fountains. They travelled upstairs on a double-decker bus, and that evening her aunt welcomed her to Clapham with a pot of gungo pea soup.

Vilma arrived in England at the tail-end of a long, hot summer; the new lime-green cardigan was yet to come into its own, and much as in Jamaica she was able to wear her light cotton florals. It now began to dawn on Vilma that Aunt Ivy's views of life were more relaxed than those of her mum. Saturday came. The question of church arose – and subsided again. After all, finding a Seventh-day Adventist church and congregation around Clapham Common wasn't going to be straightforward, and Ivy's family were casual Catholics. She let the matter of her religion drop, and there it lay, neglected and forgotten. 'The sad thing was, I just had no guilt about it!'

But Aunt Ivy was energetic in encouraging her shy young niece to apply for nursing college. By chance Cousin Roddy's girlfriend was training to be a nurse in Eastbourne, and so it was agreed that to Eastbourne she must go. In the meantime, while applying, she must contribute to the household and support herself. Her first port of call was a sausage factory, full of labourers clad in rubberised overalls and wellington boots. To Vilma's relief, her lack of sausage-making experience disqualified her from this messy work. Instead, she happily accepted a job in a factory, making and lining presentation boxes for the deluxe perfume market. All her co-workers were older white women, and occasionally she found their ways clashed with hers, but unassuming and happy to learn from them as she was, Vilma had no difficulty fitting in. The work was pleasant, and it felt glamorous too, tapping into her new taste for cosmetics and feminine trappings:

> You had to line the boxes with satin and silk. I loved doing it. I worked on things like Blue Grass, Norman Hartnell, Coty. And there was something about those beautiful boxes that made you think, 'That's out of my reach . . .' I knew I wouldn't have been able to afford to buy their contents.

Nonetheless, she was now earning money that she could, for the first time, spend on herself.

> I started buying my own clothes. And I was very much in the fashion – I used to wear those wide rock'n'roll skirts you know? And we used to use a hot comb and straighten our hair.
>
> And my cousins, they would go to parties – and take me with them, and I would DANCE!

Away from home, Vilma's confidence rocketed. Nobody told her she was too young to have a boyfriend either. She went ahead and had lots – 'and it was fun!' – but always West Indian ones. Why not white? On some inexpressible level Vilma remained fearful that her colour made her a target for taunts, and it wasn't a risk she was prepared to run. 'I wasn't entertaining it.' It was safer to stay with one's own kind, and safer not to have to deal with romantic culture clashes, should they happen. On her eighteenth birthday, Vilma celebrated by getting helplessly drunk. It might have been on gin – she can't remember – but she does remember the room spinning around her and, somewhere, the indistinct voice of Aunt Ivy saying, 'For goodness' sake, give her a coffee.' 'And then they took me home.'

In all ways – apart from the colour of her skin – Vilma was indistinguishable from a white English teenager, and she was enjoying every minute of it.

> I was like a little girl in a candy shop. After a while I didn't even
> have to use my cousin's make-up – I had my own!
> I was just sort of set free.

At last the day came when a letter arrived saying that her application to the Eastbourne teaching hospital had been accepted. Overjoyed that her plans to better herself were falling into place, Vilma danced into work that Friday morning and delightedly informed her workmates that she had gained a place to study nursing. But to her astonishment, there was no general pleasure at her achievement. The women looked wary; grudgingly, they acknowledged that she would be moving on to higher things. And at lunchtime she was handed her cards by the supervisor. That was it. She was out.

> It didn't dawn on me to question it. It didn't dawn on me to say,
> 'Well why?' Or to challenge it . . .

This was the first time that Vilma felt her colour made a difference. Realising that as a black woman she was not supposed to rise above her ordained place, even less to blow her own trumpet at having done so, was sobering. As she returned home, chastened and dismayed, from her lovely job in the luxury box factory, the bright colours of the candy shop seemed dulled.

Spring came. Eastbourne is only an hour and a half from London by train, but for Vilma it might as well have been another country. In the late 1950s the Princess Alice Hospital stood on a leafy site near the centre of that sedate seaside town. Institutional and lugubrious, its dour red brick buildings had once housed a minor boys' public school. Since the war it had been taken over by the National Health Service, its classrooms and dormitories converted to wards and nurses' accommodation. Vilma, who was one of only three West Indian trainee nurses, did her best to settle in. She was allocated a room, and measured for her uniform, which did not appeal to her newly forming fashion sense. 'The skirt was fourteen inches from the ground.' As for the food at the hospital, it was not just unfamiliar, it was awful. One lamb chop was considered sufficient nourishment after a day on the wards. 'I found the portions really small! But they were never without potato. Ham was boiled – not like the way we do it in Jamaica. And cabbage was always boiled too. Boiled and boiled . . .'

In that first year at the Princess Alice, loneliness and a sense of alienation settled on Vilma and refused to lift. The hustle and bustle of London, its throbbing life – red buses, neon lights and crowds – were replaced by temperance and tedium. In Eastbourne most of the inhabitants seemed old, and they were unremittingly white. It felt like living in a sanatorium.

Vilma worked hard; her mother had saved and made sacrifices to send her to this sad town, and she knew that when she returned to Jamaica in three years' time, it had to be with a qualification. But she was unprepared for the complex demands made on her by theoretical courses in anatomy and pharmacology. What did they mean by tachycardia? What were forceps? 'The medical terms were pretty daunting!' She passed through nevertheless, and was taken on to the wards. But if she had expected now to enter a world of patient ministrations and encounters with glamorous consultants, that idea was quickly ruled out. Junior nurses were never spoken to by the doctors. Here she also encountered another facet of the health hierarchy commonly experienced at her level: namely, hours spent doing menial jobs in the sluice room. Those hours were all the longer, because being black meant she was at the very bottom of the pile, and because a proportion of patients took the view that hospitals were fundamentally *white* by nature, and refused to be nursed by her. Thus a great deal of Vilma's time was spent dusting lockers, cleaning windows, washing out sick containers, emptying commodes and bedpans and disposing of waste urine and faecal samples. 'I felt,' she says with restraint, 'that some of the senior staff were less than fair in the way we black nurses were treated.'

Time off from the wards didn't offer much in compensation for the long, aching days at the Princess Alice.

> There wasn't much to do. I'd go to the cinema with my friends, or we'd go for walks on the beach together. We'd walk along past the old people sitting on benches on the promenade. They used to look oddly at us and we felt very self-conscious for being black . . .

But sometimes her companions' unthinking racism was so undisguised as to be positively distressing. At the end of term the students in Vilma's year were rehearsing an entertainment to be performed in front of visiting relatives. Costumes were devised, and a chorus-line of tap-dancing nurses practised high kicks. Of course, Vilma couldn't join the fair-faced soubrettes in their synchronised spectacular; instead, she was approached to play the part of a merry negro minstrel. But what was this thing that they handed her so well-meaningly? 'I'd never seen a grass skirt before!' Dance, they said. Black savages wear grass skirts, and you're black . . .

> I didn't know what to do. Did they think I was from Tahiti, or Hawaii? I remember protesting – I said, 'I can't do this,' and in the end I just refused to go on.
>
> The whole thing made me feel quite sad . . .

Vilma spent a lot of her time in Eastbourne crying. The bright-eyed optimism of her early days in London crumbled. She was reverting to the timid and self-effacing child who had left her mum just six months earlier. On summer evenings the sun set late. Off-duty, with the shadows lengthening, she would find her way to the nurses' sitting-room. It was often deserted. A chill descended as the evening's last light gleamed through the tall windows, and as it did so the bright memories flooded in. Thousands of miles away, another sun warmed her homeland. At her granny's house near Kingston the orchard trees would bow under the weight of their fruit: mangoes, pears, ginepa berries, custard apples, naseberries – 'all sorts of lovely fruits that I could get in Jamaica'. The chickens would be scratching in the yard, her little brothers playing under the trees. Inside the house, sewing, scolding the boys, or preparing pone tied up in a banana skin, would be her beloved mother. Thinking of them, Vilma's young heart would almost crack with sorrow.

> I was all right right through the day – but when I saw the sun setting I think it just reminded me of Jamaica so much. I know it would have disappointed my mum, because she wanted me to continue my training, but I remember missing home, my family and friends with such longings that if I could have walked home I would certainly have done so.
>
> And somehow I think I must have been looking for that feeling, because I could always find it.

But it was to be fourteen years before Vilma would return to Jamaica.

Leading Ladies

We all know that trying to make sense of a decade is an arbitrary, irrational undertaking. When does New Year's Day ever feel like anything other than a disappointment, as one realises, waking up, that 1 January is just the same as 31 December? But the human propensity to derive significance from parcelled-up portions of time is a way we use to understand and explain ourselves. I have tried in this book to illustrate the character of the years 1950–60 by allowing the women who lived through them to tell their own stories, most of them forgotten, though all of them, I hope, revealing. But I want to end by touching on the lives of two of the 1950s' leading ladies, whose differing fortunes throw a raking light on the challenges of being a woman at the junction point between that decade and the next. Both of them were called Margaret.*

In 1955, when she first visited Vilma Owen's homeland, its welcoming inhabitants dubbed Princess Margaret Rose 'the Dolly Princess'. In years to come, the white, palm-fringed beaches and turquoise seas of the Caribbean would bring solace in a life that had had more than its share of sorrows. A sixty-cigarette-a-day habit and a taste for Famous Grouse probably played their part too.

At the age of twenty, the Queen's sister was entranced by life and its wealth of promises; her beauty, brilliance and charisma epitomised 1950s femininity. But she also came of age under the shadow of an ancien régime. In the late fifties that régime was far from burnt out. Here was a young woman who could never forget that she was a royal, nor that all subordinates must walk a pace behind her. Friends and courtiers alike would be subjected to the Princess's famously glacial stare. By turns affable and imperious, she oscillated between the demands made on her by her public role, and her own pulsating desires. When a pack of archbishops, newspaper editors, senior royal advisers and politicians – all male – closed ranks and told her that she must not marry the love of her life, she, not surprisingly, capitulated. But

* In 1924, 1934 and 1944 Margaret topped the charts as the most popular girl's name.

the regret would not go away, nor with it the human urge to seek love.

History moulds us, as we mould it. In Princess Margaret's case, the tensions of the 1950s were perhaps extreme. The tug-of-war between society and the individual is a constant; what changes is sets of expectations, moral certainties, the zeitgeist. We tip from decade to decade, swayed by human longings, but too often trapped or propelled by forces outside our control.

In March 1958, three years after Princess Margaret's relationship with Group Captain Peter Townsend crashed and burned, the couple re-met; and once more, as rumours of a rapprochement went out of control, the press pack swarmed around them. Denials were issued. In October 1959 the Princess received a letter from him; he was getting married. She wiped away her tears, straightened her back, drew on all her reserves of royal dignity, and turned for consolation to an attractive new suitor. At the outset, it looked as if she and Antony Armstrong-Jones might find happiness; they shared interests, for he was fascinatingly artistic and high-spirited, and early in 1960 he proposed. It is true there were reservations among Tony's closest friends, who thought the match ill-omened. According to his biographer,★ it was no secret that he was inclined to flirt almost as much with men as with women. But after the cruel meltdown of her previous relationship nobody thought to stop Princess Margaret in her tracks. That spring, London's processional streets were decked out with flowers again, and on a brilliantly sunny Friday morning in May a King's daughter married a commoner for the first time in four centuries of British history.

I remember my mother coming to fetch me early from my

★ *Snowdon: The Biography* by Anne de Courcy (2008) exposes and unravels Tony Armstrong-Jones's colourful and tangled life. At the time of the book's publication Lord Snowdon told a journalist, 'I want to put the record straight.'

nursery school to watch the Westminster Abbey ceremony on a bulbous television set in some friend's crowded sitting-room. In my memory, even the crackly picture couldn't cloud the brilliance of her flashing diamond tiara. Later that day the newlyweds boarded the royal yacht *Britannia*, caught the tide in the Pool of London, and set sail for a dream honeymoon in the Caribbean. Calypsos were written in their honour at every island they visited.

But the marriage was doomed. Tony didn't respect boundaries, least of all royal ones. He was capricious and could be cruel; she was argumentative and suffered from mood swings. Sixties excess and hedonism came on a collision course with the imperiousness and hauteur of an earlier age. There were rows, and infidelities. One of his friends recalled, 'They were both centre-stage people – but only one person can occupy the centre at any given moment . . .' As the Princess and her new husband basked on the royal yacht moored off the Grenadine Islands, Camilla Fry – who was married to one of Tony's closest friends – was giving birth to his probable love-child in a four-poster bed in the English shires.

*

In the summer of 1958 thirty-four-year-old mother of two Margaret Thatcher was selected as Conservative candidate for the safe seat of Finchley. One of her competitors, Molly Huggins, went before the Committee knowing she didn't stand a chance, since her husband, Sir John Huggins, former Governor of Jamaica, had run off with her dressmaker a fortnight earlier, and the scandal would not improve her popularity. It was goodbye to Molly Huggins's political ambitions, but for Mrs Thatcher it was just the beginning.

At the end of a Conservative-dominated decade, the Labour Party felt an (unjustified) optimism that they would win the next election. But the party was split, and the electorate was reaping the benefits of the late 50s economic boom. Although some women in northern towns were still donkey-stoning their doorsteps, many more perfect wives in ideal homes were twirl-ing the household wash into a shiny new twin-tub washing machine, and thanking Harold Macmillan's government, which, since taking the helm in 1957, had given them the feeling that they had 'never had it so good'.

The Prime Minister went to the country in October 1959. With him went a sprinkling of Conservative women candidates – twenty-nine in all – of whom sixteen stood a sporting chance of winning their seats.* In the run-up to the election, Mrs Thatcher briskly brought her constituency to heel. She spoke out in support of the birch, and voiced caution about the new comprehensive schools. Polling day (8 October) saw a clear win for the Tories. At the Finchley count, Margaret Thatcher waited in trepidation for the result. When the announcement came, she had gained 29,697 votes: a majority of over 16,000, and an increase of nearly 3,500 over her predecessor. Thus our first and only female Prime Minister entered parliament.

Soon after making her maiden speech in the House of Com-mons Mrs Thatcher was interviewed about her debut. Had it been an ordeal? Indeed it had. Did being a woman make it harder? No, not noticeably.

> Q: And have you been able to combine your political life with looking after a family, running a home?
> A: Well, I mainly do the catering here. I like cooking – I do the shopping . . . I do a batch of cooking at the weekend, and of course there are the parliamentary recesses which coincide with the school holidays so I can see quite a good bit of the children

*In all, 1,536 candidates contested the 1959 election. Eighty-one were women, of whom just twenty-five (4 per cent of the total) were elected.

and take them out, and at half-term they come up to the House of Commons and have lunch with me . . .

The grocer's daughter from Grantham was no shirker. But despite her eminent success as a female candidate and her subsequent extraordinary rise to the highest office in the land, a part of Mrs Thatcher would always embrace the worthy, upright, thrifty values of the 1950s – a decade which encompassed her adulthood from twenty-five to thirty-five. For many a woman, that is a time of life when one becomes established in one's self-image. Later, it may be hard to change.

Mrs Thatcher would govern our country as if through a time-warp. In many ways she was another quintessential woman of the 1950s, who would become an anachronism in her own lifetime. The tailored suits, the familiar, discreet string of pearls, the quiet sparkle of costume jewellery twinkling on her lapel, the court shoes and iconic patent leather handbag, the pill-box hats, diaphanous pussy-bows and sculpted hairstyles were essentially the same in 2013 as they had been sixty years earlier. Her look belongs unmistakably, unchangingly to a breed of middle-class women whom we recognise again from that 1959 issue of *Good Housekeeping*: headmistresses, clergy wives and the wives of merchants and landowners, minor dignitaries, honorary secretaries of small charities, leading lights of the Women's Institute. They are those same 'enchantingly unruffled' fifty-year-olds, at the constant bidding of husband, family and 'several social organisations'. They were, and are, the salt of the earth.

Mrs Thatcher shared many of their values. Those who knew her remember her conscientiousness, her perfect manners, her patriotism and overriding Englishness, her housewifely virtues, her frugality. She would remain forever proud of having made her own curtains. She was 'Christian but not churchy', an inexhaustible organiser and planner, and a socially ambitious wife and mother who 'pursued the haut-bourgeois dream'. The look, and the convictions, took root; for over thirty years Mrs Thatcher would wave the banner for a set of beliefs, many of which belonged to the early Elizabethan era.

In Sussex, farmer's wife and mother-of-six Liz Monnington was typical of those who most admired her. As Chairman of the Conservative Women's Constitutional Committee, Liz was deputed to play hostess to visiting speakers, and thus found herself lunching with Margaret Thatcher in the early 1960s:

> Well, she looked beautiful, smart without being over-smart, nicely made-up, a beautiful complexion, very charming, very polite, and very down-to-earth. And over lunch we talked about politics, and about living in the country, and about going up to London to the area meetings and so on.
>
> And when she got up to go she shook my hand, and her last words to me were: 'Goodbye, my dear.' And then she hesitated a bit and looked round, and said: 'I *do* hope having *all* these children won't stop you going *far* in politics!'
>
> And then she left.

For Mrs Thatcher was insurmountably ambitious. An exact contemporary of the Queen,* she maintained that her phenomenal drive and indefatigable energy drew from that very royal example:

> A young Queen, the loveliest ever to reign over us, now occupies the highest position in the land.
>
> If, as many earnestly pray, the accession of Elizabeth II can help to remove the last shreds of prejudice against women aspiring to the highest places, then a new era for women will indeed be at hand . . .

Those words were written by Mrs Thatcher in 1952, when she was still the youngest female candidate at the 1950 and 1951

---

* Margaret Thatcher was born on 13 October 1925; the Queen was born just six months later, on 21 April 1926.

elections. Gender-phobia was no hindrance to her ambitions; her husband took a back seat. After 1959 she would become unstoppable, powering through obstacles with the thrust of a jet engine. In the late 1960s and early 70s, while the Women's Liberation movement was gathering momentum, Mrs Thatcher was systematically demolishing her opponents through the opportunistic manipulation of an obsolete femininity. Her unyielding black handbag came to symbolise the woman herself: no mere accessory, but an almost mythic repository of female power. She was later quoted as saying, 'I owe nothing to women's lib.'

*

For Princess Margaret and Margaret Thatcher, and for many other less illustrious women whose names and life experiences have appeared in this book, the tug-of-war I have described was a daily reality: between society and the individual, prohibition and permissiveness, conformity and independence, passivity and ambition. Between identity – and the empty shell. And the feminism versus femininity debate continues today. Though the 1950s can seem like another planet, there can be few female readers of this book who won't recognise some of the dilemmas faced by our mothers and grandmothers: work, or motherhood? Sex or celibacy? Skirts or trousers?

In July 1959 the catchy hit blaring from everyone's transistor was Cliff Richard's 'Living Doll' . . .

> Got myself a crying, talking, sleeping, walking,
> Living doll –
> Got to do my best to please her
> Just 'cause she's a
> Living doll . . .

And that summer our family moved house. My father's job was taking him from Newcastle-upon-Tyne to Leeds; my mother, aged forty-three, was a full-time housewife. Louis Quinze furniture was not really their style, but *Good Housekeeping* would doubtless have approved of her taste in floor-length brocade dresses. My father, being bohemian in spirit, was undemanding; in any case, he thought his wife perfect as she was.

We settled into a comfortable house not far from Roundhay Park. We had coal fires; a radiogram but no television. My parents put up a washing line in the back garden; once a week the grocer called with his delivery of bacon, cheese and tinned mandarin oranges. Mornings for me were spent at a nursery school; at home my baby sister crowed in her playpen while our mother got through her chores with the help of Mrs Hardy from across the way.

And here, only a whisker away on the respectable fringes of suburban Roundhay, a young woman aged seventeen stands hesitantly on the brink of the new decade. Her name is Sheila. What will she become? She has grown up intensely susceptible to poetry, rock'n'roll, religion, clothes and boys. She reads widely and indiscriminately: the Bible, *Vogue*, Mary Wollstonecraft, *True Confessions*, and Byron. She is high-minded, romantic, needy, earnest, an outsider – and passionately motivated by a desire to escape from Roundhay. 'Oh to get away so I could exhaust myself with intense experiences, where everyone spoke of intense subjects and *never* said "pass the bread and butter."' Sheila models herself on a combination of Juliette Greco and Simone de Beauvoir. She adopts the existentialist 'uniform' – tight skirts, a shapeless black sweater, black stockings and black high heels; her face is eerily whitened. 'Nothing like it was seen in Roundhay in 1959.' People stop her on the shopping parade and ask 'You an art student?' She smiles mysteriously.

My close women friends, like me, were all straining beyond our backgrounds. Art school, university, we were going out of Yorkshire and nothing could stop us. Life was what you made it . . .

[We were] heading towards sub-cultures, which as yet did not exist, and which we could envisage only hazily . . .

Sheila Rowbotham will escape from Roundhay; she will go to France and have a love affair with a pavement artist, then to Oxford, where she will read Marx and become a socialist. She will join CND, demonstrate against the Vietnam War, write for a radical left-wing paper, live in a Hackney commune, and become part of the fledgling Women's Liberation Movement.

Sheila's voice is a new voice, the voice of the nineteen-sixties:

We assumed we were going to change the world.

Afterword

Stories should certainly have endings. But the stories in this book are true, not fiction, and real life can't always be fitted in to the artificial constraints of a decade. My sympathies, however, are with the tidy-minded, so for them, here is a brief round-up of loose ends.

⋆

'You'll never last,' they said to her.

The comment put steel in Valerie Gisborn's soul, when early in 1958 she waved goodbye to her parents and set off for Staffordshire to train as a policewoman. Over the years that followed, that determination stood her in good stead as a woman in an exceptionally laddish world, where prejudice, discrimination and sexual harassment were her everyday lot. The timid, reserved factory girl had become a confident, steadfast officer of the law, directing traffic, catching criminals (including sex offenders), controlling crowds, tracing missing persons and, over the course of a long career, working in eight murder incident rooms. Almost unexpectedly, at the age of forty-four, she married a widower. 'I'd got the police as a career, and I hadn't thought about marriage really.' By the time she retired in 1984, after nearly twenty-seven years with Leicestershire Police, Valerie was their longest-serving policewoman. 'I carried the knowledge that my life had been useful and busy.'

Butlin's redcoat Sheila McKenzie did three seasons at Clacton-on-Sea; in 1957, while doing an off-season job as a demonstrator in Selfridge's toy department, she met fellow redcoat Bob Just, a handsome clean-limbed swimming instructor who had been working at a Butlin's hotel pool; six weeks later they became engaged. They were married in October 1958. After an interlude as a mum and home-maker, Sheila turned to teaching. She and Bob still keep in touch with the other redcoats, and both retain a characteristically 'Butlin's' sense of fun and welcome. Perhaps that is the secret of their marriage, for in 2015 they will have been together for fifty-seven years.

In 2014 Lorna Arnold died aged ninety-eight. In December 2011 I spent three and a half hours interviewing this modest, intelligent and articulate nonagenarian in her Oxford sitting room. We talked about women's education and expectations, about being a woman in the Foreign Office, about single mother-hood and the pressures of a sexually incompatible marriage, about birth control, dead-end jobs, and civil and military nuclear power. I was awed, and unprepared for her stamina. Lorna believed in the value of her life's work, and continued to keep her mind alive by writing, and by talking to people. TV and radio producers were still coming to her for interviews; she continued to correspond with journalists and political scientists, retaining a fierce grip on the academic advances in her chosen field. In a memoir published not long before her death she wrote, 'I do not yet feel quite retired.'

Joan Bakewell, as everybody knows, found her métier in the media. Being trapped at home with a baby, while her husband engaged with the wider world of radio drama, was not for her. 'My mind was turning to porridge.' Bakewell's candid and inti-mate autobiography *The Centre of the Bed* tracks the progress of her career and breakdown of her marriage in the 1960s and 70s. In her eighties Baroness Bakewell continues to write and broad-cast with her customary pungency and insight.

In 1950 radio presenter Jean Metcalfe was already a household name; she gave up broadcasting to raise a family, for in her world view 'Mrs Michelmore' largely took precedence over Miss Metcalfe, but in the 1970s her voice was heard again on the BBC. In her autobiography Jean wrote that, if anyone were to ask her for her reflections on life, they would be 'Thank God for a marvellous husband and children. And I wish I had dyed my hair *years* ago.'

Rose Hendon kept Jimmy Shine waiting for five years before she married him in 1964. 'My twin sister, she got married at nineteen, and I thought, "You're not enjoying yourself . . ." That was what put me off. I wanted to see a bit and live a bit . . .' Jimmy was a glazier; Rose stayed at home, but later rubbed shoulders with the stars while working as a receptionist at White City Stadium, west London's glamorous dog-racing Mecca. But her own moment in the spotlight came in 2005, by which time Rose was a grandmother. The pictures Ken Russell had taken of her Teddy girl gang back in 1955 came to light in the forgotten archive of *Picture Post*, and because of his fame they were put on exhibition. At the opening, Rose Shine was guest of honour. She treasures her press cuttings: 'the only known professional photographs of the teddy girls . . .'; 'a rare and unique glimpse of a little recognized and under-documented subculture of austere post war Britain'.

Christine Finch left Cambridge in 1952, carrying with her a first-class honours degree, and the taint of having briefly belonged to the student Communist Party. In 1953 she married her fellow student Jack Margolis and their paths led them to settle in Leeds. Christine, who now had a child, continued to find the role of 'university wife' oppressive; her valiant efforts to uphold equal status in her marriage ran up – not so much against Jack, who was an enlightened partner – but against colleagues and contemporaries of both sexes. Christine's world view continued to be underpinned by a tenacious feminism. Looking back, she feels 'the fifties really was a terrible time for women'. Today, having obtained a doctorate and – eventually – a professorship, Christine Margolis has an established academic reputation as a housing and planning historian. It is many years since her marriage ended.

In 1958, before leaving Oxford, Sarah Myers went to the University Appointments Board and asked how to become a political writer. '"Oh," they said, "there aren't any women political writers. You should take a shorthand typing course and then you can get a job in the typing pool."' She knocked on doors, and finally landed a job on the *Times Educational Supplement*; in 1960 she married the deputy editor of the *Literary Supplement* next door. Wifehood and motherhood took over, but for Sarah politics never died. In 1974 she stood as Liberal candidate for Enfield North, polling an impressive 20 per cent of the vote, and since then has given much of her energy to social causes such as the Family Planning Association.

On 29 June 1962, air hostess Angela Austin's nine-hour flight from Freetown, Sierra Leone landed at Gatwick airport. In her high heels, Angela stepped from the passenger stairs, passed through Crew Customs, went home and took off her uniform for the last time. She was almost thirty, and after five years on the flight paths, had begun to hope that the wealthy businessman who had been paying for her London flat might leave his wife and give her the stability she had started to crave. As it turned out, this was not part of his plan. 'He claimed he was getting a divorce, but he didn't. So that all came to an abrupt halt.' Though the sixties were starting to swing, Angela was back home, living with her parents in Golders Green, and nursing a broken heart. At the earliest opportunity she accepted a job as far away from home as she could get: with a major American oil company, in Tripoli, Libya. 'And on the first blind date of my life I met my husband.' Harry Waller was American, divorced, a geologist. Today Angela too is a naturalised American citizen. But it is hard to believe that she is now over eighty years old. Smiling, spry and elegant, she exudes the warm and practised welcome of the expert flight attendant; she's beautifully made-up, carefully dressed, and still prefers high heels to flats. She writes, volunteers and is frequently invited to tell her stories to audiences, about the long-ago time 'Before There Were Trolley Dollies'.*

Flora Calder put her narrow-minded Scottish background behind her when she came to London and got a job with *Woman* magazine. She was working hard and playing hard, enjoying all that London had to offer. Her fears of commitment were disarmed, however, when she found herself being chatted up by a talented artist who was peddling his portfolio in her office. 'We married very quickly . . .' Even so, on her wedding day, Flora tried to wriggle out at the last minute. And the echo of her mother's awful warnings about childbirth still kept her apprehensive about the prospect of having babies. Two daughters were born, nonetheless, but Flora's marriage to the mercurial, funny, brilliant, angry artist didn't stay the course. Her mischievous humour and earthy appetites remained keen, however; while – at over eighty – her urge to draw is still irrepressible. 'It's always been as natural to me to draw as it is to write. It just comes out that way; it gives me a grip on life.'

Audrey Alssebrook still lives barely three miles from where she was born, grew up and married. Len, her late, much-loved husband, was as hefted to the Derbyshire coalfields as she was. Here she raised their family, and here she endured as tragedy visited. In 1969 Audrey's son Malcolm, the pride of her pram, the apple of her eye, died painfully of cancer of the lymph glands aged twenty-three.

---

* Angela Waller's very amusing book of that name is published by Pen Press (2009).

That's our Malcolm, look, in that photo. That were took three weeks before he died. He had a very short life, but a very happy life. He were lovely though. You never get over that you know . . .

But I tell you what saved my life. I was a midday meals supervisor for special children. I were a dinner lady, and let me tell you, I *loved* that job. And it saved my life when our Malcolm died.

And I did it for twenty-two years and to this day the kids call me 'Miss' if they see me . . .

Audrey's mantelpiece is full of framed family photos, with not an inch to spare.

The tragedies of her long life might have broken a lesser person than Dora Russell. From 1954 she had cared for her son John, a severe schizophrenic. Her younger son Roddy, who was eligible for compulsory military service, refused the call-up to fight in the Korean war, opting instead to work in a Yorkshire mine. While there, a pit accident rendered him paraplegic at the age of twenty-four, and he was to spend the remainder of his short life in a wheelchair. Years later her beloved granddaughter Lucy burnt herself to death in an act of protest against the Vietnam War. Dora agonised over the fear that her own left-wing political stance had contributed to the tragic loss of these much-loved family members. Despite being a lifelong chain-smoker, she died at the age of ninety-two, upbeat to the end, guided by indomitable self-belief and by the cheerful, reckless spirit of optimism which in 1958 had launched the Women's Caravan of Peace.

Vilma Owen had only intended to stay in England for three years. The 1960s would see her qualified as a nurse, married and – by the end of that decade – a mother of three herself. With a family to support, she couldn't afford the fare home. At long last, in 1972, Vilma Maduro boarded a flight to Kingston. She was crying and crying. Aged just fifty-nine, Mrs Owen had been run over as she alighted from a bus. Vilma was returning for her mother's funeral.

In so many ways Anthea York was competent, confident and clever. She was a feminist, a professional and interested in politics. But, from not understanding her sexuality, she spent the decade of the nineteen-fifties in ignorance and confusion. The culture she had grown up in was one of 'don't-talk-about-things'; shame had buried the unmentionable facts both of her father's alcoholism, and a family suicide. She found it impossible to acknowledge her feelings about women. Until 1961. That year, Anthea travelled to the USA to pursue her work in the consumer movement. For a reticent upper-class young woman, America's brashness was like a drug. Under its bracing influence the doctrines of her class faltered, then fizzled out. She fell in love. 'And I came back a different person . . .' Today, Anthea is growing old contentedly alongside her partner of many years; their relationship is one of ease and trust. The loneliness has gone and nothing but death can part them now.

Florence Fell believed she would never see her child again. Feeling as if the very guts had been emptied from her body, she returned to her parents' home to pick up her life. In her neighbourhood, the people she knew had been persuaded – or so she thought – that she had been away 'nursing'. 'Everybody at my church must have discussed it. They all knew. But nobody actually mentioned the baby to me.' Going back to nursing was no longer an option. In Stepney, she got a menial job at the Ministry of Pensions and National Insurance, but being a Civil Service post this necessitated a medical examination. A female doctor pushed her, pulled her and peered at her; she felt invaded.

Eighteen months after her return from Yateley, Florence got married. Her husband, Alf, a soldier, was a good, broad-minded man, and there was no secret between them about the baby; by 1968 there were three small boys to look after. But as the years passed Florence's grief sharpened. The little girl she had lost — where was she? 'I wonder what she's doing? Is she at school? Is she even still alive to go to school? You never know. You weren't allowed to talk to anybody, social workers and so on — not even the Minister. So you're thinking in your head all the time, maybe she died of baby things? Or got run over by a bus — and I would never, ever know.' Florence's doctor prescribed Valium. It helped, but still the anguish refused to abate.

In 1986 Florence's mother died. Relieved of her oppressive presence, the unspoken subject surfaced one day as she was returning from a shopping trip with her sister. '"Have you ever tried to find Avril?" she said. Nobody had spoken her name since I'd had her. I burst into tears in the street.' On that day she decided she must try to find her daughter.

But it took several years for Florence to trace the files relating to the mother-and-baby home at Yateley. When at last she did she was told she could leave letters; should her daughter ever seek her out, she would find them. She wrote, added some photographs, and waited.

In 2010 Florence was told that a woman had asked to see the Yateley file. Months passed. And then she heard that her daughter wanted to meet her.

> Two years ago I traced my baby. And it was the happiest day of my life when I saw her. But of course, she wasn't the baby any more . . .

Florence flips through the photos. These are the years she missed. Here is her child aged eighteen months; toddling towards the camera, concentrating, tongue poked out, proudly smiling as she achieves those first steps. And a little older, with bucket and spade by the seaside; on the farm with her adoptive grandparents; flashing forward to the 1960s, complete with trendy hairstyle, bell-bottom trousers and boyfriend. 'She later married him . . . And here's her first baby . . .' Florence hasn't yet met her three grandchildren and one great-grandchild.

She's a big tall girl now. She's fifty-four. They brought her up very well; they were lovely people. She had a bike, and she went horse-riding, they lived near a farm. Her adoptive parents are dead now. But I would love to have thanked them.

She's really a lovely person. We're learning to be friends as adults. You know, she's nothing like me at all. She's well-educated. She's been abroad too. And she's on the Board of the school governors. And the main thing is, she's confident.

She is my daughter – though she can never be as a daughter to me. But I don't mind that. It's just lovely to know that she is who she is.

Acknowledgements

No writer can do it on their own, writers of non-fiction especially, so I am in debt to the many people who made this book possible. Eleo Gordon, who has been my wonderful editor for nearly fifteen years, has supported me in every way, as a professional and as a friend. My husband, William Nicholson, always my first reader, has been unfailingly loving, wise, patient and critical in the most constructive way. Caroline Dawnay is an agent whose skills are legendary in the book world; I am one of her grateful beneficiaries. She also helped me to find one of my most interesting interviewees. Thanks too to Venetia Butterfield and Joanna Prior, who have shown consistent confidence and enthusiasm for this book. Julia Nicholson's interest in my writing (and my punctuation) has been daughterly, professional, helpful and heart-warming. This book is dedicated to her.

If it has a USP, it is that much of the research is drawn from first-hand interviews with women prepared to share the (sometimes) most intimate memories of their lives. Women all over Britain were generous, hospitable and trusting. My task has been not to betray that trust. They are: Audrey Alssebrook, Lorna Arnold, Pat Arrowsmith, Gloria Blackwood, Brenda Bullock, Flora Calder, Sarah Curtis, the Honourable Iris Dawnay MVO, Phyllis Dennis, Professor Mary Evans, Florence Fell, Lady Jacqueline Goode, Sheila Just, Janet Lovegrove, Vilma Maduro, Professor Christine Margolis, Dorothy Medhurst, Elizabeth Monnington, Eileen Mooney, Leila Mudd, Maureen Nicol, Rose Shine, Anne Stamper, Valerie Tedder, Dilys Thompson, Angela Waller and Anthea York. I also had valuable conversations with Rupert Christiansen, Lady Conran, Sue MacGregor and Pauline Williams.

Many individuals kindly sent me their suggestions for interviewees, while others went to the additional trouble of making introductions, and in many cases offered welcome hospitality; my thanks to Yaba Badoe, Terry Baker, Julian Bell, Professor Jay Blumler, Cynthia Brown, Wendy Butlin, Stephanie Calman, Steve Condie, Claire Days, Bevolin Garneth, Alan Gascoyne, Peter Grimsdale, Sophia Hartland, Sophie Henderson, Julian Henriques, Dave Hopper, Colin Hyde, Sarah Jelly, Sue McAlpine, Angela McKeith, Nick Milner-Gulland, Anne Morrison, Caroline Muir, Jamie Muir, Iram Naz, Michael Poole, Sandra Shakespeare, Dr Richard Smith, Ron Stanway, Paula Thompson and Sheila Walker.

I owe particular thanks to Sharon Chen, who gave me invaluable support with her research expertise, quick intelligence, and convenient access to the Social Sciences library at the London School of Economics; also to Paul Beecham, who travelled to the (less convenient, and now obsolete) Colindale Library to find me newspaper articles about his speciality, which is Teddy boys. Charles Anson, Juliet Gardiner, David Kynaston, Kate Murphy, Angela Neuberger, Professor Gill Plain, Jane Robinson, Otto Saumarez Smith and Marina Warner have provided me with useful advice and erudite recommendations. Thank you all; and also to Carmen Callil for her unfailingly warm encouragement. And thank you to Mary McPherson, who kindly sent me a copy of her interesting autobiography.

I am also grateful to Sir Peter Bazalgette, Valerie Grove and Russ Kane for helping to clear the undergrowth lying around certain research routes, while family, friends and acquaintances have been ready to help with answers to the oddest queries. Augusta Skidelsky's mathematical talents merit a warm acknowledgement, as do Sulaiman Hakemy's patient and detailed responses to my enquiries regarding the use of the mihrab, Teddy Nicholson's conscientious descriptions of the interiors of Embassy residences, and Norman Stone's explanations of the tenets of the Congregationalist church. A particular thank you to Maria Nicholson for her methodical approach to the extra-curricular task I assigned her of dealing with certain literary estates.

My warmest thanks to the librarians and archivists who have made their treasure-troves available to me – the manuscript boxes, folders, tapes and microfilms that reveal the unmediated past lives of so many women. They are Hannah Ishmael at the Black Cultural Archives, Fiona Courage and her team at the University of Sussex Special Collections, Jenny Brattle and Hannah Lowery at the University of Bristol Special Collections, Sonia Gomes at the Women's Library, Paula Gerrard at the archive of Brunel University, Dr Lesley Hall at the Wellcome Institute Library; also the staff of the London Library and those at the British Library – particularly in the recorded sound collections – who helped me to access their oral history recordings.

Last (but never least), thank you to Annie Lee for her meticulous copy-editing, and to my admired associate Douglas Matthews for the index. And thank you too to the team at Viking, especially Jillian Taylor, Poppy North, Keith Taylor and Catriona Hillerton.

★

In addition, the author gratefully acknowledges the kind permission of copyright holders to quote from a number of authors and sources, as follows: excerpts from *The Centre of the Bed* by Joan Bakewell, copyright © 2003 Joan Bakewell, reproduced by permission of Hodder & Stoughton Ltd; an excerpt from

'Business Girls' from *Collected Poems*, by John Betjeman, © 1955, 1958, 1962, 1964, 1968, 1970, 1979, 1981, 1982, 2001, reproduced by permission of John Murray (Publishers), an imprint of Hodder & Stoughton Ltd; *A Pocket with a Hole: A Birmingham Childhood of the 1940s and 1950s, Over the Wall: A Working-class Girl at University in the 1950s,* and *Reflected Glory*, by Brenda Bullock, published by Brewin Books, Studley, Warwickshire, all excerpts reprinted by kind permission of the author; *A Good School: Life at a Girls' Grammar School in the 1950s*, The Women's Press Ltd, London, by Mary Evans, all excerpts reprinted by kind permission of the author; *Hidden Lives: A Family Memoir*, by Margaret Forster, all excerpts reprinted by kind permission of the author; extracts from *Janey and Me* by Virginia Ironside are published by permission of Quercus Editions Ltd; *Austerity Britain, 1945–51* and *Family Britain, 1951-57*, by David Kynaston, all excerpts reprinted by kind permission of the author; *Post War Blues*, A Living History Publication published by Leicester City Council, and *You'll Never Last: One Policewoman's Story from 1958–1984*, by Valerie A. Tedder, both published by United Press Ltd, London, all excerpts reprinted by kind permission of the author; Jean Hart of Wormley Women's Institute, permission granted for quotations to be included from the book *Turning Back the Clock*, a Wormley W I publication; acknowledgements to The Orion Publishing Group, London, for permission to reprint excerpts from *Call the Midwife* by Jennifer Worth, © Jennifer Worth 2002; material from the Mass Observation archive reproduced with permission of Curtis Brown Ltd, London, on behalf of the Trustees of the Mass Observation Archive, copyright © The Trustees of the Mass Observation Archive; excerpts from *We Called on Europe: The Story of the Women's Caravan of Peace 1958* by Dora Russell reprinted with the permission of the Feminist Archive South, University of Bristol Library Special Collections; a verse from 'Last Night I Had the Strangest Dream' by Ed

McCurdy, © 1950, 1951 and 1955 Folkways Music Pub. Co. Inc., USA, assigned to Kensington Music Ltd of Suite 2.07, Plaza 535 Kings Road, London sw 10 0sz, International copyright secured, all rights reserved, used by permission.

Acknowledgements are also due for use of material transcribed from the Millennium Memory Bank held by the British Library, and for use of quotations transcribed from the Personal Predicament letters sent to the Abortion Law Reform Association and now held in the Wellcome Institute Library.

Acknowledgements to the following whose works have been quoted from: Anonymous, *Streetwalker*; Margaret Argyll, *Forget Not: The Autobiography of Margaret Duchess of Argyll*; Lorna Arnold, *Windscale 1957: Anatomy of a Nuclear Accident*; Diana Athill, *Stet: An Editor's Life*; Deirdre Beddoe (ed.), *Changing Times: Welsh Women Writing on the 1950s and 1960s*; Violet Bonham Carter, *Daring to Hope: Diaries*; Barbara Cartland, *Marriage for Moderns*; Mark Clapson, *Invincible Green Suburbs, Brave New Towns, Social Change and Urban Dispersal*; Lucie Clayton, *The World of Modelling and How to Get the London Model-girl Look*; Becky E. Conekin, *The Autobiography of a Nation: The 1951 Festival of Britain*; Jennifer Craig, *Yes Sister, No Sister: My Life as a Trainee Nurse in 1950s Yorkshire*; Stella Dadzie, *The Heart of the Race, Black Women's Lives in Britain*; Rosamund Essex, *Woman in a Man's World*; Leonora Eyles, *Sex for the Engaged*; Winifred Foley, *Shiny Pennies and Grubby Pinafores*; Jill Gardiner, *From the Closet to the Screen: Women at the Gateways Club* . . .; Geoffrey Gorer, *Exploring English Character*; Pip Granger, *Up West: Voices from the Streets of Post-war London*; Mary Grieve, *Millions Made My Story*; Grace Hall, *How to Get Your Man!*; Teresa Hayter, *Hayter of the Bourgeoisie*; Peter Hennessy, *Having It So Good: Britain in the Fifties*; Richard Hoggart, *The Uses of Literacy*; Judith Hubback, *Wives Who Went to College*; Ruth Jennings, *One Woman's Work . . . and Other Disasters*; Betty Kenward, *Eighty-five Years of*

Fun and Functions; Emily Kimbrough, *Forty Plus and Fancy Free*; Leonore King, *Glorify Yourself*; Alfred Kinsey, *Sexual Behavior in the Human Female*; Jill Liddington, *The Road to Greenham Common: Feminism and Anti-militarism in Britain* . . .; John Lucas, *Next Year Will Be Better: A Memoir of England in the 1950s*; Ethel Mannin, *Brief Voices: A Writer's Story*; Laura Duchess of Marlborough, *Laughter from a Cloud*; Cliff Michelmore and Jean Metcalfe, *Two Way Story*; Charles Moore, *Margaret Thatcher: The Authorized Biography,* Volume 1: *Not for Turning*; Eric Morley, *The Miss World Story*; Alva Myrdal and Viola Klein, *Women's Two Roles*; John Newsom, *The Education of Girls*; Frances Partridge, *Everything to Lose: Diaries 1945-1960*; Margaret Pringle, *Dance Little Ladies: The Days of the Debutante*; Elizabeth Roberts, *Women and Families: An Oral History 1940-1970*; Lorna Sage, *Bad Blood*; Dodie Smith, *Look Back with Gratitude*; Noel Streatfeild, *The Years of Grace*; Elizabeth Stucley, *Teddy Boys' Picnic*; Edith Summerskill, *Letters to my Daughter*; Maureen Sutton, *'We Didn't Know Aught': A Study of Sexuality, Superstition and Death in* . . .; Peter Townsend, *Time and Chance: An Autobiography*; Christopher Warwick, *Princess Margaret: A Life of Contrasts*; Priscilla West, *Reminiscences of Seven Decades at St Hugh's: One Hundred Years of Women's Education in Oxford*; Katharine Whitehorn, *Selective Memory: An Autobiography*; Mary Whitehouse, *Who Does She Think She Is?*; Phyllis Whiteman, *Speaking as a Woman*; Amabel Williams-Ellis, *The Art of Being a Woman*; Michael Young and Peter Willmott, *Family and Class in a London Suburb*; Ferdynand Zweig, *The Worker in an Affluent Society*.

While every effort has been made to obtain clearances from copyright holders, the publishers would be glad to correct any errors of omission or commission in future editions.

Notes on Sources

The following notes give only principal sources consulted, and are aimed at the general reader rather than the scholar. For all publication details, please refer to the Select Bibliography on page 493.

Where reference is made to monetary values I have often referred to a website which calculates what sums in the past would be worth today. This calculator is available through http://www.thisismoney.co.uk/money/index.html

Statistical references are not credited throughout. Principal statistical sources are:

Mark Abrams, *The Teenage Consumer*
Paul Addison, *No Turning Back: The Peacetime Revolutions of Post-war Britain*
Dr Eustace Chesser, *The Sexual, Marital and Family Relationships of the English Woman*
David Clark (ed.), *Marriage, Domestic Life and Social Change*
Geoffrey Gorer, *Exploring English Character*
A. H. Halsey (ed.), *Trends in British Society since 1900*
Cate Haste, *Rules of Desire*
Peter Hennessy, *Having It So Good*
Pearl Jephcott, *Married Women Working*
George Joseph, *Women at Work: The British Experience*
David Kynaston, *Family Britain, 1951–57*
Jane Lewis, *Women in Britain since 1945*
John Montgomery, *The Fifties*

Alva Myrdal and Viola Klein, *Women's Two Roles: Home and Work*
Elizabeth Roberts, *Women and Families: An Oral History, 1940–1970*
Stephanie Spencer, *Gender, Work and Education in Britain in the 1950s*
Virginia Wimperis, *The Unmarried Mother and Her Child*
Ferdynand Zweig, *The Worker in an Affluent Society*

Certain sources recur throughout the book. For the sake of brevity, they are abbreviated as follows:

AA/A   Audrey Alssebrook, author interview.

AW/A   Angela Waller née Austin, author interview.

AW/BTD   Angela Waller, *Before There Were Trolley Dollies*.

AY/A   Anthea York, author interview.

BB/A   Brenda Bullock née Nash, author interview.

BB/OW   Brenda Bullock, *Over the Wall*.

BB/PH   Brenda Bullock, *Pocket with a Hole*.

BB/RG   Brenda Bullock, *Reflected Glory*.

CW/PM   Christopher Warwick, *Princess Margaret: A Life of Contrasts*.

DM/A   Dorothy Medhurst née Maskell, author interview.

Ei/A   Eileen Mooney née Hawe, author interview.

EM/A   Elizabeth Monnington née Jones, author interview.

FC/A   Flora Calder, author interview.

FF/A   Florence Fell, author interview.

FM/LC   Fiona MacCarthy, *Last Curtsey*.

FP/EL   Frances Partridge, *Everything to Lose*: *Diaries 1945–1960*.

ID/A   The Hon. Mrs Iris Dawnay née Peake, author interview.

JB/CB   Joan Bakewell, *The Centre of the Bed*.

JL/A   Janet Lovegrove née Bourne, author interview.

JM/TWS   Cliff Michelmore and Jean Metcalfe, *Two-way Story*.

JW/CM   Jennifer Worth, *Call the Midwife*.

LA/A   Lorna Arnold née Rainbow, author interview.

LA/SC   Lorna Arnold, *My Short Century*.

LM/A   Leila Mudd née Williams, author interview.

LM/BQ   *The Beauty Queen Business*, chapter 18 of Leila Mudd's unpublished autobiography.

ME/GS   Mary Evans, *A Good School*.

MF/HL   Margaret Forster, *Hidden Lives*.

MM/BL   Millennium Memory Bank, British Library.

MN/A   Maureen Nicol née Johnson, author interview.

MN/CS   Maureen Nicol, 'You Opened the Door', in *The Unsung Sixties: Memoirs of Social Innovation*, ed. Helene Curtis and Mimi Sanderson.

MP/NY   Mollie Panter-Downes, 'Letter from London', *The New Yorker*.

MS/WLL   Maureen Sutton, *'We Didn't Know Aught': A Study of Sexuality, Superstition and Death in Women's Lives in Lincolnshire during the 1930s, '40s and '50s*.

NL/50s   P. and R. Malcolmson (eds.), *Nella Last in the 1950s*.

P/Cine   Pathé Cinemagazine clip available at http://www.britishpathe.com/pages/cinemagazines.

P/News   Pathé newsreel available at http://www.britishpathe.com/pages/newsreels.

PT/TC   Peter Townsend, *Time and Chance – an Autobiography*.

RH/UL   Richard Hoggart, *The Uses of Literacy*.

RS/A   Rose Shine née Hendon, author interview.

SC/A   Sarah Curtis née Myers, author interview.

SJ/A   Sheila Just née McKenzie, author interview.

VM/A   Vilma Maduro née Owen, author interview.

VT/A   Valerie Tedder née Gisborn, author interview.

VT/PWB   Valerie A. Tedder, *Post War Blues*.

VT/YNL   Valerie A. Tedder, *You'll Never Last*.

WF/BF   Winifred Foley, *Back to the Forest*.

WW/B   Deirdre Beddoe (ed.), *Changing Times: Welsh Women Writing on the 1950s and 1960s*.

1: Elizabethans

pp. 1–9. 'In 1999 a community history unit . . .': VT/PWB.

p. 5. 'the ultimate goal . . .': feature by Monica Dickens in *Woman's Own* entitled 'Don't Try to be the Boss', 6 October 1955.

p. 7. '. . . bright adornments for my lady . . .': cited in Becky E. Conekin, *The Autobiography of a Nation: The 1951 Festival of Britain*.

p. 9. 'I am toying with the idea . . .': Miss Prudence Moss is the pseudonym of an anonymous Mass Observation diarist, writing between April and June 1953.

p. 10. '. . . the most she could have earned . . .' (and footnote): statistics from Freda Conway, *School Teachers' Salaries, 1945–1959*.

p. 13. 'Now she would be queen . . .': JB/CB.

pp. 13–14. 'Janet Bourne, her contemporary . . .': JL/A.

p. 14. 'Observing these details . . .': Betty Kenward, *Jennifer's Memoirs: Eighty-five Years of Fun and Functions*.

pp. 14–15. '. . . the American journalist . . .': Emily Kimbrough, *Forty Plus and Fancy Free*.

p. 15. '. . . sixty-one-year-old Betty Hodge . . .': from Mass Observation Diarist 5338, 14 May 1953.

p. 15. 'That same day . . .': FP/EL.

pp. 17–18. '. . . Constance Spry was invited . . .': Sue Shephard, *The Surprising Life of Constance Spry*.

pp. 18–19. 'Another name . . .': JM/TWS.

pp. 20–21. 'Over the weeks . . .': Mary Whitehouse's broadcast text, *Who Does She Think She Is?* from http://www.mediawatchuk.org.uk/index.php?option=com_content&task=view&id=211&Itemid=93.

pp. 22–3. 'That night Angela Austin . . .': AW/A.

pp. 24–5. 'On that raw, wet morning . . .': Rosamund Essex, *Woman in a Man's World*.

pp. 24, 27. 'The blanco ran off . . .': Wormley Women's Institute, *Turning Back the Clock: Personal Memories spanning the 20th Century*.

p. 27. 'Florence Fell's parents . . .': FF/A.

p. 28. 'The Queen had . . .': ID/A.

pp. 28–9. 'With her view . . .': Felicity Fisher's recollections of Coronation day are available on http://www.bbc.co.uk/dna/memoryshare/home.

pp. 29–30. 'Emily Kimbrough sat . . .': Kimbrough, cited above.

p. 29. 'Would it be regarded . . .': MP/NY 13 June 1953.

p. 30. '. . . one who is little more than a girl . . .': 'Inside the Abbey', Joan Reeder writing in the *Daily Mirror*, Wednesday 3 June 1953.

p. 31. 'Princess Margaret came up to me . . .': see Jean Rook, *Majesty Magazine*, August 1990, cited in CW/PM; see also PT/TC.

p. 31. 'I doubt whether . . .': quoted in 'Rosemary Hume's Coronation Chicken', *Daily Telegraph*, Monday 17 September 2012.

p. 31. 'Coronation Chicken was . . .': FM/LC.

p. 32. 'We had a nine-inch television . . .': AA/A.

p. 32. 'In Leicester Valerie Gisborn . . .': VT/PWB.

pp. 32–3. 'In Liverpool . . .': SJ/A.

p. 33. 'In Sussex Elizabeth Monnington . . .': EM/A.

p. 34. '. . . in "unexpectedly bridal" attire . . .': MP/NY 13 June 1953.

pp. 34–5. 'In the down-at-heel . . .': BB/PH.

p. 35. 'Over 4,000 miles away . . .': author interview with Gloria Blackwood.

pp. 35–7. 'Vilma Owen, whose story . . .': VM/A.

pp. 37–8. '. . . ex-debutante Anthea York . . .': AY/A.

p. 38. 'Another Cambridge student . . .': JB/CB.

pp. 38–9. 'In 1953 Flora Calder . . .': FC/A.

p. 41. 'The Princess was very calm . . .': PT/TC.

2: Her True Calling

p. 42. 'Writing about her Essex childhood . . .': *Memories of my Childhood in Kelvedon in the 1930s*, by Kath Lewis (née Langstone), 2006.

pp. 42–3. 'For Margaret Duchess of Argyll . . .': *Forget Not: The Auto-biography of Margaret Duchess of Argyll*.

p. 43. '. . . there was right and wrong . . .': NL/50s.

pp. 43–4. 'The great majority of married women . . .': *The Beveridge Report*, 1942, para. 108; and 'The attitude of the housewife . . .', paras 114 and 117.

p. 45. 'Diana Athill, co-director . . .': Diana Athill, *Stet*.

p. 47. 'America has the A-bomb . . .': NL/50s.

p. 47. 'Another visitor from America . . .': cited in David Kynaston, *Family Britain 1951–57*.

p. 48. 'Among Joan Rowlands's memories . . .': JB/CB.

pp. 48–9. 'Virginia Ironside recalled . . .': Virginia Ironside, *Janey and Me*.

pp. 49–50. 'Liz Jones was seventeen . . .': EM/A.

pp. 51–3. 'Maureen dates her passion . . .': MN/A. See also MN/CS.

p. 53. 'Gradually a feeling . . .'. NL/50s.

pp. 54–6. 'I think probably . . .': EM/A.

p. 58. '*The Housewives' Pocket Book* . . .': ed. Carlton Wallace.

p. 59. 'Audrey Alssebrook was another . . .': AA/A.

p. 59. 'And Nella Last recorded . . .': NL/50s.

pp. 59–60. 'The young East End midwife . . .': JW/CM.

p. 60. 'And we had our steps . . .': AA/A.

pp. 61–2. 'One boy who grew up . . .': Mike Shaw, *Donkey Stones*, available on http://www.openwriting.com.

p. 62. 'Another young . . . health worker . . .': Jennifer Craig, *Yes Sister, No Sister*.

p. 62. '. . . not for Mrs Phillips . . .': in Amabel Williams-Ellis, *The Art of Being a Woman*.

p. 63. 'Never was I so barren . . .': Mass Observation Diarist No. 5447.

pp. 63–9. 'But in 1950 Eileen Hawe . . .': Ei/A.

p. 69. 'Richard Hoggart's assertion . . .': RH/UL.

pp. 69–70. 'Honest to God . . .': AA/A.

p. 70. 'I shall never forget . . .': Janet Lee, MM/BL.

pp. 70–71. 'She started her periods . . .': Joan Hilditch, *Sweet Sixteen*, in WW/B.

p. 71. 'In Birmingham, teenager Brenda Nash . . .': BB/PH.

pp. 71–2. 'Jennifer Craig was well . . .': Jennifer Craig, *Yes Sister, No Sister*.

p. 72. 'Her mother was educated . . .': ME/GS.

pp. 72–4. 'For a girl like Florence . . .': FF/A.

3: Lovely in Every Way

pp. 76–8. 'HOW TO GET YOUR MAN!': by Grace Hall.

p. 80. 'Writing about her teenage years . . .': FM/LC.

pp. 80–81. 'Every girl cannot be beautiful . . .': Noel Streatfeild (ed.), *The Years of Grace*.

p. 83. 'Jennifer Hocking . . .': cited in Lucie Clayton, *The World of Modelling*.

p. 83. 'The Clayton students . . .': P/Cine.

pp. 84–8. 'His name was Eric Morley . . .': see entry in *The Dictionary of National Biography*, also Eric Morley, *The Miss World Story*.

pp. 88–93. 'Certainly, Leila Williams didn't . . .': LM/A, also LM/BQ.

pp. 94–5. 'Princess Margaret couldn't . . .': see CW/PM.

pp. 94–5. 'Her lady-in-waiting . . .': ID/A.

pp. 95–6. 'Nella Last, when she heard . . .': NL/50s.

p. 96. 'We queued up for hours . . .': AW/A.

pp. 97–8. 'That crisp winter's morning . . .': RS/A.

pp. 98–9. 'Iris Peake, who had only . . .': ID/A.

pp. 99–101. 'Peter Townsend was one . . .': PT/TC; see also CW/PM.

p. 101. 'Eileen Hawe was no princess . . .': Ei/A.

p. 102. 'This Bill seeks . . .': *The Times*, Tuesday 17 February 1953.

pp. 102–3. 'Listen to some of them . . .': quotations from letters to the Abortion Law Reform Association, held in the Wellcome Archive.

p. 104. 'When Jessie Butler . . .': BB/PH.

pp. 104–6. 'In Dublin, Eileen Hawe . . .': Ei/A.

pp. 106–12. 'Lorna Arnold's remarkable career . . .': LA/A, also LA/SC.

p. 112. 'I often wondered . . .': JW/CM.

p. 112. 'My wife is on staff . . .': cited in Ferdynand Zweig, *The Worker in an Affluent Society*.

p. 113. 'Having sex with a condom . . .': cited in Lorna Sage, *Bad Blood*.

p. 113. 'They take away the pleasure . . .': cited in RH/UL.

p. 113. 'He couldn't always time it . . .': cited in MS/WLL.

p. 113. 'It was like getting off . . .': cited in Elizabeth Roberts, *Women and Families: An Oral History, 1940–1970*.

pp. 113–15. 'Lorna Arnold described . . .': LA/A, also LA/SC.

4: Paved with Gold

pp. 117–18. 'At the start of the 1950s . . .': AW/A.

p. 123. 'Dr Wand, the Bishop of London . . .': Hansard, 5 April 1951.

p. 123. 'Oh well, Thursday's my day . . .': cited in Pip Granger, *Up West*.

pp. 124–5. 'It was twilight time . . .': ibid.

p. 126. 'On Friday nights . . .': Henrietta Moraes, *Henrietta*.

p. 126. 'ten bob and find your own railings . . .': cited in Granger, above.

p. 127. 'noise and loud music . . .': JW/CM.

p. 127. 'Liverpool shop assistant . . .': Joyce Kearney, MM/BL.

p. 132. 'When I first fell in love . . .': Ruth Ellis, 'My Love and Hate', *Sunday Mirror*, 17 July 1955.

p. 137. 'I thought England was broke . . .': cited in David Kynaston, *Family Britain 1951–57*.

pp. 137–8. 'Even Leicester Square . . .': Dodie Smith, *Look Back with Gratitude*.

pp. 139–40. 'This is Sally . . .': 'A Girl versus London', *Good Housekeeping*, 1951.

p. 140. 'It was a golden time . . .': Mrs Mary White, correspondence with author.

pp. 140–48. 'Flora Calder never lived . . .': FC/A.

pp. 148–52. 'During the war Dot . . .': DM/A.

pp. 152–3. 'Ancient folklore survived . . .': see MS/WLL.

pp. 153–4. 'In 1952 Elaine Morgan . . .': Elaine Morgan, *Living at the End of the World*, in WW/B.

p. 154. 'Who would willingly . . .': see WF/BF.

p. 154. 'Post-war, the Women's Institute . . .': see Jane Robinson, *A Force to be Reckoned With: A History of the Women's Institute*.

5: *When I Grow Up* . . .

p. 157. 'Most of my teachers . . .': JB/CB.

p. 158. 'John Newsom was . . .': John Newsom, *The Education of Girls*.

pp. 159–61. '. . . the social scientist Mary Evans . . .': ME/GS.

pp. 161–4. 'Brenda Nash was growing up . . .': BB/PH.

p. 164. 'A careers-advice book . . .': Eva Isabel Marian Primrose and the Countess of Rosebery, *The Ambitious Girl*, cited in Stephanie Spencer, *Gender, Work and Education in Britain in the 1950s*.

p. 166. 'as in the case of Valerie Gisborn . . .': VT/PWB.

p. 166. 'Brenda broke the mould . . .': BB/PH.

pp. 167–8. 'What woman *doesn't* dream . . .': P/Cine.

p. 169. 'As a girl . . .': letter to author from Mrs Patricia Moore.

p. 169. 'I left school in 1950 . . .': letter to author from Liz Balmforth.

p. 169. 'I wanted to be a teacher . . .': author interview with Anne Stamper.

p. 171. 'In Carlisle Margaret Forster . . .': MF/HL.

pp. 171–2. 'Joan Rowlands was possessed . . .': JB/CB.

p. 173. 'Ruth Barnet from Merseyside . . .': Ruth Jennings, *One Woman's Work . . . and other disasters*.

pp. 174–5. 'When Anne Howarth went . . .': author interview with Anne Stamper née Howarth.

p. 175. 'Ann Owen was another . . .': Ann Rodgers née Owen, *College Days*, in WW/B.

pp. 175–6. 'When Joan Rowlands arrived . . .': JB/CB.

pp. 176–7. 'Anthea York was . . .': AY/A.

p. 177. 'The dominant social element . . .': Teresa Hayter, *Hayter of the Bourgeoisie*.

pp. 177–84. 'For Christine Finch . . .': author interview with Christine Margolis née Finch.

pp. 184–5. 'Sarah Myers from Preston . . .': SC/A.

p. 185. 'I am convinced . . .': Priscilla West, *Reminiscences of Seven Decades* in *St Hugh's: One Hundred Years of Women's Education in Oxford*, ed. Penny Griffin, Macmillan, Basingstoke, 1986.

pp. 186–7. 'Joan Rowlands, too . . .': JB/CB.

pp. 187–8. 'They either didn't . . .': SC/A.

p. 188. 'Years later, in 1984 . . .': Sarah Curtis, *Origins and Outcomes*, in Penny Griffin (ed.), cited above.

pp. 188–9. 'Judith Hubback was born . . .': Judith Hubback, *From Dawn to Dusk*.

pp. 192–3. 'But she herself . . .': ibid.

pp. 194–5. 'Meanwhile, the correspondence pages . . .': in *The Times*, June 1958.

pp. 195–6. 'Seriously depressed . . .': Hubback, cited above.

pp. 196–7. 'At the height of McCarthyism . . .': author interview with Christine Margolis née Finch.

6: Queen of Her Castle

p. 198. 'She came to Jamaica . . .': author interview with Phyllis Dennis.

p. 199. 'But Vilma Owen's family . . .': VM/A.

pp. 199–200. 'At the start of 1955 . . .': CW/PM; also ID/A.

p. 200. 'The reality was that Townsend . . .': PT/TC and CW/PM.

pp. 200–201. 'Well, I married . . .': vox pops quoted from *Princess Margaret: A Love Story*, BBC documentary 2005.

p. 201. 'If Princess Margaret marries . . .': cited in *The Times*, 31 October 1955.

p. 203. 'Women are no longer content . . .': Royal Commission on Marriage and Divorce 1956, para 45.

p. 204. '[This] is one of the great . . .': Michael Young and Peter Willmott, *Family and Kinship in East London*.

p. 204. 'When *Woman's Realm* published . . .': *Woman's Realm*, 15 March 1958.

p. 204. 'The working out . . .': RCMD cited above, para 45.

p. 205. 'A leaflet published . . .': A. Joseph Brayshaw, *The Stability of Marriage*.

pp. 205–6. 'If [a man] wants . . .': Phyllis Whiteman, *Speaking as a Woman*.

p. 206. 'Every husband expects . . .': ibid.

p. 206. 'Love him, feed him . . .': Grace Hall, *How to Get Your Man!*

p. 206. '1,400 married women . . .': in Dr Eustace Chesser, *The Sexual, Marital and Family Relationships of the English Woman*.

pp. 206–7. '. . . Geoffrey Gorer surveyed . . .': Geoffrey Gorer, *Exploring English Character*.

p. 209. 'As Geoffrey Gorer commented . . .': ibid.

p. 209. 'Barbara Cartland warned . . .': Barbara Cartland, *Marriage for Moderns*.

pp. 209–10. 'We sent away for the first . . .': AA/A.

p. 210. 'Lady Isobel Barnett . . .': Isobel Barnett, *My Life Line*.

p. 213. 'The National Marriage Guidance Council . . .': National Marriage Guidance Council publication, *Sex in Marriage*.

p. 213. 'When Eustace Chesser interviewed . . .': Chesser, cited above.

pp. 213–14. 'I had intercourse . . .' and others: in MS/WLL.

p. 214. 'Janet Lee, a housewife . . .': Janet Lee, MM/BL.

p. 214. 'He came up to bed . . .': in WF/BF.

p. 215. 'He'd be home around ten . . .': cited in David Kynaston, *Family Britain 1951–57*.

pp. 215–16. 'I love my husband . . .': Leonora Eyles, *The New Commonsense about Sex*.

p. 217. 'One self-help author . . .': Cartland, cited above.

pp. 218–21. 'Nineteen-year-old Liz Jones . . .': EM/A.

pp. 221–4. 'The story of the Mooney . . .': Ei/A.

pp. 224–8. 'To this day . . .': author interview with Lady Marion Turnbull.

p. 229. 'As Nella Last wrote . . .': NL/50s.

pp. 230–32. 'The academic Richard Hoggart . . .': RH/UL.

pp. 234–6. 'In most respects . . .': AA/A.

pp. 236–40. 'A generation earlier . . .': WF/BF.

p. 237. 'People do not realise . . .': Hilda Price, *A Political Life* in WW/B.

p. 238. 'Never before had we . . .': cited in Mark Clapson, *Invincible Green Suburbs, Brave New Towns: Social Change and Urban Dispersal in Postwar England*.

p. 238. 'It's just like . . .' and 'When I walked . . .': Marion Hill (ed.), *Bigger, Brighter, Better: The Story of Bletchley*.

p. 238. 'I felt like the Queen': from Clapson, cited above.

p. 241. 'The 1951 Exhibition hosted . . .': see *Home and Country* (magazine of the Women's Institute), March 1951 issue.

p. 241. 'In 1955 C.O.S.M.I.T.H. . . .': leaflet on *The C.O.S.M.I.T.H. Kitchen* published for the *Daily Mail* Ideal Home Exhibition.

p. 241. 'That year Pathé's cameras . . .': P/Cine.

pp. 241–2. 'House of the Future . . .': JM/TWS.

pp. 242–3. 'When Maureen Johnson moved . . .': MN/A; also MN/CS.

p. 244. 'The politician Edith Summerskill . . .': Edith Summerskill, *Letters to my Daughter*.

pp. 245–8. 'Before moving to Westcott Road . . .': BB/A; also BB/PH.

7: *What's My Line?*

p. 249. 'My first job . . .': RS/A.

pp. 250–51. 'Girls like my sisters . . .': BB/A.

p. 251. '. . . social researcher Pearl Jephcott . . .': Pearl Jephcott, *Some Young People*.

pp. 251–2. '. . . social scientist Mark Abrams . . .': Mark Abrams, *The Teenage Consumer*.

pp. 251–2. 'In her teens Margaret Forster . . .': MF/HL.

p. 252. 'What favours you doin' . . .': cited in John Lucas, *Next Year will be Better*.

p. 253. 'One survey claimed . . .': Elizabeth Roberts, *Women and Families: An Oral History, 1940–1970*.

p. 253. 'Midwife Jennifer Worth . . .': JW/CM.

p. 253. 'The Liverpool shop assistant . . .': Joyce Kearney, MM/BL.

p. 254. 'According to Pearl Jephcott . . .': Pearl Jephcott, *Some Young People*.

pp. 254–6. 'In 1957 Valerie Gisborn . . .': VT/PWB, VT/A, VT/YNL.

pp. 256–61. 'Joyce Kearney was one . . .': Joyce Kearney, MM/BL.

pp. 261–3. '. . . north Londoner Patricia Saville . . .': Patricia Saville's unpublished memoir is held in the Burnett Archive of Working Class Autobiographies at Brunel University.

p. 264. 'Margery Hurst, founder . . .': Margery Hurst, *No Glass Slipper*.

pp. 264–5. 'However the sociologist . . .': Dr Ferdynand Zweig, *Women's Life and Labour*, cited in Alva Myrdal and Viola Klein, *Women's Two Roles: Home and Work*.

pp. 265–6. 'Bowlby was a caring . . .': John Bowlby, *Child Care and the Growth of Love*.

p. 266. '. . . Joan Bakewell was working . . .': JB/CB.

p. 266. 'As Mary Stott . . .': Mary Stott, *Forgetting's No Excuse*.

pp. 267–70. 'Lorna Rainbow married . . .': LA/A and LA/SC.

pp. 272–3. 'Pathé's Cinemagazine producers . . .': P/Cine.

pp. 273–4. '[they] thought that in engineering . . .': see Stephanie Spencer, *Gender, Work and Education in Britain in the 1950s*.

pp. 276–7. 'Jean Hart, who was . . .': from Jean Hart's memoir in *Turning Back the Clock*, a publication by Wormley Women's Institute.

p. 277. 'Your employer will . . .': from Noel Streatfeild, *The Years of Grace*.

pp. 277–83. 'When I became an air hostess . . .': AW/A and AW/BTD.

p. 282. 'During the London Season . . .': in FM/LC.

pp. 283–7. 'Dilys Hughes was . . .': author interview with Dilys Thompson née Hughes.

pp. 287–8. 'This is morally wrong . . .': Edith Summerskill, *Letters to my Daughter*.

p. 290. 'But in 1956 . . .': Dilys Thompson, cited above.

p. 292. 'In her memoir . . .': FM/LC.

p. 292. 'The Hon. Emma Tennant . . .': Emma Tennant, *Girlitude*.

pp. 292–5. 'Or, like Laura Charteris . . .': Laura Duchess of Marlborough, *Laughter from a Cloud*.

8: On Parade

pp. 296–300. 'Sheila McKenzie left . . .': SJ/A.

p. 296. 'Butlin's was the brainchild . . .': see entry on Billy Butlin in *The Oxford Dictionary of National Biography*, and B. Butlin and P. Dacre, *The Billy Butlin story: 'A Showman to the End'*.

p. 300. 'One of Eden's . . .': see Charles Moore, *Margaret Thatcher: The Authorized Biography*.

p. 301. 'Among the first . . .': Butlin, cited above.

p. 301. 'If this goes on . . .': P/News.

pp. 301–2. 'Eden must be raving mad . . .': FP/EL.

p. 302. 'Rosamund Essex immediately . . .': Rosamund Essex, *Woman in a Man's World*.

p. 302. 'Sir, – I am one of millions . . .': *Daring to Hope: The Diaries and Letters of Violet Bonham Carter 1946–1969*.

pp. 302–3. 'Never before had I seen . . .': Edith Summerskill, *A Woman's World*.

p. 303. 'Sarah Myers, newly . . .': SC/A.

pp. 303–4. '. . . Anthea York was working . . .': AY/A.

p. 304. 'The Middle East situation . . .': Mass Observation Diarist No. 5338.

p. 304. '[They were] carrying . . .': Mass Observation Diarist No. 5445.

p. 304. 'But Mollie Panter-Downes . . .': MP/NY, 10 November 1956.

p. 305. 'I know it were . . .': author interview with Vera Brydon.

p. 305. 'Something happens to men . . .': DM/A.

p. 305. 'I took over . . .': author interview with Dilys Thompson née Hughes.

p. 305. 'The society diarist . . .': Betty Kenward, *Jennifer's Memoirs*.

p. 306. 'Lord Franks, post-war . . .': cited in Peter Hennessy, *Having It So Good*.

pp. 307–14. 'I gave myself a deadline . . .': LM/A, also LM/BQ.

pp. 314–18. 'Sheila McKenzie looked . . .': SJ/A.

p. 321. 'You gave us the glamour . . .': Margaret Payton's post on http://www.butlinsmemories.com/index.htm.

p. 322. 'Two-guinea tickets . . .': MP/NY, 13 May 1950.

pp. 322–3. '"Good" girls were expected . . .': ME/GS.

p. 323. 'Virginia Ironside, recalling . . .': Virginia Ironside, *Janey and Me*.

p. 323. 'Barbara Hulanicki, another . . .': *From A to Biba: The Autobiography of Barbara Hulanicki*.

pp. 323–4. 'A coy clip from 1953 . . .': P/Cine.

p. 324. 'Girls could wear trousers . . .': Lorna Sage, *Bad Blood*.

p. 325. '. . . like Sarah Myers . . .': SC/A.

p. 325. 'You just didn't . . .': JL/A.

p. 326. '. . . midwife Jennifer Worth . . .': JW/CM.

p. 326. '. . . Isobel Barnett recollected . . .': Lady Isobel Barnett, *My Life Line*.

p. 326. 'For Barbara Cartland . . .': Barbara Cartland, *I Search for Rainbows*.

p. 326. 'When Gracie Fields . . .': P/Cine.

pp. 327–8. 'One memoirist . . .': John Lucas, *Next Year Will Be Better: A Memoir of England in the 1950s*.

p. 328. 'Sheila McKenzie had one . . .': SJ/A.

p. 328. 'The Glaswegian . . .': FC/A.

p. 329. 'Fiona MacCarthy hazards . . .': FM/LC.

p. 329. '"Are my seams straight?" . . .': JW/CM.

pp. 329–30. 'They were wonderful . . .': VT/PWB.

p. 330. 'At her Vogue offices . . .': JL/A.

p. 330. 'A writer in . . .': Women's Institute magazine, *Home and Country*, July 1950.

p. 330. 'In Eye-Witness . . .': Mass Observation diarist 5447, 8 February 1950.

p. 330. 'Shop girls were going . . .': cited in Marcus Sieff, *Don't Ask the Price*.

pp. 330–31. 'One chronicler . . .': John Montgomery, *The Fifties*.

p. 331. 'One memoirist describes . . .': Lucas, cited above.

p. 332. 'I could stand . . .': Mary Grieve, *Millions Made my Story*.

p. 332. 'On a tight budget . . .': Hazel, in Terry Jordan, *Growing Up in the Fifties*.

pp. 332–3. 'We dreamt of America . . .': Mary Quant, *Autobiography*.

9: Keeping up with the Joneses

pp. 334–6. 'Anthea's privileged country . . .': AY/A.

pp. 336–7. 'Mitford's witty piece . . .': in Alan S. C. Ross, *Noblesse Oblige: An Enquiry into the Identifiable Characteristics of the English Aristocracy*.

p. 337. 'Leila Williams's ambitious . . .': LM/A, also LM/BQ.

p. 337. '. . . happened to Joan Rowlands . . .': JB/CB.

pp. 337–8. 'I had been horrified . . .': Betty Kenward, *Jennifer's Memoirs*.

p. 338. '. . . numbers of presentations . . .': figures from Margaret Pringle, *Dance Little Ladies*.

pp. 339–40. 'Philippa Pullar was . . .': Philippa Pullar, *Gilded Butterflies*.

p. 340. 'I never really forgave . . .' and 'The whole operation . . .': in Pringle, cited above.

p. 341. 'The Season is here . . .': Nancy Banks-Smith in the *Daily Herald*, cited in Pringle, above.

p. 341. 'Princess Margaret expressed . . .': cited in FM/LC.

pp. 341–2. 'Pushing her pram . . .': see P/Cine.

pp. 342–4. 'Grocery stores . . .': see Dolly Scannell, *Dolly's Mixture*, and Marion Hill (ed.), *Bigger, Brighter, Better: The Story of Bletchley 1944–1966 Told by its Residents*.

p. 344. 'The national economy . . .': MP/NY 13 August 1955.

p. 345. 'None of this impressed Nella Last . . .': NL/50s.

p. 346. 'I've tried it . . .': cited in Elizabeth Roberts, *Women and Families: An Oral History, 1940–1970*.

p. 346. 'Cradock specialised . . .': See P/Cine. See also entry on Fanny Cradock in the *Oxford Dictionary of National Biography*.

p. 348. '. . . the feminist writers . . .': Alva Myrdal and Viola Klein, *Women's Two Roles*.

p. 348. 'When Janet Bourne got married . . .': JL/A.

p. 349. 'Pearl Jephcott's survey . . .': Pearl Jephcott and others, *Married Women Working*.

p. 349. 'My wife is always . . .' and 'As soon as next door . . .': cited in Peter Willmott and Michael Young, *Family and Class in a London Suburb*.

p. 349. 'London itself . . .': FP/EL.

p. 349. 'Another chronicler . . .': John Montgomery, *The Fifties*.

pp. 349–50. 'As a teenager . . .': Margaret Forster, MF/HL.

p. 351. 'Mary Grieve, editor of *Woman* . . .': Mary Grieve, *Millions Made My Story*.

p. 352. '. . . the Bermondsey wives . . .': Jephcott, cited above.

p. 352. 'In Harlow . . .': see Judy Attfield, 'Inside Pram Town: A Case Study of Harlow House Interiors, 1951–61' in Attfield and Kirkham (eds.), *A View from the Interior: Women and Design*.

p. 353. 'Every Friday . . .': AA/A.

p. 353. 'Nan Marshallsay was . . .': in MF/HL.

p. 354. 'It was an era . . .': AY/A.

p. 355. 'Eirlys Roberts's courage . . .': see entry on Eirlys Roberts in the *Oxford Dictionary of National Biography*.

p. 355. 'A whole new world . . .': Mary Grieve, *Millions Made My Story*.

pp. 355–8. 'Rose Hendon was one . . .': RS/A.

p. 359. 'Rock and roll burst . . .': Sheila Rowbotham, 'Revolt in Roundhay', in Liz Heron (ed.), *Truth, Dare or Promise: Girls Growing Up in the Fifties*.

p. 359. 'It's easy to see . . .' and 'The music, so wild . . .': Denis Price, *When Buddy Holly Came to Hull*, and Agedrocker's *Memory of 1st April 1954*, posts on http://www.bbc.co.uk/dna/memoryshare.

pp. 359–60. '. 'I remember going . . .': RS/A.

pp. 361–2. '. . . like Joan Hilditch . . .': Joan Hilditch, 'Sweet Sixteen', in WW/B.

p. 363. 'The writer and journalist . . .': Ethel Mannin, *Brief Voices: A Writer's Story*.

p. 363. 'Another head-wagger . . .': Leonora Eyles, *Sex for the Engaged*.

p. 364. 'There are two kinds . . .': Rose Hacker, *Telling the Teenagers*.

p. 364. '. . . the shining El Dorado . . .': Katharine Whitehorn, *Selective Memory*.

pp. 364–5. 'Glaringly showy . . .': RH/UL.

p. 364. '*Absolute Beginners* . . .': by Colin MacInnes.

pp. 365–7. 'Betty Stucley was another . . .': Elizabeth Stucley, *Teddy Boys' Picnic*.

p. 367. 'In 1956 new arrivals . . .': figures from Anthony H. Richmond, *The Colour Problem – A Study of Racial Relations*.

pp. 368–77. 'Florence Fell was . . .': FF/A; also an unpublished recollection by Florence Fell.

p. 373. 'Run since 1945 . . .': See Valerie Kerslake, *The Haven in Yateley*, available at http://yateley.hampshire.org.uk/haven.

p. 373. 'Sin, shame and heartache . . .': Sister Ruby Burt, *The Haven Story*.

10: Under the Radar

pp. 378–9. 'When the plug . . .': Lorna Arnold, *Windscale 1957, Anatomy of a Nuclear Accident*.

pp. 379–81. 'We last saw Lorna . . .': LA/A, and LA/SC.

p. 381. 'When Nella Last . . .': NL/50s.

pp. 381–2. 'Frances Partridge found . . .': FP/EL.

p. 382. 'Am rather horrified . . .': Mass Observation Diarist No. 5338.

p. 382. 'I've come to the conclusion . . .': Mass Observation Diarist No. 5445.

p. 382. 'We were, some of the time . . .': Katharine Whitehorn, *Selective Memory*.

pp. 382–3. 'Meanwhile in Leeds . . .': Jennifer Craig, *Yes Sister, No Sister*.

pp. 386–8. 'One of these was Pat Arrowsmith . . .': author interview with Pat Arrowsmith.

p. 389. 'But women's voices . . .': for Peggy Duff and others, see entries in the *Oxford Dictionary of National Biography*.

p. 390. 'I remember having . . .': Lindsey Miller, cited in *Campaigners Look Back at Historic CND Protest*, in the *Watford Observer*, 15 February 2009.

p. 390. 'When they joined . . .': Peggy Duff, *Left, Left, Left*.

pp. 390–98. 'Among those thousands . . .': see Dora Russell, *The Tamarisk Tree*, vols 1 and 3; the *Oxford Dictionary of National Biography*; and Dora Russell, *We Called on Europe: The Story of the Women's Caravan of Peace, 1958*, unpublished, held in the Feminist Archive, University of Bristol.

pp. 398–9. 'In general I suppose . . .': Arrowsmith, cited above.

p. 399. 'But in her study . . .': ME/GS.

pp. 399–400. 'I didn't know . . .': AY/A.

pp. 402–4. 'At 239 King's Road . . .': see Jill Gardiner, *From the Closet to the Screen – Women at the Gateways Club, 1945–85*.

pp. 405–13. 'Brenda Nash was not . . .': BB/A; also BB/PH, BB/RG and BB/OW.

11: *A Living Doll*

pp. 415–20. 'Maureen Nicol was thirty . . .': MN/A; also MN/CS.

pp. 417–18. 'Mary Stott's sympathies . . .': Mary Stott, *Forgetting's No Excuse*; obituary of Mary Stott in *The Guardian*, and entry in the *Oxford Dictionary of National Biography*.

p. 422. 'Television masts seem . . .': MP/NY, 29 August 1959.

p. 422. 'The tellie keeps . . .': cited in Hannah Gavron, *The Captive Wife*.

p. 423. 'The passion for these dresses . . .': Mary Quant's *Autobiography*.

p. 423. 'She dialled a number . . .': See P/Cine.

pp. 423–4. 'In 1957 Lord Altrincham . . .': see Ben Pimlott, *The Queen: Elizabeth II and the Monarchy*.

pp. 425–33. 'In the late summer . . .': LM/A, also LM/BQ.

pp. 433–6. 'At her school in Kingston . . .': VM/A.

p. 437. 'It was strange . . .': Daphne Cover, interviewed in Z. Nia Reynolds (ed.), *When I Came to England – An Oral History of Life in 1950s and 1960s Britain*, Black Stock, 2001.

p. 437. 'When we come to Waterloo . . .': Bertha Williamson, interviewed in *Sorry, No Vacancies: Life Stories of Senior Citizens from the Caribbean*, London Borough of Hammersmith and Fulham, 1992.

p. 437. 'I clearly remember . . .': Matilda Lewis in Reynolds (ed.), cited above.

p. 437. 'It was a cold . . .': cited in Elyse Dodgson, *Motherland: West Indian Women to Britain in the 1950s*.

p. 437. 'The accent . . .': Dodgson, cited above.

p. 437. 'There was no fruit. . .': Dodgson, cited above.

p. 437. 'The first Monday . . .': Cecilia Wade in *Sorry, No Vacancies*, cited above.

p. 437. 'If you went and knocked . . .': Joyce Douglas in Reynolds (ed.), cited above.

p. 438. 'I remember once . . .': in Dodgson, cited above.

p. 438. '. . . between 1952 and 1958 . . .': statistics from Anthony H. Richmond, *The Colour Problem*.

p. 438. 'Pathé News denounced . . .': P/News.

p. 438. 'They were told . . .': see http://www.bbc.co.uk/learning-zone/clips/notting-hill-race-riots/7681.html.

p. 439. 'We united and fought back . . .': Stella Dadzie, *The Heart of the Race*.

pp. 439–45. 'Vilma showed her British passport . . .': VM/A.

pp. 446 8. 'At the age of twenty . . .': see CW/PM.

p. 448. 'They were both centre-stage . . .': cited in the *Daily Mail*, 31 May 2008.

pp. 448–52. 'In the summer of 1958 . . .': see Charles Moore, *Margaret Thatcher – The Authorized Biography*.

p. 448. 'One of her competitors . . .': Molly Huggins, *Too Much to Tell*.

pp. 449–50. 'And have you been able . . .': http://www.youtube.com/watch?v=b2zNYUCAEzU.

p. 451. 'In Sussex, farmer's wife . . .': EM/A.

p. 451 'A young Queen . . .' : Margaret Thatcher, article in the *Sunday Graphic*, 17 February 1952.

p. 452. 'I owe nothing to women's lib . . .': Margaret Thatcher, cited in the *Daily Telegraph*, 8 April 2013.

pp. 453–4. 'Oh to get away . . .': Sheila Rowbotham, 'Revolt in Roundhay', in Liz Heron (ed.), *Truth, Dare or Promise: Girls Growing Up in the Fifties*.

Afterword

p. 455. 'You'll never last . . .': VT/A, VT/YNL.

pp. 455–6. 'Butlin's redcoat Sheila McKenzie . . .': SJ/A.

p. 456. 'In 2014 Lorna Arnold . . .': LA/A, and LA/SC.

p. 456. 'Joan Bakewell . . .': JB/CB.

pp. 456–7. 'In 1950 radio presenter . . .': JM/TWS.

p. 457. 'Rose Hendon kept . . .': RS/A.

p. 457. 'the only known . . .': *Sunday Times Magazine*, 5 March 2006.

p. 457. 'a rare and unique glimpse . . .': http://lightbox.time.com/2011/12/20/cool-cats-and-tom-boys-ken-russells-the-last-of-the-teddy-girls/#1.

pp. 457–8. 'Christine Finch left Cambridge . . .': author interview with Christine Finch.

p. 458. 'In 1958, before leaving . . .': SC/A.

pp. 458–9. 'On 29 June 1962 . . .': AW/A. and AW/BTD.

p. 459. 'Flora Calder put . . .': FC/A.

pp. 459–60. 'Audrey Alssebrook still lives . . .': AA/A.

p. 460. 'The tragedies . . .': see Dora Russell, *The Tamarisk Tree*, vols 1 and 3; the *Oxford Dictionary of National Biography*; and Dora Russell, *We Called on Europe – The Story of the Women's Caravan of Peace, 1958*, unpublished, held in the Feminist Archive, University of Bristol.

pp. 460–61. 'Vilma Owen had only . . .': VM/A.

p. 461. 'In so many ways . . .': AY/A.

pp. 461–3. 'Florence Fell believed . . .': FF/A, also an unpublished recollection by Florence Fell.

Select Bibliography

I consulted over 250 books while doing the research for this one. The following list is not comprehensive, but lists the main sources which those studying the period and subject-matter may find useful.

Biography, Memoirs, Diaries, Autobiography, Oral Histories

Anonymous, *Streetwalker*, The Bodley Head, London, 1959.

Argyll, Margaret, *Forget Not: The Autobiography of Margaret, Duchess of Argyll*, W. H. Allen, London, 1976.

Arnold, Lorna, *My Short Century: Memoirs of an Accidental Nuclear Historian*, Cumnor Hill Books, Palo Alto, CA, 2012.

Athill, Diana, *Stet: An Editor's Life*, Granta, London, 2000.

Bakewell, Joan, *The Centre of the Bed: An Autobiography*, Hodder & Stoughton, London, 2003.

Barnett, Lady Isobel, *My Life Line*, Hutchinson, London, 1956.

Beddoe, Deirdre (ed.), *Changing Times: Welsh Women Writing on the 1950s and 1960s*, Honno, Dinas Powys, 2003.

Bonham Carter, Violet, *Daring to Hope: The Diaries and Letters of Violet Bonham Carter 1946–1969*, ed. Mark Pottle, Weidenfeld & Nicolson, London, 2000.

Brighton Ourstory Project, *Daring Hearts: Lesbian and Gay Lives of 50s and 60s Brighton*, QueenSpark Books, Brighton, 1992.

Bullock, Brenda, *A Pocket with a Hole: A Birmingham Childhood of the 1940s and 1950s*, Brewin Books, Studley, Warwickshire, 1996.

Bullock, Brenda, *Over the Wall: A Working-class Girl at University in the 1950s*, Brewin Books, Studley, Warwickshire, 1998.

Bullock, Brenda, *Reflected Glory*, Brewin Books, Studley, Warwickshire, 1996.

Cartland, Barbara, *I Search for Rainbows*, Hutchinson, London, 1967.

Coxhead, Elizabeth, *Constance Spry: A Biography*, Luscombe, London, 1975.

Craig, Jennifer, *Yes Sister, No Sister: My Life as a Trainee Nurse in 1950s Yorkshire*, Random House, London, 2002.

Essex, Rosamund, *Woman in a Man's World*, Sheldon Press, London, 1977.

Evans, Mary, *A Good School: Life at a Girls' Grammar School in the 1950s*, The Women's Press, London, 1991.

Foley, Winifred, *No Pipe Dreams for Father*, Macdonald & Co., London, 1978.

Foley, Winifred, *Back to the Forest*, Macdonald & Co., London, 1981.

Forster, Margaret, *Hidden Lives: A Family Memoir*, Viking, London, 1995.

Goldsmith, Lady Annabel, *Annabel: An Unconventional Life, The Memoirs of Lady Annabel Goldsmith*, Weidenfeld & Nicolson, London, 2004.

Grieve, Mary, *Millions Made My Story*, Victor Gollancz, London, 1964.

Hayter, Teresa, *Hayter of the Bourgeoisie*, Sidgwick & Jackson, London, 1971.

Heron, Liz (ed.), *Truth, Dare or Promise: Girls Growing up in the Fifties*, Virago Press, London, 1985.

Hill, Marion (ed.), *Bigger, Brighter, Better: The Story of Bletchley 1944–1966 Told by its Residents*, Living Archive, 1996.

Howard, Elizabeth Jane, *Slipstream: A Memoir*, Macmillan, London, 2002.

Hubback, Judith, *From Dawn to Dusk: Autobiography*, Chiron Publications, Wilmette, Illinois, 2003.

Huggins, Molly, *Too Much to Tell*, Heinemann, London, 1967.

Hurst, Margery, *No Glass Slipper*, Arlington Books, London, 1967.

Ironside, Virginia, *Janey and Me: Growing up with My Mother*, Fourth Estate, London and New York, 2003.

Jennings, Ruth, *One Woman's Work . . . and Other Disasters*, Matador, Leicester, 2011.

Jordan, Terry (ed.), *Growing Up in the Fifties*, Macdonald & Co., London, 1990.

Kenward, Betty, *Jennifer's Memoirs: Eighty-five Years of Fun and Functions*, HarperCollins, London, 1992.

Kimbrough, Emily, *Forty Plus and Fancy Free*, Harper & Bros, New York, 1954.

Last, Nella, *Nella Last in the 1950s: Further Diaries of Housewife, 49*, ed. Patricia and Robert Malcolmson, Profile Books, London, 2010.

Lee, Carol Ann, *A Fine Day for a Hanging: The Real Ruth Ellis Story*, Mainstream Publishing, Edinburgh and London, 2012.

Lucas, John, *Next Year Will Be Better: A Memoir of England in the 1950s*, Five Leaves Publications, Nottingham, 2010.

MacCarthy, Fiona, *Last Curtsey: The End of the Debutantes*, Faber & Faber, London, 2006.

Mannin, Ethel, *Brief Voices: A Writer's Story*, Hutchinson, London, 1959.

Marlborough, Laura, Duchess of, *Laughter from a Cloud*, Weidenfeld & Nicolson, London, 1980.

Meynell, Dame Alix, *Public Servant, Private Woman*, Gollancz, London, 1988.

Michelmore, Cliff, and Metcalfe, Jean, *Two-way Story*, Hamish Hamilton, London, 1986.

Moore, Charles, *Margaret Thatcher: The Authorized Biography, Volume One: Not for Turning*, Allen Lane, London, 2013.

Morley, Eric, *The Miss World Story*, Angley Books Ltd, Maidstone, Kent, 1967.

Partridge, Frances, *Everything to Lose: Diaries 1945–1960*, Victor Gollancz, London, 1985.

Pimlott, Ben, *The Queen: Elizabeth II and the Monarchy*, HarperCollins, London, 2001.

Plath, Sylvia, *Letters Home: Correspondence 1950–1963*, selected and edited by Aurelia Schober Plath, Faber & Faber, London, 1976.

Pullar, Philippa, *The Shortest Journey*, Hamish Hamilton, London, 1981.

Roberts, Elizabeth, *Women and Families: An Oral History, 1940–1970*, Blackwell, Oxford, and Cambridge, MA, 1995.

Russell, Dora, *The Tamarisk Tree: Volume 3, Challenge to the Cold War*, Virago, London, 1985.

Sage, Lorna, *Bad Blood*, Fourth Estate, London, 2000.

Scannell, Dorothy, *Dolly's Mixture*, Macmillan, London, 1977.

Shephard, Sue, *The Surprising Life of Constance Spry*, Macmillan, London, 2010.

Sieff, Marcus, *Don't Ask the Price: The Memoirs of the President of Marks & Spencer*, Weidenfeld & Nicolson, London, 1987.

Smith, Dodie, *Look Back with Gratitude*, Muller, Blond & White, London, 1985.

Stott, Mary, *Forgetting's No Excuse*, Faber & Faber, London, 1973.

Stucley, Elizabeth, *Teddy Boys' Picnic*, Anthony Blond, London, 1958.

Summerskill, Edith, *Letters to my Daughter*, Heinemann, London, 1957.

Tedder, Valerie A., *Post War Blues*, published by Leicester City Council, 1999.

Tedder, Valerie A., *You'll Never Last: One Policewoman's Story from 1958–1984*, United Press Limited, London, 2010.

Tennant, Emma, *Girlitude: A Portrait of the 50s and 60s*, Jonathan Cape, London, 1999.

Townsend, Peter, *Time and Chance: An Autobiography*, Collins, London, 1978.

Waller, Angela, *Before There Were Trolley Dollies*, Pen Press, Brighton, 2009.

Warwick, Christopher, *Princess Margaret: A Life of Contrasts*, André Deutsch, London, 2000.

Watts, Marthe, *The Men in my Life: The Story of the Messina Reign of Vice in London*, Christopher Johnson, London, 1960.

Whitehorn, Katharine, *Selective Memory: An Autobiography,* Virago Press, London, 2007.

Wormley Women's Institute, *Turning Back the Clock: Personal Memories Spanning the 20th Century*, published by Wormley Women's Institute.

Worth, Jennifer, *Call the Midwife: A True Story of the East End in the 1950s*, Weidenfeld & Nicolson, London, 2007.

History, Sociology, Psychology, Advice

Abrams, Mark, *The Teenage Consumer*, London Press Exchange Ltd, London, 1959.

Adam, Ruth, *A Woman's Place: 1910–1975*, Chatto & Windus, London, 1975.

Addison, Paul, *No Turning Back: The Peacetime Revolutions of Post-war Britain*, Oxford University Press, 2010.

Addison, Paul, *Now the War is Over: A Social History of Britain 1945–51*, British Broadcasting Corporation and Jonathan Cape Ltd, London, 1985.

Akhtar, Miriam, and Humphries, Steve, *The Fifties and Sixties: A Lifestyle Revolution*, Boxtree, Basingstoke and London, 2001.

Arnold, Lorna, *Windscale 1957: Anatomy of a Nuclear Accident*, Macmillan, London, 1992.

Attfield, Judy, and Kirkham, Pat (eds.), *A View from the Interior: Women and Design*, Women's Press, London, 1995.

Baker, Niamh, *Happily Ever After? Women's Fiction in Postwar Britain 1945–1960*, Macmillan, London, 1989.

Banton, Michael, *The Coloured Quarter: Negro Immigrants in an English City*, Jonathan Cape, London, 1955.

Black, Lawrence, and Pemberton, Hugh (eds.), *An Affluent Society? Britain's Post-war 'Golden Age' Revisited*, Ashgate, Aldershot, 2004.

Booker, Christopher, *The Neophiliacs: A Study of the Revolution in English Life in the Fifties and Sixties*, Collins, London, 1969.

Bourke, Joanna, *Working-class Cultures in Britain 1890–1960: Gender, Class and Ethnicity*, Routledge, London and New York, 1994.

Bowlby, John, *Child Care and the Growth of Love*, Pelican Books, London 1953.

Brayshaw, A. Joseph, *The Stability of Marriage*, published by the National Marriage Guidance Council, 1952.

British Council of Churches publication, *Your Neighbour from the West Indies*, 1955.

Brittain, Vera, *Lady into Woman*, Andrew Dakers, London, 1953.

Bruley, Sue, *Women in Britain Since 1900*, Palgrave, Basingstoke and New York, 1999.

Bryan, Beverley, Dadzie, Stella, and Scafe, Suzanne, *The Heart of the Race: Black Women's Lives in Britain*, Virago, London, 1985.

Cartland, Barbara, *Marriage for Moderns*, Herbert Jenkins, London, 1955.

Chesser, Dr Eustace, *Humanly Speaking*, Hutchinson's Scientific and Technical Publications, London, New York, Toronto, 1953.

Chesser, Dr Eustace, *The Sexual, Marital and Family Relationships of the English Woman*, Hutchinson's Medical Publications, London, New York, Toronto, 1956.

Clapson, Mark, *Invincible Green Suburbs, Brave New Towns: Social Change and Urban Dispersal in Postwar England*, Manchester University Press, Manchester and New York, 1998.

Clark, David (ed.), *Marriage, Domestic Life and Social Change: Writings for Jacqueline Burgoyne (1944–88)*, Routledge, London and New York, 1991.

Clayton, Lucie, *The World of Modelling, and How to Get the London Model-girl Look*, George G. Harrap, London, 1968.

Collins, Sydney, *Coloured Minorities in Britain: Studies in British Race Relations based on African, West Indian and Asiatic Immigrants*, Lutterworth Press, London, 1957.

Conekin, Becky E., *The Autobiography of a Nation: The 1951 Festival of Britain*, Manchester University Press, Manchester, 2003.

Cooke, Rachel, *Her Brilliant Career: Ten Extraordinary Women of the Fifties*, Virago, London, 2013.

C.O.S.M.I.T.H. [Council of Scientific Management in the Home] pamphlets:

> *The Women's Group on Public Welfare Sub-Committee on Scientific Management in the Home: Report of an Enquiry into the Effect of the Designs of the Temporary Prefabricated Bungalow on Household Routines*, 1951.

> *Daily Mail Ideal Home Exhibition, 1955, The C.O.S.M.I.T.H. Kitchen.*
> *Meals in Modern Homes*, 1955.

Davidson, Caroline, *A Woman's Work is Never Done*, Chatto & Windus, London, 1982.

Dennis, Norman, Henriques, Fernando, and Slaughter, Clifford, *Coal is Our Life: An Analysis of a Yorkshire Mining Community*, Eyre & Spottiswoode, London, 1956.

Dodgson, Elyse, *Motherland: West Indian Women to Britain in the 1950s*, Heinemann Educational Books, London, 1984.

Egginton, Joyce, *They Seek a Living*, Hutchinson, London, 1957.

Eyles, Leonora, *The New Commonsense about Sex*, Victor Gollancz, London, 1956.

Eyles, Leonora, *Sex for the Engaged*, Robert Hale Ltd, London, 1960.

Frame, Pete, *The Restless Generation*, Omnibus, London, 2007.

Francis, Vivienne, *With Hope in Their Eyes: The Compelling Stories of the Windrush Generation*, The X Press, London, 1998.

Fyvel, T. R., *The Insecure Offenders: Rebellious Youth in the Welfare State*, Chatto & Windus, 1961.

Gardiner, Jill, *From the Closet to the Screen: Women at the Gateways Club, 1945–85*, Pandora Press, London, Sydney, Chicago, 2003.

Gavron, Hannah, *The Captive Wife: Conflicts of Housebound Mothers*, Routledge & Kegan Paul, London, New York, 1966.

Glass, Ruth, assisted by Harold Pollins, *Newcomers: The West Indians in London*, published by the Centre for Urban Studies and George Allen & Unwin Ltd, London, 1960.

Good Housekeeping, *Good Housekeeping: The Best of the 1950s*, Collins & Brown, London, 2008.

Good Housekeeping Institute, *The Happy Home: A Universal Guide to Household Management*, published by the Good Housekeeping Institute, London, 1955.

Gorer, Geoffrey, *Exploring English Character*, The Cresset Press, London, 1955.

Granger, Pip, *Up West: Voices from the Streets of Post-war London*, Transworld, London, 2009.

Hacker, Rose, *Telling the Teenagers: A Guide to Parents, Teachers and Youth Leaders*, André Deutsch, London, 1957.

Hall, Grace, *How to Get Your Man!* Pitt's Bookshop, Exeter, 1951.

Hall, Lesley A., *Outspoken Women: An Anthology of Women's Writing on Sex, 1870–1969*, Routledge, London and New York, 2005.

Halsey, A. H. (ed.), *Trends in British Society since 1900: A Guide to the Changing Social Structure of Britain*, Macmillan, London and Basingstoke, 1972.

Haste, Cate, *Rules of Desire: Sex in Britain, World War I to the Present*, Chatto & Windus, London, 1992.

Hennessy, Peter, *Never Again: Britain 1945–51*, Jonathan Cape, London, 1992.

Hennessy, Peter, *Having It So Good: Britain in the Fifties*, Allen Lane, London, 2006.

Hoggart, Richard, *The Uses of Literacy*, Chatto & Windus, London, 1957.

Holdsworth, Angela, *Out of the Dolls House: The Story of Women in the Twentieth Century*, BBC Books, London, 1988.

Hubback, Judith, *Wives Who Went to College*, Heinemann, London, 1957.

Humble, Nicola, *The Feminine Middlebrow Novel, 1920s to 1950s: Class, Domesticity and Bohemianism*, Oxford University Press, Oxford, 2001.

Jephcott, Pearl, *Some Young People*, George Allen & Unwin Ltd, London, 1954.

Jephcott, Pearl (with Nancy Seear and John H. Smith under the direction of Professor Richard Titmuss), *Married Women Working*, George Allen & Unwin Ltd, London, 1962.

Joseph, George, *Women at Work: The British Experience*, Philip Allan Publishers Ltd, Oxford, 1983.

King, Leonore (and others), *Glorify Yourself*, Psychology Publishing Co. Ltd, Marple, Cheshire, 1953.

Kinsey, Alfred (and others), *Sexual Behavior in the Human Female*, W. B. Saunders Company, Philadelphia and London, 1953.

Kynaston, David, *Austerity Britain, 1945–51*, Bloomsbury, London, Berlin, New York, 2007.

Kynaston, David, *Family Britain, 1951–57*, Bloomsbury, London, Berlin, New York, 2009.

Kynaston, David, *Modernity Britain, Opening the Box, 1957–59*, Bloomsbury, London, Berlin, New York, 2013.

Lewis, Jane, *Women in Britain since 1945: Women, Family, Work and the State in the Post-war Years*, Blackwell, Oxford, and Cambridge, MA, 1992.

Lewis, Peter, *The Fifties*, Book Club Associates in association with William Heinemann Limited, London, 1978.

Liddington, Jill, *The Road to Greenham Common: Feminism and Anti-militarism in Britain Since 1820*, Syracuse University Press, Syracuse, NY, 1991.

Little, Jo, Peake, Linda, and Richardson, Pat (eds.), *Women in Cities: Gender and the Urban Environment*, Macmillan Education, London, 1988.

Macaulay, Mary (M.B., Ch.B, J.P.), *The Art of Marriage*, De Lisle, London, 1952.

Mann, Jessica, *The Fifties Mystique*, Quartet Books, London, 2012.

Marwick, Arthur, *British Society since 1945*, Allen Lane, 1982.

McNally, Fiona, *Women for Hire: A Study of the Female Office Worker*, Macmillan, London, 1979.

Mitford, Nancy (ed.), with contributions by Alan S. C. Ross and Evelyn Waugh, *Noblesse Oblige: An Enquiry into the Identifiable Characteristics of the English Aristocracy*, Hamish Hamilton, London, 1956.

Montgomery, John, *The Fifties,* George Allen and Unwin Ltd, London, 1965.

Myrdal, Alva, and Klein, Viola, *Women's Two Roles: Home and Work*, Routledge & Kegan Paul, London, 1956.

National Magazines, *Good Housekeeping's Book of Entertaining*, published by the National Magazine Company Limited, London, 1955.

National Marriage Guidance Council pamphlet, *Sex in Marriage*, published by the National Marriage Guidance Council, 1958.

Newsom, John, *The Education of Girls*, Faber and Faber, London, 1948.

Opie, Robert (compiled by), *The 1950s Scrapbook*, New Cavendish Books, London, 1998.

Pringle, Margaret, *Dance Little Ladies: The Days of the Debutante*, Orbis Publishing, London, 1977.

Pullar, Philippa, *Gilded Butterflies: The Rise and Fall of the London Season*, Hamish Hamilton, London, 1978.

Ravetz, Alison, with Turkington, Richard, *The Place of Home: English Domestic Environments 1914–2000*, E. and F. N. Spon (Chapman and Hall), London etc., 1955.

Richmond, Anthony H., *The Colour Problem: A Study of Racial Relations*, Penguin, London, 1955, revised edition 1961.

Robinson, Jane, *A Force to be Reckoned With: A History of the Women's Institute*, Virago Press, London, 2011.

Rolph, C. H., *Women of the Streets: A Sociological Study of the Common Prostitute*, Secker & Warburg, London, 1955.

Ryan, Maud, Edgcombe, Margot, and Chance, Janet, *Back-Street Surgery: A Study of the Illegal Operation, which is performed probably about 100,000 times a year in England and Wales*, published by the Abortion Law Reform Association, Fordingbridge, Hants, 1947.

Sandbrook, Dominic, *Never Had it So Good: A History of Britain from Suez to the Beatles*, Little, Brown, London, 2005.

Short, John R., *Housing in Britain: The Post-war Experience*, Methuen, London and New York, 1982.

Spencer, Stephanie, *Gender, Work and Education in Britain in the 1950s*, Palgrave Macmillan, Basingstoke, 2005.

Streatfeild, Noel (ed.), *The Years of Grace*, Evans Brothers Limited, London, 1950.

Sutton, Maureen, *'We Didn't Know Aught': A Study of Sexuality, Superstition and Death in Women's Lives in Lincolnshire during the 1930s, '40s and '50s*, Paul Watkins, Stamford, 1992.

Szreter, Simon, and Fisher, Kate, *Sex Before the Sexual Revolution: Intimate Life in England 1918–1963*, Cambridge University Press, Cambridge, 2010.

Wallace, Carlton (ed.), *The Housewives' Pocket Book*, Evans Brothers Ltd, London, 1953.

Weddell, Margaret, *Training in Home Management*, Routledge & Kegan Paul Ltd, London, 1955.

Whiteman, Phyllis, *Speaking as a Woman*, Chapman & Hall, London, 1953.

Williams-Ellis, Amabel, *The Art of Being a Woman*, The Bodley Head, London, 1951.

Willmott, Peter, and Young, Michael, *Family and Class in a London Suburb*, Routledge & Kegan Paul, London, 1960.

Wimperis, Virginia, *The Unmarried Mother and Her Child*, George Allen and Unwin Ltd, London, 1960.

Wright, Helena, *Sex Fulfilment in Married Women*, Williams & Norgate Ltd, London, 1947.

Zweig, Ferdynand, *The Worker in an Affluent Society*, Heinemann, London, 1960.

Zweiniger-Bargielowska, Ina, *Women in Twentieth-century Britain*, Pearson Education Ltd, London, 2001.

Fiction

Cochrane, Louise, *Social Work for Jill*, Chatto & Windus, London, 1954.

Dawson, Stella, *Joanna in Advertising*, Chatto & Windus, London, 1958.

MacInnes, Colin, *Absolute Beginners*, MacGibbon & Kee, London, 1959.

Portobello, Petronella (pseudonym of Lady Flavia Anderson), *How to Be a Deb's Mum*, Victor Gollancz, London, 1957.

Spark, Muriel, *The Girls of Slender Means*, Macmillan, London, 1963.

Scholarly Articles and Theses

Birmingham Feminist History Group (Lucy Bland, Angela Coyle and others), *Feminism as Femininity in the Nineteen-Fifties*, in *Feminist Review*, No. 80, 2005.

Freeguard, Joyce, *It's Time for Women of the 1950s to Stand Up and Be Counted*, D.Phil thesis, University of Sussex, 2004.

Langhamer, Claire, *The Meanings of Home in Postwar Britain*, in *Journal of Contemporary History*, Vol. 40, No. 2, April 2005.

Lloyd, Justine, and Johnson, Lesley, *The Three Faces of Eve: The Postwar Housewife, Melodrama and Home 1*, in *Feminist Media Studies*, Vol. 3, No. 1, 2003.

Todd, Selina, *Domestic Service and Class Relations in Britain 1900–1950*, in *Past and Present*, No. 203, May 2009.

Archives

Abortion Law Reform Association papers held at the Wellcome Library.

Black Cultural Archives.

Dora Russell's papers, including the manuscript of *We Called on Europe: The Story of the Women's Caravan of Peace, 1958,* held at the Feminist Archive, University of Bristol.

Family Planning Association papers held at the Wellcome Library.

Mass Observation Archive, University of Sussex.

Millennium Memory Bank Oral History Collection held at the British Library.

The Women's Library @ LSE.
Working-class Autobiographies collection held at Brunel University.

Newspapers and Magazines

Until recently the British Newspaper Archive was held at the British
   Library's Colindale premises. Their complete collection is now
   divided between the British Library at St Pancras and the Boston site.
Newspapers and magazines consulted include:
   Home and Country (the magazine of the Women's Institute)
   News of the World
   Peace News
   Radio Times
   Sunday Despatch
   Sunday Graphic
   The Daily Express
   The Daily Mail
   The Daily Mirror
   The Daily Sketch
   The Manchester Guardian
   The Observer
   The Times
   Woman
   Woman and Home
   Woman's Own
   Woman's Realm

A Few Useful Websites

British Pathé at http://www.britishpathe.com
Butlin's memories at http://www.butlinsmemories.com/index.htm

Fashion through history on http://www.fashion-era.com/index.htm

Historic Inflation calculator at http://www.thisismoney.co.uk

Memories posted by the public on http://www.bbc.co.uk/dna/memoryshare

The *New Yorker* online archive at http://www.newyorker.com/archive

The Oxford Dictionary of National Biography at www.oxforddnb.com

Teddy Boys at http://edwardianteddyboy.com

Index

NOTE: Ranks and titles are generally those applying
at the time of latest mention